Better Policies, Better Schools
Theories and Applications

Bruce S. Cooper

Fordham University

Lance D. Fusarelli

Fordham University

E. Vance Randall

Brigham Young University

Boston ■ New York ■ San Francisco
Mexico City ■ Montreal ■ Toronto ■ London ■ Madrid ■ Munich ■ Paris
Hong Kong ■ Singapore ■ Tokyo ■ Cape Town ■ Sydney

Series Editor: *Arnis E. Burvikovs*
Editorial Assistant: *Christine Lyons*
Marketing Manager: *Tara Whorf*
Editorial-Production Service: *Omegatype Typography, Inc.*
Composition and Prepress Buyer: *Linda Cox*
Manufacturing Buyer: *Andrew Turso*
Cover Administrator: *Linda Knowles*
Electronic Composition: *Omegatype Typography, Inc.*

For related titles and support material, visit our online catalog at www.ablongman.com.

Between the time Website information is gathered and then published, it is not unusual for some sites to have closed. Also, the transcription of URLs can result in typographical errors. The publisher would appreciate notification where these errors occur so that they may be corrected in subsequent editions.

Library of Congress Cataloging-in-Publication Data

Cooper, Bruce S.
    Better policies, better schools : theories and applications / Bruce S. Cooper, Lance D. Fusarelli, E. Vance Randall.
        p.   cm.
    Includes bibliographical references and index.
    ISBN 0-205-32152-6
    1. Education and state—United States.   2. Educational change—United States.   I. Fusarelli, Lance D. (Lance Darin)   II. Randall, E. Vance.   III. Title.

LC89 .C66 2004
379.73—dc21

2002038411

Printed in the United States of America

10   9   8   7   6   5   4   3   2   1   08   07   06   05   04   03

To my beloved parents, Louis and Harriet Cooper, and my wife, Nancy,
and my children, and grandchildren.
—B. S. Cooper

In loving memory of my father.
—L. D. Fusarelli

To my wife, Vickie, a true saint and a scholar.
—E. V. Randall

Contents

Foreword

Better Policies, Better Schools: Theories and Applications, by Bruce S. Cooper, Lance D. Fusarelli, and E. Vance Randall, is a welcome addition to the literature on education policymaking. Because the field of education policy analysis is relatively young, many theories and case analyses have accumulated in recent decades. Consequently, the field has competing theories and conceptual approaches, with relatively little attention to comparing or reconciling these different perspectives. Moreover, because most contributors to the field have been concerned about specific education issues and problems, visitors to this field confront a vast, fragmented landscape of studies that seem unrelated, even contradictory, to one another.

Education policy analysis is not unique in its eclecticism. Any new area of intellectual inquiry is likely to share this same characteristic. The field needs cartographers to create a roadmap for first-time visitors. In fact, many of those who are knowledgeable about one part of the field can also benefit from this roadmap, to provide them with "the big picture" with a sense of how their concerns fit into a larger sociopolitical framework. These individuals include not only students, but also academics, policymakers, and practitioners, among others.

This book comes to the rescue, addressing problems of fragmentation and isolation. The authors "examine the current 'state of the art' in our thinking about education policymaking and apply those concepts to specific policies and policy issues." In undertaking this task, the authors display a remarkable grasp of the breadth and depth of work already undertaken in this field.

In Part I of *Better Policies, Better Schools: Theories and Applications,* Drs. Cooper, Fusarelli, and Randall introduce the field, its history, and its emerging research directions. They then review theories of education policymaking, offering insightful comments on both the strengths and shortcomings of various theoretical approaches. This section of the book then moves to a conceptual framework for understanding policymaking in education. The four frames they identify are the normative frame, structural frame, constituentive frame, and technical frame. At the core of this four-dimensional framework is a concern for ethics and social justice, which the authors argue have received inadequate attention in the traditional policy studies literature.

In Part II of the book, the authors apply this four-dimensional framework to the policymaking process. This section includes important topics such as the role of problem definition, agenda setting, policy formulation, policy implementation, and using evaluation to improve education. Because their four analytic frames are so powerful, the authors bring together an impressive collection of topics and issues not often covered adequately in books on education policy. The use of policy "vignettes" offers the reader concrete examples to illustrate problems, conflicts, and dilemmas, as well as opportunities for policy improvement.

The inclusion of seminal works and references will help readers who wish to delve into particular topics in greater detail. The use of classroom assignments, conveniently located at the ends of chapters, should be welcomed by instructors of courses and will prove to be an invaluable aid to students. Indeed, the skillful weaving together of theoretical insights, historical contributions, legal precedents, and practical issues really sets this book apart as a truly original contribution to the literature on education policymaking.

With this foundation provided, in Part III of the book the authors provide additional applications and cases. In Chapters 6–11, they cover policies for improving school governance; curriculum, standards, and testing; accountability and school reform; improving teacher personnel policies; school finance; and charter schools. In many cases, their approach to these topics offers the reader material that is rarely found in conventional discussions of these critical policy areas. For example, their discussion of governance (Chapter 6) addresses many of the philosophical questions at the heart of governance debates. Drawing on the work of Amy Gutmann, for example, they ask who should have the ultimate authority in deciding what constitutes good education? Once again, their four-dimensional framework helps the reader view educational governance through different policy lenses.

Better Policies, Better Schools: Theories and Applications, by Bruce S. Cooper, Lance D. Fusarelli, and E. Vance Randall, is an exciting addition to the study of education policymaking. In its conceptual sweep and its grasp of the many complex issues in the field of education policy, this book is a tour de force. As such, the book should be valued highly by a wide range of stakeholders—scholars, students, teachers, school executives, policymakers, and other practitioners.

James G. Cibulka
Dean, University of Kentucky–Lexington

Preface

Better Policies, Better Schools: Theories and Applications is a comprehensive overview of the burgeoning field of education policy analysis—combining recent theoretical advances in education policy studies with concrete case studies of actual school policies. The book examines the politics surrounding policymaking in education and presents a theoretical framework for analyzing education policy and the politics surrounding those policies. It is intended to be useful to both scholars and practitioners interested in gaining a better understanding of how education policy is made and how the political environment shapes the policy process.

As suggested by the title, the purpose of this book is to apply various theories or lenses of policymaking to a series of critical issues in education policy in an effort to use the theories to improve schools. Despite the importance of policies affecting education—as both a process for reaching decisions and as a guide for implementing and shaping action—few books have applied models of policymaking systematically and critically to policies in one of society's key public concerns: the education of its citizens. We seek to be both theoretical and practical. By applying theory to practice, being normative and real, clear-headed and dirty-handed, grounded and conceptual, we hope to change and improve education by helping scholars and practitioners become more reflective of the multiple actors, forces, and factors shaping education policy.

We seek to empower educators, parents, school and community leaders, and legislators to engage in the great policy debates of our time. A healthy democracy depends on active membership and involvement in the policy discourse. Because information is power, a purpose of this book is to arm teachers, administrators, school board members, parents, legislators, policy analysts, and state education officials with the constructs and tools needed to understand and improve the critical policies affecting our nation's schools. This book is also useful as an advanced graduate text in educational policy and administration, policy studies, public affairs, and political science. Most graduate-level texts in political science and policy studies contain little discussion of educational issues. Conversely, education texts (even those with a policy bent) place little emphasis on recent theoretical developments in political science and the policy sciences, rarely moving beyond overly simplistic "how a bill becomes a law" analyses.

This book corrects for these deficiencies: we review several key policy theories (we call them "lenses"), integrate them into a coherent conceptual framework, and apply this framework to six key policy issues, including school finance, accountability, charter schools, labor relations and teacher personnel policies, curriculum, and governance. This approach demonstrates that the processes, production, and application of education policy are both more complex and simpler than previously thought. Education policy formation and reform are more *complex* because changing lenses generates a different set of questions, theories, and analyses; and is *simpler* because these lenses or frameworks can be applied again and again to a variety of issues, providing a common analytical treatment to a host of changing education policy areas.

Using a coherent conceptual framework gives shape to the field of education policy studies, which has verged on intellectual chaos at times and an atheoretical bias at others. In fact, a survey of the major writings on school policy shows a paucity of theoretical treatment—and almost never is more than one lens used to explore a policy area. The book's format allows the reader to examine policy from both the macro-level (federal and state) and the micro-level (district and school), encouraging the reader to think about specific policies within the larger political, policymaking environment. The book is divided into three sections, described briefly in the following paragraphs.

In Part I of the book, readers are introduced to the field of education policy studies. Several diverse theoretical approaches are used to conceptualize policymaking in education. Particular emphasis is placed on recent advances in political science and sociology. Theories used include systems theory, neo-pluralist advocacy and interest group theories, institutional theory, critical theory, feminism, postmodernism, and various ideological perspectives. A unifying four-dimensional framework is introduced, providing a conceptual tool to integrate the theories and apply them to critical educational policies discussed in Part III.

In Part II, the policymaking *process* in education is examined, with each chapter focusing on a different aspect (commonly and inaccurately referred to as stages) of the process, including problem definition, agenda setting, and policy formulation, implementation, and evaluation. Part III applies the four-dimensional framework to six critical policy issues: governance, curriculum, accountability, teacher personnel policies, school finance, and charter schools.

Special Features

In an effort to make the book as useful as possible for practitioners, scholars, and graduate students, we have included the following special features:

- *Policy Vignettes:* Most chapters contain policy vignettes illustrating key concepts and ideas utilized in the chapter. Each vignette will highlight different aspects of theory—affording the reader an opportunity to make a connection between theory and practice.

- *Matrix Structure:* One convenient way to conceptualize the book is as a matrix with four dimensions: normative, structural, constituentive, and technical. Applying different theoretical frames or lenses to the six policy areas highlights the importance of different actors within each dimension—actors that often have a determinant effect on the outcome of policy. Once students master the ability to apply the matrix to the six topics, it is easy to "plug in" other topics (such as teacher retirement policy or facilities and construction policy). Professors, too, can adapt the framework to new, emerging topics as they become salient in different settings.
- *Discussion Questions and Chapter Activities:* Each chapter concludes with a series of key discussion questions or chapter activities, which can be used to frame discussion and debate over the key concepts discussed in each chapter.
- *Seminal Works:* A short list of seminal works is provided at the end of each chapter to provide readers with a synopsis of key works discussed in the chapter.
- *References:* A complete list of references is included at the end of each chapter to make it more convenient for readers to look up sources used in the text. Books in which references are massed alphabetically or even grouped by chapter and located in the back of books are too cumbersome to be of much use to readers (be they researchers, students, or practitioners). By locating references at the end of the chapter, this book makes it easier for readers to use each chapter as a self-contained work—offering maximum pedagogical flexibility for scholars, students, and policymakers.

Acknowledgments

The authors would like to thank Arnis Burvikovs, our editor at Allyn and Bacon, for his assistance, gentle prodding, and great patience in ensuring the completion of this manuscript. Thanks also go to James Cibulka, Dean of the Graduate School of Education at the University of Kentucky, for generously agreeing to write the Foreword to this book. The authors appreciate the thoughtful suggestions of the reviewers who took time from their busy schedules to critique thoroughly and improve the manuscript: Patricia A. Bauch, The University of Alabama; Gus Douvanis, University of West Georgia; Carolyn Herrington, Florida State University; Betty Malen, University of Maryland, Dennis McNaughten, Tarleton State University; Davis J. Parks, Virginia Tech; Barba Patton, University of Houston–Victoria; and Kenneth Wong, Vanderbilt University.

About the Authors

Bruce S. Cooper, Ph.D., is professor and vice chair, Division of Educational Leadership, Administration, and Policy at the Fordham University Graduate School of Education. His Ph.D. is from the University of Chicago and he has taught at the University of Pennsylvania and Dartmouth College, where his research includes school finance and teacher unionism. Recent books include *The Promises and Perils Facing Today's School Superintendent,* coedited with Lance Fusarelli (Scarecrow Press, 2002); *Advocacy or Accuracy: The Politics of Research in Education,* coedited with Vance Randall (Sage, 1999); and *Optimizing Education Resources* (JAI Press, 1998).

Lance D. Fusarelli, Ph.D., is assistant professor in the Division of Educational Leadership, Administration, and Policy at Fordham University. He received his M.A. in government and Ph.D. in educational administration from the University of Texas at Austin. His research interests include educational politics and policy (state-level), school choice, and the superintendency. He recently completed *The Political Dynamics of School Choice* (St. Martin's, in press) and coedited with Bruce Cooper *The Promises and Perils Facing Today's School Superintendent* (Scarecrow Press, 2002).

E. Vance Randall, Ph.D., is an associate professor and chair of the Department of Educational Leadership and Foundations at Brigham Young University, Provo, Utah. His scholarly interests are in the field of social and political philosophy of education and policy studies. Specific research topics include private education and privatization both domestically and internationally, governance, equity, normative policy analysis, and culture and education. He is the author of two books: *Private Schools and Public Power: A Case for Pluralism* (Teachers College Press, 1994) and *Advocacy or Accuracy: The Politics of Research in Education,* coedited with Bruce Cooper (Sage, 1999).

1

Introduction

We live and work in an age when educational leaders—superintendents, school board members, central office administrators, even principals—need to be well informed and familiar with education policy and the politics surrounding the creation and implementation of those policies. Traditionally, however, few have paid attention to the macro-level forces and actors who often create school policies, preferring instead to focus on the day-to-day operations of individual schools or districts. Increasingly, however, school leaders (particularly urban superintendents) perceive their major problems as statewide and national in both scope and origin (Kowalski, 1995).

This perception reflects the view that U.S. education is controlled by and reformed within a "web" of public policies (see Wirt & Kirst, 1997), some as old as the "one best system" itself (Tyack, 1974). Others are as new as federal legislation to test school children in grades 3–8. Whatever their age and stage, better policies hold the key to improving education for *all* children. These policies seek to change the vision and mission of education; enhance the way teachers work and what they teach; increase the human, capital, and financial resources to schools; and ensure that standards are high and results forthcoming. In fact, all these policy areas need to work in concert—purpose, teaching, funding, standards, and assessment—if schools are to improve. Porter (1998) wrote that,

> Most important, all the policy levers have to speak in the same direction [if not the same language]. They have to be consistent if the effect is going to be achieved; if they are not consistent, trouble results. For example, Florida gave the minimum competency test at the same time it required more units in math. As a result, students took remedial math and not college preparatory math. Meanwhile, no science test was administered, so students took more ambitious classes. (p. 170)

Porter's comments highlight the often unintended consequences of education policies and their effects on students. This is not surprising, because we are working in a highly diverse, rich field where the federal government and courts, fifty state legislatures and departments of education, and some 14,200 local education authorities (including mayors and school boards) all engage in policymaking. The field has deep roots and a rich history, dating back to the origins of universal, tax-supported public schooling. Policies were created and implemented, not whole or in coordination, but slowly, haltingly, unevenly, and incrementally, all leading to what Tyack (1974) called "the one best system." However, it is not "one" system, but many interacting systems across the country. It started small, locally, and voluntaristically; it became universal, mandatory, and extensive, as policymakers sought to make education accessible, affordable, equitable, and excellent for students.

It is clear, in the midst of this milieu, that policymakers of all stripes and persuasions—legislators, academics, and practitioners—and at all levels—federal, state, and local—need to develop and refine the craft of education policymaking if we are to promote policies to improve schools. As Kerr (1976) asserted a quarter century ago, "The quality of our actions can be no greater than the quality of our understandings" (p. iii). Throughout this book, we will examine the current state of the art in our thinking about educational policymaking and apply those concepts to specific policies and policy issues. Through the application of theory to practice, we shall highlight the strengths and weaknesses of various approaches and suggest methods and avenues for improvement.

Policy Defined

Despite the increasing importance of using the policy process to change and improve education, the field of policy analysis and policymaking is rather new and ill-defined. In fact, the very definition of *policy* in general, and *education policy* in particular, is complex and confusing. Is a policy a law, a regulation, or a rule that governs the education process? Can inaction constitute a policy? Or is policy far broader and more contextual, even cultural? To what degree is it the whole environment that makes schools function the way they do? In part, the plethora of definitions and terms signals that the field is vital, changing, and new. It also means that as an academic discipline, "policy studies" and "education policy studies" are not yet well delineated and are developing to meet new needs and challenges, as evidenced by a review of recent symposiums and papers sponsored by Division L (Education Politics and Policy) of the American Education Research Association.

A review of definitions of policy reveals just how disparate the field has become. This reflects the fact that studies of policy and policymaking come from a number of disciplines, including political science, public administration, sociology, history, education, and anthropology. As a result, discussion of policy across (and even within) disciplines often degenerates into a "babel of tongues in which participants talk past rather than to one another" (Bobrow & Dryzek, 1987, p. 4).

Defining policy is a bit like trying to define obscenity—you know it when you see it, but it varies from place to place. Harman (1984) views policy as "courses of purposive action . . . directed towards the accomplishment of some intended or desired set of goals" (p. 13). Dye (1992) defines (public) policy as "whatever governments choose to do or not to do" (p. 2), suggesting that government inaction constitutes policy. Agreeing with Dye, Cibulka (1995) includes "both official enactments of government and something as informal as 'practices.' Also, policy may be viewed as the inactions of government" (p. 106).

Earlier, Easton (1965) suggested a normative dimension to policy when he argued policy represents the "authoritative allocation of values" for society (and thus politics as the mechanism through which these values are allocated). In her review of definitions of policy, Fowler (2000) listed seven distinct definitions before proffering her own: "Public policy is the dynamic and value-laden process through which a political system handles a public problem. It includes a government's expressed intentions and official enactments as well as its consistent patterns of activity and inactivity" (p. 9). Public policies are those decisions or actions taken by government to meet "perceived social problems" (Dror, 1971, p. 49). Thus, policy involves a set of goals and choices, setting in motion a set of actions and events (Lasswell, 1951, 1971).

We believe a useful way to define policy is to view it as *a political process where needs, goals, and intentions are translated into a set of objectives, laws, policies, and programs, which in turn affect resource allocations, actions, and outputs, which are the basis for evaluation, reforms, and new policies.* The political process infuses all aspects of our definition of policy—in determining what our needs are, how the problem is defined, what objectives and programs are considered and adopted, the evaluation of outcomes, and what new reforms and policies (if any) are needed. Like Taylor, Rizvi, Lingard, and Henry (1997), we view policy "as a compromise which is struggled over at all stages by competing interests" (p. 24). It is a product of contested terrain.

Formation of a Field: Policy Studies

Considering early writings, human beings have long worked to give meaning to public life. One could read the Hebrew Scriptures from a public policy perspective, understanding how an ancient people sought to organize its religious, moral, and civic life around the Mosaic Code. One could even argue, as does Robert Dahl in his book *On Democracy* (1998), that democratic policy ideals of human dignity and responsibility are "consistent with the most fundamental ethical beliefs and principles. That we are equally God's children is a tenet of Judaism, Christianity, Islam; Buddhism incorporates a somewhat similar view" (p. 66).

Although public policy is as old as civilization itself, the systematic analysis of policy is a relatively new endeavor, compared to more traditional areas of inquiry within the social sciences, such as political science and sociology. The advent of World War II, coupled with the development of operations research and advances in economics and social psychology, "helped point the way to a more systematic and empirical investigation of policy making" (McCool, 1995, p. 1). In 1951, Harold Lasswell conceptualized "policy science" as an emerging field of inquiry. Despite these early efforts, "It was not until the late 1960s" with the Great Society programs of the Johnson administration, "that the study of public policy began to blossom and gain credibility" (McCool, 1995, p. 3). As Robertson and Judd determined, "the explicit study of policy processes and outcomes evolved because of the proliferation of government programs in the 1960s and 1970s" (1989, p. vii).

During the late 1960s and early 1970s, a number of significant policy studies were conducted, as the federal government made substantial funds available for policy research. Among the most important studies of the period were James S. Coleman et al.'s *Equality of Educational Opportunity* (1966) and Christopher Jencks et al.'s *Inequality* (1972). Using large-scale databases, both studies examined the effect of demographics and schooling on the educational achievement of children. The Coleman study is "arguably, the most important and influential study ever concerned with the administration of America's schools" (Haller & Kleine, 2001, p. 21). Among the study's many findings, Coleman and colleagues documented the degree of racial segregation in schools, particularly in northern cities. Widespread achievement gaps among ethnic groups were documented as well. Coleman and colleagues determined that family background factors, school facilities and curriculum, teacher quality, and student body characteristics accounted for only 16 percent of the variation in student achievement. In *Inequality*, Jencks et al. (1972) found that educational opportunity, cognitive skills, educational credentials, occupational status, income, and job satisfaction were all inequitably distributed in society, with important implications for the education of children. Jencks concluded, however, that "equalizing educational opportunity would do very little to make adults more equal" and recommended government intervention to ensure a more equitable distribution of income throughout society (p. 255).

As is evident from these early studies, the emergent field of policy studies is much like "a child growing up . . . struggling for a clear identity" (Cibulka, 1995, p. 106), reflecting both the relative newness of the field and its multidisciplinary nature. Policy studies draw scholars and policymakers from education, political science, management, sociology, public administration, history, and psychology, to name only a few. This intellectual eclecticism, as Cibulka (1995) observes, is both a strength and a weakness. It is a strength insofar as the field is dynamic, important, and attractive to scholars from a variety of fields. Intellectual eclecticism is a weakness because we see no agreement whatsoever on methods or approaches; not even one singular conference brings these diverse scholars together.

Formation of a Sub-Field: Policy Studies in Education

During the last three decades, policy studies have proliferated in virtually all areas of public life, including education (Cibulka, 1995; Dye, 2002; Mawhinney, 1993). Early researchers seemed adept at describing and analyzing the political actors involved and the rather mechanistic processes of policymaking and change. However, often the questions of why policies change and to what ends (who benefits and who loses?) were not as well understood. Consequently, research is better at describing what happens to whom, why, and when, and often less able to figure out better ways of crafting policy in education (Bennett & Howlett, 1992).

Policy studies in education gained prominence as a vital field of endeavor in the United States in the 1950s and 1960s, as federal and state governments created new policies and sought more resources to cope with such critical problems in education as: how to educate twelve million returning World War II soldiers (the G.I. Bill); how to win the race for space and the escalating Cold War (National Science Foundation and the National Defense Education Act); and how to overcome racial and social injustice (the *Brown* court decisions and Title I of the Elementary and Secondary Education Act of 1965). These needs, accompanied by vast appropriations for federal research grants, spurred the creation of the subfield of policy studies in education within political science and related disciplines.

Most of the early analysis of U.S. education policy focused on a single issue or policy, such as the passage and implementation of ESEA (see Bailey & Mosher, 1968), the first significant federal education law for K–12 public education. Scholars also tended to apply only one theory, if any, such as "interest group politics"— concentrating on questions of which power groups supported the law and which ones resisted it, and how their interactions and compromises shaped both the final policy and how it was implemented.

Would not a different lens, or a multitude of lenses, produce other equally important questions and, perhaps, different conclusions? For example, critical theorists would question the sources of support for ESEA in 1965 and thereafter, such as the Civil Rights movement and national efforts to extend equal education opportunity to the poor and children of color. A critical theorist or postmodernist might view the law as largely symbolic, pointing out that once rich suburban school districts realized that twelve poor, low-achieving students led to federal funding for an ESEA Title I teacher (and a resource room), low-income students became a useful commodity and federal aid was forthcoming. The overwhelming majority (95 percent) of the nation's school districts, whether rich or poor, receive Title I aid. The result of the nearly universal access to federal largess built a powerful coalition of poor, middle-class, and wealthy districts. This new power bloc meant that ESEA policies have become politically popular and virtually sacrosanct—even congressional Republicans have been willing to support increases in aid above those recommended by Democratic presidents (Traub, 2000).

Some policy scholars argue that this ESEA coalition formed as much around money as the needs of poor students, explaining in large part what happened when President Nixon tried repeatedly to repeal the law, and President Reagan pressed to privatize it four times through Chapter I vouchers for eligible children in private and parochial schools. Both presidents failed to kill or radically change the Title I (Chapter I) program, developments best understood using both interest group theory to explain the broad coalition in support of ESEA and the critical theorist/postmodernist perspective to show the ability of the middle classes to capitalize on programs designed for the poor. Analysis of the effects of *Sesame Street* on television is another example of the continuing ability of the middle and upper classes to take advantage of new societal opportunities, like federal education programs, while the poor often get left behind.

Emerging Research Directions

Incorporating History into Education Policy Studies

Traditional policy studies often become trapped in the "fallacy of presentism"—the tendency in policy studies to ignore the effects of past policies and their programmatic, institutional, cultural, and organizational histories. "Research studies tend to focus exclusively on the present rather than past or future trends" (Majchrzak, 1984, p. 20). However, as Fuhrman (1989) observed in her six-state analysis of implementation and reform, context really matters. Any social phenomenon "must be understood in its historical context" (Tuchman, 1994, p. 306). The context is more than historical—it is also highly personal, temporal, and ideological. Neustadt and May (1986) assert that "decision-makers always draw on past experience, whether conscious of doing so or not" (p. xxi). Time, too, may properly be conceived of as a stream of events, somehow connected to previous decisions (Neustadt & May, 1986).

Failure, then, to consider adequately the role and effects of history and context leads to a poor conceptualization of the policy process and a lack of understanding that (1) history repeats itself, as the same education problems and programs reappear under different names and labels; (2) history influences current decisionmaking, as we are all captives of our past experiences; and (3) history shapes the conditions under which education change and reform occurs. How could one even consider school reform for inner-city African American students without knowing the history of slavery, Jim Crow, Reconstruction, Civil Rights, and the culture of the black family? Yet repeatedly, policy "solutions" are offered that ignore the history and context of educational problems, presenting them as if new and undiscovered.

Longitudinal analysis may help to compensate for the fallacy of presentism by illuminating the underlying forces, the "grid of social regularities" (Scheurich,

1994, p. 313) that shape and often determine the scope and nature of policy change. While researchers have long been aware of the need for history and context, they frequently ignored or dismissed the structural character and connections of social and educational problems when conducting their analysis. According to Warren (1978), "linear studies of particular policy issues hold some [intrinsic] interest, but a more significant contribution is the analysis of such developments within broader social and cultural contexts" (p. 16). Because we believe that policy must be contextually understood and developed, the theories presented in Chapter Two focus particular attention on this oft-overlooked aspect of policymaking and reform.

Viewing Policy through Multiple Lenses

Education policy needs to be examined through multiple theories or lenses because many traditional policy analyses are too narrow and static, leading to inadequate conceptualizations of complex sociopolitical phenomena (Hall, 1993; Mazzoni, 1995; Sroufe, 1995). In her critique of traditional policy studies in education, Young (1999) asserted that traditional policy studies "do not provide a comprehensive understanding of the policy problems being researched and, thus, should not be used as the sole basis for making educational policy" (p. 677). Often, theories or models of education policy analysis, particularly those using a traditional, rationalist frame such as David Easton's "systems" framework, fail to explain adequately what occurs within the "black box," as policy inputs are converted to policy outputs. Mawhinney (1994), for example, states that "there is general agreement that current frameworks of policy fail to guide understanding of the politics of policy change" (pp. 1–2). "Many of our efforts to chronicle policy events are unsatisfactory because they lack attention to the basic political structure and processes, thereby providing an incomplete and, frequently, erroneous understanding" (Sroufe, 1995, p. 79). "The field of inquiry is too broad and varied to fit within a single theoretical framework or set of methodologies" (Dresang, 1983, p. ix).

Several recent approaches to policy studies, such as Sabatier and Jenkins-Smith's (1993) advocacy coalition model, are improvements over traditional approaches insofar as they improve our understanding of (1) who participates in the policy process; (2) the dynamics of the policymaking process; and (3) the ways in which institutions interact with one another and with various interest groups, media, and policy communities. Lasswell (1951) argued for the creation of a rigorous, scientific approach to policy studies that could be used to craft good policy. However, critics such as Doron (1992) assert that we are no closer to achieving these goals today than we were in the 1950s. Lamented McCool (1995), "it seems that just about every educational construct that we have developed has been debunked or discarded" in the postmodernist era (p. 390).

The study of public policy in general and education policy in particular suffers under the burden of complexity and confusing models and theories. It is not that the field has too few theories; rather, it has too many. The field offers analysts a confusing array of perspectives and therefore a lack of discipline, direction, and scientific rigor. It is not the absence of theory but the "plethora" of theories of policy studies that contradicts the once prominent view that policy analysis was "atheoretical and limited" (Blair & Maser, 1977, p. 282). As McCool (1995) points out, "there has been undeniable progress in the development of policy theory. It would be a serious mistake to conclude that we do not have a rich theoretical tradition in policy science" (p. 291). What is needed is "to figure out how all these concepts, theories, and approaches relate to each other" (McCool, 1995, p. 393). "To a great extent the future success and direction of policy studies will be determined by the extent to which policy theorists investigate and resolve this balkanization of policy theory" (McCool, 1995, p. 393).

It is this balkanization of theories in educational policymaking that this book attempts to remedy. We believe policy theories should be practical; they should be "directly relevant to applied policy problems" (McCool, 1995, p. 396). "If we can determine the appropriate role of theory in relation to . . . practice, then we can go far toward determining how to make good use of the various frames" (Bobrow & Dryzek, 1987, p. 16). For far too long, argues Young (1999), "Policy studies has remained a narrow and undertheorized area, relying upon functionalist, rational, and scientific models of operationalization and explanation" (p. 678). "Alternatives to positivism, along with traditional positivist approaches," according to McCool (1995), "provide an epistemological diversity that increases our ability to match theory to application" (p. 400).

These alternatives include critical theory, institutional theory, feminism, and postmodernist/poststructuralist theories of policymaking. This book applies this epistemological diversity to six critical educational policy issues, highlighting the utility of theory for improving schools. The theories are also applied to the policy process itself—to the processes of problem definition, agenda setting, policy formulation, implementation, and evaluation. To simplify the analytic process, the theories are placed within a four-dimensional framework: the normative, structural, constituentive, and technical frames. These evolve around the central themes of ethics and social justice, which we believe are the primary, core values around which all educational policies should be developed.

Theories of Education Policymaking: An Overview

Seven primary theories of education policymaking are discussed in this book. Like Young (1999), we believe that examining educational policy (both process and product) through multiple lenses and frameworks "may help us better understand the policy problems we study; the relationships among policy discourse, planning, implementation, and practice; the dynamics of policy contexts; and the impact of policy and practice on individuals" (p. 679). Like Young, we see these theories and lenses as complementary, not as contradictory. After all, the purpose of theory, lenses, and frameworks is to help us better understand policy problems in all their complexity. As H. L. Mencken once said, "For every complex problem there is a simple solution. And it is always wrong." Likewise, given the inherently complex, multifaceted nature of educational problems and the crafting of policies to address those problems, we believe it unwise for policy researchers to unnecessarily limit themselves when they seek to address the significant questions of educational policy.

1. *Systems theory* provides a means for analyzing the "policy inputs" including demands, needs, and resources, the "throughputs" that involve the key actors who implement policy, and "policy outputs" such as educated, civic-minded students or improved economic productivity (see Easton, 1965; Senge, 1990; Wirt & Kirst, 1997). Systems theory has the distinct advantage of a long history, great adaptability, and a useful framework for handling almost any policy problem.

2. *Neopluralist advocacy coalition and interest group theories* are grounded in a political science perspective that seeks to answer "who gets what, when, and how," as key coalitions struggle to obtain from government the resources and support they believe necessary (see Sabatier & Jenkins-Smith, 1993). These key actors (legislators, governors, mayors, superintendents, school boards, etc.) work out their interest group concerns in a variety of arenas, depending on the level in the federalist system (federal, state, county, city, school district, and individual schools). Bringing interest groups and their arenas together provides a useful means of understanding how laws are passed, shaped, implemented, and evaluated.

3. *Neoinstitutional theory* posits that the structure of societal and political organizations exerts independent effects on policy (see Crowson, Boyd, & Mawhinney, 1996; Peters, 1999; Scott, 1995). In fact, it would be difficult to analyze school policies without understanding both the political institutions that enact and enforce laws and regulations and the schools and classrooms where policy is implemented. The structure, culture, leadership, and demands of organizations that pass and implement education policy are essential to any true understanding of policymaking in education.

4. *Critical theory* questions the existing economic, political, and social purposes of schooling and examines policy through the lens of oppressed groups, with a normative orientation toward freeing disenfranchised groups from conditions of domination and subjugation (see Freire, 1970; Habermas, 1971, 1975, 1983, 1988; Held, 1980). Primarily concerned with issues of equity and social justice, policy analysis from the perspective of critical theory focuses on the hidden (and often unequal) uses of power through which policy is transformed into practice.

Using this approach, critical theorists are able to focus attention on the effects of policy on various groups and the ways in which policy reproduces (and reinforces) societal inequities.

5. *Feminist theory* is concerned primarily with the often unequal effects of education policies on issues relating to gender and sexual difference, including how education policies are translated through institutional processes that serve to reinforce or encourage gender inequity (see Gilligan, 1982; Marshall, 1993, 1997; Marshall & Anderson, 1995). Related issues for policy analysis from a feminist theoretical perspective include policies affecting women's access and choice within the educational system, women's "ways of knowing," and the (re)structuration of power relations through policy.

Feminist theorists question and problematize seemingly neutral policies and institutions, such as bureaucracy, seeking to understand the "subtleties of power and control" that shape patterns of dominance and subordination (Ferguson, 1984, p. 5). For example, in her classic feminist analysis of the nature of bureaucracy, Ferguson (1984) argued, "Once bureaucracy is seen as an *issue,* rather than as simply a fact of modern life or a neutral method of organizing activity, questions about it appear in a fundamentally different light. A critical analysis of bureaucracy entails an analysis of the history and structure of bureaucratic society, a society permeated by both the institutional forms and the language of instrumental rationality" (p. 6).

6. *Postmodernism* takes a much different view of education policy and outcomes than traditional policy studies. It rejects out of hand the "scientific," more positivistic perspectives on policymaking and argues that policy is contextually defined by those in authority and has little validity when separated from its setting (see Scheurich, 1994). These critics argue that the neutral, scientific pretense of policy analysis merely screens the highly racist, sexist, and classist nature of most policies. The reason, according to the postmodernist, that schools do not readily improve is that privileged elites in society seek to maintain the status quo, allowing the predominately upper class, Anglo, male leadership to remain in authority at the expense of the poor, women, and people of color.

7. *Ideological theories of policymaking* place policy into a partisan, politically value-laden structure, hoping to gain insight into the econo-political context surrounding key policies (see Cibulka, 1999). In its simplest form, is the particular policy associated with a left-liberal perspective, stressing equity, involvement, or multicultural, multilingual values? Or is the policy sponsored and supported by a right-wing, neoconservative coalition that stresses competition, choice, minimal government involvement, and more free market, privatized approaches? Besides the left–right perspective on policy, this ideological lens permits a more fine-tuned look at subtle value differences held on both the right and left: as between the radical religious right or the moderate economic right versus the radical left, socialist, Marxist, moderate, or neoliberal positions. Although European scholars are more comfortable with such terms and analysis, U.S. analysts eschew such labels, sacrificing the kind of ideological-political sophistication in scholarship commonly found in international research on education policy (Fowler, 1995).

A Call for Theoretical Pluralism

In *Essence of Decision,* Graham Allison (1971) used three different models (rational actor, organizational process, and governmental process) to explain the decision-making processes involved in the Cuban missile crisis. Allison noted that each model produced "different answers to the same question. But as we observe the models at work, what is equally striking are the differences in the ways the analysts conceive of the problem, shape the puzzle, unpack the summary questions, and pick up pieces of the world in search of an answer" (p. 249). In *Reframing Organizations,* Lee Bolman and Terrence Deal (1991) used four frameworks—structural, human resource, political, and symbolic—to understand the complex world of modern organizations. The authors believe that viewing organizational problems through multiple lenses enables leaders to better understand both the problems being confronted and to consider a wider range of possible policy options for addressing those problems.

In a similar vein, Gareth Morgan's (1997) *Images of Organization* employs various metaphors to help readers understand organizational processes, including organizations as machines, as organisms, as brains, as cultures, as political systems, as psychic prisons, as instruments of domination, and in flux and in transformation. Morgan asserts that "no single theory will ever give us a perfect or all-purpose point of view" but can provide "fresh ways of seeing, understanding, and shaping the situations that we want to organize and manage" (pp. 5–6). Morgan argues that viewing organizations through the lenses of competing metaphors better enables readers to understand the strengths and weaknesses of each theory and to adopt a more reflective approach to grappling with organizational issues. Thus, when examining policy, we must examine it through multiple lenses, through different perspectives, if we are to understand policy issues and problems in all their glorious complexity.

Each of the perspectives discussed in this book adds new insight into education policy. Although they may appear quite distinct, in fact some of these lenses can be applied in combination, sometimes to strengthen one another, other times calling conclusions into question. Systems theory, advocacy coalitions, and institutional perspectives seem somewhat compatible, because various interest groups in different institutions can be subsumed by the systems theorists as just another policy "input." The theories focus attention on how policy is made—its structure and process. Interpretive and ideological theories of policymaking share similar concerns, presuppositions, and foci, particularly a critical, skeptical, and reflexive view of the structure and processes of policymaking in education. These theories explore the critical question of for whom policy is made. Who benefits?

Who loses? How could education policy be made more ethical and just to benefit disenfranchised groups?

As we apply these lenses to key education policies, the limits and usefulness of each of the theories discussed in Chapter 2 will become more apparent. The cases will highlight the utility of various theories in accurately capturing and explaining school policies, identifying what is most significant about the policies, representing each theory's congruence with political reality, and suggesting avenues for further research and inquiry. Given the pressure placed on school systems by increasingly activist and interventionist state governments, a pressing need exists to craft better educational policies to improve schools. It is only through better policies that we can produce better schools.

Structure of the Book

The authors discussed at length how best to organize and present a policy perspective on education reform. Should we make the book issue-oriented, theoretical, or both? How might theory and example, concepts and practices, be combined for best effect? To what degree should the book focus on the processes of policymaking in education, the policies themselves and their implementation, or the effects of policy? To what extent was historical context essential in explaining the evolution of such education issues as equity, choice, standards, union–management relations, finance, curriculum, testing, and governance? To what degree do theories make much sense without examples? And which theories and issues should be included?

We chose to examine several major theories or lenses of policy analysis in education, drawn from the major schools of thought in research on educational policy. Incorporating both traditional policy approaches and newer, alternative theories of policy analysis, the book reflects the diversity of approaches in the field of education policy analysis. Given this diversity, we recognize that omissions have been made. No text could possibly cover in detail all the various theories and approaches used by scholars and policymakers in education—the field is simply too broad and ill-defined. Drawing from Kerr (1976), we assert that "the quality of our making and implementing of educational policies depends, in large measure, upon the quality of our individual maps of the conceptual and normative terrain of educational policy" (p. iii). By grouping the theories into practical, conceptual boxes, we hope to accomplish two objectives: (1) bring some conceptual clarity to the field of education policymaking and analysis and (2) provide a framework to help policymakers create usable knowledge.

The theories examined include systems theory, advocacy coalition theory, institutional theory, critical theory, feminist theory, postmodernist theory, and ideological perspectives. These theories are integrated into a coherent, conceptual four-dimensional framework to facilitate the viewing of policy from multiple perspectives. We then apply this theoretical framework to six education policies—again having to select from the scores of important areas. The policies examined include those affecting school organization and governance, labor relations, curriculum, finance, charter schools, and student personnel. To some degree, however, once we show the uses of theory in explaining policy practices across these areas, it is possible to then apply these lenses to new issues as they arise.

Chapter Discussion Questions

1. What difference, if any, do the various definitions of policy make for our understanding of studies of education policy?

2. In education, theoretical pluralism is considered a virtue. What effect does this pluralism have on our understanding of policy? On the evaluation of policy? Is there a downside to this pluralism?

Seminal Works

Several works provide an excellent overview of the policy process, although most use the traditional stage model of the process. Among the most popular is Thomas Dye's (2002) *Understanding Public Policy,* now in its tenth edition. Dye examines different models of politics and policymaking, including group theory, elite theory, rationalism, incrementalism, game theory, public choice theory, and systems theory. Dye devotes a chapter to several policy areas, including education, and explores agenda setting and policy evaluation.

Typically, edited anthologies would not be considered seminal works. However, because most graduate students lack solid disciplinary backgrounds in political science and public policy, we believe it important to include two anthologies that contain selections from several leading authors in the field of policy studies. Daniel McCool's (1995) edited anthology *Public Policy Theories, Models, and Concepts: An Anthology* consists of a collection of classic and more recent essays on public policy theories within political science, including works by David Truman, David Easton, Charles Lindblom, Theodore Lowi, Hugh Heclo, and Paul Sabatier. The text provides a solid overview of how political scientists view and conceptualize the study of public policy. Another excellent collection of readings in public policy is Stella Theodoulou and Matthew Cahn's (1995) *Public Policy: The Essential Readings,* which contains selections from Robert Dahl, Murray Edelman, C. Wright Mills, John Kingdon, Eugene Bardach, Aaron Wildavsky, and Stuart Nagel.

For students interested in applying multiple models or lenses to the study of policy problems, the following three studies are recommended: In 1971, Graham Allison produced his instant classic, *Essence of Decision,* in which he used the rational actor, organizational process, and governmental politics models to explain the Cuban missile crisis. Twenty years later, in *Reframing Organizations,* Lee Bolman and Terrence Deal (1991) used four frameworks—structural, human resource, political, and symbolic—to understand the complex world of modern organizations.

This work quickly became a leading text in administrator preparation programs nationwide. Another classic applying various models or lenses to organizations is Gareth Morgan's (1997) *Images of Organization*. The first edition of Morgan's book was also used extensively in graduate-level administrator preparation courses throughout the country. Morgan employs various metaphors to help readers understand organizational processes, including organizations as machines, as organisms, as brains, as cultures, as political systems, as psychic prisons, as instruments of domination, and in flux and in transformation.

References

Allison, G. T. (1971). *Essence of decision: Explaining the Cuban missile crisis.* Boston: Little, Brown and Company.

Bailey, S. K., & Mosher, E. K. (1968). *ESEA: The Office of Education administers a law.* Syracuse, NY: Syracuse University Press.

Bennett, C. J., & Howlett, M. (1992). The lessons of learning: Reconciling theories of policy learning and policy change. *Policy Sciences, 25,* 275–294.

Blair, J., & Maser, S. (1977). Axiomatic versus empirical models in policy studies. *Policy Studies Journal, 5,* 282–289.

Bobrow, D., & Dryzek, J. (1987). *Policy analysis by design.* Pittsburgh, PA: University of Pittsburgh Press.

Bolman, L. G., & Deal, T. E. (1991). *Reframing organizations.* San Francisco: Jossey-Bass.

Cibulka, J. G. (1995). Policy analysis and the study of the politics of education. In J. D. Scribner & D. H. Layton (Eds.), *The study of educational politics* (pp. 105–125). Washington, DC: Falmer Press.

Cibulka, J. G. (1999). Ideological lenses for interpreting political and economic changes affecting schooling. In J. Murphy & K. Seashore Louis (Eds.), *Handbook of research on educational administration* (2nd ed., pp. 163–182). San Francisco: Jossey-Bass.

Coleman, J. S., Campbell, E. Q., Hobson, C. J., McPartland, J., Mood, A. M., Weinfeld, F. D., & York, R. L. (1966). *Equality of educational opportunity.* Washington, DC: U.S. Government Printing Office.

Crowson, R. L., Boyd, W. L., & Mawhinney, H. B. (Eds.). (1996). *The politics of education and the new institutionalism: Reinventing the American school.* London: Falmer Press.

Dahl, R. (1998). *On democracy.* New Haven, CT: Yale University Press.

Doron, G. (1992). Policy sciences: The state of the discipline. *Policy Studies Review, 11,* 303–309.

Dresang, D. (1983). Foreword. In D. Paris & J. Reynolds. *The logic of policy inquiry* (pp. i–xiv). New York: Longman.

Dror, Y. (1971). *Design for policy sciences.* New York: American Elsevier.

Dye, T. (1992). *Understanding public policy* (7th ed.). Englewood Cliffs, NJ: Prentice Hall.

Dye, T. (2002). *Understanding public policy* (10th ed.). Englewood Cliffs, NJ: Prentice Hall.

Easton, D. (1965). *A framework for political analysis.* Chicago: University of Chicago Press.

Ferguson, K. E. (1984). *The feminist case against bureaucracy.* Philadelphia: Temple University Press.

Fowler, F. C. (1995). The international arena: The global village. In J. D. Scribner & D. H. Layton (Eds.), *The study of educational politics* (pp. 89–102). Washington, DC: Falmer Press.

Fowler, F. C. (2000). *Policy studies for educational leaders: An introduction.* Upper Saddle River, NJ: Merrill.

Freire, P. (1970). *Pedagogy of the oppressed.* (M. Bergman Ramos, Trans.). New York: Seabury Press.

Fuhrman, S. H. (1989). State politics and education reform. In J. Hannaway & R. Crowson (Eds.), *The politics of reforming school administration* (pp. 61–75). New York: Falmer Press.

Gilligan, C. (1982). *In a different voice.* Cambridge, MA: Harvard University Press.

Habermas, J. (1971). *Knowledge and human interests.* Boston: Beacon Press.

Habermas, J. (1975). *Legitimation crisis.* Boston: Beacon Press.

Habermas, J. (1983). *The theory of communicative action, Vol. 1.* Boston: Beacon Press.

Habermas, J. (1988). *The theory of communicative action, Vol. 2.* Boston: Beacon Press.

Hall, P. A. (1993). Policy paradigms, social learning, and the state: The case of economic policymaking in Britain. *Comparative Politics, 25*(3), 275–296.

Haller, E. J., & Kleine, P. F. (2001). *Using educational research: A school administrator's guide.* New York: Longman.

Harman, G. (1984). Conceptual and theoretical issues. In J. R. Hough (Ed.), *Educational policy: An international survey* (pp. 13–29). London: Croom Helm.

Held, D. (1980). *Introduction to critical theory: Horkheimer to Habermas.* Berkeley: University of California Press.

Jencks, C., Smith, M., Acland, H., Bane, M. J., Cohen, D., Gintis, H., Heyns, B., & Michelson, S. (1972). *Inequality.* New York: Basic Books.

Kerr, D. H. (1976). *Educational policy: Analysis, structure, and justification.* New York: David McKay.

Kowalski, T. J. (1995). *Keepers of the flame: Contemporary urban superintendents.* Thousand Oaks, CA: Corwin Press.

Lasswell, H. (1951). The policy orientation. In D. Lerner & H. Lasswell (Eds.), *The policy sciences* (pp. 3–15). Stanford, CA: Stanford University Press.

Lasswell, H. (1971). *A pre-view of policy sciences.* New York: American Elsevier.

Majchrzak, A. (1984). *Methods for policy research.* Newbury Park, CA: Sage.

Marshall, C. (Ed.). (1993). *The new politics of race and gender.* Washington, DC: Falmer Press.

Marshall, C. (Ed.). (1997). *Feminist critical policy analysis* (Vols. 1–2). London: Falmer Press.

Marshall, C., & Anderson, G. L. (1995). Rethinking the public and private spheres: Feminist and cultural studies perspectives on the politics of education. In

J. D. Scribner & D. H. Layton (Eds.), *The study of educational politics* (pp. 169–182). Washington, DC: Falmer Press.

Mawhinney, H. B. (1993). *An interpretive framework for understanding the politics of policy change.* Unpublished doctoral dissertation, University of Ottawa, Ottawa, Canada.

Mawhinney, H. B. (1994). *An interpretive framework for understanding the politics of policy change.* Paper presented at the Annual Meeting of the Canadian Association for Studies in Educational Administration. Calgary, Alberta, Canada.

Mazzoni, T. L. (1995). State policymaking and school reform: Influences and influentials. In J. D. Scribner & D. H. Layton (Eds.), *The study of educational politics* (pp. 53–73). Washington, DC: Falmer Press.

McCool, D. C. (Ed.). (1995). *Public policy theories, models, and concepts: An anthology.* Englewood Cliffs, NJ: Prentice Hall.

Morgan, G. (1997). *Images of organization* (2nd ed.). Thousand Oaks, CA: Sage.

Neustadt, R. E., & May, E. R. (1986). *Thinking in time: The uses of history for decision-makers.* New York: The Free Press.

Peters, B. G. (1999). *Institutional theory in political science.* London: Pinter.

Porter, A. (1998). The effects of upgrading policies on high school mathematics and science. In D. Ravitch (Ed.), *Brookings papers on education policy, 1998* (pp. 123–172). Washington, DC: The Brookings Institution Press.

Robertson, D., & Judd, D. (1989). *The development of American public policy.* Glenview, IL: Scott-Foresman.

Sabatier, P. A., & Jenkins-Smith, H. C. (Eds.). (1993). *Policy change and learning: An advocacy coalition approach.* Boulder, CO: Westview Press.

Scheurich, J. J. (1994). Policy archaeology: A new policy studies methodology. *Journal of Education Policy, 9*(4), 297–316.

Scott, W. R. (1995). *Institutions and organizations.* Thousand Oaks, CA: Sage.

Senge, P. (1990). *The fifth discipline: The art and practice of the learning organization.* New York: Doubleday.

Sroufe, G. E. (1995). Politics of education at the federal level. In J. D. Scribner & D. H. Layton (Eds.), *The study of educational politics* (pp. 75–88). Washington, DC: Falmer Press.

Taylor, S., Rizvi, F., Lingard, B., & Henry, M. (1997). *Educational policy and the politics of change.* London: Routledge.

Theocoulou, S. Z., & Cahn, M. A. (Eds.). (1994). *Public policy: The essential readings.* New York: Prentice Hall.

Traub, J. (January 16, 2000). What no school can do. *The New York Times Magazine*, pp. 52–57, 68, 81, 90–91.

Tuchman, G. (1994). Historical social science. In N. K. Denzin & Y. S. Lincoln (Eds.), *Handbook of qualitative research* (pp. 306–323). Thousand Oaks, CA: Sage.

Tyack, D. B. (1974). *The one best system: A history of American urban education.* Cambridge, MA: Harvard University Press.

Warren, D. R. (1978). A past for the present. In D. R. Warren (Ed.), *History, education, and public policy* (pp. 1–20). Berkeley, CA: McCutchan.

Wirt, F. M., & Kirst, M. W. (1997). *The political dynamics of American education.* Berkeley, CA: McCutchan.

Young, M. D. (1999). Multifocal educational policy research: Toward a method for enhancing traditional educational policy studies. *American Educational Research Journal, 36*(4), 677–714.

2

Theories of Education Policymaking

POLICY VIGNETTE • *President Signs First Major Federal Aid to Education Bill*

On September 12, 1965, on the front porch of a one-room schoolhouse in Stonewall, Texas, where he had taught, President Lyndon B. Johnson made history, signing the Elementary and Secondary Education Act (ESEA), the largest and arguably most important piece of federal legislation for public education in U.S. history. Its main purpose, under Title I (later renamed Chapter I), was to assist the nation's poorest, most disadvantaged children, offering them extra help in the basic subjects of reading, writing, and mathematics. Since 1965, over $200 billion has gone to states and school districts to give assistance to the nation's neediest students.

ESEA has been reauthorized eight times, has been changed and augmented, and has been the subject of several key court cases, but remarkably its initial shape and purpose have survived legal challenges, conservative Republican administrations, and attacks from various interest groups. ESEA is a useful case to introduce theories of education policymaking, because the laws, policies, and programs have been examined repeatedly by policy analysts. In fact, we can safely say that ESEA and its descendents were the watershed developments for the field of education policy. Its passage, implementation, evaluation, and re-authorizations have been exhaustively reviewed from a number of conceptual perspectives, allowing us to illustrate a number of "lenses" or theoretical viewpoints examined in this chapter.

Positivist Theories of Policymaking in Education

Systems Theory

Systems theory is among the oldest, most common approaches to explain both the policy process and its outcomes. It became fashionable during the Vietnam War, as leaders such as Secretary of Defense Robert F. McNamara stressed a "systems approach" to weapons development, sometimes leading to disaster. For example, once the Secretary selected a single, multipurpose F-15 fighter aircraft, instead of two planes of different designs, to take off from Navy aircraft carriers and land at Air Force bases. The plane turned out to be somewhat too small and limited for the Air Force and a bit too large and heavy for the Navy—and actually cost more than two conventional planes.

In the policy vignette described above, systems theory views the political demands to help poor children as a key policy "input," along with demands from key groups, resources, and votes. These policy inputs, then, are translated into legislation and implemented as part of the policy through-put process. According to David Easton (1965), early innovator of systems analysis in politics, policies and programs become the key policy outputs. As shown in Figure 2.1, as updated by Wirt and Kirst (2001), systems theory has been applied extensively by political analysts, where the politics shapes the pressures and the process, and the policies become one output.

A systems model—whether biological, physical, or social—has certain key elements that can be applied to education policy. A "system" is a purposive arrangement of "subsystems" that:

- *inputs* resources (whether oxygen and calories, as with a living system; gasoline and oxygen, as in an internal combustion engine; or people, know-how, and resources, as with a school, hospital, or other social system);
- *throughputs* these resources (to convert them into energy in a living organism, productivity in a physical system, or teaching and learning, in the case of schools);
- *outputs* the finished product (whether mobility, fertility, and respiration in organic systems, a new car in a factory, or a high school graduate in a social system).

The concept of systems analysis, useful in understanding education policymaking for several reasons, breaks the policy effort into its component parts, while preserving the sense of the interdependencies of the processes. Senge (1990), for example, notes that "systems thinking is a conceptual framework, a body of knowledge and tools that have developed over the past fifty years" (p. 7). Applied to education, systems theory views education policy as a series of stages in which various political actors and interest groups shape the outcome of policy through institutions.

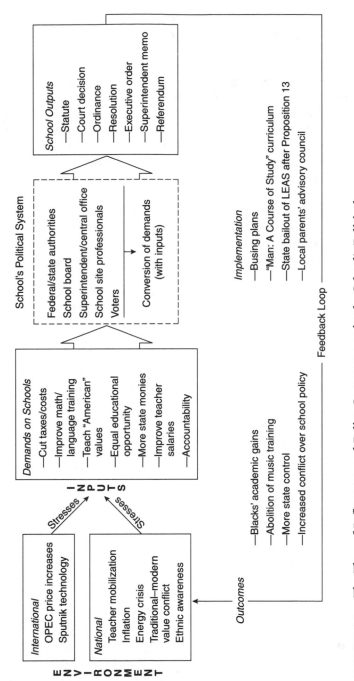

FIGURE 2.1 *The Flow of Influences and Policy Consequences in the School's Political System*

Source: Frederick M. Wirt and Michael W. Kirst, *The Political Dynamics of American Education*, 2nd ed., 2001. Richmond, CA: McCutchan.

The systems approach is comprehensive, emphasizing the "influence relationships among key actors—individuals, groups, and coalitions—as demands are converted into decisions" (Mazzoni, 1993, p. 359). The value of this approach is that it is all-encompassing, accounting for the various forces, actors, and institutions that affect policy. Senge (1990) observes that "we tend to focus on snapshots of isolated parts of the system" (p. 7), rather than the whole. However, "you can only understand the system . . . by contemplating the whole, not any individual part of the pattern" (p. 7). Thus, systems theory has the benefit of integrating the individual parts into a coherent, interrelated theoretical framework. The continued popularity and extensive use of Senge's *The Fifth Discipline* in administrator preparation programs is testament to the utility of systems theory when applied to issues in education.

Systems theory rests on the notion that policymaking and implementation take place in an open systems environment. Again, using the biological and physical systems model, we can see that no organism is totally self-contained. It must gather resources from its immediate environment, although it must be able to maintain and manage its boundaries—the semi-permeable membrane that separates an amoeba from its water, or a school from its immediate community. Although some social systems are more closed than others—say, a prison or military training base—all social systems must remain open to their setting and context.

During policymaking, for example, political bodies (Congress, the White House, the U.S. Department of Education, state legislatures) are all subjected to a kaleidoscope of interest groups, demands, and requirements. These forces include, to quote Bailey and Mosher (1968), "competing interest groups, legislative forerunners, academic colloquies, bureaucratic innovations, and personal political and administrative initiatives," which often come together to shape policy—or to block it (p. 206). Other inputs include the "views and wishes of constituencies, testimonials, and the 'give-and-take' of colleagues, superiors, staff opinions, existing policies, and preconceived attitudes" (Majchrzak, 1984, p. 55). This approach led Abrams (1993) to observe that

> the range of relevant contingencies and organizational and political constraints bearing upon education policy leaders is very broad, extending from constitutional and statutory provisions of formal authority and role, to the dynamically changing configurations of informal organizational power . . . in which the rank and file play a central role, to the very human considerations of personal liking or dislike, friendship, trust or distrust, commitment and loyalty. (pp. 169–170)

As shown in Figure 2.1, each of the contingencies and constraints listed by Abrams can be placed within the model of systems theory.

Another advantage of analyzing education policy through the lens of systems theory is that it emphasizes the critical role of the immediate environment in shaping policy—not only at the formation (or formulation) stage, as when the law is being developed and passed, but also at the implementation and evaluation stages of education policies (see Nakamura & Smallwood, 1980). The systems approach, then, allows us to witness the complex processes of making policy and what happens once the law or policy is put to use in the school system. Several scholars stress the significant societal forces that affect policymaking and policy enactment, the entire "change process" (Heclo, 1974). In his analysis of the formation of policy at the federal level, Redman (1973) argues that even the best policies can be derailed by outside forces. For example, global and interstate economic competition affect "arenas and processes in the policy process, as well as the outcomes" (Mazzoni, 1993, p. 367).

Nakamura and Smallwood (1980) go so far as to argue that the policy process actually occurs in three distinct environments, not one. One setting formulates policy, involving interest groups, lobbyists, legislators, and other political entities. Implementation occurs in yet a second policy environment, where regulators and bureaucrats seek to interpret the intent of laws and policies to end-users. When governments want to determine whether a policy is implemented and working as intended, a third environment is created, evaluation, with yet another group of actors and concerns. In each of these three environments—formulation, implementation, and evaluation—politics plays a role, as key actors, institutions, and agencies seek to control the process to their own advantage.

We assert, however, that although the strategies and tactics of interest groups, lobbyists, politicians, bureaucrats, and administrative agencies may differ in each of the three stages outlined by Nakamura and Smallwood, each stage does not bring about an entirely new set of policy activists. Losers in the policy formulation stage simply continue the conflict in the implementation and evaluation phases, attempting to control the outcome and effects of policies, which, as part of the feedback loop, affect future inputs.

Shortcomings of Systems Theory.   One of the merits of systems theory for understanding education policy is that it attempts to include all the forces at all the stages that affect policies. However, in an effort to create an all-encompassing "grand theory" that explains everything, systems theory may explain little in the end. Sabatier (1991a) asserts that such models are inadequate for two reasons. First, they are not causal in the strict sense: rather, they try to be inclusive and predictive. It is their "rationality" that makes them both attractive and vulnerable, because policymaking and enacting cannot possibly anticipate all exigencies and contingencies, no matter how hard social scientists work to account for all the variables in the policy process.

A second shortcoming of systems analysis is that it contains "no coherent assumptions about what forces are driving the process from stage to stage and very few falsifiable hypotheses" (Sabatier, 1991a, p. 145). Sabatier notes that "the result is weakened theoretical coherence across stages" (p. 145). Furthermore, is it not possible that change in education policy is neither linear nor predictable? Wise

(1991) makes us aware that "legislating [not to mention implementing policy] is not so much a mechanistic process that occurs within a defined structure as it is a political and social dynamic within a particular governmental [and cultural] context—a context that itself is altered in response to changes in the wider political and social milieu" (pp. xii–xiii). Confirming this statement by Wise, Weiss (1991) observes that

> given the fragmentation of authority across multiple bureaus, departments, and legislative committees, and the disjointed stages by which actions coalesce into decisions, the traditional model of decisionmaking is a highly stylized rendition of reality. . . . The complexity of government decisionmaking often defies neat compartmentalization. (p. 26)

And neither Wise nor Weiss takes into consideration the chaos that often occurs as fifty states and some 15,000 school systems attempt to implement these laws in 88,000 schools. Thus, one might be tempted to agree with Mawhinney (1994) when she concludes that the systems model fails to "capture the true dynamics of policymaking" (p. 8), leading us to share her argument that the field of education policy analysis "must move beyond conceptions of discrete stages to encompass a focus on policy dynamics" (p. 14).

Besides being overly rational, stage-oriented, and linear, systems theory is virtually empty of cultural context, local color, and style, and thus is robbed of its richness. Policymaking in state capitals varies widely, between Honolulu, Hawaii and Albany, New York; Columbia, South Carolina and Sacramento, California. Besides the obvious differences in partisan party control (Republican versus Democratic) in different legislatures at different times, systems theory seems oblivious to the "learning curve" that surrounds many education issues. States and localities do gain experience and wisdom concerning which laws and policies to pass, how best to couch and phrase them, and the most effective ways to carry these new policies out.

Look at what happened, as described by Bailey and Mosher, between 1965 and 1968, as the federal government set out to implement ESEA. The testing and accountability movement of the 1990s is "learning" much about the trials and tribulations of trying to test all fourth graders in a state (for example, New York and New Jersey). Mistakes are made. New York, for example, included four "practice items" from the preparation booklets on the actual test, seriously endangering the reliability of the entire testing enterprise. New Jersey found that only 18 percent of the students made passing marks on its statewide ESPA test, setting off a screaming protest from upper-class communities whose students had always done well on statewide norm-referenced tests.

It appears that often systems theory ignores the messy details affecting the inputs, throughputs, and outputs of policymaking, while the real world of policymaking is far messier and more interesting. Yet, the model has the value of providing a ready framework for tracking the laws and policies through stages and developments, from conceptualization to policy outcomes, finessing to some degree the "black box" problem of what really happens in each school and classroom (the throughput). Systems theory also has problems explaining what doesn't happen: the laws that never get introduced, are killed off in committee or voted down, or that are legislated and die on the floor for lack of support.

For example, vocational education, the nation's oldest federal program dating back to the 1914 Smith-Lever and Smith-Lanham Acts, has virtually dried up in many communities as districts have ended tracking and found vocational education programs to be the dumping grounds for the "non-college bound" students. In Germany, on the other hand, industrial training is reserved for able students who wish to learn a skill or trade (welding, auto design and repair, computer science, lathe operations). The "slow death" of policies and programs goes unnoticed and unanalyzed, not fitting the stages and rationality of systems theories of policymaking. The real world is more complex and more interesting than mechanistic, step-by-step, linear, unidirectional theories suggest.

It's as though the systems metaphor—represented by mechanical and biological systems—is too blunt an instrument to capture the subtlety and complexity of human social, cultural, and political activity. Systems theory carries us just so far, and no farther. Other policy perspectives and models are necessary, including those that concentrate on the underlying values and ideologies, cultural and social contexts, and overt political and factional arenas in which policy is made and enacted.

Neopluralist Advocacy Coalition and Interest Group Theories

For those wishing to apply an interest group perspective to school policymaking, an examination of political coalitions and the location of political decision-making is critical. Such approaches date from the seminal work of interest group politics by David Truman in the early 1950s, with substantial revisions and modifications made in the last decade (why we refer to them as neopluralist approaches). Truman (1951) explained that much human interaction revolves around groups that exert power on government policy through the need to affiliate. In fact, Truman (1951) explains that:

> The institutions of government are centers of interest-group power; their connections with interest groups may be latent or overt and their activities range in political character from the routinized and widely accepted to the unstable and highly controversial. To make claims, political interest groups will seek access to the key points of decision within these institutions. Such points are scattered throughout the structure, including not only the formally established branches of government but also the political parties in their various forms and the relationships between governmental units and other interest groups. (p. 506)

A growing number of scholars working within the neopluralist tradition in political science take Truman's analysis a step further, asserting that policy is the product of the interactions of competing advocacy or interest groups operating within specific political arenas. Sabatier (1991b) observes that

> one of the conclusions emerging from the policy literature is that understanding the policy process requires looking at an inter-governmental policy community or *sub-system*—composed of bureaucrats, legislative personnel, interest group leaders, researchers, specialist [newspaper] reporters with a substantive policy area—as the basic unit of study. (p. 148)

Note the use of the term "sub-system," showing the influence of systems language on advocacy coalition theories.

Unlike systems theory, which is less concerned about the time factor in policymaking, advocacy coalition theorists study the complex processes of formation and change within interest groups that support or resist a policy or program. As Jenkins-Smith and Sabatier (1994) explain, "understanding the process of policy change—and the role of learning therein—requires a time perspective of a decade or more" (p. 178). For example, the evolution of desegregation policy took decades, as states and communities adjusted to the U.S. Supreme Court ruling against racial segregation (the *Brown* cases in 1954 and 1955), leading from the "war on poverty" and the New Frontier in the mid-1960s to magnet schools and public school choice in the 1970s and 1980s—all different attempts to counter the effects of racial isolation and poverty. Coalition theorists examine the processes of policy formation across decades, as various interest groups join together in the struggle to shape policies that attack segregation and poverty, and their effects on children's learning and achievement.

A second premise of interest group and advocacy coalition models is that key actors from different arenas and institutions interact, form coalitions and factions, fight among themselves, and attempt to hammer out a compromise that will "win" in both the legislature and the field. It is the struggle, the hog trading, and the give-and-take around mutual interests that drive the policies. Which actors want what? From which arenas or institutions? And what will they give up to gain sufficient unity to pass laws and policies? As Jenkins-Smith and Sabatier (1994) observe, "the most useful way to think about policy change over such a time span is through a focus on policy sub-systems, i.e., the interaction of actors from different institutions who follow, and seek to influence, governmental decisions in a policy area" (p. 178).

While public education lobbyists have much to disagree about, whether they represent management (the superintendents and school boards), employees (teachers' unions), parents (PTA and PTO groups), or business and community groups (chambers of commerce), they come together around several key policy issues: allocating more public resources for education, creating new and better programs for schools (e.g., early childhood and kindergarten for all students), and resisting attempts by lawmakers and other interest groups to privatize education, whether through vouchers, out-sourcing programs, or other programs that diminish public control. It becomes, then, a smart strategy to avoid divisive issues (such as merit pay, which divides management and labor within the ranks of public education associations).

Third, interest group pluralism rests on a shared set of beliefs and priorities—not only about the nature of the policy itself, but also about the means and ends to be sought. Hence, groups may agree about the ends but fight over the means, or vice versa. Everyone may agree that all children need to learn to read and write English, but groups differ about whether to adopt a policy of English immersion or bilingual education. Similarly, interest groups may agree that all children should attend four years of high school but not agree on exactly what the secondary school curriculum should be: vocational preparation, college prep, or something in between. Thus, "public policies or programs can be conceptualized in the same manner as belief systems, i.e., as sets of value priorities and causal assumptions about how to realize them" (Jenkins-Smith & Sabatier, 1994, p. 178).

Given the great differences in values, beliefs, and priorities, one would predict ongoing conflict about which policies to pass and implement, and how. Competition in the policy marketplace (arenas), then, shapes and fashions the policy outcomes—a different view than traditional systems theory, where the process produces the "best" or optimum policy. Jenkins-Smith and Sabatier (1993) argue that within the constraints of the policy sub-system, three processes affect policy change (Figure 2.2):

> The first concerns the interaction of competing *advocacy coalitions* within a policy subsystem. An advocacy coalition consists of actors from a variety of public and private institutions at all levels of government who share a set of basic beliefs (policy goals plus causal and other perceptions), and who seek to manipulate the rules, budget, and personnel of government institutions in order to achieve these goals over time. The second set of processes concern *changes external to the subsystem* in socioeconomic conditions, system-wide governing coalitions, and output from other subsystems that provide opportunities and obstacles to the competing coalitions. The third set involves the effects of *stable system parameters*—such as social structure and constitutional rules—on the constraints and resources of the various subsystem actors. (p. 5)

According to the advocacy coalition model, networks of actors learn how best to play the political game to achieve policy objectives. Learning becomes a key factor, getting away from the assumption in much of systems theory that experts know it all and simply impose their will on the process.

Note the use of the nomenclature of neopluralist, advocacy coalition analysis, with the added dimensions of (a) inter-institutional relations, which take into account that more than one "system" or sub-system may be involved; (b) rivalry,

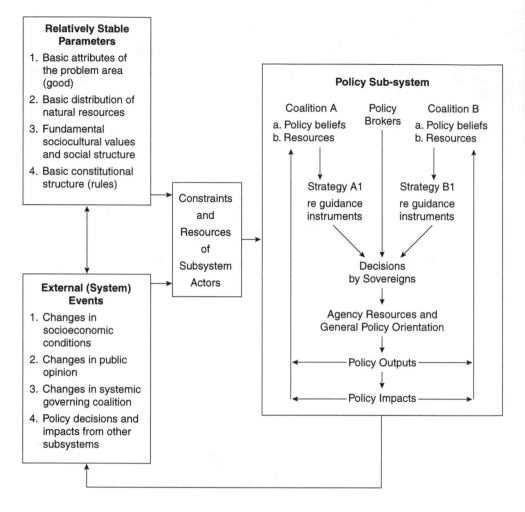

FIGURE 2.2   *The Advocacy Coalition Model of Policymaking*

Source: Paul A. Sabater and Hank C. Jenkins-Smith, *Policy Change and Learning: An Advocacy Coalition Approach,* 1993. Boulder, CO: Westview Press.

if not outright competition, between key interest groups for access and control of the policymaking apparatus; (c) differing beliefs and values that divide and re-unite key groups or coalitions; and (d) the key role of the social structure, rules, constitution, and other constraints on the policymaking process. Advocacy coalition perspectives give greater depth and context to the rather flat, uni-dimensional, and sterile view of systems theory.

This approach has several advantages over the more rational-actor approach inherent in systems theory. Stewart (1991) explains that

> In looking at change in public policy, particularly over an extended period of time, the advocacy coalition approach brings some important elements more explicitly into the analysis than does the rational actor approach. In particular, the role of new information, ideas, or assumptions can be considered in ways other than just as rational actions within organizations. (p. 171)

A number of studies of the policymaking process in education support the theories of interest groups, advocacy coalitions, and their interactions. Burlingame and Geske (1979), for example, found that "the politics of education at the state level is still a politics of interest groups" (p. 71). Similarly, in Canadian policymaking, "the Ontario education policy community is tightly knit with well-defined sets of assumptions and norms" (Mawhinney, 1993, p. 412). This finding suggests that policy communities (another term for a system of interest groups) have a significant impact on the nature, direction, and scope of policy change in education. Mazzoni (1993), in his analysis of changes in state education policymaking over twenty years in Minnesota, found that advocacy coalitions were a driving force behind the school reform movement and argues that Minnesota's state school policy system can be characterized as a far-flung coalition of reform advocates. Mazzoni (1993) states that

> linking together government, business, education, foundation, parent and civic actors—led by elected officials—this coalition has become a potent force in setting forth a restructuring agenda and in influencing the policy system to adopt public school choice as the central element of that agenda. (p. 375)

According to Mazzoni, advocacy coalitions in Minnesota "have repeatedly squared off during the past decade over issues of school reform, with their struggle appearing to have been spawned by a fundamental cleavage over the impact of multiple changes in a turbulent external environment" (p. 377).

Education interest group politics in Pennsylvania appears quite similar, where Feir (1995) found that a coalition of business leaders, media, two governors, and a string of chief state school officers were actively engaged in education reform, while traditional education interest groups played only a minor role in the transformation of the state's education policymaking landscape in the mid-1980s. Feir notes that "the expansion of the conflict over education reform to include business, political, and media leaders, coupled with the substantial neutralization of education interest groups, provided opportunities for new actors to set the agenda" (1995, p. 29). Weaver and Geske (1996) also noted the shifting advocacy coalitions and their key role in promoting policies. According to these researchers, leaders from different agencies and interest groups were "usually able to coalesce on major educational issues" (p. 1). The advocacy coalitions created via this process were able to exert substantial pressure on the legislature to promote their preferred policy solutions.

A major advantage of this approach to the study of education policy is that models of advocacy coalitions incorporate a change component into the theory, freeing it from the static, status quo elements common in other theories. While systems theory stresses regularity and step-by-step processes, advocacy coalition theory expects pressures, changes, and conflict (competition) for scarce resources. Systems theory is "mechanical" in the best sense of the word; advocacy coalition theory is more interactive, dynamic, changing, and flexible. While systems theorists view conflict and competition as "noise" in the process, scholars studying interest group interactions look for competition among contending groups for control and power, and build their predictions around these conflicts and compromises.

Traditional systems theory does incorporate change (vis-à-vis a feedback loop) into the analytical framework (see Figure 2.1). As such, advocacy coalition models share some of the elements of systems thinking. In fact, it should be obvious that much of the intellectual groundwork of interest group analysis rests on systems theory. However, systems theory is not a testable or verifiable theory of policy change so much as a laundry list of factors affecting policy development and change. It lacks the necessary parsimony of desirable theory.

Shortcomings of Advocacy Coalition and Interest Group Models.   Despite their obvious appeal, advocacy coalition and interest group models of policymaking suffer three major weaknesses, some of which are similar to the shortcomings of systems theory. First, while advocacy coalition theory is more sensitive to environmental pressures, it still lacks a fully developed sense of the cultural, micropolitical context. It tends to ignore the structure of organizations in which policy change is to be implemented, as well as differences among schools, districts, and states. We know from years of research that once the lobbying is over, the policy may be changed by street-level bureaucrats. Thus, policymaking does not simply end when the policy is enacted under the watchful eye of competing interest groups. In fact, the next stages are equally important, as local school systems shape and change a policy—a process called "mutual accommodation" by those who study the change process.

Second, in some ways, neopluralist interest group analysis is only half a theory of policymaking and implementation. It is particularly strong in describing and helping to analyze those forces that shape the passage of new laws and policies; unlike systems theory that links policy inputs to program outputs, advocacy coalition and interest group theories lack the tools for tracing policies through to their logical end. True, advocacy groups may influence how a particular policy is to be implemented, where, when, and to whose benefit; who will evaluate the results of a policy and how; and whether a particular policy was successful in reaching its goals and purposes. Advocacy coalition theory, however, appears more concerned about the processes of lobbying than to what happens later in the process.

Finally, advocacy coalition theory appears to lack the language and methods for comparing purpose to outcomes, while input-output theory assumes a feedback loop and some comparison between what goes into the political process and what comes out. As such, advocacy coalition theory is less useful as a tool to evaluate the effectiveness of policy—analysis of effects is limited to what each actor or group learns from the outcome of the political conflict.

Neoinstitutional Theory

An alternative model developed in the fields of political science and organizational theory focuses not on actors and interest groups as change agents but rather on the effects of institutions in helping to shape and mediate policies. Sometimes referred to as the "new institutionalism" or "historical institutionalism," it encompasses a variety of perspectives from rational choice theory to normative institutionalism. The core idea of this approach is the recognition that institutions of the state exert an independent effect on policy, shaping it in profound ways.

First, institutions play a key role in defining individual, group, associational, and societal identities and are, it is believed, much more than simple mirrors or reflectors of societal forces (March & Olsen, 1989). Second, institutions are skillful at raising and focusing resources—whether during the passage of laws or when the policies and resources are being distributed to constituents. Third, because schools—the very centerpiece of education policy—are themselves institutions, we can see the importance of relating the policy, its processes, and its effects to institutional variables. Take one obvious example: a law changing the curriculum of schools will have a profound effect on the organization of the school day, the deployment of teachers, and the activities of staff and students. Neoinstitutional theory helps to place policy into its organizational context and to see the effects of these changes on future actions.

This perspective contrasts sharply with the behavioral point of view, incorporated into both systems and advocacy coalition theories, whereby institutions are "portrayed simply as arenas within which political behavior, driven by more fundamental factors, occurs" (March & Olsen, 1989, p. 1). Renewed attention to institutional variables "grew out of a critique of the behavioral emphasis" that "often obscures the enduring socioeconomic and political structures that mold behavior" (Thelen & Steinmo, 1992, p. 1). According to Thelen and Steinmo (1992),

> Interest group theories that focused on the characteristics and preferences of pressure groups themselves could not account for why interest groups with similar organizational characteristics (including measures of interest group "strength") and

similar preferences could not always influence policy in the same way or to the same extent in different national contexts. (p. 5)

Neoinstitutional theory "can be understood as an attempt to reassert the importance of institutions in modern life, as ideological and structural devices for arranging the social, cultural, and political order" (Cibulka, 1997, p. 318). For example, Senge (1990) argues that "we must look into the underlying structures which shape individual actions and create the conditions where types of events become likely" (p. 43). The structural context "is the means by which politics is either thwarted or translated into action" (Peterson, 1993, p. 395). This includes "various rules of procedure, including the constitution, statutes, prescribed jurisdictions, precedents, customary decision-making modes, and other legal requirements," as well as the mood of the public and the preferences of various politicians and interest group members (Kingdon, 1984, p. 217). One might also add the particular organizational structures of government, which provide opportunities and access for these actors, especially advocacy group members. For example, a federal system of governance facilitates institutional fragmentation (Robertson & Judd, 1989), thereby providing multiple opportunities for interest groups to exert their influence on policymaking and implementation. A different institutional structure would produce different policy outcomes.

Institutions, then, are the object of this mode of policy analysis. Skocpol (1992) asserts that "political activities, whether carried on by politicians or social groups [are] conditioned by the institutional configurations of government and political party systems" (p. 41). Not only does the institutional context help to shape the passage of key policies, but policies are also implemented and shaped by the education settings (whether the U.S. Department of Education, state departments of education, local school boards, individual schools, or classrooms) in which laws and policies are enforced. Therefore, the outcomes of politics are mediated by the institutional setting within which these contests occur (Ikenberry, 1988).

Institutional approaches explicitly link political preferences to institutional processes. Previous research often assumed "that class, geography, ideology, and religion all affect politics but are not significantly affected by politics" (March & Olsen, 1989, p. 4). Drawing from Krasner (1984), the preferences of public officials are constrained by the administrative apparatus, legal order, and enduring beliefs. However, March and Olsen (1984) state that "if political preferences are molded through political experiences, or by political institutions, it is awkward to have a theory that presumes preferences are exogenous to the political process" (p. 739). This suggests that public policy, as an outcome of institutional processes, can shape private (interest group) preferences (Katzenstein, 1978a). March and Olsen (1989) explain that

> analysis of the effects of institutional variables on policy outcomes invites theoretical development of models of the ways in which interests and preferences de-

velop within the context of institutional action, the ways reputations and expectations develop as a result of the outcomes of politics, and the ways in which
the process of controlling purposive organizations produce unanticipated consequences and are tied to a symbolic system that evolves within an institution.
(p. 17)

Institutional structures, therefore, affect individual political behavior and
shape policy (Pal, 1992). "The ability of a political leader to carry out a policy is
critically determined by the authoritative institutional resources and arrangements existing within a given political system" (Krasner, 1984, p. 228). Further,
Cibulka (1997) explains that

institutions both shape and constrain the choices actors make. They do this in numerous ways: by creating symbols and legitimating myths about the institution,
by structuring the environment, and by creating structures and processes for addressing goals and mediating conflicts, and so on. (pp. 318–319)

Thus, both the goals and strategies that political agents pursue "are shaped by the
institutional context" (Thelen & Steinmo, 1992, p. 8), with institutions functioning as "sites of autonomous action, not reducible to the demands or preferences
of any social group" (Skocpol, 1992, p. 42).

Neoinstitutional theory views institutions such as state government or the
school system as autonomous actors capable of bias and not merely as neutral,
disinterested arbiters of conflicting interests. This approach goes well beyond the
neopluralists who emphasize policy change as the product of competing advocacy
coalitions within a given arena. For example, Hall (1993) believes that "the state
has an important impact of its own on the nature of public policy and considerable independence from organized social interests and electoral coalitions that
might otherwise be said to drive policy" (p. 275). Internal institutional processes
affect, for example, the distribution of resources and power (March & Olsen,
1989). Decisions are always "deeply affected by the position and relative power
of those who make them" (Roberts & King, 1996, p. 17). The state mediates "the
many interacting forces of change that shape education as a public good" and cannot be assumed to act in a neutral manner (James, 1991, p. 177).

Schattschneider (1960) recognized this long ago when he asserted that "the
function of institutions is to channel conflict; institutions do not treat all forms of
conflict impartially" (p. 70). Schattschneider went on to argue that "all forms of
political organization have a bias in favor of the exploitation of some kinds of conflict and the suppression of others because organization is the mobilization of bias.
Some issues are organized into politics while others are organized out" (p. 69).
Thus, while "bureaucratic agencies, legislative committees, and appellate courts
are arenas for contending social forces," they are also "collections of standard operating procedures and structures that define and defend values, norms, interests,
identities, and beliefs" (March & Olsen, 1989, p. 17).

Neoinstitutional theory places the state at the center of analysis, while not ignoring the crucial role of interest groups and coalitions in shaping policy change vis-à-vis institutional processes. For example, in one of the earliest analyses using historical institutionalism, Katzenstein (1978a) notes that "the governing coalitions of social forces in each of the advanced industrial states find their institutional expression in distinct policy networks which link the public and private sector" (p. 19). These coalitions and networks are central agents of policy change, utilizing the institutional structure to achieve their policy objectives. These objectives, in turn, are "shaped largely by the ideological outlook and material interests of the ruling coalition. Such coalitions combine elements of the dominant social classes with political power-brokers finding their institutional expression in the party system" (Katzenstein, 1978b, p. 306).

Several studies document the effects of institutions on shaping education policy. In his study of reform during the Progressive Era, Plank (1988) asks,

> If the changes that occurred in urban public school systems in the Progressive era were not elements in a unitary reform agenda, and if the success or failure of particular reforms was determined by the vagaries of a pluralistic political system that varied in significant ways across cities, why were similar packages of reforms implemented in cities across the country, and why did urban school systems come to resemble one another so closely? (p. 35)

Plank and others attribute the similarities to "underlying organizational imperatives" (Peterson, 1985, p. 205) such as the "need to adapt to changing urban environments," including rapid growth in urban populations, the increasing popular demand for schooling, and "the increasing size and complexity of urban school systems" (Plank, 1988, pp. 35, 39). Crawford and Fusarelli (2001) examined autonomy and innovation in charter schools through the lens of neoinstitutional theory and found that "The deep institutional structure of education, both its formal policies and procedures as well as its informal norms, exerts tremendous pressure on charter schools to conform to the traditional model of education" (p. 8).

Neoinstitutional theorists stress the importance of the state in shaping education policy. James (1991) found a "growing state presence in shaping educational policy" (p. 190), brought about by an expansion in state capacity (Mazzoni, 1993; Rosenthal, 1977) and "the use of law as an instrument for managing local schools" (James, 1991, p. 187). This expansion in state capacity extends well beyond education to all areas of policy and is evident in increased state-level policy activism (Beyle, 1989).

Drawing from Robertson (1993), the policymaking capacity of the state can be gauged on three dimensions:

> First, the formal boundaries of legitimate government intervention (that is, what it is permissible for government to do); second, government's fiscal ability (the

ability to raise revenues and fund policy initiatives); and third, the professionalism and expertise of legislators and public administrators. (p. 24)

Factors associated with the expansion of state capacity include states' adoption of annual meetings, the movement toward single-member districts, unlimited sessions, presession organization, uniform rules, growth of professional staff, and legislative management improvements such as electronic voting, bill-introduction deadlines, and the installation of "electronic data-processing equipment to track bills and reveal their contents" (Reeves, 1990, p. 88; Rosenthal, 1977, 1989). Robertson and Judd (1989) note that "over time, Congress and state legislatures, the president and state governors, and bureaucracies at all levels of government have grown larger, and more professional" (p. 10).

This growth has enabled actors within state governments to be increasingly active in shaping education policy and initiating policy change. "We have mounting evidence," Doyle, Cooper, and Trachtman (1991) argue, "that, indeed, the states did take charge, with all fifty making important changes in their schools during the decade" (p. 1). Murphy (1990) observes that there "has been a dramatic increase in the capacity of state governments to engage in educational issues" (p. 21). State legislatures and their staffs have become more professionalized and judicial interventions and gubernatorial initiatives have increased (Kirst & Somers, 1981). This has enabled state governments to "use the means at their disposal to influence schooling at the local level" to a degree unprecedented in U.S. history (Firestone, 1990, p. 146).

Thus, neoinstitutional theory contains a built-in dimension allowing for organizational change, which many policy scholars have used to explain changes over time in American education. As Rowan and Miskel (1999) argue, "Over the past 30 years, concerted institution-building by the education professions, government agencies, and private sector organizations has begun to produce a more elaborate technical environment for schooling, one that includes not only an increasingly sophisticated theory of educational productivity, but also the technical capacity to inspect instructional outcomes in schools. As a result, it appears that schools now face much stronger demands for technical performance than they did in the past, without also experiencing a decline in demands for institutional conformity" (p. 365), a point made in studies of accountability that conclude that such policies tend to induce institutional conformity (Crawford, 2001).

Coupled with the institutional fragmentation of a federal system of governance in which education is primarily a state (and local) responsibility, the institutional structure of the state gives well-positioned participants, such as the chairs of education committees and their finance subcommittees, the power to structure the agenda-setting process (Mazzoni, 1993; Weaver & Geske, 1996). The committee structure provides considerable institutional influence over policy outcomes (Weaver & Geske, 1996). Mazzoni (1993) observed that "all other would-be initiators must deal with the preferences, power, and personalities of these key lawmakers" (p. 365), allowing participants to set the terms or parameters of debate and ultimately play a decisive role in determining the outcome of the policy change (Bosso, 1994; Mazzoni, 1993; Rochefort & Cobb, 1994).

Perhaps the greatest utility of neoinstitutional theory, when applied to improving education policy, is that it reminds us (as systems theory does) that "policies, once enacted, restructure subsequent political processes" (Skocpol, 1992, p. 58). Robertson (1993), a proponent of neoinstitutional theory, asserts that "past decisions shape the institutional constraints and opportunities of later periods, including the present" (p. 19). This belief is consistent with Crowson and Boyd's (1996) observation that "there is a systemic character to schooling . . . where the reality of organizational life nevertheless displays a breadth far beyond any of its immediate environments" (p. 207). Thus, as politics create policies, policies may be said to remake politics (Skocpol, 1992). These policies "affect the social identities, goals, and capabilities of groups that subsequently struggle or ally in politics" (Skocpol, 1992, p. 58).

Neoinstitutional theory encourages researchers to look beyond existing political alliances and incorporate a historical dimension into their analyses (Skocpol, 1992). This step is necessary because "decisionmakers always draw on past experience, whether conscious of doing so or not" (Neustadt & May, 1986, p. xxi). For example, "previous decades of policy activism create conditions which constrain or make inevitable political action" (Mawhinney, 1994, p. 19). Within a policy community, "the capacity of each actor to influence a policy change is the product of past policy debates and changes" (Mawhinney, 1994, p. 20). Skocpol (1992) asserts that "the importance of policy feedbacks is one of the best reasons why any valid explanation of the development of a nation's social policies [particularly education policy] must be genuinely historical, sensitive to processes unfolding over time" (p. 59). Such a historical approach "furnishes a span of institutional time embracing a wide variety of changing conditions and variables" (Swift & Brady, 1991, p. 61).

Weir (1992) suggests that researchers should look for connections among policies over time and view policy innovations as part of a policy sequence. Applying this logic to charter schools and vouchers, one might view the school choice movement as part of a general political trend toward neoconservatism and market-based educational reforms. The argument situates school choice within the context of larger political and historical forces and views policy change through a historical, contextual lens.

The failure to consider adequately the effects of history and context leads to inadequate conceptualizations of social phenomenon (Neustadt & May, 1986). Thus, one of the greatest strengths of neoinstitutional theory is that it seeks to develop theory at the middle range, allowing researchers to "integrate an understanding of general patterns of political history with an explanation of the contingent nature of political and economic development, and especially the role of political agency, conflict, and choice, in shaping that development"

(Thelen & Steinmo, 1992, pp. 11–12). Thelen and Steinmo argue that neoinstitutional theory

> structures the *explanation* of political phenomena by providing a perspective for identifying how these different variables relate to one another. Thus, by placing the structuring factors at the center of the analysis, an institutional approach allows the theorist to capture the complexity of real political situations, but not at the expense of theoretical clarity. (p. 13)

Neoinstitutional theory is useful in illuminating the after-effects of the passage of ESEA, described in the policy vignette. Once Congress passed ESEA, it virtually transformed several key agencies (particularly the fifty sleepy state departments of education) and the U.S. Office of Education itself (another nearly comatose institution) into active, growing, influential organizations. Bailey and Mosher (1968) analyzed the institutional-transforming effects of ESEA as federal dollars, programs, and mandates flowed from Washington through the state capitals and education agencies, to districts, schools, and children.

In *ESEA: The Office of Education Administers a Law* (1968), Bailey and Mosher detail the transformative effects of the law and how education and governmental institutions were changed and reborn under the effects of the federal legislation. Later, too, researchers noted the reverse effect: local institutions, such as school systems, were successful in changing the purposes and implementation of ESEA. One example was the early tendency of some districts to reduce their local budget by the amount of the federal money, blunting the effect of the resources. This effort to supplant local efforts with federal funds—the effect of local institutional incentives to "let Uncle Sam pay for it"—was later confronted, and rules were made that federal dollars must supplement program resources for poor children, not supplant what was already there.

Shortcomings of Neoinstitutional Theory. Despite its growing popularity as a method for understanding education policy (see Crowson, Boyd, & Mawhinney, 1996), neoinstitutional theory suffers from two significant weaknesses: lack of substance and lack of focus. First, scholars working from a neoinstitutional perspective have been unable to flesh out theoretical propositions that would be useful to researchers and practitioners. Aside from the blinding insight that "institutions matter," policy scholars have been unable to explain clearly *how* institutions affect behavior. How can similar institutions cause people to behave differently? Why? Conversely, why do different institutions cause some people to behave in a similar manner?

The second major weakness in the theory is that it is really several different branches of one theory, with each branch differing in significant ways. Peters (1999), for example, identified seven different, conceptually distinct neoinstitutional theories, including normative institutionalism, rational choice theory, historical institutionalism, empirical institutionalism, sociological institutionalism, interest group institutional theory, and international institutionalism. Rational choice theory, which enjoys a long tradition in political science and economics, and empirical institutionalism are firmly rooted in the positivistic tradition. Normative institutionalism, on the other hand, rejects the "value-free," predictive assumptions on which such theories are based. Historical and sociological institutionalism trace their origins to Marxist thought, while interest group institutionalism is similar to neopluralist advocacy coalition theory minus the well-developed theoretical schema.

Interpretivist Theories of Policymaking in Education

More recent theorizing about the nature of policymaking in general and the policy process in education in particular has attacked the very root of traditional policy theories. These interpretivist perspectives assert that the casting of theory, the purposes and processes of determining how society educates its citizenry, and the results of policy change are all closely related to the division of power in society. According to Marshall and Anderson (1995), social theories, when used heuristically, serve as

> lenses or windows that provide a particular view of social phenomena, opening up vistas not to be seen from other windows/theories. In this way, new theoretical perspectives can make visible those aspects of traditional educational phenomena made invisible by previous theoretical frames. New theories can also illuminate previously ignored phenomena, opening up new areas for critical examination. (p. 169)

Interpretive approaches directly dispute the seemingly value-neutral assumptions of traditional policy analyses, questioning their positivistic, rational premises. These newer approaches, including critical theory, feminist critical policy analysis, cultural studies, postmodernism, policy archaeology, and poststructuralism, serve as alternative lenses for viewing policy, seeing policy as the product of issues of power, authority, control, participation, representation, gender, race and ethnicity, social class, and sexual differences (Young, 1999).

With rare exception, including early work from a left-Marxist perspective by Katz (1971) and Bowles and Gintis (1976), traditional policy scholars ignore such issues. Instead, in education policy, interpretive approaches "have problematized and politicized areas of education that previously, if viewed at all, were viewed as nonproblematic and nonpolitical" (Marshall & Anderson, 1995, p. 170). To give readers a flavor of these alternative approaches to policy studies in education, four major interpretive lenses are discussed. These include critical theory, feminist theory, postmodernism, and ideological perspectives.

Critical Theory

Critical theory "rejects a sharp distinction between political and social life, and focuses on hidden uses of power through such means as socialization and use of language" (Cibulka, 1995, p. 116). Key analytical constructs of critical theory include notions of power, "contradiction, dialectics, exploitation, domination, and legitimation" (Torres, 1999, p. 92). Critical theorists study how power is used and employed in school systems to privilege some actors while excluding or marginalizing others (Popkewitz, 1999). Critical theory enables researchers to "study the situated, performative qualities of their conversations and texts and realize how far broader institutional and structural questions of power, class, culture, ethnicity and control manifest themselves in daily speech, writing, and gesture" (Forester, 1993, p. 2). By exposing the insidious effects of these forces, critical theory seeks to transform individuals from dominated objects into active subjects who are self-determining (Comstock, 1982; Foster, 1986; Held, 1980).

As such, critical theory has an explicitly emancipatory purpose. It emphasizes individual self-knowledge, self-actualization, awareness, and freedom. Reflecting its ideological roots in Marxism and the Frankfurt School, critical theory seeks to help individuals to transcend repressive social structures (Held, 1980). Critical theory is readily made for and increasingly used in studies of education policy. Research has focused on issues such as the role of administrative practices in reproducing societal inequities and traditional power arrangements (Foster, 1986; Scheurich & Imber, 1991), how schools engage in patterns of systematic exclusion (Fine, 1993), and the ideological justifications that support such behavior (Reyes & Capper, 1991).

One weakness of this approach is that it treats as insignificant the role of policy processes in shaping policy, while focusing explicitly on power arrangements (Cibulka, 1995). Another weakness includes the tendency of many critical theorists "to minimize the importance of social values other than equality, such as efficiency, productivity, and market choice. Also, their analyses often can explain better how a social system preserves the status-quo than how that system changes and progresses" (Cibulka, 1995, p. 116).

Feminist Theory

Feminist theory—and feminist critical policy analysis—"begin[s] with the assumption that gender inequity results from purposeful (if subconscious) choices to serve some in-group's ideology and purpose" and is concerned with "identifying how the political agenda benefiting males is embedded in school structure and practices" (Marshall & Anderson, 1995, p. 172). In full bloom, feminist critiques are based on the belief that society favors males and disadvantages females. As such, policies grow out of a sexist institutional setting, are enacted and implemented to the disadvantage of women, and result in further reinforcing the sexist nature of schools.

Education policies that are anti-feminist include lower pay for elementary principals (where most female administrators work), fewer job opportunities, and fewer chances for promotion for women. Unfortunately, education is a classic case: with 83 percent of all teachers being females, we see only 12 percent of the nation's school superintendents who are women, up from about 7 percent in 1990 (Fusarelli, Cooper, & Carella, in press). It's a clear case of women as passive workers and men as dominant/dominating managers. In education, feminist scholars examine differential socialization and barriers to opportunities (Ferguson, 1984; Marshall, 1993) that limit females' access and choice (Marshall and Anderson refer to this as "Liberal Feminism"), women's ways of knowing (Gilligan, 1982), ethics (Noddings, 1984), and decisionmaking ("Difference Feminism").

Postmodernism

Drawn from the poststructuralist work of Foucault, postmodernism focuses on the social construction of "problems" and "reality." Rejecting value-neutral assumptions inherent in positivist, rationalist policy studies, "refusing the acceptance of social problems as natural occurrences, [postmodernism or policy archaeology] examines closely and skeptically the emergence of the particular problem" (Scheurich, 1994, p. 300). Scheurich, who developed a method for applying postmodernism to policy studies, asks "by what process did a particular problem emerge, or better, how did a particular problem come to be seen as a problem? What makes the emergence of a particular problem possible? Why do some 'problems' become identified as social problems while other 'problems' do not achieve that level of identification?" (1994, p. 300). Rochefort and Cobb (1994) stress the need to focus on the antecedent conditions of policy, particularly how problems are defined as legitimate and in need of remedy. "At the nexus of politics and policy development lies persistent conflict over where problems come from, and based on the answer to this question, what kinds of solutions should be attempted" (Rochefort & Cobb, 1994, p. 3).

According to Hogwood and Gunn (1984), "We each create our own 'reality,' and this is nowhere more true than in the way we identify problems or issues, and interpret and relate them to our mental map of some larger situation" (p. 109). How we perceive reality has a determining effect on policy analysis. For example, in the late 1980s, teenage pregnancy became a great concern, rising to the level of a "crisis." Oddly enough, this crisis occurred at a time when teen pregnancy was actually in decline (NCHS, 1992, cited in Pillow, 1997). Pillow (1997) questions whether the problem is teen pregnancy or unwed teen pregnancy, and asks how issues of race and class "impact what we think about who should be pregnant or who should not be" (p. 146).

A number of scholars have begun to study education policy through a postmodern lens. For example, Opfer (2001) conducted a postmodern policy analysis of charter school accountability and found that the state's overriding emphasis on accountability severely constrained the freedom and flexibility promised in the charter school movement. She argued, "The charter school model, when paired with accountability, does not encourage states to relinquish their control of the educational process to the school level. With this pairing, the charter school concept is meaningless beyond a superficial level, merely offering a symbolic gloss of popular democracy and freedom from (usually local) bureaucracy" (p. 209).

One significant difference between postmodernism and critical theory (in fact, between critical theory and other interpretive approaches discussed in this section) is that critical theory, although designed to be emancipatory, relies on reason as its underlying premise. In this sense, it may be thought of as a special type of postpositivist lens. Habermas (1971, 1975, 1983, 1988), for example, believed in the existence of true knowledge and insisted that it could be distinguished from justificatory ideologies. Postmodernists reject such universal or "true" knowledge, asserting that all knowledge represents some form of justification or rationalizing ideology. Postmodernism disputes the notion of impartial rationality in policymaking, that somehow "policy is or can be objective or idcologically neutral" (Rosenau, 1993, p. 3).

Ideological Perspectives: From Left to Right

Within the political system, policy is often shaped, sponsored, and promulgated by "experts" from a particular political position. Thus, during the administration of President Lyndon Johnson, we expected and did see a raft of "liberal" education policy, including compensatory education, equity, and help for disadvantaged, "at-risk" students. When Ronald Reagan became president, the nation witnessed a slew of right-wing, neoconservative policies and programs, the most famous including *A Nation at Risk* (National Commission on Excellence in Education, 1983), attempts to legislate choice, markets, higher standards, and even national Title I vouchers for poor children to attend parochial schools.

Whether from the left or the right, neoconservative, neoliberal, socialist or libertarian, policy can be understood in political-ideological terms, as the platform of a particular political group or faction. This ideological perspective shares several characteristics with "interest group" politics, because one way to categorize and analyze factional behaviors is to expose their values and beliefs. Many conservative Republicans want to privatize, marketize, and consumerize education, while liberal Democrats prefer radical equality, controlled by socialistic, monopolistic systems of education that stress equity over choice. Like postmodernism (and, interestingly enough, neopluralist advocacy coalition theories), ideological perspectives acknowledge the importance of deeply held values and beliefs in shaping policy inputs.

Yet, ideological perspectives are less self-conscious about the roots of their values because these values are more obvious to adherents of that political party. Prayer in school, for example, may be fundamental to some religious groups and associated with a conservative viewpoint, while affirmative action in schools is a policy long supported by the liberal left. The strength of the political ideology approach is that it has a behavioral referent: voting behavior and other actions of actors from these parties or perspectives. One can count the votes, hear the debate, and read the platforms. Stone (1988) refers to this as a "policy argument."

ESEA, discussed in the policy vignette, provides an interesting application of ideological perspectives to education policy studies. In the early 1960s, a central tenet of the Republican Party was that education was primarily a local and state matter, that the U.S. government's role in policymaking was mainly to collect data and to try new ideas—but certainly not to fund programs directly for students. It was the smashing defeat of Arizona Republican Barry Goldwater in his bid for the presidency in 1964 that cleared the way for the liberal, Democratic victory of Lyndon Johnson and brought to Congress the youngest, most diverse, and most ideologically liberal group since Franklin D. Roosevelt was elected president. Not only were more Democrats and fewer Republicans elected to the House and Senate than at any time in the twentieth century, but these were liberal Democrats at that. This brought about a fundamental shift in the federal government's policies toward and role in shaping education policy. This changing of elites brought about an immense ideological shift in the federal government's policies toward education—an ideological shift that remained unchallenged for nearly two decades.

Shortcomings of Interpretivist Theories of Policymaking

One weakness of interpretivist theories of policymaking is that they treat as insignificant the role of policy processes in shaping policy, while focusing explicitly on power arrangements (Cibulka, 1995). Another weakness is the tendency of many interpretivist scholars "to minimize the importance of social values other than equality, such as efficiency, productivity, and market choice. Also, their analyses often can explain better how a social system preserves the status-quo than how that system changes and progresses" (Cibulka, 1995, p. 116).

The popularity of interpretivist theories in the field of education in the last two decades has had a significant impact on education policy analysis. These analysts have questioned the positivistic, scientific assumptions of traditional education policy, focused much needed attention on the effects of education policy on marginalized groups, and helped us to realize the limits of what can be accomplished through the manipulation of policy. However, interpretivist theories of education policymaking have also witnessed a backlash of criticism—most of which centers on the notion inherent in these theories, particularly postmodernism, that knowledge is "socially constructed." Although this phrase is now a mantra in many schools of education, critics have questioned whether we really mean what the phrase implies: that no knowledge or policies are better than others, and that knowledge and policies are merely products of our current conditions, ideologies, views, or biases. Such pronouncements sound ridiculous to many practitioners.

Indeed, the title of this book, *Better Policies, Better Schools,* suggests that we can improve education with better education policies. The entire school improvement movement rests on this premise. Thus, although the critical, interrogative, dialogic aspect of interpretivist theories is a crucial and long-missing component of studies of education policy, we need to exert great care not to go to the extreme of pronouncing that everything is relativistic and that improving schools through better policy, by extension, is irrelevant or impossible. As Kerr (1976) has argued, "Policy choices do matter. If they did not, there would be no point in making a policy" (p. 177). Progress can be made in improving our policies and improving our schools. Otherwise, the entire schooling enterprise is unnecessary and doomed to failure.

A Conceptual Framework for Understanding Policymaking in Education

To make sense of the growing number of theoretical perspectives, models, and concepts permeating the field, we have developed a four-dimensional conceptual framework that is both comprehensive and simple. As shown in Figure 2.3, various theories and models of policymaking in education can be grouped along four dimensions:

• *Normative dimension:* includes the beliefs, values, and ideologies that drive societies to seek improvement and change. To the extent that all policies are expressions of the purposes of society, they are highly normative. Even so-called "scientific" policy efforts indicate a set of assumptions and beliefs about the rationality of human action and the "scientific" nature of social actions. Postmodernism and ideological perspectives inform work in this dimension.

• *Structural dimension:* includes the governmental arrangements, institutional structure, systems, and processes that promulgate and support policies in education. Analysis of the role and effects of federal, state, and local institutional structures is critical to adequately understanding the way institutions shape education policy. Neoinstitutional theory informs research in this dimension.

• *Constituentive dimension:* includes theories of the networks, elites, masses, interest groups, ethnic/gender groups, providers and "end users," and beneficiaries who influence, participate in, and benefit from the policymaking process. Issues needing to be addressed in this dimension include who has access to power, how these interest groups make their needs felt, and the degree to which competing

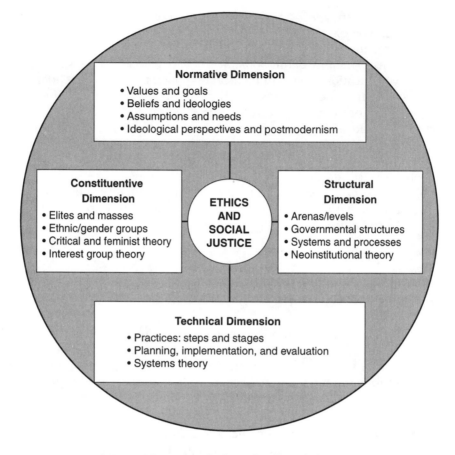

FIGURE 2.3   *A Four-Dimensional View of Policy Theory*

interests can work out a compromise solution or have their needs met. In this dimension, policies are formed and fashioned by the constituent groups that favor and oppose them—formally through governmental structure and informally through their ability to influence other groups. Neopluralist advocacy coalition and interest group models, as well as critical and feminist theories, focus attention on actors in this dimension.

• *Technical dimension:* includes educational planning, practice, implementation, and evaluation—the nuts and bolts of policymaking. Systems theory is useful to understand developments in this dimension as we trace the technical and instrumental effects of policies. Because "the devil is in the details," no analysis of policy is complete without examining policy effects and consequences.

Each of the four dimensions in Figure 2.3 is applied to all education policies. Understanding education policy, therefore, requires that policymakers consider the impact and effects of proposed policies along these dimensions. For example, ESEA may be best understood by viewing it along its normative, structural, constituentive, and technical dimensions. What are the values and beliefs embedded in the policy? Whose ideology does the policy reflect? Which groups benefit from the policy? Who loses? How did various interest groups shape the content of the policy and its implementation? How did the institutional structure of the process affect the policy, both in its formation and implementation? How has the policy been implemented and evaluated? And what do we still need to know about the policy to improve schools?

These are the types of questions that must be considered within the four-dimensional framework of policy outlined above. Failure to do so leads to inadequate conceptualizations of education policy and, by extension, bad policy. By adopting a holistic, four-dimensional policy framework, policymakers can improve their practice—the practice of school improvement.

Ethics and Social Justice: The Core of the Four-Dimensional Framework

Our conceptual framework is rooted in a deep concern for ethics and social justice. Seldom do those engaged in crafting, implementing, and evaluating policy consciously examine and reflect on the ethical issues raised in their work. In fact, few texts used to prepare policy analysts give adequate treatment to the role of ethics in policy studies, traditionally ignoring ethics altogether; "built on the foundations of logical positivism, there is a lingering sense that the entire domain of ethics is soft and subjective and therefore suspect" (Warwick & Pettigrew, 1983, p. 338). For example, in a recent introduction to the policy process, Birkland (2001) fails to mention ethics or social justice at all.

A few political theorists such as Amy Gutmann (1980, 1987) and Kenneth Strike (1982) have asserted that policymakers need to pay greater attention to the implications of education policies for equity and social justice. In *Liberal Equality*, Gutmann explores the tension between equality of opportunity and equality of outcome—and fashions a combination of these approaches into a form of liberal egalitarianism linking equality with liberty, with the explicit purpose of more effectively integrating individuals into social and political life. In *Democratic Education*, Gutmann examines a range of education policies such as sex education, creationism, school finance, busing, funding for parochial schools, and book censorship, among others. Again, she explores the basic tension between local (citizen) control and non-discrimination and non-repression in crafting ethical and equitable education policy.

Strike (1982) commented on the tension in liberal political thought when he observed, "For liberals a compensatory role for schooling becomes problematic because it can lead schools to distribute resources in apparently unequal ways and because it can lead to expanding the role of the state in education, an expansion which may threaten other liberal views" (p. 189). According to Strike, "If school opportunities are equal, then the results of schooling should be affected primarily by such characteristics as ability and willingness to learn. But if poverty, let us say, affects the student's ability or willingness to learn, then equal schooling will result in unequal achievement. Poor students will do less well than their affluent peers because they are less capable of profiting from the opportunity. The result of equal opportunity is that those who enter school behind will leave it behind" (p. 209). As Strike suggests, equitable educational policies should achieve at least roughly equal results "among social groups, not among individuals" (pp. 209–210).

Consistent with the theory of liberal equality, Strike suggests that contemporary education policy should work toward the development of "social organizations (including schools) which are smaller and more intimate and in which authority and the organization of activity are more democratic and less bureaucratic" (p. 255), a point echoed by several other scholars (see Fine, 1993; Fusarelli, 1999b; Meier, 1995; NASSP, 1996; Sergiovanni, 1995, 1996). Strike further asserts that the foremost need of education policy is "restoring citizenship to its role as the predominant public task of the school and reducing the subserviance of schools to the values of economic efficiency" (p. 255), a point made by critics who charge that "education is more than numbers" and who recognize the critical role of schools in transmitting and preserving our democratic heritage (Fusarelli, 1999a, p. 97; Barber, 1984; Strike, 1989, 1993; Wood, 1992).

The failure of policy studies to treat ethics and social justice in any systematic way has filtered down into the various topical areas or subfields of the discipline, including education. Despite a resurgence of interest in ethics in education (Kallio, 1999), such concerns are focused more on administrator preparation and decisionmaking, and less on education politics and policy. As evidenced by a recent *Politics of Education Yearbook* devoted to the politics of education research (Cooper & Randall, 1999), concern is growing over the politicization of policy research and analysis, although significantly it took three decades before a *Yearbook* exploring the political dimensions of research in education was published. Even then, however, only one chapter by Catherine Emihovich in the 1999 *Yearbook* explicitly discusses ethics.

Drawing from Amy (1987), we examine ethics and social justice in the larger sense and call on those involved in crafting education policy to reexamine and carefully analyze the moral premises of their work. This is an important, if underexamined, aspect of policymaking because, as Amy (1987) observed, "Being concerned about the ethical implications of public policies serves to make one more sensitive to what is actually happening to real people in the world" (p. 51). To understand education in the United States, we must begin by examining the ethical dimensions of policies that affect children. If policy represents the authoritative allocation of values of society, then "the [most] important questions concerning policy analysis have as much to do with the 'should' questions as with the 'can' questions. That is, most important policy decisions involve an assessment of what should be done by government as much as they involve the feasibility question of what government can do" (Peters, 1986, p. 311).

Policy studies in public education have long triggered intense debate, as evidenced by battles over achievement testing, the Coleman report, desegregation, Head Start, bilingual education, school choice, and a host of other reforms. All policies have an ethical dimension. For example, in the 1960s and 1970s, a major goal of federal educational policy was "to provide equal opportunity for all students, with particular emphasis on the needy" (Larson, 1980, p. 66). Ethical concerns are rooted explicitly in conflicting interpretations of "the good society" (Bellah, Madsen, Sullivan, Swidler, & Tipton, 1991) over competing concerns of public philosophy.

At its core, crafting better education policy entails confronting conflicting values, particularly because education "is, and always has been, inseparable from broader social, political, and economic goals" (Pratte, 1978, p. 161). At a minimum, these values include choice, efficiency, equity, and quality (excellence), although numerous other values could be included (Stout, Tallerico, & Scribner, 1995). According to Johnson (1999), "Multiple actors driven by diverse agendas interact in numerous ways to produce policy outcomes" (p. 20). In an environment of scarcity, amidst competing values, the battle occurs over which values should take priority over others. As will be demonstrated throughout this book, no facet of the education policy process is value neutral; therefore, normative questions cannot be ignored. As Randall, Cooper, and Hite (1999) note, "the cloak of neutrality in both research and education is being discarded as researchers begin to acknowledge the political nature of their work" (pp. 1–2).

Barriers to Ethical Considerations in Education Policy

According to Warwick and Pettigrew (1983), "There are distinctive ethical problems that arise in policy research" (p. 339). First, the technocratic ethos of policy analysis minimizes ethical considerations of policy (Amy, 1987). For example, cost-benefit analyses favor quantifiable values at the expense of intangible, qualitative variables. In education, it is much easier to quantify student learning in terms of test scores rather than portfolios of students' performance. Similarly, it is easier to emphasize student achievement as the primary goal or purpose of education because this goal is presumably quantifiable and measurable, whereas other goals such as preparing students to live in a democracy are more difficult to capture (Fusarelli, 1999a). Second, "the social sciences entertain a greater range of permissible, even conflicting conceptualizations because there are few widely accepted theoretical models" and allow "a greater range of permissible research designs and methods" (Warwick & Pettigrew, 1983, p. 341).

Third, the client-centered nature of policy studies, wherein policy analysts typically work for (or are funded by) clients inside and outside government, can produce pressure to conform the analysis to the client's preferences. Since analysts have professional and personal incentives to maintain good relationships with clients, ethical dimensions of policy reports are seldom explored (Amy, 1987). "Not all groups have an interest in emphasizing the moral dimensions" of policy (Amy, 1987, p. 65). Even when ethical concerns are incorporated into the analysis, the results are often interpreted by others as biased—no matter how carefully designed the study may have been.

The scientific veneer of policy analysis is often used to advance partisan interests, thus crossing an imaginary line into policy advocacy (Cibulka, 1995). As Cibulka (1995) observed, the line between policy research and policy argument (the use of research to fit a predetermined position) is razor thin, becoming even more problematic when research is funded by a government agency or foundation. Whenever policy analysts are contracted to evaluate a program or conduct an implementation evaluation, they are answerable to their employers or sponsors (Browne & Wildavsky, 1984).

To a large extent, the line between policy research and advocacy in education is nonexistent: "Education is by its very nature a profoundly political enterprise because it is the means and the message by which worldviews are transmitted, cultures are reproduced, a way of life is passed on, and a person is created" (Randall, Cooper, & Hite, 1999, p. 2). As Johnson (1999) so aptly pointed out in his analysis of research-information use in education policy, "Given the large number of actors and political needs, it should come as no surprise to see the same set of information used by competing interests to buttress opposing arguments" (p. 21).

A fourth barrier that inhibits policymakers from incorporating an ethical dimension into their work is the psychological risks of engaging in ethical analysis (Amy, 1987). Questioning long held assumptions and moral commitments can be unsettling. As Amy (1987) explains, "Ethical analysis involves asking questions that can be disturbing to the analyst" (p. 59). As various interpretivist theorists point out, current policy largely benefits children from white middle- and upper-class families. Incorporating ethical considerations into policy development and analysis forces policymakers to confront existing societal inequities, requiring them to craft policies that would explicitly threaten the existing ethnic-economic order, something policymakers are reluctant to do.

Incorporating Ethics and Social Justice into Education Policy Studies

If we truly want to craft better policies for better schools, we must center our education policies around concerns for equity and social justice. As our framework suggests, these values should be at the heart of education policy. Some would argue that orienting policies toward efficiency and excellence—such as standards and accountability—precludes emphasis on concerns for equity and social justice, implying that these values are somehow incompatible with each other. We disagree with this overly simplistic, narrow position—one rooted in an outdated ontological worldview of policy as a zero-sum game, as though this was the only possible outcome (Scribner, Reyes, & Fusarelli, 1995). In fact, it does not take much imagination to view policymaking as a positive-sum game in which excellence for *all* children is the realized objective of policymaking, as we believe it should be.

As Haller and Strike (1986) observe, "Educational institutions perform a distributive function," influencing who gets what (p. 11). After all, note the researchers, "What happens in educational institutions affects an individual's life chances" (p. 11). Haller and Strike suggest that crafting equitable educational policies requires that at least three conditions be met: (1) policies must ensure and preserve the dignity and respect of people, (2) policies must be impartial, and (3) echoing the Habermasian notion of an ideal speech community, the policy process must ensure "the equal consideration of interests" (p. 12).

Although these conditions are difficult to dispute, we argue that, due to the profound societal inequities in the United States, crafting better policies for better schools necessitates creating policies that favor children most at risk—policies that, by definition, are partial, biased, and unequal. The United States has the highest percentage of families and children living in poverty of any advanced, industrial nation *in the world*. And evidence shows that the gap between rich and poor is widening; it is wider today than in 1940 (Reyes, Wagstaff, & Fusarelli, 1999). Given an unlevel playing field, only redistributive policies offer the possibility of equalizing educational opportunity. For example, if policymakers believe vouchers will level the playing field, then only voucher plans targeted toward the poor and disenfranchised—not toward the wealthy, or even the middle class—should be promulgated (this is, essentially, Viteritti's argument in *Choosing Equality*).

We assert, somewhat paradoxically, that crafting equitable educational policies necessitates preferential consideration and treatment of children most at risk. This position is echoed in Strike's (1982) seminal work, *Educational Policy and the Just Society*, in which he argues that "The liberal society must permit rewards to reflect ability in one generation and at the same time prevent the resulting inequalities from causing rewards to fail to reflect ability in the next generation" (p. 175). Therefore, contends Strike, people who differ "should be treated differently" (p. 178).

Many popular school reforms, such as standards, accountability, and school choice, represent concerns for equity as well as efficiency, excellence, and choice. For years, African American and Latino students have received a dumbed-down curriculum in a system unresponsive to their needs. Contrary to the assertions of some liberal elite critics such as Kohn (2000), mounting evidence indicates that reforms such as higher standards, testing, and accountability are narrowing the performance gaps between Anglo, Hispanic, and African American students (Scheurich, Skrla, & Johnson, 2000). In fact, many of the "conservative" school reforms of the past two decades have received strong support from groups representing minority interests—many of which have become impatient with decades-old promises of good schools for minority children. Thus, we caution readers, and educational historians, not to conclude that equity is not a concern in supposedly "conservative" eras. Such views reflect an oversimplification of the size, scope, and diversity of the school reform movement.

Although we accept the postmodern caveat that researchers who study policy and those who craft it can never be ideologically neutral, we disagree with the implication that distinctions cannot be made with respect to differences in the quality of policy analyses. If all policy studies are inherently biased, as postmodern critics assert, it does not follow that all policy studies are *equally* biased. Some studies may be, and are, more biased than others, creating a space or place to situate ethics in policy studies. By striving to craft policy studies in an ethical manner, we can limit the amount of bias that inevitably filters into policymaking and analysis.

We agree with Emihovich (1999) that researchers and policymakers should articulate "a normative framework that embodies our commitment to ethics and community," in the process, becoming "public intellectuals"—individuals who "recognize that the perceived contradictions between reason and passion are false dichotomies, and that a search for rational solutions to pressing social problems can be pursued within a framework of commitment to the public good and caring for those in need" (p. 34).

Ultimately, any effort to craft more ethical educational policies must begin with a realistic assessment of educational opportunities and outcomes within schools, considering socioeconomic class, ethnic group, and gender. It is no secret that schools have "failed many minority children and the poor" (Hudson, 1999, p. 139). Poor students and students of color "have been traditionally underserved in the public education system," and by nearly all indices continue to score far below standard (Peebles, 2000, p. 192). This finding is not surprising given that minorities, especially Latinos, are significantly less likely to be placed in advanced or gifted curricular tracks than either Anglo or Asian students (Howe, 1994). Educational policies grounded in ethical concerns would be devoted, for example, to reducing or eliminating the overplacement of minority children in low-track curriculum (Lucas, Henze, & Donato, 1990; Romo & Falbo, 1996).

To this day, schools (and student performance within them) are divided along racial and class lines. Although the literature is replete with examples of schools that successfully narrow the performance gaps among student subgroups (Edmonds, 1979; Reyes, Scribner, & Scribner, 1999), such examples still constitute the exception rather than the norm. If we accept the premise that schools "have a moral obligation to provide minority students a quality education" (Hudson, 1999, p. 139), then the inability (or unwillingness) of educational leaders, and the policies they promulgate, to provide a high quality education for all children constitutes the single greatest failure of ethical policymaking in the history of U.S. education.

Unfortunately, ethical considerations rooted in a concern for equity and social justice are frequently ignored in promulgating education policy. Policies that promise to narrow the achievement gap between ethnic groups or that provide a better education for poor children are often bypassed because they are "too expensive" or "impractical"—problems easily overcome in the more affluent suburbs. For example, large, urban schools containing in excess of 3,000 students are not uncommon in central cities—whose population is overwhelmingly children of color, poor, and most at risk. It has long been known that breaking up large schools—creating smaller schools where administrators, teachers, students, and their families know each other and can establish a high quality, caring environment—is a key ingredient in improving education, particularly urban education (Fusarelli, 2000).

For decades, numerous calls have been made by various professional educator organizations to do just that (see Gregory & Smith, 1987). Some scholars have even pointed out that charter schools, despite some well-documented problems, at least provide at-risk children with an opportunity to learn in a small school setting (charter schools are about one-third the size of traditional public schools) (Fusarelli, 1999b). Unfortunately, "building construction is seldom a high priority in the reform game" as politicians seek more cost effective (i.e., cheaper) alternatives (Fusarelli, 2000, p. 234).

Lack of political will and the constraints of crafting education policy in a highly politicized environment dominated by competing interests, answer in part Ennis's question, "Why is it that even though there is so much agreement on equality of educational opportunity as an ideal, there is so much disagreement about its application?" (1978, p. 169). Although education is the single largest expenditure in each state's budget, it competes with thousands of other state initiatives, often in a tight fiscal environment.

Despite more than forty years of research on at risk students, the condition of urban education has not substantially improved and, in fact, may have gotten worse (Emihovich, 1999). To incorporate ethical concerns for equity and social justice into education policy studies, researchers must use their *moral imagination*, conceptualizing a future in which schools are places where children are nurtured and given full opportunity to develop their talents and realize their potential. As

Emihovich (1999) has noted, policymakers exhibit far too little imagination when developing proposals to improve social conditions. Because education is fundamentally a moral enterprise, policy studies in education—in all phases and stages— must be infused with ethical concerns for equity and social justice. Only then can real progress be made in improving education for all children.

Chapter Discussion Questions _____

1. How do different theories of policy affect our understanding of studies of education policy?

2. Evaluate the four-dimensional policy framework discussed in this chapter. What revisions would you make to the framework?

3. Compare and contrast the theories of policymaking discussed in the chapter. How do these theories relate to one another and to the four dimensional framework?

Seminal Works _____

A wide array of theories and approaches have been discussed in this chapter. Accordingly, we highlight a few works that serve as representative samples of scholarship within each area. First, David Easton's (1965) *A Framework for Political Analysis* presents the classic formulation of systems theory. One of the most oft-cited works in political science in the past half century, Easton's framework is used widely in policy courses as a primer for policy analysis. In *The Political Dynamics of American Education*, Frederick Wirt and Michael Kirst (2001) applied systems theory to the study of educational institutions, paying particular attention to the impact of political turbulence on education policymaking at the local, state, and federal levels.

Paul Sabatier and Hank Jenkins-Smith's (1993) edited volume, *Policy Change and Learning: An Advocacy Coalition Approach*, reflects recent advances in interest group theory. This book explores the key elements of and methodology employed in using the advocacy coalition framework for understanding policy change. Several chapters explicitly test the theory, using both quantitative and qualitative methods.

Richard Scott's (1995) *Institutions and Organizations* provides an excellent overview of early as well as contemporary institutional theory. Scott devotes particular attention to the effects of institutions on societal systems, organizational fields, populations, structure, and organizational performance. Guy Peters's (1999) *Institutional Theory in Political Science* explores in detail the differences inherent in the multiple strands of neoinstitutional theory, including normative, historical, empirical, sociological, and international institutionalism, as well as rational choice theory and interest representation. It is an excellent primer for scholars and students interested in the important differences among these varied approaches to studying institutions. Students interested in the application of institutional theory to education should read Robert Crowson, William Boyd, and Hanne Mawhinney's (1996) edited volume, *The Politics of Education and the New Institutionalism,* which addresses topics such as school reform and restructuring, environmental adaptation and selection, choice and control, the social structure of education, and reinvented schooling.

Within the field of education, William Foster's (1986) *Paradigms and Promises* contains a solid overview of various interpretivist approaches to studying educational issues. Catherine Marshall's (1997) two-volume edited work, *Feminist Critical Policy Analysis,* contains a comprehensive, incisive application of critical and feminist theory to education policy. In a somewhat similar vein, James Scheurich's (1994) work on policy archaeology provides a stimulating example of the application of postmodernism to education policy analysis.

References

Abrams, D. M. (1993). *Conflict, competition, or cooperation? Dilemmas of state education policymaking.* Albany: State University of New York Press.

Amy, D. J. (1987). Can policy analysis be ethical? In F. Fischer & J. Forester (Eds.), *Confronting values in policy analysis* (pp. 45–67). Newbury Park, CA: Sage.

Bailey, S. K., & Mosher, E. K. (1968). *ESEA: The Office of Education administers a law.* Syracuse, NY: Syracuse University Press.

Barber, B. R. (1984). *Strong democracy: Participatory politics for a new age.* Los Angeles: University of California Press.

Bellah, R. N., Madsen, R., Sullivan, W. M., Swidler, A., & Tipton, S. M. (1991). *The good society.* New York: Vintage Books.

Beyle, T. L. (Ed.). (1989). *State government: CQ's guide to current issues and activities, 1987–88.* Washington, DC: Congressional Quarterly Inc.

Birkland, T. A. (2001). *An introduction to the policy process.* Armonk, NY: M. E. Sharpe.

Bosso, C. J. (1994). The contextual bases of problem definition. In D. A. Rochefort & R. W. Cobb (Eds.), *The politics of problem definition: Shaping the policy agenda* (pp. 182–203). Lawrence: University Press of Kansas.

Bowles, S., & Gintis, H. (1976). *Schooling in capitalist America: Educational reform and the contradictions of economic life.* New York: Basic Books.

Browne, A., & Wildavsky, A. (1984). Implementation as mutual adaptation. In J. L. Pressman & A. Wildavsky (Eds.), *Implementation* (3rd ed., pp. 206–231). Berkeley: University of California Press.

Burlingame, M., & Geske, T. G. (1979). State politics and education: An examination of selected multiple-state case studies. *Educational Administration Quarterly, 15*(2), 50–75.

Cibulka, J. G. (1995). Policy analysis and the study of the politics of education. In J. D. Scribner & D. H. Layton (Eds.), *The study of educational politics* (pp. 105–125). Washington, DC: Falmer Press.

Cibulka, J. G. (1997). Two eras of schooling: The decline of the old order and the emergence of new organizational forms. *Education and Urban Society, 29*(3), 317–341.

Comstock, D. E. (1982). A method for critical research. In E. Bredo & W. Feinberg (Eds.), *Knowledge and values in social and educational research* (pp. 370–390). Philadelphia: Temple University Press.

Cooper, B. S., & Randall, E. V. (1999). *Accuracy or advocacy: The politics of research in education.* Thousand Oaks, CA: Corwin Press.

Crawford, J. R. (2001). Teacher autonomy and accountability in charter schools. *Education and Urban Society, 33*(2), 186–200.

Crawford, J. R., & Fusarelli, L. D. (2001). *Autonomy and innovation in charter schools: Less than meets the eye.* Paper presented at the Annual Meeting of the American Educational Research Association, April 12, 2002, Seattle, WA.

Crowson, R. L., & Boyd, W. L. (1996). The politics of education, the new institutionalism, and reinvented schooling: Some concluding observations. In R. L. Crowson, W. L. Boyd, & H. B. Mawhinney (Eds.), *The politics of education and the new institutionalism: Reinventing the American school* (pp. 203–214). London: Falmer Press.

Crowson, R. L., Boyd, W. L., & Mawhinney, H. B. (Eds.). (1996). *The politics of education and the new institutionalism: Reinventing the American school.* London: Falmer Press.

Doyle, D. P., Cooper, B. S., & Trachtman, R. (1991). *Taking charge: State action on school reform in the 1980s.* Indianapolis, IN: Hudson Institute.

Easton, D. (1965). *A framework for political analysis.* Chicago: University of Chicago Press.

Edmonds, R. (1979). Some schools work and more can. *Social Policy, 9*(2), 28–32.

Emihovich, C. (1999). Compromised positions: The ethics and politics of designing research in the postmodern age. In B. S. Cooper & E. V. Randall (Eds.), *Accuracy or advocacy: The politics of research in education* (pp. 31–41). Thousand Oaks, CA: Corwin Press.

Ennis, R. H. (1978). Equality of educational opportunity. In K. A. Strike & K. Egan (Eds.), *Ethics and educational policy* (pp. 168–190). London: Routledge & Kegan Paul.

Feir, R. E. (1995). *Political and social roots of education reform: A look at the states in the mid-1980s.* Paper presented at the Annual Meeting of the American Educational Research Association. San Francisco.

Ferguson, K. E. (1984). *The feminist case against bureaucracy.* Philadelphia: Temple University Press.

Fine, M. (1993). [Ap]parent involvement: Reflections on parents, power, and urban public schools. *Teachers College Record, 94,* 682–710.

Firestone, W. A. (1990). Continuity and incrementalism after all: State responses to the excellence movement. In J. Murphy (Ed.), *The educational reform movement of the 1980s: Perspectives and cases* (pp. 143–166). Berkeley, CA: McCutchan.

Forester, J. (1993). *Critical theory, public policy, and planning practice: Toward a critical pragmatism.* Albany: State University of New York Press.

Foster, W. (1986). *Paradigms and promises: New approaches to educational administration.* Buffalo, NY: Prometheus.

Freire, P. (1970). *Pedagogy of the oppressed.* M. B. Ramos (Trans.). New York: Seabury Press.

Fusarelli, L. D. (1999a). Education is more than numbers: Communitarian leadership of schools for the new millennium. In L. T. Fenwick (Ed.), *School leadership: Expanding horizons of the mind and spirit* (pp. 97–107). Lancaster, PA: Technomic.

Fusarelli, L. D. (1999b). Reinventing urban education in Texas: Charter schools, smaller schools, and the new institutionalism. *Education and Urban Society, 31*(2), 214–224.

Fusarelli, L. D. (2000). Leadership in Latino schools: Challenges for the new millennium. In P. M. Jenlink (Ed.), *Marching into a new millennium: Challenges to educational leadership* (pp. 228–238). Lanham, MD: Scarecrow Press.

Fusarelli, L. D., Cooper, B. S., & Carella, V. (in press). Who will serve? An analysis of superintendent mobility, satisfaction, and perceptions of crisis. *Journal of School Leadership.*

Gilligan, C. (1982). *In a different voice: Psychological theory and women's development.* Cambridge, MA: Harvard University Press.

Gregory, T. B., & Smith, G. R. (1987). *High schools as communities: The small school reconsidered.* Bloomington, IN: Phi Delta Kappa Educational Foundation.

Gutmann, A. (1980). *Liberal equality.* Cambridge, MA: Cambridge University Press.

Gutmann, A. (1987). *Democratic education.* Princeton, NJ: Princeton University Press.

Habermas, J. (1971). *Knowledge and human interests.* Boston: Beacon Press.

Habermas, J. (1975). *Legitimation crisis.* Boston: Beacon Press.

Habermas, J. (1983). *The theory of communicative action, Vol. 1.* Boston: Beacon Press.

Habermas, J. (1988). *The theory of communicative action, Vol. 2.* Boston: Beacon Press.

Hall, P. A. (1993). Policy paradigms, social learning, and the state: The case of economic policymaking in Britain. *Comparative Politics, 25*(3), 275–296.

Haller, E. J., & Strike, K. A. (1986). *An introduction to educational administration: Social, legal, and ethical perspectives.* New York: Longman.

Heclo, H. (1974). *Modern social politics in Britain and Sweden: From relief to income maintenance.* New Haven, CT: Yale University Press.

Held, D. (1980). *An introduction to critical theory.* London: Hutchinson.

Hogwood, B. W., & Gunn, L. A. (1984). *Policy analysis for the real world.* Oxford, UK: Oxford University Press.

Howe, C. K. (1994). Improving the achievement of Hispanic students. *Educational Leadership, 51*(8), 42–44.

Hudson, J. (1999). Leadership for culturally responsive schools. In L. T. Fenwick (Ed.), *School leadership: Expanding horizons of the mind and spirit* (pp. 139–144). Lancaster, PA: Technomic.

Ikenberry, G. J. (1988). Conclusion: An institutional approach to American foreign economic policy. In G. J. Ikenberry, D. A. Lake, & M. Mastanduno (Eds.), *The state and American foreign economic policy* (pp. 219–243). Ithaca, NY: Cornell University Press.

James, T. (1991). State authority and the politics of educational change. *Review of Research in Education, 17:* 169–224.

Jenkins-Smith, H. C., & Sabatier, P. A. (1993). The study of public policy processes. In P. A. Sabatier & H. C. Jenkins-Smith (Eds.), *Policy change and learning: An advocacy coalition approach* (pp. 1–9). Boulder, CO: Westview Press.

Jenkins-Smith, H. C., & Sabatier, P. A. (1994). Evaluating the advocacy coalition framework. *Journal of Public Policy, 14*(2), 175–203.

Johnson, B. L., Jr. (1999). The politics of research-information use in the education policy arena. In B. S. Cooper & E. V. Randall (Eds.), *Accuracy or advocacy: The politics of research in education* (pp. 17–30). Thousand Oaks, CA: Corwin Press.

Kallio, B. R. (1999). Ethics education in school administrator preparation programs. In L. T. Fenwick (Ed.), *School leadership: Expanding horizons of the mind and spirit* (pp. 222–230). Lancaster, PA: Technomic.

Katz, M. B. (1971). *Class, bureaucracy, and schools: The illusion of educational change in America.* New York: Praeger.

Katzenstein, P. J. (1978a). Introduction: Domestic and international forces and strategies of foreign economic policy. In P. J. Katzenstein (Ed.), *Between power and plenty: Foreign economic policies of advanced industrial states* (pp. 3–22). Madison: University of Wisconsin Press.

Katzenstein, P. J. (1978b). Conclusion: Domestic structures and strategies of foreign economic policy. In P. J. Katzenstein (Ed.), *Between power and plenty: Foreign economic policies of advanced industrial states* (pp. 295–336). Madison: University of Wisconsin Press.

Kerr, D. H. (1976). *Educational policy: Analysis, structure, and justification.* New York: David McKay Co., Inc.

Kingdon, J. W. (1984). *Agendas, alternatives, and public policies.* Boston: Little, Brown, and Co.

Kirst, M. W., & Somers, S. A. (1981). California educational interest groups: Collective action as a logical response to proposition 13. *Education and Urban Society, 13*(2), 235–256.

Kohn, A. (2000). *The case against standardized testing.* Greenwich, CT: Heinemann.

Krasner, S. D. (1984). Approaches to the state: Alternative conceptions and historical dynamics. *Comparative Politics, 16*(2), 223–246.

Larson, J. P. (1980). *Why government programs fail.* New York: Praeger.

Lucas, T., Henze, R., & Donato, R. (1990). Promoting the success of Latino language-minority students: An exploratory study of six high schools. *Harvard Educational Review, 60*(3), 315–340.

Majchrzak, A. (1984). *Methods for policy research.* Newbury Park, CA: Sage.

March, J. G., & Olsen, J. P. (1984). The new institutionalism: Organizational factors of political life. *American Political Science Review, 78,* 734–749.

March, J. G., & Olsen, J. P. (1989). *Rediscovering institutions: The organizational basis of politics.* New York: The Free Press.

Marshall, C. (1993). The new politics of race and gender. In C. Marshall (Ed.), *The new politics of race and gender* (pp. 1–8). London: Falmer Press.

Marshall, C. (1997). *Feminist critical policy analysis* (Vols. 1–2). London: Falmer Press.

Marshall, C., & Anderson, G. L. (1995). Rethinking the public and private spheres: Feminist and cultural studies perspectives on the politics of education. In J. D. Scribner & D. H. Layton (Eds.), *The study of educational politics* (pp. 169–182). Washington, DC: Falmer Press.

Mawhinney, H. B. (1993). *An interpretive framework for understanding the politics of policy change.* Unpublished doctoral dissertation, University of Ottawa, Ottawa, Ontario, Canada.

Mawhinney, H. B. (1994). *An interpretive framework for understanding the politics of policy change.* Paper presented at the Annual Meeting of the Canadian Association for Studies in Educational Administration. Calgary, Alberta, Canada.

Mazzoni, T. L. (1993). The changing politics of state education policymaking: A 20-year Minnesota perspective. *Educational Evaluation and Policy Analysis, 15*(4), 357–379.

Meier, D. (1995). *The power of their ideas.* Boston: Beacon Press.

Murphy, J. (1990). The educational reform movement of the 1980s: A comprehensive analysis. In J. Murphy (Ed.), *The educational reform movement of the 1980s: Perspectives and cases* (pp. 3–55). Berkeley, CA: McCutchan.

Nakamura, R. T., & Smallwood, F. (1980). *The politics of policy implementation.* New York: St. Martin's Press.

National Association of Secondary School Principals. (1996). *Breaking ranks: Changing an American institution.* Reston, VA: Author.

National Commission on Excellence in Education. (1983). *A nation at risk: The imperative for educational reform.* (Stock No. 065-000-00177-2). Washington, DC: U.S. Government Printing Office.

Neustadt, R. E., & May, E. R. (1986). *Thinking in time: The uses of history for decision-makers.* New York: The Free Press.

Noddings, N. (1984). *Caring, a feminine approach to ethics and moral education.* Berkeley: University of California Press.

Opfer, V. D. (2001). Charter schools and the panoptic effect of accountability. *Education and Urban Society, 33*(2), 201–215.

Pal, L. A. (1992). *Public policy analysis: An introduction* (2nd ed.). Scarborough, ON: Nelson Canada.

Peebles, L. D. (2000). Millennial challenges for educational leadership: Revisiting issues of diversity. In P. M. Jenlink (Ed.), *Marching into a new millennium: Challenges to educational leadership* (pp. 190–211). Lanham, MD: Scarecrow Press.

Peters, B. G. (1986). *American public policy: Promise and performance* (2nd ed.), London: MacMillan.

Peters, B. G. (1999). *Institutional theory in political science.* London: Pinter.

Peterson, M. A. (1993). Political influence in the 1990s: From iron triangles to policy networks. *Journal of Health Politics, Policy and Law, 18*(2), 395–438.

Peterson, P. E. (1985). *The politics of school reform, 1870–1940.* Chicago: University of Chicago Press.

Pillow, W. S. (1997). Decentering silences/troubling irony: Teen pregnancy's challenge to policy analysis. In C. Marshall (Ed.), *Feminist critical policy analysis: A perspective from primary and secondary schooling* (pp. 134–152). London: Falmer Press.

Plank, D. N. (1988). Educational reform and organizational change: Atlanta in the Progressive era. *Journal of Urban History, 15*(1), 22–41.

Popkewitz, T. S. (1999). Introduction: Critical traditions, modernisms, and the "posts." In T. S. Popkewitz & L. Fendler (Eds.), *Changing terrains of knowledge and politics* (pp. 1–13). New York: Routledge.

Pratte, R. (1978). Cultural diversity and education. In K. A. Strike & K. Egan (Eds.), *Ethics and educational policy* (pp. 147–167). London: Routledge & Kegan Paul.

Randall, E. V., Cooper, B. S., & Hite, S. J. (1999). Understanding the politics of research in education. In B. S. Cooper & E. V. Randall (Eds.), *Accuracy or advocacy: The politics of research in education* (pp. 1–16). Thousand Oaks, CA: Corwin Press.

Redman, E. (1973). *The dance of legislation.* New York: Simon & Schuster.

Reeves, M. M. (1990). The states as polities: Reformed, reinvigorated, resourceful. *Annals of the American Academy of Political and Social Science, 509,* 83–93.

Reyes, P., & Capper, C. A. (1991). Urban principals: A critical perspective on the context of minority student dropouts. *Educational Administration Quarterly, 27*(4), 530–557.

Reyes, P., Scribner, J. D., & Scribner, A. P. (Eds.). (1999). *Lessons from high-performing Hispanic schools.* New York: Teachers College Press.

Reyes, P., Wagstaff, L. H., & Fusarelli, L. D. (1999). Delta forces: The changing fabric of American society and education. In J. Murphy & K. Seashore Louis

(Eds.), *Handbook of research on educational administration* (2nd ed., pp. 183–201). San Francisco: Jossey-Bass.

Roberts, N. C., & King, P. J. (1996). *Transforming public policy: Dynamics of policy entrepreneurship and innovation.* San Francisco: Jossey-Bass.

Robertson, D. B. (1993). The return to history and the new institutionalism in American political science. *Social Science History, 17*(1), 1–36.

Robertson, D., & Judd, D. (1989). *The development of American public policy.* Glenview, IL: Scott-Foresman.

Rochefort, D. A., & Cobb, R. W. (Eds.). (1994). *The politics of problem definition.* Lawrence: University Press of Kansas.

Romo, H. D., & Falbo, T. (1996). *Latino high school graduation: Defying the odds.* Austin: University of Texas Press.

Rosenau, P. V. (1993). Anticipating a post-modern policy current? *Policy Currents, 3,* 1–4.

Rosenthal, A. (1977). The emerging legislative role in education. *Compact, 11*(4), 2–4.

Rosenthal, A. (1989). The new legislature: Better or worse and for whom? In T. L. Beyle (Ed.), *State government: CQ's guide to current issues and activities, 1987–88* (pp. 69–70). Washington, DC: Congressional Quarterly Inc.

Rowan, B., & Miskel, C. G. (1999). Institutional theory and the study of educational organizations. In J. Murphy & K. Seashore Louis (Eds.), *Handbook of research on educational administration* (2nd ed., pp. 359–383). San Francisco: Jossey-Bass.

Sabatier, P. A. (1991a). Political science and public policy. *PS: Political Science & Politics, 24*(2), 144–147.

Sabatier, P. A. (1991b). Toward better theories of the policy process. *PS: Political Science & Politics, 24*(2), 147–156.

Sabatier, P. A., & Jenkins-Smith, H. C. (Eds.). (1993). *Policy change and learning: An advocacy coalition approach.* Boulder, CO: Westview Press.

Schattschneider, E. E. (1960). *The semi-sovereign people: A realist's view of democracy in America.* Hinsdale, IL: Dryden Press.

Scheurich, J. J. (1994). Policy archaeology: A new policy studies methodology. *Journal of Education Policy, 9*(4), 297–316.

Scheurich, J. J., & Imber, M. (1991). Educational reforms can reproduce societal inequities: A case study. *Educational Administration Quarterly, 27*(3), 297–320.

Scheurich, J. J., Skrla, L., & Johnson, J. F. (2000). Thinking carefully about equity and accountability. *Phi Delta Kappan, 82*(4), 293–299.

Scott, W. R. (1995). *Institutions and organizations.* Thousand Oaks, CA: Sage.

Scribner, J. D., Reyes, P., & Fusarelli, L. D. (1995). Educational politics and policy: And the game goes on. In J. D. Scribner & D. H. Layton (Eds.), *The study of educational politics* (pp. 201–212). London: Falmer Press.

Senge, P. (1990). *The fifth discipline: The art and practice of the learning organization.* New York: Doubleday.

Sergiovanni, T. J. (1995). Small schools, great expectations. *Educational Leadership, 53*(3), 48–53.

Sergiovanni, T. J. (1996). *Leadership for the schoolhouse.* San Francisco: Jossey-Bass.

Skocpol, T. (1992). *Protecting soldiers and mothers: The political origins of social policy in the United States.* Cambridge, MA: Harvard University Press.

Stewart, J., Jr. (1991). Policy models and equal educational opportunity. *PS: Political Science & Politics, 24*(2), 167–173.

Stone, D. A. (1988). *Policy paradox and political reason.* New York: HarperCollins.

Stout, R. T., Tallerico, M., & Scribner, K. P. (1995). Values: The 'what?' of the politics of education. In J. D. Scribner & D. H. Layton (Eds.), *The study of educational politics* (pp. 5–20). Washington, DC: Falmer Press.

Strike, K. A. (1982). *Educational policy and the just society.* Urbana: University of Illinois Press.

Strike, K. A. (1989). *Liberal justice and the Marxist critique of education.* New York: Routledge.

Strike, K. A. (1993). Professionalism, democracy, and discursive communities: Normative reflections on restructuring. *American Educational Research Journal, 30*(2), 255–275.

Swift, E. K., & Brady, D. W. (1991). Out of the past: Theoretical and methodological contributions of congressional history. *PS: Political Science & Politics, 24*(1), 61–64.

Thelen, K., & Steinmo, S. (1992). Historical institutionalism in comparative politics. In S. Steinmo, K. Thelen, & F. Longstreth (Eds.), *Structuring politics: Historical institutionalism in comparative analysis* (pp. 1–32). Cambridge, MA: Cambridge University Press.

Torres, C. A. (1999). Critical theory and political sociology of education: Arguments. In T. S. Popkewitz & L. Fendler (Eds.), *Changing terrains of knowledge and politics* (pp. 87–115). New York: Routledge.

Truman, D. B. (1951). *The governmental process: Political interests and public opinion.* New York: Knopf.

Viteritti, J. P. (1999). *Choosing equality: School choice, the constitution, and civil society.* Washington, DC: Brookings Institution Press.

Warwick, D. P., & Pettigrew, T. F. (1983). Toward ethical guidelines for social science research in public policy. In D. Callahan & B. Jennings (Eds.), *Ethics, the social sciences, and policy analysis* (pp. 335–368). New York: Plenum Press.

Weaver, S. W., & Geske, T. G. (1996). *Educational policy-making in the state legislature: Legislator as policy expert.* Paper presented at the Annual Meeting of the American Educational Research Association. New York.

Weir, M. (1992). Ideas and the politics of bounded innovation. In S. Steinmo, K. Thelen, & F. Longstreth (Eds.), *Structuring politics: Historical institutionalism in comparative analysis* (pp. 188–216). Cambridge, MA: Cambridge University Press.

Weiss, C. H. (1991). Policy research in the context of diffuse decision-making. *Journal of Higher Education, 53,* 619–640.

Wirt, F. M., & Kirst, M. W. (2001). *The political dynamics of American education* (2nd ed.). Berkeley, CA: McCutchan.

Wise, C. R. (1991). *The dynamics of legislation: Leadership and policy change in the congressional process.* San Francisco: Jossey-Bass.

Wood, G. H. (1992). *Schools that work: America's most innovative public education programs.* New York: Dutton.

Young, M. D. (1999). Multifocal educational policy research: Toward a method for enhancing traditional educational policy studies. *American Educational Research Journal, 36*(4), 677–714.

3

The Birth of Policy

Problem Definition, Agenda Setting, and Policy Formulation

In his popular public policy textbook, Thomas Dye (2001) comments that policy issues do not just "happen." Policies affecting education have a point (or multiple points) of origin, emerging from what Kingdon (1995) refers to as the "policy primeval soup" (p. 116). This chapter focuses on three key, interrelated aspects of policy formation: problem definition, agenda setting, and policy formulation. After all, what is policy but a set of answers to questions, a series of solutions to problems? Yet, how policy is formulated is dependent in large measure on how problems are defined within the policy arena and how agendas are set within the context of the policymaking environment. In many respects, problem definition is the single most important part of the policy process, because how problems are defined affects their position on the policy agenda, presages what alternatives are considered and adopted, and determines how the policy is implemented and evaluated (Dye, 1992). A simple case illustrates the importance of problem definition in the policy process.

POLICY VIGNETTE • *The Problem of Defining Desegregation*

On its face, school segregation seems a relatively simple problem, one readily addressed through policy. Segregation and desegregation are not complex concepts to understand. Yet, segregation remains a persistent issue in U.S. education. A number of researchers point out that public schools are as segregated today as they were before the *Brown* decision in 1954 (Orfield, Eaton, & Jones, 1997). But does this constitute a problem? The answer to this question depends on several factors, including whether dominant policy elites consider segregation a problem and, if they do, how it is defined within the political arena. If segregation is primarily a product of individual, residential choice, then is segregation really a problem? Can the state restrict individual choice in the name of the "greater good"? However, if segregation is the result of racism or discrimination, and segregation perpetuates inequality, then it becomes a policy problem requiring action.

What would a truly desegregated school or school system look like? Should each school mirror the ethnic makeup of the local community or should the "community" be defined as the larger metropolitan statistical area (MSA)? What should be the target ethnic mix in each school? How should this be achieved? What policy mechanisms would be required? And if segregation reflects, in part, individual choice, then how can actors balance the conflict between the competing values of equity and choice? Furthermore, it could be argued that even if schools had an equitable ethnic mix of students, they would still be segregated. As Oakes (1986) found in her research on tracking, many schools that appear to be integrated at the schoolhouse door are incredibly segregated by curricular track. The overwhelming majority of Anglo and Asian students follow an advanced curricular track consisting of Advanced Placement and honors courses, while most Latino and African American students are placed in vocational or general curricular tracks. Therefore, how desegregation is defined is a key determinant of which policy mechanisms to use to achieve the policy objective.

Problem Definition

"At the nexus of politics and policy development lies persistent conflict over where problems come from and, based on the answer to this question, what kinds of solutions should be attempted" (Rochefort & Cobb, 1994, p. 3). Dye (2001) asserts that agenda setting and problem definition constitute the most important stage of the entire policymaking process. In law, for example, scholars—particularly legal literary analysts—have noted that "the very way in which we use law to talk about problems determines their resolution" (Grossberg, 1993, p. 112). Problem definition entails not only what issues are elevated to the level of problems (and thus require action) but also "preventing certain conditions in society from becoming policy issues," what Dye calls non-decisionmaking (Dye, 1992, p. 336).

Problem definition, a crucial stage of the policy process, "has to do with what we choose to identify as public issues and how we think and talk about these concerns" (Rochefort & Cobb, 1994, p. vii). The description of a social problem "can effect its rise or decline before government" (Rochefort & Cobb, 1994, p. vii). Problem definition and redefinition are often used as tools by opposing sides to gain advantage. As Fowler (2000) observed, "If a policy issue is not well defined, it will not be perceived as important," making it difficult to "attract enough attention to reach the policy agenda" and become policy (p. 167).

Policy actors who are successful in deciding how problems are defined and agendas are set wield enormous power in the policymaking process. "How an issue is defined or redefined, as the case may be, influences: (1) the type of politicking which will ensue around it; (2) its chances of reaching the agenda of a particular political institution; and (3) the probability of a policy outcome favorable to advocates of the issue" (Petracca, 1992, p. 1). What Schattschneider (1960) wrote over four decades ago remains true today: "the definition of the alternatives is the supreme instrument of power" (p. 68).

Conditions and Problems

To understand how some issues rise quickly on the policy agenda, while others languish for months or years without being addressed, it is important to distinguish between conditions and problems. A problem is a condition that can be addressed through policy. Put another way, problems are conditions that have solutions attached to them. This conceptualization is a bit different from Kingdon's (1995) distinction between a condition and a problem. Kingdon argues that the difference lies in intentionality: "Conditions become defined as problems when we come to believe that we *should* do something about them" (emphasis added) (p. 109). However, even if policymakers want to address a problem such as poverty, absent a proposed solution or plan of action, the problem cannot be addressed and will remain a condition.

Sometimes, solutions determine how problems are defined. Wildavsky (1979) argues that public officials will not take a problem seriously unless there is a proposed course of action attached to it. He stated, "a problem is a problem only if something can be done about it" (p. 42). A good example of the distinction between a condition and a problem is drawn from Kingdon, quoting a lobbyist who said, "If you have only four fingers on one hand, that's not a problem; that's a situation [a condition]" (p. 109). Good intentions alone cannot change this condition into a problem; only intent coupled with capacity or a solution turns the condition into a problem. Thus, we might best conceptualize the difference between conditions and problems as this: conditions become defined as problems when policymakers have the technical ability and political will to address them.

Agenda Setting

It is important to view policy as a political battle over problem definition and agenda setting, rather than as a process by which policy is the product of impartial rationality. "Before a policy choice can be made, a problem in society must have been accepted as a part of the agenda of the policymaking system—that is, as a portion of the range of problems deemed amenable to public action and worthy of the attention of policymakers" (Peters, 1986, p. 39). "Cultural values, interest group advocacy, scientific information, and professional advice all help to shape the content of problem definition" (Rochefort & Cobb, 1994, p. 4). One of the major contributions of postmodernism to policy studies is in the rejection of the notion that policy "is or can be objective or ideologically neutral" (Rosenau, 1993, p. 3). Decades of policy research demonstrate that problem definition and agenda setting are never purely technical exercises but rather political activities offering "substantial control over ultimate policy choices" (Peters, 1986, p. 42; see also Cooper & Randall 1999; Dery, 1984; Hogwood & Gunn, 1984; Wildavsky, 1979).

Several factors affect the agenda setting process, including the "extremity, concentration, range, and visibility of problems" (Peters, 1986, p. 46). The more people affected by a problem, the more likely the item will receive priority on the legislative agenda, particularly if the effects are concentrated and serious or extreme. Highly visible events, such as a school shooting, generate immediate policy responses, despite the fact that such occurrences are rare. Peters (1986) discusses two other kinds of agenda setting: spillover and analogous agenda setting. Spillover effects occur when policy has unintended effects, producing the need for other policies and programs. For example, the development of the interstate highway system and associated federal transportation policies were major factors in the suburbanization of the United States. However, these policies also effectively walled in urban, predominately minority neighborhoods, destroying many viable low-income communities and encouraging white flight from the urban core, thereby increasing segregation in schools (Reyes, Wagstaff, & Fusarelli, 1999; Wilson, 1997). These spillover effects led, in part, to the development of other education policies, such as the Elementary and Secondary Education Act (ESEA), designed to ameliorate the negative effects of segregation, poverty, and economic isolation created by national transportation policies.

Analogous agenda setting occurs when new issues are framed within the context of an earlier policy referent. "The more a new issue can be made to look like an old issue, the more likely it is to be placed on an agenda" (Peters, 1986, p. 47). For example, improving urban education through charter schools, rather than through vouchers, provides greater school choice while restricting choice to the public sphere. If charter schools were not "public schools," and if other public school choice options did not exist, then charter schools would appear to be a radical policy proposal—one encountering much opposition. However, the existence of interdistrict and intradistrict choice policies in many states, magnet schools, and alternative schools (such as the alternative high school system in New York City) makes charter school proposals look like an extension of public school choice—not really radical at all. In fact, one of the criticisms leveled against charter schools is that, because they remain tied to the public school system and cannot operate outside it, the expected benefits of choice and competition will not accrue. Thus, the charter school reform could be interpreted as a conservative policy response, not the radical reform touted by proponents (Nathan, 1996).

The Role of the Media

With the advent of television in the 1950s and cable, CNN, and the Internet today, the media are omnipresent and play a major role in the agenda setting process. More Americans can name a nightly news anchor than can identify their state senator. Cognizant of this power, a number of scholars in a variety of disciplines (journalism, history, political science, sociology, and education, to name but a few) have studied the effects of the mass media in shaping the policy agenda. Graber (1984) examined the effects of the media on political beliefs, attitudes, and activities. She concluded that when political elites disagree about an issue, the media have the power to amplify those disagreements, thereby turning issues into public controversies. A book-length example of this process may be found in Snyderman and Rothman's (1988) analysis of the media's role in the IQ controversy. The authors' major findings include: (1) media coverage of the IQ controversy was inaccurate; (2) erroneous reporting of technical issues; and (3) journalists repeatedly misrepresented scholarly views and research findings—suggesting greater controversy and disagreement than actually existed.

While the media may not have the power to create or set the policy agenda, they play a crucial role in determining how quickly agenda items rise to prominence on the political agenda. However, other scholars, such as Spitzer (1993), go much further, arguing that TV news magazines such as "60 Minutes" and its offspring intentionally seek to shape government policymaking. Drawing from Schattschneider, Spitzer asserts, "More than any other single force in national politics, the media controls the scope of politics, since the scope of politics is most often regulated by modern mass communication organizations" (p. 9). Snyderman and Rothman (1988) characterize the media as the "new strategic elites" (p. 255). Although disagreement exists among scholars as to precisely how the media influences policy, there is little disagreement that such influence extends into all stages of the policy process. Commenting on this phenomenon, Paletz (1998) stated, "Media influence on the process and content of policies varies according to type of issue, stage of process, time frame, and political and media systems. Under certain circumstances, the media can be a crucial player. It depends on what is covered, how often, and how it is framed" (p. 234).

Related to the media's ability to frame issues, focusing or triggering events often enable problems to rise to the top of policymakers' agendas (Baumgartner & Jones, 1993). Focusing events are "sudden, relatively rare events that spark intense media and public attention because of their sheer magnitude or, sometimes, because of the harm they reveal" (Birkland, 2001, p. 116). A dramatic example of a focusing event was the Columbine school shooting in 1999. Although focusing events elevate dormant problems to the front of policy agendas, they can mislead policymakers by making a problem appear bigger than it is. In the case of school shootings, for example, data collected by the F.B.I. indicate that schools overall are quite safe—incidences of violent crime among juveniles are declining and school shootings are rare. But policymakers and the public are led to believe otherwise and demand action—possibly diverting resources from other, more urgent problems.

On the other hand, triggering events can force policymakers to address issues that otherwise would be ignored. Fowler (2000) uses the example of school construction and renovation. School buildings in many of our nation's large, urban systems are in decay. It is likely that some buildings are unsafe. However, policymakers are notorious for their unwillingness to allocate sufficient funds for renovation and new school construction, in large part because it is expensive (particularly in urban areas such as New York City, Chicago, or Los Angeles). Providing sufficient funding might necessitate a tax increase, which politicians are understandably reluctant to support. However, as Fowler (2000) notes, if a roof were to collapse, injuring fifty children, the catastrophe could act as a triggering event, "attracting media attention, causing a public outcry, and almost forcing the state legislature to act" (p. 183).

POLICY VIGNETTE • *Agenda Setting, Sputnik, and Education Policy*

In 1957, at the height of the Cold War, the Soviet Union launched the Sputnik satellite into orbit. Almost immediately, the launch created a crisis in U.S. education. It appeared that the United States had fallen behind in the technology race into space and that the United States was in danger of losing the Cold War. Predictably, the educational system was blamed. Critics charged that science, mathematics, and technology instruction in schools was poor quality (or nonexistent) and in need of immediate improvement. Schools were not producing enough students well educated in science, math, technology, and foreign languages. In response, Congress passed the National Defense Education Act. Curriculum was upgraded and more advanced courses offered in these critical areas. The launch of Sputnik was a triggering event with significant effects on American education. Congressional action redirected resources toward science, math, and language programs, as well as freeing up resources for school districts to purchase new technology.

Triggering events are, by definition, impossible to predict, complicating efforts at educational planning and forecasting. An example is the terrorist attack on the World Trade Center in New York City on September 11, 2001. Prior to the attack, a major issue in the mayoral primary was how large a raise the city's teachers, represented by the United Federation of Teachers (UFT), should receive, as they had been operating without a contract for several months (and were not inclined to negotiate with New York City's then mayor, Rudolph Giuliani, who was perceived as hostile toward the union). After the attack, the issue disappeared off the radar screen. The attack accelerated the economy's downward spiral into recession. The enormous cost of rebuilding, projected well into the billions, left less city and state money available for other services, including a major teacher raise.

The tragedy placed the union in the difficult position of advocating for a substantial pay raise during an unprecedented tragedy, amidst enormous pain and suffering. As many union members expressed to the authors, the timing was incredibly unfortunate. Just as the union was gearing up for a major public relations campaign dramatizing the plight of the city's teachers, the story line dramatically changed, creating a potential PR nightmare for the union. After all, how do you advocate a major teacher salary increase without appearing greedy, particularly in light of the enormous suffering of others around you? Entire fire companies were lost in the tragedy (mothers and fathers, sons and daughters, not to mention the cost of replacing very expensive equipment). Police, EMS, and Port Authority personnel were also lost, including thousands of workers in the Twin Towers themselves. The attack, acting as a triggering event, dramatically altered the city's political agenda, placing teacher concerns on the back burner.

The Power of Language in Problem Definition and Agenda Setting

At its core, problem definition requires the expression or symbolic representation of policy problems in words.[1] How words are used, how arguments are structured, represent "the essence of problem definition" (Stone, 1988, p. 108). All problems are social constructions—they reflect the ways "in which we as a society and the various contending interests within it structure and tell the stories about how problems come to be the way they are" (Birkland, 2001, p. 122). Language is an expression of power relations. The structuration of language has

---

[1]We devote considerable attention to the role of language and rhetoric in problem definition, agenda setting, and policy formulation because we believe language plays a crucial, and oft-overlooked, role in the policy process—both in shaping our perceptions and understanding of problems and in the courses of action or solutions developed in response to those problems.

the power to shape our perceptions and suspend skepticism (Stone, 1988). As Edelman (1964) remarked in *The Symbolic Uses of Politics*, "Language becomes a sequence of Pavlovian cues rather than an instrument for reasoning and analysis if situation and appropriate cue occur together" (p. 116). "Virtually every word and phrase used in casual speech and thought bears a heavy connotative burden which opens the way to socially approved conclusions and inhibits the recognition of possibilities that are not culturally condoned" (Edelman, 1964, pp. 119–120).

Stone (1988) identifies four aspects of symbolic representation critical to problem definition: (1) narrative stories (explanations of how the world works), (2) synechdoches (a part is used to represent the whole), (3) metaphors (the most common in education discourse), and (4) ambiguity (the capacity to have multiple meanings—a useful political tool). Language, particularly the use of metaphors and analogies, is used "to control people's evaluations of policy alternatives" (Stone, 1988, p. 200). Language structures decisionmaking insofar as it can favor a particular result and diminish the consideration or adoption of alternatives (Riker, 1986). How is this favored result achieved? Language is employed either to expand or narrow the scope of conflict because "every change in the scope of conflict has a bias; it is partisan in its nature" (Schattschneider, 1960, p. 4). For example, issues may be defined in procedural or technical language in order to restrict participation, thereby narrowing the scope of conflict and enabling dominant policymakers to control the policymaking process (Nelkin, 1975; Schattschneider, 1960). Conversely, "to heighten participation, issues may be connected to sweeping social themes, such as justice, democracy, and liberty" (Rochefort & Cobb, 1994, p. 5).

"As political discourse, the function of problem definition is at once to explain, to describe, to recommend, and, above all, to persuade" (Rochefort & Cobb, 1994, p. 15). For example, the word *crisis* is "used by claims-makers to elevate a concern when facing an environment overloaded with competing claims" (Rochefort & Cobb, 1994, p. 21). In another example, the *A Nation at Risk* report used stark, militaristic terminology to claim a crisis in public education and provided a set of readily adoptable reforms to address the crisis. More recently, the perceived shortage of school administrators, particularly superintendents, has been elevated to crisis proportions, although there is continuing dispute among scholars as to whether this crisis is real, a problem but not yet a crisis, or not really a problem at all but rather a social construction of the media, superintendent associations, and scholars (Fusarelli, Cooper, & Carella, in press; Glass, Bjork, & Brunner, 2000).

Related to language is the power of symbols in American politics and policy. According to Peters (1986), "The more closely a particular problem can be linked to certain important national symbols, the greater its probability of being placed on the agenda" (p. 48). In the policy vignette discussed earlier in this chapter, educational deficiencies in science, mathematics, technology, and foreign language required national intervention in much greater scope than in the past. As a result, the programs and policies designed to address the deficiency employed the rhetoric of national defense—hence, the National *Defense* Education Act (NDEA) (Peters, 1986, p. 48, emphasis in original). Similarly, the federal government's major welfare program was originally titled Aid to Families with Dependent *Children* (AFDC) (Peters, 1986, p. 48, emphasis in original).

When policies are couched in terminology with mass appeal, they generate greater popular (and political) support. In the case of NDEA, it is difficult to oppose educational policies that strengthen our country's defenses in the face of perceived aggression. Similarly, in the case of AFDC, providing support to needy children is a popular political position (Grossberg, 1993), whereas a welfare program providing benefits to poor, single, unemployed mothers would engender less support. Even the program's new title, Temporary Assistance for Needy Families (TANF), emphasizes the transitory nature of governmental assistance. Note also that the word *children* was removed from the program's title, because Temporary Assistance to Needy Children might foster a political backlash against welfare reformers (it would, in fact, appear mean-spirited).

Linguistic representations such as those discussed above construct reality (Fennimore, 2000). Language conveys intentionality through its power to create desired outcomes and to influence relationships through shared social meanings (Putnam, 1994). Edelman (1988) argues that

> the critical element in political maneuver for advantage is the creation of meaning: the construction of beliefs about events, policies, leaders, problems, and crises that rationalize or challenge existing inequalities. The strategic need is to immobilize opposition and mobilize support. While coercion and intimidation help to check resistance in all political systems, the key tactic must always be the evocation of interpretations that legitimize favored courses of action and threaten or reassure people so as to encourage them to be supportive or to remain quiescent. (pp. 103–104)

The choice of words used, and the care in which they are crafted into policy arguments, open windows of opportunity for some actors or groups, while closing off others from policy discourse. In policy debates, the structuration of language confers legitimacy because "It is language that confers status on reality, not reality on language" (Prawat & Peterson, 1999, p. 214).

Meaning is derived from its use in language games, which is to say that meaning is dependent on the way in which issues are framed in political discourse (Brand, 1979; Wittgenstein, 1974). In his study of presidential campaigns, Riker (1996) found that "campaigns are rhetorical exercises: attempts to persuade voters to view issues in the way the candidate wishes them to" (p. 4). And as Garman and Holland (1995) assert in their analysis of the rhetoric of school reform reports, "rhetoric matters" (p. 106). It shapes practice insofar as it influences the thoughts and actions of the audience. Arguments appeal to emotion, rather than reason, and the "sacred" remains "beyond challenge or question" (p. 106). Once ideas become axiomatic in policy discourse, refutation becomes nearly impossible. As Norton (1993) has argued, "The force of a political idea lies in its capacity to transcend thought," becoming "a set of principles unconsciously adhered to, a set of conventions so deeply held that they appear (when they appear at all) to be no more than common sense" (p. 1).

By problematizing political discourse and the context within which it takes place, we may better understand how language games shape educational policymaking. For example, Tyack (1974) and Hansot and Tyack (1982) documented the success political progressives of the early twentieth century had in removing public control from educational decisionmaking and placing the process in the hands of "experts." By defining spheres of activity and policy as beyond the political realm, or as nonpartisan, professionals were able to insulate key areas of educational decisionmaking from popular pressures (Katznelson & Weir, 1985). Similarly, by contracting the sphere in which lay people could participate, school professionals were able to implement their policy solutions largely without opposition (Katznelson & Weir, 1985). By redefining partisanship as a form of deviancy, partisanship was sanitized out of political discourse, leaving nonpartisanship or expert control as the preferred solution. By manipulating language in this manner, school professionals were able to exclude the voices of the public from the policy dialogue. Thus, far from being a neutral transmitter of ideas, language serves to structure policy debates, privileging some while excluding others.

The political manipulation of language plays a key role in agenda setting when political rhetoric and policy discourse are linked to dominant cultural values. For example, Bastian (1995) notes that opposing school choice "is a bit like being asked to burn the American flag at a VFW meeting. You have every right to do it, but do you want to? After all, choice is a bedrock American value" (p. 205). Bartolome and Macedo (1997) assert that "The illusion of choice . . . creates a pedagogy of entrapment that makes it undemocratic to argue against school choice. Thus school choice becomes part of a discourse that brooks no dissension or argument, for to argue against it is to deny democracy" (p. 233). Choice, then, is viewed within the cultural referents of individualism, liberty, and democracy. To argue against choice, opponents are placed in the unenviable position of opposing cultural values widely held among both policy elites and the general populace. Policy change is difficult when it conflicts with strongly held public values in the political culture (Bosso, 1994). Conversely, policy change is facilitated when it reflects commonly held public values.

All policy discourse is framed within a cultural context that carries "its own characteristic perspectives and ways of framing issues" (Rein & Schon, 1993, p. 156). Words are carefully chosen, appropriate metaphors and analogies used, which appeal to popular cultural markers or referents. Lather argues that this seemingly transparent use of language is not innocent. "The way we speak and write reflects the structures of power in our society" (Lather, 1991, pp. 11–12). According to Lather (1996), "speech is part of a discursive system, a network of power that has material effects" (p. 528). Drawing from Cherryholmes (1988), language "determines what counts as true, important, or relevant" (p. 35). In the context of school choice, arguing against choice is un-American. As a result, few policymakers oppose school choice; many, in fact, argue for more choice but differ with respect to the type of choice—whether it be magnet schools, charter schools, various open-enrollment plans (inter- and intradistrict choice options), or vouchers. The language game becomes how best to frame choice within the education policymaking context.

POLICY VIGNETTE • *Defining Pathology: Who's At Risk?*

Throughout the United States, multiple indicators are used to determine and classify at risk children. A child may be categorized as at risk if he or she "exhibits high absenteeism, has been retained, performs poorly in class, indicates a 'previolent' disposition," is emotionally disabled (ED) or learning disabled (LD), is pregnant, poor, lives in a single parent household, or speaks English as a second language (ESL) (Fine, 1993, p. 104). Fine (1993) reminds us that "The cultural construction of a group defined through a discourse of risk represents a quite partial image, typically strengthening those institutions and groups that have carved out, severed, denied connection to, and then promised to 'save' those who will undoubtedly remain 'at risk' " (p. 91). She asks, "Who benefits from the ideological and material construction 'youth at risk'?" (p. 104).

In effect, the multiple indicators used to define children at risk exclude the majority of Anglo, middle- and upper-class students, because they are less likely to fit this profile. The indices, which reflect upper- and middle-class norms of what constitute "disadvantage" or, perhaps more accurately, "social pathology," are constructed in such a manner that most children of the dominant group do not fit the definition—in effect, defining the problem as one of deficiencies with "other people's children" (Delpit, 1995).

The Role of Political Culture in Agenda Setting: The Normative Dimension

What is most remarkable about the problem definition and agenda setting processes is that in any given arena—whether it be Congress, a state legislature, or a school district—remarkably few alternatives are actually considered. The political culture in a given arena or location plays a significant role in determining the range of alternatives given serious consideration at any time. Culture imposes boundaries that serve to confine our thinking within well-defined parameters (Bosso, 1994). In the United States, "a powerful and enduring political culture (as distinct from an arguably much more variegated popular culture) helps to whittle down the range of 'legitimate' alternatives to a pitiful few long before any quasi-pluralist 'conflict' over problem definition ever ensues" (Bosso, 1994, p. 184).

This "received" culture (Goodwyn, 1978) shapes in large measure people's perceptions of reality—of what policy options are legitimate and acceptable. Generally, these perceptions coalesce around a set of core beliefs in individual liberty, private property, capitalism, the Protestant work ethic, meritocracy, civic duty, faith in progress, democracy, and freedom (Bellah, Madsen, Sullivan, Swidler, & Tipton, 1985, 1991; Bosso, 1994). The national ideology of free-market capitalism and minimal government intervention is so potent "that anyone who suggests real alternatives is labeled quickly a radical or dreamer, an image that ultimately exiles advocates to the margins of mainstream discourse" (Bosso, 1994, p. 185).

States that have a reformist or progressive tradition in their political culture tend to be leaders in policy innovation (Mazzoni, 1993). For example, Minnesota boasts a long tradition of progressive education reform. In 1958, the state legislature "piloted a plan that allowed at-risk students to exit their own neighborhood districts to obtain remedial instruction in other public and private schools" (Viteritti, 1999, pp. 62–63). That same year, lawmakers adopted a proposal allowing "high school juniors and seniors to take courses at public and private colleges" (Viteritti, 1999, p. 63), a policy now in use throughout the country. In 1991, the Minnesota legislature passed the nation's first charter school law. It is unlikely that such extensive, progressive policy activism in education, over such a lengthy period, would have been possible absent a supportive political culture. Because problem definition and agenda setting are predominately normative enterprises, the normative dimension of policy formulation is crucial to understanding this stage of the policy process.

Institutional Effects on Agenda Setting: The Structural and Technical Dimensions

The processes of problem definition and agenda setting are not only affected by culture, values, and prevailing norms, but also by the formal structure of governing institutions and procedures within which these processes take place. According to David Truman (1964) in his classic study of the governmental process, institutional configurations determine the pathways through which conflict is channeled. These institutions, be they legislatures, courts, or local school boards, shape the way we understand and evaluate policy alternatives, shaping problem definition and agenda setting within a given cultural frame (Skocpol, 1992). In education, the power of institutions, particularly state legislatures and courts, has expanded rapidly in the last twenty-five years. State legislative staffs have grown and become more professionalized. State departments of education have greater capacity than ever to monitor and, when necessary, to intervene directly in taking over troubled school districts.

Because power and policymaking are spread throughout our federal system of governance, interest groups denied success at one level or by one branch of government often seek to achieve policy objectives through other institutions. For example, when Congress and state legislatures denied African Americans equal educational opportunity, they turned to the courts to address their concerns. Baumgartner and Jones (1993) refer to this as venue shopping. Another significant institutional constraint on problem definition and agenda setting is "constitutionality" (Fowler, 2000, p. 179). Constitutions, and the case law on which they are interpreted, set broad parameters within which educational issues are defined. For example, significant constitutional constraints prohibit religious activity in schools (Fowler, 2000). Such constraints serve as external checks on how school policies are written and issues defined in this area.

The structural context "is the means by which politics is either thwarted or translated into action" (Peterson, 1993, p. 395). This includes various rules and procedures, such as the Constitution, statutes, jurisdictions, precedents, customary decisionmaking modes, and other legal requirements as well as the mood of the public and the preferences of various politicians and interest group members (Kingdon, 1995). One might add as well that the particular organizational structure of government provides opportunities and access for these actors, especially interest group members. For example, a federal system of governance facilitates institutional fragmentation (Robertson & Judd, 1989), thereby providing multiple opportunities for interest groups to exert influence on policy formulation.

Students interested in the role of institutions in the agenda setting process should explore the well-developed literature in political science on executive-legislative dynamics. Within this extensive literature, the work of Paul Light (1982, 1999) stands out. Throughout the last two decades, Light has examined presidential policymaking from Kennedy through Clinton. His research demonstrates the complexity of executive leadership in modern times, wherein the domestic policy agendas of presidents are constrained by greater competition from Congress over control of the policy agenda and by the increased complexity of policymaking at the national level. Light concludes that presidents face a paradox of power: presidential influence over the domestic policy agenda decreases over time, while their effectiveness (learned expertise) increases during that same period. As a result, presidents are most powerful (in the political stream) when they are least knowledgeable.

Light's work has interesting implications for leadership at the state and local levels. For example, it could be extended to governors, mayors, superintendents, and principals—with significant implications for school change and reform. It might be the case that new superintendents have the greatest opportunity to initiate reforms early in their tenure, during which they are often least knowledgeable about local conditions, norms, and values—"the way things are done around here." This dynamic may be true particularly when the new superintendent is an outsider. We believe such leadership studies at the state and local levels would add much to our understanding of school change and reform—and are an example of how research outside education can be extended and applied to the study of educational leadership, politics, and policy.

Interest Groups and Policy Formulation: The Constituentive Dimension

Like all areas of public policy, the field of education is populated by an enormous number of interest groups—each with its own agenda. Attempting to list all the interest groups involved in policy formulation in education would be a pointless exercise, as the number stretches nearly to infinity. Significant, however, are the interest groups that have risen to prominence in shaping education policy within the last decade. Spurred on by hundreds of national and state blue ribbon commissions and reports (Ginsberg & Plank, 1995), education has witnessed an explosion of interest group activity at all levels—national, state, and local. Fowler (2000) identifies a loosely linked group of institutions that she refers to as the education policy planning and research community (EPPRC), which includes corporations, the wealthy elite, U.S. Department of Education, foundations (Carnegie, Danforth, Ford, etc.), think tanks (Brookings, Manhattan Institute, RAND, etc.), universities, and education associations. What is significant about much of this interest group activity, and what distinguishes it from previous activism, is the prominence of non-educators leading reform efforts.

In their review of major multiple-state case studies in education, Burlingame and Geske (1979) assert that "the politics of education at the state level is still a politics of interest groups" (p. 71). Mawhinney (1993) found that "the Ontario educational policy community is tightly knit with well-defined sets of assumptions and norms" (p. 412), suggesting that policy communities have a significant impact on the nature and direction of policy change. In his analysis of changes in state educational policymaking over twenty years in Minnesota, Mazzoni (1993) found that advocacy coalitions were a driving force behind the educational reform movement. Mazzoni argues that Minnesota's state school policy system can be characterized as an advocacy coalition of innovative reformers. He observed that "linking together government, business, education, foundation, parent, and civic actors—and led by elected officials—this coalition became a potent force in setting forth a restructuring agenda and in influencing the policy system" (p. 375). According to Mazzoni, Minnesota's advocacy coalitions "have repeatedly squared off during the past decade over issues of school reform, with their struggle appearing to have been spawned by a fundamental cleavage over core beliefs, by stable structural features of the institutional setting, and by the impact of multiple changes in a turbulent external environment" (p. 377).

The findings of Mazzoni's research are consistent with Feir's (1995) analysis of education policymaking in Pennsylvania. Feir found that a coalition of business leaders, media, governors, and chief state school officers were actively engaged in educational reform, while traditional education interest groups played minor roles in the reforms of the mid 1980s. Feir (1995) notes that "the expansion of the conflict over education reform to include business, political, and media leaders, coupled with the substantial neutralization of education interest groups, provided opportunities for new actors to set the agenda" (p. 29). Weaver and Geske (1996) also note the existence of shifting advocacy coalitions and their role in promoting policy change. According to the researchers, leaders from different agencies and groups were "usually able to coalesce on major educational issues" (p. 1). The advocacy coalitions created via this process were able to exert substantial pressure on the legislature to promote their preferred policy solutions.

Chapter Discussion Questions

1. Are there differences among students and, if so, should not educators create policies and programs to provide resources to students to address their needs?

2. If you answered yes to both parts of question one, how would you craft a policy, using nonexclusionary language descriptors, to identify eligible students, the target population?

Seminal Works

Students interested in agenda setting and policy formulation should begin with a careful reading of E. E. Schattschneider's (1960) classic, *The Semi-Sovereign People*. Rarely has such a concise work of scholarship contained so many profound and important insights into the scope and nature of political conflict—with particular emphasis on the role of institutions in shaping the context of agenda setting and problem definition and in influencing the outcome of conflict.

John Kingdon's (1995) *Agendas, Alternatives, and Public Policies*, now in its second edition, is perhaps the most definitive study of agenda setting currently in print. Winner of the 1994 Aaron Wildavsky award, Kingdon explores the development of public policy over time at the national level in the areas of health and transportation. Interviewing policy actors both inside and outside government, Kingdon seeks to answer the question, "How does an idea's time come?" In answering this question, Kingdon explores the nuances of three distinct, yet interrelated process "streams"—streams of problems, policies, and politics. These streams come together at certain critical junctures to produce policy change.

Perhaps the single best analysis of problem definition is David Rochefort and Roger Cobb's (1994) edited book, *The Politics of Problem Definition,* which examines problem definition in several diverse areas, including industrial plant closings, air transportation policy, sexual harassment, antidrug policy, agriculture, traffic congestion, and AIDS policymaking. Research by Murray Edelman, particularly *The Symbolic Uses of Politics* (1964) and *Constructing the Political Spectacle* (1988), provides a unique social-psychological analysis of the manipulation of language for political purposes. In a similar vein, Deborah Stone's (1988) *Policy Paradox and Political Reason* examines how different types of language are used to support various policy arguments and positions.

A classic study of the media's effect on agenda setting is Doris Graber's (1984) *Mass Media and American Politics* (2nd ed.), which covers all aspects of media involvement in influencing the political stream. Chapters include analysis of the newsmaking process; the media's impact on individual attitudes and behavior; television's impact on elections, the relationship between the media, the White House, Congress, and the courts; the media as policymakers; and media coverage of crises and foreign affairs.

Paul Light's decades-long research into the president's role in setting and controlling the domestic policy agenda has had a major impact on studies of presidential influence, decisionmaking, and leadership. In 1982, Light published *The President's Agenda: Domestic Policy Choice from Kennedy to Carter;* seventeen years later, in the third edition of his book, Light extended his work to include the presidencies of Ronald Reagan, George H. W. Bush, and Bill Clinton. These studies are useful to students interested in understanding the president's role in setting the domestic policy agenda—a particularly important function in education given recent passage of the "No Child Left Behind Act," initiated by President George W. Bush.

References

Bartolome, L. I., & Macedo, D. P. (1997). Dancing with bigotry: The poisoning of racial and ethnic identities. *Harvard Educational Review, 67*(2), 222–246.

Bastian, A. (1995). Is public school "choice" a viable alternative? In D. Levine, R. Lowe, B. Peterson, & R. Tenorio (Eds.), *Rethinking schools: An agenda for change* (pp. 205–208). New York: The Free Press.

Baumgartner, F. R., & Jones, B. D. (1993). *Agendas and instability in American politics.* Chicago: University of Chicago Press.

Bellah, R. N., Madsen, R., Sullivan, W. M., Swidler, A., & Tipton, S. M. (1985). *Habits of the heart.* New York: Harper & Row.

Bellah, R. N., Madsen, R., Sullivan, W. M., Swidler, A., & Tipton, S. M. (1991). *The good society.* New York: Vintage Books.

Birkland, T. A. (2001). *An introduction to the policy process.* Armonk, NY: M. E. Sharpe.

Bosso, C. J. (1994). The contextual bases of problem definition. In D. A. Rochefort & R. W. Cobb (Eds.), *The politics of problem definition* (pp. 182–203). Lawrence: University Press of Kansas.

Brand, G. (1979). *The essential Wittgenstein* (R. E. Innis, Trans.). New York: Basic Books.

Burlingame, M., & Geske, T. G. (1979). State politics and education: An examination of selected multiple-state case studies. *Educational Administration Quarterly, 15*(2), 50–75.

Cherryholmes, C. H. (1988). *Power and criticism: Poststructural investigations in education.* New York: Teachers College Press.

Cooper, B. S., & Randall, E. V. (1999). *Accuracy or advocacy: The politics of research in education.* Thousand Oaks, CA: Corwin Press.

Delpit, L. (1995). *Other people's children: Cultural conflict in the classroom.* New York: The New Press.

Dery, D. (1984). *Problem definition in policy analysis.* Lawrence: University Press of Kansas.

Dye, T. R. (1992). *Understanding public policy* (7th ed.). Englewood Cliffs, NJ: Prentice Hall.

Dye, T. R. (2001). *Understanding public policy* (10th ed.). Englewood Cliffs, NJ: Prentice Hall.

Edelman, M. (1964). *The symbolic uses of politics.* Urbana: University of Illinois Press.

Edelman, M. (1988). *Constructing the political spectacle.* Chicago: University of Chicago Press.

Feir, R. E. (1995). *Political and social roots of education reform: A look at the states in the mid-1980s.* Paper presented at the Annual Meeting of the American Educational Research Association. San Francisco, CA.

Fennimore, B. S. (2000). *Talk matters: Refocusing the language of public schooling.* New York: Teachers College Press.

Fine, M. (1993). Making controversy: Who's "at risk?" In R. Wollons (Ed.), *Children at risk in America* (pp. 91–110). Albany: State University of New York Press.

Fowler, F. C. (2000). *Policy studies for educational leaders.* Upper Saddle River, NJ: Prentice Hall.

Fusarelli, L. D., Cooper, B. S., & Carella, V. (in press). Who will serve? An analysis of superintendent mobility, satisfaction, and perceptions of crisis. *Journal of School Leadership.*

Garman, N. B., & Holland, P. C. (1995). The rhetoric of school reform reports: Sacred, skeptical, and cynical interpretations. In R. Ginsberg & D. N. Plank (Eds.), *Commissions, reports, reforms, and educational policy* (pp. 101–117). Westport, CT: Praeger.

Ginsberg, R., & Plank, D. N. (Eds.). (1995). *Commissions, reports, reforms, and educational policy.* Westport, CT: Praeger.

Glass, T., Bjork, L., & Brunner, C. C. (2000). *2000 study of the American school superintendency.* Arlington, VA: American Association of School Administrators.

Goodwyn, L. (1978). *The populist movement: A short history of the agrarian revolt in America.* Oxford, UK: Oxford University Press.

Graber, D. A. (1984). *Mass media and American politics* (2nd ed.). Washington, DC: Congressional Quarterly Press.

Grossberg, M. (1993). Children's legal rights? A historical look at a legal paradox. In R. Wollons (Ed.), *Children at risk in America* (pp. 111–140). Albany: State University of New York Press.

Hansot, E., & Tyack, D. B. (1982). A usable past: Using history in educational policy. In A. Lieberman & M. W. McLaughlin (Eds.), *Policy making in education* (pp. 5–10). Chicago: University of Chicago Press.

Hogwood, B. W., & Gunn, L. G. (1984). *Policy analysis for the real world.* London: Oxford University Press.

Katznelson, I., & Weir, M. (1985). *Schooling for all: Class, race, and the decline of the democratic ideal.* New York: Basic Books.

Kingdon, J. W. (1995). *Agendas, alternatives, and public policies* (2nd ed.). New York: Longman.

Lather, P. (1991). *Getting smart: Feminist research and pedagogy with/in the postmodern.* New York: Routledge.

Lather, P. (1996). Troubling clarity: The politics of accessible language. *Harvard Educational Review, 66*(3), 525–545.

Light, P. C. (1982). *The president's agenda: Domestic policy choice from Kennedy to Carter.* Baltimore: Johns Hopkins University Press.

Light, P. C. (1999). *The president's agenda: Domestic policy choice from Kennedy to Clinton* (3rd Ed.). Baltimore: Johns Hopkins University Press.

Mawhinney, H. B. (1993). *An interpretive framework for understanding the politics of policy change.* Unpublished doctoral dissertation. University of Ottawa, Ottawa, Ontario, Canada.

Mazzoni, T. L. (1993). The changing politics of state education policymaking: A 20-year Minnesota perspective. *Educational Evaluation and Policy Analysis, 15*(4), 357–379.

Nathan, J. (1996). *Charter schools: Creating hope and opportunity for American education.* San Francisco: Jossey-Bass.

Nelkin, D. (1975). The political impact of technical expertise. *Social Studies of Science 5,* 35–54.

Norton, A. (1993). *Republic of signs: Liberal theory and American popular culture.* Chicago: University of Chicago Press.

Oakes, J. (1986). *Keeping track: How schools structure inequality.* New Haven, CT: Yale University Press.

Orfield, G., Eaton, S. E., & Jones, E. R. (1997). *Dismantling desegregation: The quiet reversal of Brown v. Board of Education.* New York: The New Press.

Paletz, D. L. (1998). The media and public policy. In D. Graber, D. McQuail, & P. Norris (Eds.), *The politics of news, the news of politics* (pp. 218–237). Washington, DC: Congressional Quarterly Press.

Peters, B. G. (1986). *American public policy: Promise and performance* (2nd ed.). London: MacMillan.

Peterson, M. A. (1993). Political influence in the 1990s: From iron triangles to policy networks. *Journal of Health Politics, Policy and Law, 18*(2), 395–438.

Petracca, M. P. (1992). Issue definitions, agenda-building, and policymaking. *Policy Currents, 2,* 1–4.

Prawat, R. S., & Peterson, P. L. (1999). Social constructivist views of learning. In J. Murphy & K. Seashore-Louis (Eds.), *Handbook of research on education administration* (2nd ed., pp. 203–226). San Francisco: Jossey-Bass.

Putnam, H. (1994). *Words and life.* Cambridge, MA: Harvard University Press.

Rein, M., & Schon, D. (1993). Reframing policy discourse. In F. Fischer & J. Forester (Eds.), *The argumentative turn in policy analysis and planning* (pp. 145–166). Durham, NC: Duke University Press.

Reyes, P., Wagstaff, L. H., & Fusarelli, L. D. (1999). Delta forces: The changing fabric of American society and education. In J. Murphy & K. Seashore Louis (Eds.), *Handbook of research on educational administration* (2nd ed., pp. 183–201). San Francisco: Jossey-Bass.

Riker, W. H. (1986). *The art of political manipulation.* New Haven, CT: Yale University Press.

Riker, W. H. (1996). *The strategy of rhetoric.* New Haven, CT: Yale University Press.

Robertson, D. B., & Judd, D. R. (1989). *The development of American public policy: The structure of policy restraint.* Glenview, IL: Scott-Foresman.

Rochefort, D. A., & Cobb, R. W. (1994). Problem definition: An emerging perspective. In D. A. Rochefort & R. W. Cobb (Eds.), *The politics of problem definition* (pp. 1–31). Lawrence: University Press of Kansas.

Rosenau, P. V. (1993). Anticipating a post-modern policy current? *Policy Currents 3,* 1–4.

Schattschneider, E. E. (1960). *The semi-sovereign people: A realist's view of democracy in America.* Hinsdale, IL: Dryden Press.

Skocpol, T. (1992). *Protecting soldiers and mothers: The political origins of social policy in the United States.* Cambridge, MA: Harvard University Press.

Snyderman, M., & Rothman, S. (1988). *The IQ controversy: The media and public policy.* New Brunswick, NJ: Transaction Books.

Spitzer, R. J. (1993). Introduction: Defining the media-policy link. In R. J. Spitzer (Ed.), *Media and public policy* (pp. 1–15). Westport, CT: Praeger.

Stone, D. A. (1988). *Policy paradox and political reason.* Glenview, IL: Scott-Foresman.

Truman, D. B. (1964). *The governmental process: Political interests and public opinion.* New York: Knopf.

Tyack, D. B. (1974). *The one best system: A history of American urban education.* Cambridge, MA: Harvard University Press.

Viteritti, J. P. (1999). *Choosing equality: School choice, the constitution, and civil society.* Washington, DC: The Brookings Institution.

Weaver, S. W., & Geske, T. G. (1996). *Educational policy-making in the state legislature: Legislator as policy expert.* Paper presented at the Annual Meeting of the American Educational Research Association. New York.

Wildavsky, A. (1979). *Speaking truth to power.* Boston: Little, Brown.

Wilson, W. J. (1997). *When work disappears: The world of the new urban poor.* New York: Knopf.

Wittgenstein, L. (1974). *Philosophical grammar* (R. Rhees, Ed., A. Kenny, Trans.). Berkeley: University of California Press.

4

Education Policy Implementation

In an increasingly turbulent policymaking environment—amidst tough international competition, declining resources, an aging, increasingly impoverished and ethnically diverse population—schools are under intense pressure to produce results (Reyes, Wagstaff, & Fusarelli, 1999). "The institutional environment of education is changing in the United States" with "greater emphasis on monitoring organizational performance" and "a growing attempt to develop more coherent education policy" (Rowan & Miskel, 1999, p. 379). School systems throughout the country are experiencing much stronger demands for technical performance and are under increasing pressure to improve student achievement (Rowan & Miskel, 1999). The result is increased state and federal involvement through mandates and the implementation of top-down reforms such as national standards, testing, and accountability, exemplified by the federal No Child Left Behind Act. Cohen and Spillane (1992) observe that "Major efforts are under way to mobilize much more consistent and powerful direction for instruction from state or national agencies . . . to create state and national curricula and tests to pull instruction in the same direction" (pp. 3–4). Under the guise of education reform, President Bush signed legislation mandating state testing of students at *every* grade level between grades 3 and 8.

This chapter examines a critical, if sometimes overlooked, aspect of policymaking—policy implementation. Some policy scholars have observed a tendency in the public's imagination and fueled by the popular press to assume that once bills become law, once policy is enacted, things change (Fischer, 1995). However, as Peters (1986) notes, "Once enacted, laws do not go into effect by themselves" (p. 84). Policies, like laws, are neither self-explanatory nor self-executing. Policies, no matter how well designed, must be implemented successfully to achieve their intended effects. "After all, a good solution is only useful if people adopt it, if its implementation enables them to really make it their own" (Evans, 1996, pp. 15–16). And the nature of public policymaking in a democracy is difficult even under the best circumstances, especially in policy arenas such as education, dominated by intense value conflicts. Amidst all the talk of education reform and change, we need to examine more closely the issues and intricacies of policy implementation in education. After all, educational reform and change are impossible if policies are not implemented properly. As Birkland (2001) notes, "learning from implementation problems can foster learning about better ways to structure policies to ensure that they have the effects that designers of these policies seek" (p. 177).

Compared to other subfields in political science and policy studies, the study of public policy implementation is relatively new. Implementation is what "takes place between the formal enactment of a program by a legislative body (or, in some instances, a chief executive or the courts) and its intended and unintended impacts" (Mazmanian & Sabatier, 1981, p. xi). It consists of the "relevant actions and inactions of public officials who are responsible for helping to achieve objectives" of programs or policies (Baum, 1981, p. 39). Essentially, implementation is what happens when a policy is (or is not) carried out (Sabatier & Mazmanian, 1981). We find it useful to view the process, as Bardach (1977) does in *The Implementation Game,* as "(1) a process of assembling the elements required to produce a particular programmatic outcome, and (2) the playing out of a number of loosely interrelated games whereby these elements are withheld from or delivered to the program assembly process on particular terms" (pp. 57–58).

Research on education policy came to the fore in the 1960s, when President Johnson's "Great Society" initiatives were enacted. As noted by McLaughlin (1987) in her review of policy implementation studies, "As federal, state, and local officials developed responses to these new social policies, implementation issues were revealed in all their complexity, intractability, and inevitability" (p. 171).

Early analyses of policy implementation tended to minimize the degree to which politics shaped the implementation process. As Bardach (1977) observed in his classic study of the politics of implementation,

> The bargaining and maneuvering, the pulling and hauling, of the policy-adoption process carries over into the policy-implementation process. Die-hard opponents of the policy who lost out in the adoption stage seek, and find, means to continue their opposition when, say, administrative regulations and guidelines are being written. Many who supported the original policy proposal did so only because they expected to be able to twist it in the implementation phase to suit purposes never contemplated or desired by others who formed part of the original coalition. (p. 38)

Thus, policy implementation is as enmeshed in politics as other stages of the policy process, including policy formulation, problem definition, and agenda setting. Bardach views implementation as a series of games—of political pressures and counter-pressures. From this perspective, implementation is "the continuation of politics by other means" (p. 85). Therefore, politics and policy conflict do not end after a bill becomes law or after a policy is created. Rather, the conflict enters a new phase—the implementation phase.

Despite a veritable explosion of research on policy implementation processes in the 1960s and 1970s, interest in policy implementation has noticeably decreased in the past two decades (some important exceptions are discussed below). This decline is unfortunate, because as Evans (1996) observed in his study of the failure of planned organizational change, large gaps in our knowledge about policy implementation remain. McLaughlin (1987) concurs, noting that "Perhaps the overarching, obvious conclusion running through empirical research on policy implementation is that it is incredibly hard to make something happen, most especially across layers of government and institutions" (p. 172). Implementing policy is no simple task, involving conflicts and competition as well as issues of coordination and control (Peters, 1986).

In his overview of the evolution of policy implementation in education, Odden (1991) noted that early research "showed that there was a lack of both capacity and will at all levels of government—the U.S. Office of Education, state departments of education, local district offices and local schools—to develop and implement newly created governmental programs" (p. 1). Odden goes on to say, "Research showed not only that most local educators did not want to implement such programs (the will was not there), but also that they did not know how to implement them (the capacity was not there)" (p. 1).

Lack of will is an important variable to consider when evaluating the effectiveness of policy implementation. It should not be assumed that all policies or programs have an equal opportunity to be implemented effectively. Policies originating from different institutional actors, branches of government, or political processes often differ substantially in the degree to which they are accepted by other participants. For example, Baum (1981) observes that policies promulgated by Congress and supported by the President often enjoy broad bipartisan support, whereas those arising from the judiciary, such as the *Brown* decision, frequently lack widespread public support. Lacking an enforcement mechanism and relying on public support (or at least acquiescence), implementation of judicial policy is often far more difficult and problematic than implementation of policies crafted by legislatures or chief executives. Not only do courts lack the resources to entice compliance with judicial directives, they lack (under most circumstances) the ability to impose sanctions intended to make noncompliance less attractive (Baum, 1981). Unfortunately, much of the research on policy implementation fails to consider the origins of policies, an important factor affecting successful implementation.

Stages of Education Policy Implementation Research

Odden (1991) identified three stages of education policy implementation research. The first stage (late 1960s–early 1970s) reflected preliminary lessons from efforts to implement President Johnson's Great Society programs. Many of these studies, such as Pressman and Wildavsky's (1973) study of the efforts of the Economic Development Administration to create minority jobs in Oakland, California, focused on individual case studies (Birkland, 2001). The major finding of this research was the "inevitable conflict between local orientations, values, and priorities and state or federally initiated programs," which were often met with resistance at the local level (Odden, 1991, p. 5). Given such conflict, it was often concluded that "higher level government programs simply did not work, and that local governments would never implement them faithfully" (p. 5). As Bailey and Mosher (1968) noted in their study of the implementation of the Elementary and Secondary Education Act of 1965 (ESEA), given the complexity of the process, it is a wonder that programs are implemented at all. The real "miracle" occurs when the process works successfully.

The second stage of education policy implementation research (late 1970s–mid 1980s) produced numerous studies focused on program implementation after the initial start-up years of the 1960s. Studies found that many of the initial implementation difficulties had been overcome by the late 1970s. Local school districts, for example, "had not only learned how to administer Title I in compliance with rules and regulations but also had even begun to sanction the education priorities embodied in Title I" (Odden, 1991, p. 6). As Odden (1991) explains changes over time, "local opposition was transformed into support for new program initiatives for targeted students, that local capacity was developed to run the programs in compliance with rules and regulations, and that eligible students were provided appropriate services" (p. 6). As Odden points out, "The important overall conclusion from stage two implementation research is that higher level government programs eventually get implemented locally, that the initial conflict gets worked out over time, and that the opportunity for bargaining ultimately produces a workable program for both parties. Another conclusion is that state and federal initiatives do impact local practice: there may be questions about the impact, but impact occurs" (pp. 7–8).

The third stage of education policy implementation identified by Odden (mid 1980s–early 1990s) examined program effectiveness—do the programs and policies solve the problems for which they were created? Much of this research, such as that done on the Head Start program, concluded that "the impact was small and often eroded over time" (p. 8). As a result, researchers studying implementation began to look at how to make the programs work better.

We argue that the third stage of implementation research continues to the present day, albeit in somewhat modified form. Implementation research in education has shifted from macro-level analyses of programs to micro-level studies of the particulars of implementation at the local level. In part, this reflects changes in the dominant paradigm of educational research, from macro-level quantitative studies to micro-level ethnographies and case studies (which now constitute the majority of education policy studies, particularly among doctoral dissertations). Consistent with the burgeoning literature on educational change—of which implementation research is a key, if often overlooked, aspect—much implementation research has focused on how to implement education reform initiatives more effectively and on how to create systemic change at the local level (Duke & Canady, 1991; Evans, 1996; Fullan, 1991).

Policy Implementation in Loosely Coupled Systems

Several scholars have pointed out the difficulty of crafting coherent education policy at the state and national level in a system where power and authority are decentralized to the degree found in the United States. Smith and O'Day (1990) asserted, "a fundamental barrier to developing and sustaining successful schools in the USA is the fragmented, complex, multi-layered educational policy system in which they are embedded" (p. 237). Schools are more loosely coupled than most other organizations (Weick, 1976, 1982, 2001). Goals are multiple, often conflicting, and indeterminate. Technology is unclear. The participation and involvement of members are fluid (the number of participants is exceeded only by the various degrees of involvement of stakeholders). Rules are often violated in schools, and policy implementation is uneven (Meyer & Rowan, 1977). Schools afford little daily teacher-to-teacher interaction between or within grade levels (Meyer & Rowan, 1983). Further, the work of teachers and administrators "is intrinsically uninspected and unevaluated or if it is evaluated it is done so infrequently and in a perfunctory manner" (Weick, 1976, p. 11). One need not spend extended time in schools to realize this depiction accurately captures the reality of education in the United States.

The structural looseness of education in the United States poses significant challenges to efforts to implement successfully school reform (or any policy for that matter). The sheer number of actors responsible for implementing policy creates multiple "veto points" in which policy can be manipulated and altered. The more players involved in the implementation process, the lesser the chance that the policy will be implemented in a manner consistent with the original intent of those who crafted the policy (Allison, 1969; Lipsky, 1980).

In their study of the implementation of educational innovation in an elementary school, Gross, Giacquinta, and Bernstein (1971) identified four significant barriers to effective policy implementation at the local level, including (1) lack of clarity and understanding of the innovation, (2) inadequate skills and knowledge (capability) necessary to implement innovation, (3) inadequate material resources, and (4) incompatible organizational arrangements. Successfully implementing policy is difficult. Frequently, when implementation fails, those charged with implementation blame lack of resources. However, as McLaughlin (1990) observed in her review of lessons learned from the Rand change agent study, "resources alone did not secure successful implementation" (p. 12).

All too frequently, policymakers assume that the goals and objectives of a policy are known to everyone, that everyone involved in implementing policy understands their roles and responsibilities, and that implementation is simply a matter of carrying out administrative mandates. However, as Madsen (1994) found in her study of implementation of education reform at the state level, state education personnel seldom understand and frequently underestimate the important role local administrators play in policy implementation. This problem exists across all levels of government, as evidenced by the disjuncture and misunderstandings between local (site) administrators and district administrators, state and local implementors, and federal, state, and local administrators. As Madsen (1994) points out, distrust and suspicion often develop between administrators at different levels of government responsible for implementing policy, particularly when local administrators become frustrated with the lack of direction provided by state officials.

Why? Because, as McLaughlin (1987) observed, "policymakers can't mandate what matters" (p. 172). Local decisionmakers are often "unclear about what is expected of them" (Gross, Giacquinta, & Bernstein, 1971, p. 202). Furthermore, unless they receive extensive professional development (which seldom, if ever, occurs), local personnel will be unable to implement the policy successfully. Unfortunately, policies are often simply mandated, with little attention to issues arising during the implementation phase—almost as if saying it makes it so.

The Experimental Education Project (EEP) illustrates the difficulty of implementing new policy initiatives. In the early 1970s, the National Institute of Education (NIE), now the U.S. Department of Education, sponsored the Experimental Education Project, designed to assist about four hundred at risk teens. Unfortunately, the program failed due to lack of clearly defined, realistic goals (Larson, 1980). In their study of two middle and two senior high schools implementing authentic learning and assessment over a three-year period, Prestine and McGreal (1997) found that, despite the best intentions, schools often lacked the necessary capacity, resources, and support to effectively implement policy and create change.

Furthermore, when successful policy implementation requires the involvement of actors and agencies at different governmental levels, researchers and evaluators tend to gloss over significant differences in organizational culture among participants. For example, in their traditional oversight role, state education department (SED) staff operate under a compliance paradigm, not a service orientation (Madsen, 1994). The culture of SEDs is heavily influenced by an obsession with regulatory issues and program compliance. Often, this generates resentment and resistance among street-level bureaucrats, on whom implementation success rests.

Street-Level Bureaucrats

Street-level bureaucrats are key players in determining the extent to which policies are implemented in schools. In a loosely coupled educational system, street-level bureaucrats exercise wide discretion and are relatively autonomous from higher organizational authority. For example, teachers are relatively free from supervision from administrators. Often, in a vain attempt to ensure even and effective implementation of policies and programs, administrators and state-level policymakers will try to reduce the discretion of street-level bureaucrats.

However, as Lipsky (1980) pointed out in his classic study, street-level bureaucrats "often regard such efforts as illegitimate and to some degree resist them successfully" (p. 19). How? Street-level bureaucrats can refuse "to perform work of certain kinds, by doing only minimal work, or by doing work rigidly so as to discredit supervisors" (pp. 24–25). In her studies of policy implementation, McLaughlin (1987) noted that policy implementers did "not always do as told . . . nor did they always act to maximize policy objectives" (p. 172). Teachers, for example, can refuse to implement or can substantially modify policies they dislike, such as curricular reforms. Once the classroom door closes, anything (or nothing) is liable to happen. As Prestine and McGreal (1997) observe, "if teachers do not believe in the need for the change, it is not likely to become part of their classroom repertoire" (p. 393).

Policymakers often assume that new policy initiatives are better than those they supplant, that "the 'right' policy was that contained in policy directives" (McLaughlin, 1987, p. 174). Even if teachers support the implementation of the reform, however, few policies incorporate feedback mechanisms that allow local decisionmakers "to identify and cope with barriers and problems arising during the period of attempted implementation" (Gross, Giacquinta, & Bernstein, 1971, p. 201; Jennings, 1996).

In his study of program failures in energy, health, education, the environment, and public housing, Larson (1980) identified four reasons programs fail: (1) vague or unrealistic goals, (2) poor implementation procedures, (3) the complexity of intergovernmental action, and (4) forces in the external economic environment. When policy is ill defined and unclear, implementers "will develop conflicting ideas about its content," resulting in multiple interpretations of legislative intent (p. 2). To complicate the issue further, program goals often change over time, either in response to the changing composition of political players or "in response to pressures for realistic implementation" (Larson, 1980, p. 3). During the implementation phase, goals are frequently further defined (or redefined), often as a result of political contests over implementation (Bardach, 1977).

Peters (1986) and Browne and Wildavsky (1984) identified several factors that impede implementation. These include: (1) lack of clarity and specificity in legislation, (2) lack of understanding of the actual problem the policy is designed to ameliorate (diffuse policy targets), (3) multiple, often conflicting goals, (4) organizational disunity, (5) lack of coordination, (6) improper organizational communication, (7) insufficient time, and (8) inadequate (often poor) planning. As Peters (1986) notes, "There are so many more ways of blocking intended actions than there are of making results materialize . . . it is a minor miracle that implementation is ever accomplished" (p. 84), a finding consistent with Bailey and Mosher's (1968) research on ESEA two decades earlier.

As McLaughlin (1990) concludes, "it is exceedingly difficult for policy to change practice, especially across levels of government" (p. 12), particularly when various actors are not fully committed to implementing the policy. Often, opponents will engage in "tokenism," in which participants "appear to be contributing a program element publicly while privately conceding only a small ('token') contribution" (Bardach, 1977, p. 98). Strategies such as tokenism are common when those responsible for implementing policy disagree with the policy itself (as in the case of court-ordered desegregation discussed below). Also, commitment to implementation often reflects players' judgments about how successful the program or policy is likely to be (Bardach, 1977).

Finally, there has been a tendency among both researchers and practitioners to treat local implementors as a monolithic and unified group, when in reality significant differences exist among implementors at the local level. Madsen (1994) cites disagreements among administrators at the district and building level as a major cause for the failure of policy implementation. In her study of district-level administrators, she commented, "We had many administrators with different interpretations of reform programs. If they did not agree with the program, they often sabotaged it" (p. 162). Thus, conflict is just as likely to erupt between local-level administrators as among policymakers at different governmental levels, adding yet another dimension of complexity to the policy implementation process.

POLICY VIGNETTE • *Implementing ESEA*

In 1965, Congress passed the landmark Elementary and Secondary Education Act (ESEA), the largest compensatory federal aid program for education. To ensure passage of the controversial bill, provisions were made for aid to go to both public and parochial schools, although funds could not be used for the teaching of religion. This compromise appeased Catholic voters and legislators sensitive to these constituents. Although funds were originally targeted to disadvantaged children—to help level the playing field—the bill was amended to provide impact aid to nearly every school district in the country. Thus, the bill wouldn't only provide federal aid for urban school systems, for the poor, or those with "majority-minority" populations. To guarantee bipartisan support, federal monies had to be distributed widely—and, in fact, 95 percent of all school districts in the country received funding through ESEA. With the additional funding, schools could hire teachers' aides, purchase library materials and curricular supplements, and develop compensatory education programs.

ESEA is a classic study of how policies and programs can be significantly modified through implementation. The U.S. Office of Education, responsible for implementing the legislation, did not take a proactive role in equalizing educational opportunity for disadvantaged children. Reflecting pork-barrel politics at its best, policies and regulations were developed to ensure that federal funds were distributed widely to school districts throughout the country, so that even wealthy districts with few poor children were entitled to aid. As a result, a bill originally conceived as a way to level the playing field and compensate for educational inequity was transformed through the implementation process into a mechanism that allowed wealthy districts to purchase expensive frills, while providing only basic, albeit much-needed, materials such as books for poorer districts.

Staffing was a problem in the early days of implementing ESEA. As Larson (1980) notes, "the burden of administering Title I fell on the Division of Program Operations," which was woefully understaffed and ill-equipped to implement such a massive program (p. 55). According to Larson (1980), "the USDOE was understaffed, inexperienced, and uncertain about Congressional intent in the ESEA program" (p. 59). The vague legislative goals of ESEA have been made clearer only by a host of amendments since its original passage (Larson, 1980).

Successful Policy Implementation

Normative Dimension

Lest we be too negative and discourage policymakers from attempting to implement much-needed educational reform, we should clearly identify the essential conditions that contribute to successful policy implementation. First, the program's objectives and policies should be clear and agreed on by all major stakeholder groups (Sabatier & Mazmanian, 1981). Ideally, value consensus should be achieved by all key stakeholders—those who craft the policy and those responsible for implementing it. Achieving consensus on program goals may take several years (Madsen, 1994; Pressman & Wildavsky, 1984). Local decisionmakers need to have the will to implement the policy; they should want to make it happen and should work closely with other participants to resolve value conflicts. Larson (1980) refers to this as normative justification. For a program or policy to be effective, both those charged with implementing the policy and those affected by it must agree with the program's goals.

Structural Dimension

Second, the problem that the program or policy seeks to address must be solvable. Sabatier and Mazmanian (1981) remind us that "Totally apart from the difficulties universally associated with the implementation of governmental programs, some social problems are much easier to deal with than others" (p. 6). As Bardach (1977) observed, "Any social program worth having a governmental policy about at all is likely to be a serious and complicated problem and therefore not amenable to easy solution or even amelioration" (p. 251).

Look, for example, at the four variables or conditions identified by Sabatier and Mazmanian (1981) that affect the "tractability" of problems:

1. A valid theory connects behavioral change to problem amelioration;[1] the requisite technology exists; and, measurement of change in the seriousness of the problem is inexpensive;
2. Minimal variation in the behavioral practices that cause the problem;
3. The target group constitutes an easily identifiable minority of the population within a political jurisdiction; and
4. The amount of behavioral change [required] is modest. (p. 9)

Few, if any, of these conditions are easily met in policies designed to bring about improvements in education. For example, implementing change in teaching and learning "may be a fundamentally different enterprise from implementing changes in school organization and governance" (Prestine & McGreal, 1997, p. 391). To implement change effectively, we need to examine and alter "old hierarchical structures, entrenched organizational configurations, and traditional power relationships" (Prestine & McGreal, 1997, p. 396). The personal and organizational changes required to implement educational policy successfully requires an organizational culture that fosters learning and communication. Reimers and McGinn (1997) note that "an important reason why policies do not reach schools is that there are no conditions to facilitate such dialogue and organizational learning" (p. 39).

Because of its loosely coupled nature, with multiple, competing, often conflicting interests and constituencies across many levels, unclear technology, fluid participation of members, and the significant influence of the external environ-

---

[1]Bardach (1977) also stresses the importance of policy being based on valid theory. He notes, "If this theory is fundamentally incorrect, the policy will probably fail no matter how well it is implemented" (pp. 251–252).

ment, many problems schools seek to address are far less tractable than in other areas of public policy. To overcome the barriers to implementation in loosely coupled systems, "the number of veto points in the implementation process" must be minimized, with sufficient sanctions and inducements provided to overcome resistance (Sabatier & Mazmanian, 1981, p. 14). Decision rules of implementing agencies must be "biased toward the achievement of statutory objectives" (Sabatier & Mazmanian, 1981, p. 14).

Constituentive Dimension

McLaughlin (1987) observed, "effective implementation requires a strategic balance of pressure and support" (p. 171). Pressure helps focus attention on new policy initiatives, confers legitimacy on reform efforts, and offers protection (through rules and mandates). For example, McLaughlin notes that funds targeted to the federal Chapter I program might likely have been diverted by local policymakers "in the absence of federal requirements" (p. 174). Adequate support is critical to successful implementation. After all, notes McLaughlin, "Organizations don't innovate or implement change, individuals do" (p. 174). And changing people's behavior is no simple task, particularly if they do not agree with the direction of the change (Sarason, 1982). Resistance can come from a variety of sources, including the persistence of old ways of thinking, habit, laziness, fear, and a vested interest in maintaining the status quo (Browne & Wildavsky, 1984; Evans, 1996; Weimer & Vining, 1992). To overcome these challenges, open and active communication among all participants is essential (Madsen, 1994).

In *The Human Side of School Change*, Evans's excellent analysis of our psychological resistance to change, he asserts that policymakers too often fail to understand that implementing policies, especially educational reforms, requires changing people's behavior. For example, school reform requires changing the operations of organizations as well as fundamentally modifying people's behavior—and this change often threatens people in very personal ways (Huberman & Miles, 1984). It questions their professionalism, and, by extension, their very self-concept and professional identity. It is no accident then that various school reform proposals are more readily accepted by new teachers than veterans. Reformers often naively assume reforms will be faithfully implemented when the need for reform becomes obvious— yet studies of resistance to planned change efforts demonstrate the falseness of such assumptions. In even the worst performing schools, change efforts are often met with stiff resistance.

We must remember that despite our best intentions, "there are few 'slam bang' policy effects" because policy effects are indirect and mediated by organizational context (McLaughlin, 1987, p. 175). During the implementation phase, "policy is transformed and adapted to conditions of the implementing unit" (McLaughlin, 1987, p. 175). Browne and Wildavsky (1984) view adaptation as an evolutionary characteristic of the implementation process. The authors note that policy "evolves in response to its environment as each alters the other" (p. 208). Effective strategies promote mutual adaptation (of project and institutional setting) (McLaughlin, 1990). As policy is translated into practice, effective implementation "may have different meanings in different settings" (McLaughlin, 1987, p. 175).

Technical Dimension

Local decisionmakers must have the capacity to implement the proposed reform. This includes the development of adequate professional skills and knowledge, coupled with funding, materials, resources, and compatible organizational arrangements necessary to implement the reform. We should never assume that policies and programs are created out of normative consensus and with adequate provisions for effective implementation. Often, policies lack one of these two key elements, and some policies lack both. But that seldom affects the momentum to create new policies and programs, however ill-conceived those policies may be.

Spillover Effects

In addition, it is important to remember that successfully implemented policies often produce spillover (secondary or unintended) effects. Policies that successfully address some problems may produce others (Calista, 1994). A spillover effect of the "war on drugs" serves as an illustrative case. Successfully prosecuting drug dealers may, in the short term, reduce the supply of heroin—"pushing up its price and causing addicts to commit more theft to support their addiction" (Evans, 1996, p. 10). Drug supply (and use) may decline, but violent crime may increase, as addicts struggle to feed their habits. In education, policies promoting higher standards may have the unintended result of decreasing teachers' and students' sense of efficacy—resulting in decreased engagement (and increased anomie) in schools.

Furthermore, policies with no explicit connection to education often produce significant spillover effects. For example, the federal interstate highway program of the 1950s fueled the suburbanization of the United States. As the middle class moved to the suburbs, employers and retailers followed. This mass exodus of people, jobs, and wealth threatened to destroy public education in urban areas, as urban school systems suffered under the twin burdens of a steadily declining tax base and students with ever-greater educational needs. In this case, federal transportation policy may have inadvertently contributed to the creation of good suburban schools, while facilitating the demise of urban schools. This example serves to illustrate the interconnectedness of policy, its successful implementation, and unintended outcomes.

Conclusion

As this chapter has demonstrated, implementing policy in the educational arena is a difficult yet vitally important task. Successful implementation depends on two critical factors; notes McLaughlin (1990), "What matters most to policy outcomes are local capacity and will" (p. 12). All too often, federal, state, and even local policymakers assume an abundance of both exist. Despite the difficulty of implementing education policy in a fragmented, loosely coupled system, successful implementation is possible under the conditions outlined above. The key issue is attaching the correct policies to the correct problems. Often, the failure of many policies lies not in unsuccessful implementation, but in an incorrect match between the problem and the proposed solution.

Chapter Discussion Questions

1. What impact has ESEA had on local efforts to improve the educational opportunities of at risk children in your school district?

2. Assess the implementation of ESEA in your school district. What criteria would you use and why? What is your assessment of the success of the implementation process?

Seminal Works

Although several excellent books on policy implementation have been written, four stand out as classics in the field. Three of these works—Bardach's *The Implementation Game* (1977), Lipsky's *Street-Level Bureaucracy* (1980), and Pressman and Wildavsky's *Implementation* (1973)—are notable for their comprehensive coverage of the complexities of implementation processes, vividly illustrating how and why policies succeed or fail during the implementation stage. The fourth, Odden's *Education Policy Implementation* (1991), presents a comprehensive look at implementation issues within education.

Eugene Bardach's *The Implementation Game* examines what happens after a bill becomes a law, using mental health reform in California as an example. Bardach conceptualizes implementation processes as a series of political games over resources, goals, and administration. By carefully exploring the political, organizational, and socioeconomic issues that arise during implementation, Bardach demonstrates the multiple ways in which programs and policies can be successfully blocked after a bill has become law.

Michael Lipsky's *Street-Level Bureaucracy* looks at the implementation process from the bottom up—from the perspective of local bureaucrats charged with putting policies and programs into practice. Examining issues of resources, goals, performance, relations with clients, the conditions of work, and the patterns of practice, Lipsky asserts that street-level policymakers have enormous power to undermine (or facilitate) the success of policy implementation. Since its publication in 1980, this work has served as the cornerstone of bottom-up analyses and theories of implementation processes.

Pressman and Wildavsky's book has perhaps one of the most interesting subtitles of any scholarly text: *How Great Expectations in Washington Are Dashed in Oakland; Or, Why It's Amazing That Federal Programs Work at All.* The authors analyze the Economic Development Administration's efforts in Oakland to create jobs for minorities through economic development. Beginning with the initial policy formulation stage, the authors explore different aspects of implementation, including difficulties with implementation, the complexity of joint action, implementation as evolution and mutual adaptation, and the possibility of learning from experience.

Finally, Allan Odden's *Education Policy Implementation* is one of the few books devoted entirely to implementation issues in education. This edited work contains both original research studies as well as several classic analyses of education policy implementation, such as Jerome Murphy's analysis of Title I of ESEA and Milbrey McLaughlin's evaluation of the Rand Change Agent Study.

References

Allison, G. T. (1969). Conceptual models and the Cuban missile crisis. *American Political Science Review, 63*(3), 689–718.

Bailey, S. K., & Mosher, E. K. (1968). *ESEA: The Office of Education administers a law.* Syracuse, NY: Syracuse University Press.

Bardach, E. (1977). *The implementation game: What happens after a bill becomes a law.* Cambridge, MA: MIT Press.

Baum, L. (1981). Comparing the implementation of legislative and judicial policies. In D. A. Mazmanian & P. A. Sabatier (Eds.), *Effective policy implementation* (pp. 39–62). Lexington, MA: Lexington Books.

Birkland, T. A. (2001). *An introduction to the policy process.* Armonk, NY: M. E. Sharpe.

Browne, A., & Wildavsky, A. (1984). Implementation as mutual adaptation. In J. L. Pressman & A. Wildavsky (Eds.), *Implementation* (pp. 206–231). Berkeley: University of California Press.

Calista, D. J. (1994). Policy implementation. In S. S. Nagel (Ed.), *Encyclopedia of policy studies* (2nd ed., pp. 117–155). New York: Marcel Dekker.

Cohen, D. K., & Spillane, J. P. (1992). Policy and practice: The relation between governance and instruction. *Review of Research in Education, 18,* 3–49.

Duke, D. L., & Canady, R. L. (1991). *School policy.* New York: McGraw-Hill.

Evans, R. (1996). *The human side of school change.* San Francisco: Jossey-Bass.

Fischer, F. (1995). *Evaluating public policy.* Chicago: Nelson-Hall.

Fullan, M. G. (with Stiegelbauer, S.). (1991). *The new meaning of educational change* (2nd ed.). New York: Teachers College Press.

Gross, N., Giacquinta, J. B., & Bernstein, M. (1971). *Implementing organizational innovations.* New York: Basic Books.

Huberman, A. M., & Miles, M. B. (1984). *Innovation up close.* New York: Plenum Press.

Jennings, N. E. (1996). *Interpreting policy in real classrooms: Case studies of state reform and teacher practice.* New York: Teachers College Press.

Larson, J. S. (1980). *Why government programs fail.* New York: Praeger.

Lipsky, M. (1980). *Street-level bureaucracy.* New York: Russell Sage.

Madsen, J. (1994). *Education reform at the state level: The politics and problems of implementation.* Washington, DC: Falmer Press.

Mazmanian, D. A., & Sabatier, P. A. (1981). Introduction. In D. A. Mazmanian & P. A. Sabatier (Eds.), *Effective policy implementation* (pp. xi–xv). Lexington, MA: Lexington Books.

McLaughlin, M. W. (1987). Learning from experience: Lessons from policy implementation. *Educational Evaluation and Policy Analysis, 9*(2), 171–178.

McLaughlin, M. W. (1990). The Rand change agent study revisited: Macro perspectives and micro realities. *Educational Researcher, 19*(9), 11–16.

Meyer, J. W., & Rowan, B. (1977). Institutionalized organizations: Formal structure as myth and ceremony. *American Journal of Sociology, 83*(2), 340–363.

Meyer, J. W., & Rowan, B. (1983). The structure of educational organizations. In J. W. Meyer & W. R. Scott (Eds.), *Organizational environments: Ritual and rationality* (pp. 71–97). Beverly Hills, CA: Sage.

Odden, A. R. (1991). The evolution of education policy implementation. In A. R. Odden (Ed.), *Education policy implementation* (pp. 1–12). Albany: State University of New York Press.

Peters, B. G. (1986). *American public policy: Promise and performance* (2nd ed.). London: MacMillan Education.

Pressman, J. L., & Wildavsky, A. (1984). *Implementation* (3rd ed.). Berkeley: University of California Press.

Prestine, N. A., & McGreal, T. L. (1997). Fragile changes, sturdy lives: Implementing authentic assessment in schools. *Educational Administration Quarterly, 33*(3), 371–400.

Reimers, R., & McGinn, N. (1997). *Informed dialogue: Using research to shape educational policy around the world.* Westport, CT: Praeger.

Reyes, P., Wagstaff, L. H., & Fusarelli, L. D. (1999). Delta forces: The changing fabric of American society and education. In J. Murphy & K. Seashore Louis (Eds.), *Handbook of research on educational administration* (2nd ed., pp. 183–201). San Francisco: Jossey-Bass.

Rowan, B., & Miskel, C. G. (1999). Institutional theory and the study of educational organizations. In J. Murphy & K. Seashore Louis (Eds.), *Handbook of research on educational administration* (2nd ed., pp. 359–383). San Francisco: Jossey-Bass.

Sabatier, P. A., & Mazmanian, D. A. (1981). The implementation of public policy: A framework of analysis. In D. A. Mazmanian & P. A. Sabatier (Eds.), *Effective policy implementation* (pp. 3–35). Lexington, MA: Lexington Books.

Sarason, S. B. (1982). *The culture of schooling and the problem of change* (2nd ed.). Boston: Allyn & Bacon.

Smith, M. S., & O'Day, J. (1990). Systemic school reform. In S. H. Fuhrman & B. Malen (Eds.), *The politics of curriculum and testing* (pp. 233–267). London: Falmer Press.

Weick, K. E. (1976). Educational organizations as loosely coupled systems. *Administrative Science Quarterly, 21,* 1–19.

Weick, K. E. (1982). Administering education in loosely coupled schools. *Phi Delta Kappan, 63*(10), 673–676.

Weick, K. E. (2001). *Making sense of the organization.* Malden, MA: Blackwell.

Weimer, D. L., & Vining, A. R. (1992). *Policy analysis: Concepts and practice* (2nd ed.). Upper Saddler River, NJ: Prentice Hall.

5

Using Evaluation to Improve Education

A critical, summative step in the processes of policymaking and policy improvement is evaluating the implementation and effects of laws, regulations, and programs in education. As one observer commented, "The final stage of the policy process is the assessment of what has occurred as a result of the selection and implementation of a policy, and, if it is found necessary, a change in the current policies of government" (Peters, 1986, p. 133). Another explained, "to be sure, policy researchers should give much attention to policy outcomes, as their role is to uncover what seems to work. And policies themselves should be evaluated in part on their outcomes" (Kerr, 1976, p. 212).

The systems model of education policymaking requires evaluations and feedback, as shown in Figure 2.1 (see p. 21). As Wirt and Kirst described it, policies in education are the result of new demands and inputs, which affect the way schools are organized, financed, managed, and controlled. The outputs of this systems approach are hours of education, units taught, test results of students, and presumably well-educated students, ready to take their place in society. The final step in the policy process is evaluation—feedback loops to provide information for recasting policies and more effectively implementing them.

Yet the process of policy evaluation in education is fraught with problems, some of which are normative (ideological), structural (organizational), constituentive (political), and technical (practical). For example, in an editorial, Finn (2000) attacked the federal government's attempts to gather data and evaluate federal education policies, stating that

> The researcher function has been beset with woes of every sort: shoddy work on trivial topics; research bent to conform with political imperatives and policy preferences; a skimpy budget that gets gobbled up by greedy, ineradicable "labs and

centers" and other porky projects; avoidance of promising but touchy topics; studies that seldom follow the norms of "real" science (or even social science); research that is mostly inconclusive and, when conclusive is weakly disseminated and widely ignored. (p. 48)

Trends toward Better Policy Evaluation

Despite the shortcomings of past policy evaluations in education, the future holds real promise for obtaining high-quality, timely, and well-disseminated evaluation results, leading to improved policymaking. A number of trends make the improvement of school evaluation possible.

Demands and Learning.   The pressure for better education information has reached national proportions, as policymakers seek to discover how well a particular program is working, and participants in programs wish to learn more about their own progress. Howlett and Ramesh (1995) explain that "perhaps the greatest benefit of policy evaluation is not the direct results it generates but the process of *policy learning* that accompanies it. Policy actors learn constantly from the formal and informal evaluation of policies they are engaged in, and are led to modify their positions" (emphasis added, p. 170; see also Pressman & Wildavsky, 1973).

As the standards movement takes the country by storm, the demand for better data on student performance, school quality, teacher effectiveness, and program effects, all combine to increase the demand for better tests, "value added models" of student performance and system performance data (see Sanders, 1998; Sanders, Saxton, & Horn, 1997).

Electronic Systems.   The increasing availability of electronic information provides useful data on school inputs for educators and outputs for parents and the community. Putting federal, state, and local information online is occurring at an increasing rate. School districts can now perform their own evaluations, sorting test and demographic data by student, school, and program, drilling down to information by type of student, by subject, and by school. Evaluation will someday become automatic and accepted because the data will be instantly and widely available on the Internet, a district's infra-net, and the web.

Cross-Level Alignment.   Federal and state authorities are increasingly setting the standards and requiring that test results meet certain levels or benchmarks, thus increasing the interrelationships between the state and federal levels, and school districts, as never before. Furthermore, servicing this new evaluation effort are a growing number of private, for- and not-for-profit companies that do everything from write the test questions for student assessments to analyzing standards and putting them online. These fertile new relationships (inter-governmental and inter-sectoral) are sure not only to shape the evaluation movement, increasing the demand for better evaluation, but also to provide the tools and support to accomplish these goals.

Higher Standards, Better Evaluations.   The strongest movement today in U.S. education is the effort to raise standards (see Doyle & Pimentel, 1999). When higher standards are set, they are often met, to use the Doyle phrase. And the process of "meeting the standard" requires more data, better analysis, greater access to information, and improved policy evaluation.

The Policy Evaluation Process

The process of evaluation comes toward the end of the education policymaking process, and is always complex but should be logical enough. Three questions frame the evaluation process in education:

1. To what extent was the policy implemented as conceived?
2. How effective was the policy in reaching its goals?
3. What can be done to improve education through better policies and programs?

These questions seem obvious enough. Educators should be evaluating their work regularly, although not always in a systematic, comparative way.

Defining Policy Evaluation

Policy evaluation contains some key important elements.

When?   The timing of policy evaluation may be critical. Some worry that evaluation comes too late and is an add-on when a policy is to be renewed or refunded; others contend that the true effects of a new policy may take years to achieve and to evaluate, and a few months or a year hardly gives the new program a chance to take root. So, one issue in the definition of policy evaluation in education is when to begin the evaluation, how long to continue it, and how to account for the maturation of new policies over time.

How?   Researchers sometimes argue about how best to evaluate a new policy and its effects. Would it be most effective to perform an evaluation of particular sites or programs, using the case method? Or are cross-sectional studies better, where a sampling of programs and users is attempted? Or should a more naturalistic approach be used, one that involves observations and participation of key educators, their perceptions and beliefs that may be important to the implementation and survival of school change? Others argue for a mixed design, one that uses the latest survey and statistical methods and a number of more qualitative, contextual methods to understand the meaning of a policy to those who are using it (Shapiro, 1988).

By Whom?   Another concern in trying to evaluate an education policy is who should be responsible for carrying out the studies, and who should control the process. Some argue that participating school systems and states should organize their own research efforts, to maximize participation and to give a sense of ownership for the process and the results. Others believe that real research on policy implementation and effects can only be done by an outside group or agency that has less at stake and can suggest results that may conflict with the authority figures who control the system. Thus, in defining policy evaluation, it is important to determine the agencies involved and the costs and benefits to key stakeholders.

To What End?   Another issue is the purpose of the evaluation, both stated and unstated. If a program is not working, should the results of the evaluation be to end the program, change it, or introduce a new policy altogether? Often, education policies at the state and federal levels are identified with a particular leader (e.g., the "education president or governor"), and thus evaluations may be watched closely by the leaders who helped pass the law or regulation, as well as those from the opposing party who may wish to capitalize on the failure of education programs. Policy evaluation, then, is more than a mere exercise in thinking and research; it has implications for action that are integral to the process.

To Whose Benefit?   Finally, policy evaluation may benefit some groups and disadvantage others. Careers, jobs, and reputations are often associated with the implementation of policies, both in the classroom and in the system generally. Evaluations may affect those positions: who gets promoted or demoted; who is hired or fired; and who claims credit or takes the blame if a policy fails. The cost/benefit analysis may thus be associated with political parties (Democrats and Republicans) and with key leaders (governors, presidents, superintendents, teachers' associations, and state commissioners of education).

History of Policy Analysis and Evaluation

From Charles P. Merriam's ideas on "intelligent planning," through Harold Lasswell's notions of the "policy sciences," to the work of Lindblom (1980), these studies frame a field that has developed a rich history and a growing sophistication. Garson (1986) focuses on the key role of Lasswell as someone who conceptualized the field, who understood the need for scientific rigor tempered by humanitarian and democratic concerns. Lasswell (1963) explained that policy scientists need to

> make a rapid survey of the predispositions found everywhere in the world, "predict" (retrospectively) the conditioning factors accounting for the direction and intensity of these predispositions; predict the way in which these predispositions would express themselves under the impact of any conceivable constellation of future conditioning factors; predict the probable occurrence of future conditioning constellations; outline the strategies by which the probability of future factor constellations can be modified (at stated costs in terms of values); and connect past and prospective sequences of events with specifications of goal (in our case, the goal of realizing the dignity of man—and other advanced forms of life—on the widest scale). (Lasswell, cited in Garson, 1986, p. 7)

Fry and Tompkins (1978) asserted that the research and evaluation of policies required a multi-dimensional view much like the one used in this book: Policy analysts need (1) Normative criteria, such as effectiveness, efficiency, adequacy, equity, and democracy to frame the research and to help determine the effects of a program; (2) Context, or social, economic, and policy environments in which education policies are made and then evaluated; (3) Sequence, which assumes a set of stages such as formulation, implementation, adaptation, growth, change, or ending of a particular policy or program; (4) Function, whereby policy analysts determine the role and activities of policies, from basic functions such as POSDCORB, or Planning, Organizing, Staffing, Directing, Coordinating, Reporting, and Budgeting, to more recent functions such as adjudication and mutual accommodation; and (5) Procedures including terms such as rational comprehensive procedures versus more politically mediated or "satisficing" processes (Simon, 1958). Whatever the dimension—Normative, Constituentive, Structural, or Technical—the process of evaluating school policies is critical and informative concerning the values, needs, and organization of our education systems.

Perhaps the most ambitious attempt to measure students' learning—and thus, assessments of the effectiveness of curricular and teaching policies—is the National Assessment of Educational Progress (NAEP). The National Center for Education Statistics (NCES), which administers NAEP, has encountered a "backlash from educators who say that students spend too much time taking tests" (Hoff, 2000, p. 1). Local schools in seven states did not exhibit sufficient interest to give the 45-minute math and science examinations, and withdrew. Six other states are close to the minimum number of interested schools to threaten the sample size necessary to make the test valid. Florida, for example, had to bow out because the NAEP tests coincided with the state's own tests, the Florida Comprehensive Assessment Test.

Yet Mary Lyn Bourgue (1999), of the National Assessment Governing Board, explained in the *Handbook of Educational Policy* that "NAEP has achieved a stature as a national program unlike many other federally-funded initiatives of recent memory" (p. 214). She believes that NAEP should undergo changes to make the test more compatible and useful to states that are also testing children extensively. She wrote, "It is the hope of the National Assessment Governing Board (NAGB) that the redesign of NAEP will lead to greater use of the wealth of data afforded by this large-scale assessment and that, through the mining of the data, states and other agencies will have access to the best possible technical information to help inform the policy decisions of the future" (Bourque, 1999, p. 241).

In part, states are complaining that the results of NAEP fail to help districts and schools, administrators and teachers, to evaluate their own programs, students, and policies. The state education commissioner in Colorado, William J. Maloney, for example, explained that "to local people, there is not a connection because nothing comes back to the district. It's just not on their radar screen" (Hoff, 2000, p. 11). Colorado's largest district, Jefferson County (suburban Denver), withdrew from NAEP because educators felt that students were spending too much time taking standardized tests, and because NAEP failed to deliver scores by student, schools, or district (a national random sample is used).

This case shows the difficulty of policy evaluation—even minimally, by testing students. Assessment is costly, time-consuming, and annoying. Even when agencies agree to do evaluations of policies and programs, obtaining a valid, robust sample becomes a problem. Most problematic is conceptualizing an evaluation when a policy is being conceived and then following through. Canons of research can be strict: methods include random assignment, control of external (confounding) variables, constancy of participants, pre- and post-data collection, and baseline and standardized outcomes. Fulfilling these requirements may be impossible in a school and classroom, where the needs of children are more important than the need to control the learning conditions of students. Moreover, assessing students is a necessary but not sufficient step in full policy evaluation. Other key reviews are also necessary if policy evaluators are to relate programs to student progress.

Take attempts to evaluate *choice* policies, such as voucher or charter school programs. Often, critics of choice in education complain that the more attentive, active families register their "better students" for a new school reform, while children from the poorest, neediest families cannot get organized to apply, thus skewing the results. In the language of policy evaluation, researchers are unable to control for "family effects," meaning that improved results in a choice school may be due more to the ambition, resources, knowledge, and interest of middle-class families than to the particular effects of school programs.

Peterson, Greene, and Howell (1998) confronted this issue when asked to evaluate Milwaukee's school voucher program (see also Howell & Peterson, 2002). How can policy evaluations control for variation and still be acceptable to school districts? Luckily for these researchers, students were chosen by random assignment to receive vouchers from a pool of applicants, all of whom showed the interest and energy to apply (and therefore get into the pool in the first place). Thus, when these researchers compared a "matched set" of students, those receiving and not receiving a voucher, from the same pool, they could begin to isolate the effects of voucher choices on students' performance without confronting the effects of family initiative (because all families had acted and registered their children for the voucher initiative).

Witte (1998) concluded in his study of the Milwaukee voucher experiment that "as with the effects on students and families, school effects of the Milwaukee voucher experiments are mixed" (p. 248). Meanwhile, Peterson "had unsuccessfully sought to acquire access to the data," leading to what has been described as a "feud between Witte and Peterson" (Vitteriti, 1999, p. 106).

When the smoke settled, Peterson found that Witte had compared the subset of students in the voucher schools with the *total* student body of the Milwaukee Public Schools (Davis, 1996). Because the general Milwaukee school student population was more middle class and white than the voucher applicants, the evaluation of the program suffered from the proverbial "apples-oranges" comparison. Greene, Peterson, and Du (1997), comparing the voucher cohort from those who applied but were rejected (a similar group in race and social class makeup), found that the voucher students scored five points higher in reading and twelve points higher in math than their counterparts (i.e., unsuccessful voucher applicants).

Vouchers supporters, and their opponents, have politicized the policy evaluation process, and any results are sure to be contested. Evaluation outcomes, then, will be treated as ideological because proponents firmly believe that choice improves education, and opponents see vouchers as frontal attacks on public education. Bias on both "sides" of provocative issues hampers the scientific, dispassionate reviews of such policies.

Four Dimensions of Policy Evaluation

Normative Dimension.   As we shall show, policy evaluation is highly value-laden, ideological, and contextual. When results support the belief system of researchers and practitioners, these outcomes are hailed as evidence that a particular policy is effective and should be continued and even expanded. When results run counter to the predisposition of leaders, educators, and politicians, then the data may be contested, the methods attacked, and the outcomes rejected.

Structural Dimension.   Policy evaluation in education reflects, to a large extent, the organization of education at the federal, state, and local levels. Much of the early policy research ignored the levels and structures of schooling in the United

States. We look at the *structure* of education research, as it mirrors the federal, state, and local relationships and organization of education itself. In the past, much of the debate in education policy circles revolved around the influence of federal and state programs on local schools and practices. If local educators resent the "interference" of the federal government, for example, these feelings may prejudice the evaluation of federal programs and their effectiveness (Kirst & Jung, 1991).

Constituentive Dimension.   Education policy evaluations are rarely done in a vacuum. Strong interest groups often converge around particular programs, and jobs and resources are at stake when policies are being evaluated. Without a clear understanding of whose careers are on the line, and which politicians are in support (or against) a policy, it is difficult to understand the research being conducted, the questions being asked, the methods employed, and the response to the outcomes of these studies and evaluations.

This chapter examines the evaluation process through the lens of *constituents* of education: teachers, parents, administrators, and other groups (e.g., business leaders, government officials), as well as the researchers themselves. Members of the research community have their own prejudices and beliefs that affect the methods they use and the conclusions they reach. This chapter, then, examines the meaning of policy evaluation, the needs and barriers for this research, and suggestions for improving education policies through better evaluation.

Technical Dimension.   Finally, this chapter examines the *practical*, or *technical* dimension of policy evaluation: Who should conduct such research? Under what conditions and to what ends? For example, how does the U.S. government evaluate the results of its many programs, such as bilingual education, special education, and compensatory education? Some of the limitations of education evaluations are in fact the practical problems of gathering and analyzing data across nearly 14,000 districts and 88,000 schools, in 50 states, for 55 million children.

POLICY VIGNETTE • *Evaluating Head Start*

The evaluation of Head Start began years after it was proposed, legislated, and implemented in the 1960s under President Lyndon B. Johnson. How extensively were preschool children offered the opportunity to attend Head Start programs (designed for 4- and 5-year-olds)? Did Head Start increase the skills and "readiness" of preschool children when they entered the primary grades? How far-reaching (long-lasting) were the effects of Head Start on students over their school careers?

Head Start policies were evaluated over a twenty-year period, and students were found to improve in their early years of school (1st and 2nd grades), but by the 3rd grade were no better off than non-Head Start participants. After several years, no significant differences can be seen between those who were in the program and those who were not. It seems that without reinforcement in later years, the effects of Head Start diminish over time (Aaron, 1978; Peters, 1986).

POLICY VIGNETTE • *Evaluating Title I/Chapter I*

The largest federal program for K–12 schoolchildren is the Elementary and Secondary Education Act, passed in 1965. ESEA, as it was originally called, brought extra help (compensatory education) to poor, disadvantaged students by supplementing the programs in public schools. Early evaluations of this major federal education initiative turned up an interesting development: districts were reducing local spending and off-setting these savings with the new federal dollars. By 1968, this evaluation led to a change in implementation of Title I: the principle of *supplementing*, rather than *supplanting*, was enforced, requiring that the receiving states and districts show that the new (extra) funds were providing education services to students beyond what they would have received without the money, tracking funds to Title I teachers who worked exclusively with Title I-eligible pupils.

Evaluating the academic effects of ESEA has been difficult because of the program's very general education goals: to improve the learning of at risk children; however, the exact method of instructional improvement was left for local schools and teachers to determine. Furthermore, ESEA fed large sums of federal funds through state education departments, having a profound effect on the staffing and organization of these institutions.

ESEA led to the hiring of Chapter I teachers and the establishment of resource rooms in both public and parochial schools, bridging the gap between church and state (Title I teachers were public school employees working on the premises of religious schools). Evaluating ESEA has never been attempted on a national level, other than research on the intermediate effects on state education departments and on local school districts (Bailey & Mosher, 1968; Murphy, 1991).

ESEA was the first massive intervention by the federal government into the schools and classrooms in the United States: billions of dollars have been allocated to states and then to districts to hire additional teachers and aides to help disadvantaged students in basic subjects such as reading, writing, and mathematics. Title I is so large that most evaluations of the policy and program have focused on how it was organized and implemented and less on how effective it was for children's learning.

Yet, for all the logic, common sense, and necessity of knowing whether a policy is working for the benefit of those targeted for help, it is difficult to determine what is working and what is not. Wholey and associates (1970) explained that

> Few significant studies have been undertaken. Most of those carried out have been poorly conceived. Many small studies around the country have been carried out with such lack of uniformity of design and objective that the results are rarely comparable or responsive to the questions facing policy-makers. . . . Even within agencies, orderly and integrated evaluation operations have not been established. The impact of activities that costs the public millions, sometimes billions, of dollars has not been measured. One cannot point with confidence to the difference, if any, that most social programs cause in the lives of Americans. (p. 15)

To some degree, policy evaluation is weak, late, and sometimes nonexistent because the public assumes that "once we pass a law, create a bureaucracy, and spend money, the purpose of the law, the bureaucracy, and the expenditures should be achieved" (Dye, 1992, p. 253). Although it makes perfect sense to analyze the outcomes—or at least the potential results—of policy options before deciding which program, method, or approach to use, discontinue, or improve, it is also difficult to apply sound research principles in the highly fluid, political, and complex environment of schools and school systems.

The Normative Dimension

Evaluation of policies has a strong normative component as researchers seek to determine which values to apply and how those values might affect the tools to use, norms of acceptability, and the interpretation of the results. As Kogan (1985) explained,

> Values are moral propensities or feelings about what ought to be. They underpin ideologies, which are valued preferences attached to some kind of program for, or aspirations, to action. Changes in values must be set in their context of movements in social arrangements and assumptions and in the state of the economy. . . . Values are implicit in the power and institutional relations that are both the context and the results of different value positions. (p. 11)

Often, the underlying philosophies and values are expressed in categories and even in dichotomies, although we shall argue in this chapter that these different approaches can be used in tandem to assess the overall effects of policies in education. For example, should policy evaluation be qualitative, using interviews, observations, and document review? Or should it seek to measure the effects of a policy in statistical terms, relating, for example, the level of implementation (as measured by the extent of students involved) to indicators of students' academic improvement? As we shall see, policy evaluation—along with other kinds of social research—proves to be a complex mix of values, approaches, methods, measurements, and disciplines.

Right from the beginning of efforts to evaluate policies in education, researchers disagreed about whether research in education is worthwhile, and whether the results are at all useful for improving students' education. Some have argued that although education research is well intentioned, it simply lacks the sophistication and acceptable methods to separate out the causes and effects of educational policies and programs.

Glass (1979) questioned whether the variance in education effectiveness can be determined "in terms of the influence that we can currently measure and control?" (p. 14). Although evaluative research is widely used in the natural and medical sciences, in the social science areas like education, research involves but a "minute fraction" (Biddle & Anderson, 1991, p. 4) of the time, energy, and resources of our society.

Others have rejected outright the usefulness of evaluative research. In Britain, Sir William Pile explained that "the great thing about research is that part of it is rubbish and another part . . . leads nowhere and is really indifferent. It is, I am afraid, exceptional to find a piece of research that really hits the nail on the head and tells you pretty clearly what is wrong or what is happening or what should be done" (cited in Hudson, 1986, p. 377). In the United States, Finn (1988) wrote that "to put it simply, our labors haven't produced enough findings that Americans can use or even see the use of" (p. 39).

But Finn's attack on education research has not gone unopposed. Shavelson and Berliner (1988) state that the problem is not the research community, as Finn suggested; rather, "what ails education research first and foremost is the federal government's failure, particularly the U.S. Dept. of Education's failure [where Finn was Assistant Secretary] under the current administration, to provide political leadership and financial support for education research" (p. 9).

One key controversy in the normative dimension of policy research and evaluation, then, is whether the analysis is well done or even worth doing in the first place. We argue that the drive for open access to social science data (such as test scores, student graduation rates, and even skills and standards attainment) and new information technology are making data more widely available and democratizing policy research. Parents can look to see how their children and schools are performing and make decisions based on these analyses, a change from the old days when data, if available, were the prerogative of the system alone.

Postpositivism or Science?   A second, profound division occurs between the positivist or scientific school of thought on the one side, and the postmodern, social-context perspective on the other. The postpositivists have dismissed the two major views of "scientific" inquiry, that is, both the inductive and deductive approaches to education policy evaluation and research. The *inductive* view depends on the ability to draw general conclusions from data. Also called the "empty bucket" theory (Popper, 1959), inductive researchers purportedly begin the process with few if any predispositions, values, history, or other "baggage." As Cook (1985) explains, inductive researchers "assume that some associations repeatedly occur in nature that can be validly observed by senses that bring *no prior knowledge* to bear, and from these observations general laws can be induced" (p. 44).

The *deductive* view is the opposite: that hypotheses can be generated *a priori*, and can be validated, tested, and possibly rejected. The process of deductive research is based on the assumptions that data are readily available and that theories can be created and tested using trial and error and the scientific method. Both inductive and deductive views of positivism are attacked by the postmodernists for a number of important reasons:

1. Researchers have trouble proving relationships between policy inputs and sought-after results (outputs).
2. Researchers cannot easily build predictive models that are clear and simple.
3. Causes are linked to other causes, resulting in a confusing profusion of multiple paths, contingencies, and outcomes (Cronbach & Snow, 1976).
4. Meaning is mentally and socially constructed, not simply "out there" to be gathered in an objectivized world.
5. Objective knowledge is impossible and is based instead on philosophies such as Marxist class bias, rationalist paradigms, capitalist views, or religious or humanistic beliefs.

When the positivistic/scientific view is compared to the critical/postmodern approach, a series of assumptions are made; see Table 5.1 for a comparison between scientific/positivist and postpositivist/critical theories of social science research and evaluation.

Table 5.2 shows a summary of the positive and negative ways in which the normative dimension plays itself out in evaluating education policies. On the positive side, common norms and values give a sense of unity to policy evaluators, who can work together from a similar framework, accept similar research methods and techniques, and then accept each other's results. The common belief system, then, is a key step in enhancing the effectiveness of policies, because parties spend less time fighting over basic assumptions and can concentrate on the methods and results.

Norms not only help to determine when and by whom policies in education should be evaluated, but also work to shape the conceptual/intellectual frameworks that are used and accepted. If everyone in the policy evaluation effort agreed on the theory of how to proceed, the whole process would be greatly simplified—but they do not. In its simplest form, policy evaluation rests on conceptual theories, theories of knowing, scientific and postmodern viewpoints. Is

TABLE 5.1 *Positivistic and Postpositivistic Views of Research*

Scientific/Positivist Views	*Critical Theory/Postmodernist Views*
Assumptions • Existence of a "real world" that can be studied objectively • Lawful ordering of the world • Deterministic, Predictable • Generalization of results	• The world is personally defined and contextualized • Not deterministic but probabilistic • Difficult to generalize across schools and other settings
Rules of Social Research • Research is "timeless" • Research is ahistorical • Research is impersonal • Research is objective and unbiased; applicable in all situations • Research seeks to be constant and universal	• Research is time-bound and shaped by the era in which it occurs • Research is highly personal and determined by those doing the studies • Research is subjective, biased, and applicable only to the conditions under which it was performed • Research is particularistic and uneven
Research Methods • Research is measurement-based • Research seeks stasis, stable approaches and results • Prefers random assignment of subjects in research designs • Research prefers laboratory studies that (a) control variables, (b) work in isolation, (c) control extraneous/exogenous forces and variables, and (d) use controlled experimentation	• Research is particularistic and personal • Research occurs in a highly dynamic, changing, and complex real-world environment • Prefers more naturalistic, humanistic, and qualitative methods, including observations and interviews. Not everything can be measured • Impossible to divorce bias, external realities, and beliefs from the research process
Shortcomings of Method • Tendency to reduce variables to their smallest, simplest components • Overly "reductionist" and narrow, lacking a real context and usefulness • Dependence on complex, mediating variables • Intrusive, time-consuming, and confusing • Absence of universal laws and findings	• Not always able to grasp and use the holistic contextual viewpoint • Difficult to apply naturalistic approaches to all policy evaluations • Values and judgments are common in qualitative research • Difficult to improve practices without some measurable outcomes and changes
Future Directions • Middle ground: use of grounded theory • Quasi-experimental designs • Growing use of practitioners' own experiences and opinions • Open market of "what works," as determined by end users • Increasing access to information about policies through the web and Internet	

TABLE 5.2   *Normative Dimension of Policy Evaluation in Education*

Positive Perspectives	Negative Perspectives
1. Common perspective gives unity to the purposes and values of education policy evaluations	1. Little acceptance of the basic assumptions and beliefs about research and the policies being evaluated
2. Ready acceptance of the research models and methods, based on a common philosophy and outlook	2. Contested view of the values, purposes, and uses of various research methods; methods are ideologically determined
3. Evaluations will be generally accepted and used by policymakers	3. Evaluations are often too little, too late, and lack the rigor to be convincing
4. Policy evaluations enhance the quality of decision-making and reform	4. Evaluations hardly matter in policy deliberations and change
5. Policy evaluations are based on scientific principles and rigor, and fall within the cannons of good unbiased research	5. Evaluations are contextual, political (if not politicized), and highly biased, and thus support the ideology of supporters

evaluation a rational, scientific process, or one steeped in context, beliefs, and meaning?

Philosophical Basis of Policy Evaluation.   The four-dimensional model of policymaking and analysis, around which this book is based, began with the proposition that policymaking is, first, a normative, value-laden process; second, that it is grounded in the institutional structure of policymaking and implementation; third, that policy is influenced by the constituencies that are affected; and finally, that policymaking has a technical dimension, the steps and stages of making and evaluating policy in education.

Thus, it comes as no surprise that evaluating policies, to see their shape and effect, is highly normative: as policies are created and changed, they take on symbolic and meaning-based qualities. Why are norms important in evaluation? First, values shape the meaning of the policy, how it should be evaluated, and most importantly, how results of evaluations are to be evaluated. In fact, the more dramatic the policy, the more it changes the status quo, the more controversial it becomes, and the greater conflict it will generate. Proponents of a policy will naturally seek to muster resources to show that the policy is succeeding. Detractors—people with conflicting values—will seek to demolish the program and contest positive results.

Values, then, permeate the evaluation process, in determining which research models are used; the assumptions applied; the criteria used to decide whether the policy worked; and the conflicts around the meaning of the results.

Milbrey McLaughlin (1987) recognized the shortcomings of policy evaluation and suggested that "Strategies for analysis and evaluation might become self-consciously multistaged, developmental, and iterative, keying questions and methodologies to the point in the process under study, to the needs of key decisionmakers, and to establishing a regularized system of feedback to actors at all levels of the system" (p. 177).

Evaluators hardly agree on how best to assess and determine the effects of education policies, much less sharing a common view of how to interpret the results of these studies. Two views are currently in conflict: positivistic or "scientific" means of evaluation, versus more contextual, postpositivist views. McLaughlin (1987) urges "moving away from a positivistic model to a model of social learning and policy analysis that stresses reflection and assistance to ongoing decision making" (p. 175). In effect, policy evaluation, according to this perspective, is contextual, socially formed, and ongoing, mitigating against traditional tests of student performance and static views of the effects and effectiveness of programs.

Cahill and Overman (1990) reviewed the development of "rationality," starting with Harold Lasswell's writing of *The Policy Sciences* (1963), which lead some down the path of hyper-rationality, into statistical decision theory. Cahill and Overman explain that rational models of policy evaluation are "most often validated by the use of quasi-experimental designs of social research that compare change in condition or behavior before and after a change in program or policy" (1990, p. 14). This concentration on "before and after" a policy is implemented leads the rationalists to examine systemic, institutional, and individual changes, all part of a rational framework.

Another quality of the rational or rationalist model of policy evaluation is the attempt to predict the results of a new policy on the learning of children, or the efficiency of school districts, for example. Some have argued that even the most theoretical, arcane concepts used in evaluating policies must at some point become "applied" and useful in the school and classroom.

Although research scientists seek universal, rigorous, predictive (if X, then Y), "significant" findings and knowledge, teachers want practical, particular, narrative understandings based on real-life experiences. While science seeks uniformity, practices like teaching rest on experiential and personal, "trial-and-error" approaches and tolerance for the unpredictable.

Running counter to the scientific, rationalistic perspective of policy evaluation—one based on a belief that policy effects can be measured, and changes made based on acceptable data—are a number of critical, hermeneutic, phenomenological views. All of these viewpoints call into doubt the scientific, value-free relationship between policies and change, as measured by the policy scientist. Postpositivists assert that all human endeavors, including policy evaluation, are value-intensive, are bound up with the language the researcher used, and are highly contextual. Rather than being universal and context-free, research on policies is highly relative to the audiences involved.

The Structural Dimension

Policies are often constructed and defined at one level of government (federal, state, and local) by various agencies—legislative, judicial, and so on—and implemented and evaluated at yet another: in schools and classrooms. The macro-system produces policies external to the schools, while enactment occurs internal to schools, with evaluations often undefined and late in coming. Nakamura and Smallwood (1980) argue that these different "environments" (one that formulates policy; one that implements policy; and one that evaluates policy) are disconnected and disjointed, with different key actor groups working at different levels.

Thus, a policy might be enacted by a state legislature one year, be implemented by local school districts the next year, and not be evaluated until a few years later by yet another set of players, who may or may not understand the original intent of the legislation. Lowi (1969) and others have argued that the lack of specificity at one level of government makes it difficult for lower levels to interpret and implement the change. The macro-system creates laws, and the micro-systems implement them, with issues of who should do the evaluations rarely determined ahead of time.

The quality of policies, according to political scientists, depends on the specificity and clarity of the laws and regulations. If goals are clear, laws well-written, and authority is carefully spelled out at the macro-level, it is more likely that the policy will be understood and implemented. Vague laws, embedded in unclear authority structures, make implementation and evaluation difficult if not impossible (Mazmanian & Sabatier, 1989). However laws are written, much of the real policymaking occurs at the point of implementation, as interpreted by street-level bureaucrats who translate laws and policies into services and action.

For example, policies to improve the teacher force may hold broad support from citizens and teachers alike. No one would argue for a less qualified, less professional group of teachers in our schools. Yet, evaluating teacher quality is highly controversial and value-laden, and policies that are unclear are sure to cause controversy when it is time to evaluate them.

Evaluating teacher improvement policies occurs at four levels—looking at this issue through the structural lens. First, government may wish to "raise standards" for the training and preparation of teachers, requiring more extensive courses of study, longer internships, and the passing of rigorous tests before a teacher is licensed and allowed to teach. (Of course, this assumes a connection between teacher licensing and teacher effectiveness.) But who should educate these teachers? Universities, alternative route programs like Teach for America, or school districts themselves? Who should be eligible to apply for these programs and teaching certificates? And what is considered an acceptable standard once the training is over?

Second, policies to raise teacher standards require some measure of how effective a teacher is at educating children. Do school districts, the state, or the federal government test these teachers, their students, and their schools?

And if students fail to reach basic standards, should the teachers—and their training—be blamed, or is it the student, community, the curriculum, or perhaps the family?

Third, policies are suggested for rewarding quality teaching and removing poor instructors. Merit pay, for example, has appeal to some policymakers, because it is universal, has the appearance of scientific rigor, and justifies awarding pay increases to teachers who work harder and are more successful (presuming, of course, that "good" teaching can be accurately assessed and evaluated). But severe teacher shortages (the market) undermine all these schemes. Without enough teachers, it is hard to raise entry standards, strengthen screening procedures, and push out the weaker teachers.

Finally, policies to enhance teaching through professional development are also attractive and may take the form of mid-career development, staff workshops, and mentorships. But few policies are able to align the shortcomings of teachers (e.g., the lack of knowledge, skills, and techniques) to the ongoing training they receive. Would returning to a university for a course in curriculum theory improve teachers' work in the classroom? Would putting an entire school's staff through a common workshop in classroom management meet the needs of teachers who manage students well, but have fallen behind in course content, instructional techniques, or technology?

Federal Evaluation: A View from the Structural Dimension. Understanding the complex structure of federal programs such as ESEA is essential in evaluating accurately the effects of the program on schools and students. As shown in Table 5.3, the strengths and weaknesses of the structural dimension counterpoise

TABLE 5.3 *Structural Dimension of Policy Evaluation*

Positive Qualities	*Negative Qualities*
Collaboration among levels	Tensions and competition among levels of government
Shared concepts and purposes	Competing and conflicting views of the role of government and purposes of policy
Top-down direction; bottom-up participation	Role conflict and confusion
Buy-in from levels in a shared involvement	Fundamental differences among levels of government and agencies
School-site involvement in evaluating the effects of programs on students	Unwillingness to assess students and school sites
Long-term, legitimate role of federal and state government in local policymaking	Fear of federal intervention and "big government"

the need to bring together the various levels of government—federal, state, local, and district—in determining the purposes of policy evaluation, access to data, models for analysis, and means for disseminating the results.

Again, a good illustration of the structural dimension of education policy evaluation is the more than 35-year history of ESEA and its numerous reauthorizations and changes (see Cooper & Doyle, 1989), particularly Title I (renamed Chapter I). ESEA is by far the most important federal education policy, and its genius was its ability to weld the federal and state education agencies to schools and classrooms, dedicated to helping students who are at risk. The policy reached through all fifty states into virtually all districts (even middle-class districts could locate a few dozen poor students for Chapter I remedial services at federal expense). It provided billions of dollars to hire additional resource room teachers and later to place Chapter I aides in classrooms to help needy students. Thus, the program is an ideal laboratory for examining efforts to evaluate programs across the boundaries (structures) of government. However, as Murphy (1991) explained,

> Since the beginning of the (ESEA] program, evaluation has been high on the list of federal rhetorical priorities but low on the list of actual USOE priorities. The reasons for this are many. First, they include fear of upsetting the federal-state balance; recognition that little expertise exists at the state and local levels to evaluate a broad-based reform program; and fear of disclosing failure. No administrator is anxious to show that his program is not working. (p. 20)

Much of the early evaluations functioned more as "audits," to see that school districts (and their states) were in compliance with federal regulations. When school districts tried to reduce their local spending, to take advantage of the new-found federal dollars for ESEA, the U.S. auditors accused districts of supplanting local with federal funds, rather than supplementing the education opportunities of poor children under Title I. After about three years, Martin and McClure (1969) explained that federal audits discovered serious violations of policy and regulations:

> The audit reports have brought to light numerous violations of the law and have recommended that millions of dollars be recovered by the Federal Government. Yet, in only three cases has the Office of Education sought and received restitution of illegally spent funds. . . . Even in the most flagrant cases of the unlawful uses of the money—the two swimming pools in Louisiana, for example—the office failed to act. (pp. 52–53)

Kirst and Jung (1991), also examining the assessment of Title I of ESEA, used the term "macro-case study" to describe efforts to evaluate federal programs, "tracing implementation from policy formulation through the measurement of a program's impact on intended recipients at a single point in time" (p. 17), leading to longitudinal case studies over long time periods.

Kirst and Jung (1991) concluded that "(1) initial consensus goals, often vaguely stated, are formalized *incrementally* over time in organizational routines through an on-going bargaining and compromise process; (2) that the directions of these changes are influenced by the strengths, agendas, and resources of the constituencies participating in the policy formulation and implementation process as well as broader social movements; and (3) that the evidence for longitudinal implementation studies needs to be garnered from a confluence of sources" (p. 63).

The bargaining and compromises mentioned above testify to the relationship between levels of government in establishing and evaluating education policy. To ignore the political landscape, as Kirst and Jung demonstrate, is to fail to understand the nature of policymaking and the context in which it should be evaluated. See Table 5.3 for the positive and negative effects of policy structures on the evaluation process.

The Constituentive Dimension

A third view of education policy evaluation is through the lens of key interest groups, that is, stakeholders, political parties, and affected educational associations and unions. These constituencies have a serious personal and professional stake in how a policy is rendered, implemented, and evaluated. Initially, these constituents often played a major role in legislating educational policies, implementing them, and assessing their value and effectiveness.

Where major interests are involved, interest groups may seek to control the evaluation process or to do a parallel evaluation of their own, to ensure that the reviews, analysis, publicity, and dissemination of results are favorable to the policy, if they like it. If the policies are perceived as a threat, interest groups will seek to discredit the program by trying to find negative assessments of it. On the other hand, if a key policy, such as bilingual education, comes under heavy attack, and evaluations of "immersion" programs (which obviate the need for bilingual and English as a Second Language) are found effective (as recently happened in New York and California), then the supporters of bilingual education will muster data to contradict the anti-bilingual policies.

Another controversial example of policy evaluation—illustrating the role of competing policy constituencies—was efforts to assess the effectiveness of voucher programs in Milwaukee, Cleveland, New York City, and the District of Columbia. Teacher unions watch these evaluations very closely, for these unions believe that vouchers (1) will drain valuable resources out of the public sector, resulting in fewer teachers in public schools and lower teachers' salaries; (2) will pit private schools against public and even religious schools; (3) will increase family choice and "exit" behavior (Hirschman, 1970); and (4) will weaken the social commitment to equity and social justice.

These teacher constituent groups, joined by associations of public school administrators, boards of education, and parent-teacher organizations contest the studies that find vouchers effective in raising students' test scores. Quite simply, many groups—particularly those working within the public school system—benefit greatly from the existing system and actively resist all attempts to change it, regardless of the merit of the proposed changes.

Thus, evaluation of education policies is hardly ignored by key interests. Instead, these constituents face off, helping to drive the nature of the evaluation and its acceptability and use. In England, for example, the National Union of Teachers (NUT), the nation's largest teachers' union, locked horns with the Conservative governments of Prime Ministers Margaret Thatcher (1979–1991) and John Major (1991–1998). The NUT, along with the other teachers' unions, contended that the Tory government was eroding support for state-run education. It further argued that their policies were undermining the legitimacy of public education, preventing teachers from receiving adequate pay raises, reducing job security, destroying morale among teachers, and transforming equitable schooling as legislated in the 1944 Butler Act.

Similarly, U.S. teacher unions defend the public school enterprise as their employer and the source of their profession and status. As Loveless (1998) concludes, "Teachers' beliefs are contestable; their power over implementing instructional [and other] policies is not. Instruction is conducted by teachers, so if you contend that something is wrong with contemporary instruction, then you are contending that something is wrong with contemporary teachers. . . . Teachers, informed by research and in consultation with parents, schools principals, and other local personnel, are in the best position to select the most effective strategies for teaching the children in their classrooms" (p. 300).

Table 5.4 summarizes the positive and negative qualities of the constituentive dimension of policy evaluation and change. In brief, when groups agree and share an interest in a program evaluation, the unity and drive can create strong cooperation and collaboration among, for example, teachers, administrators, school boards, and evaluation experts, around efforts to improve the schools. When, however, the key stakeholders perceive evaluation as a threat to jobs, stability, and program status, these constituents can block or obfuscate program data and undermine their efforts.

The Technical Dimension

Finally, policy evaluation requires an understanding of the practical effects of programs on the use of school time, staff, resources, and instruction—and can be evaluated "on the ground" in schools, districts, and classrooms with students. The practical or technical dimension is important if we are to understand what happens, in real terms, when a new policy is implemented.

Policy evaluation is a complex process, bringing to bear a variety of methods and skills. The history of the field shows a wide range of techniques.

TABLE 5.4   *Constituentive Dimension of Policy Evaluation*

Positive Features	Negative Features
1. Members share interest and perspectives on education evaluation	1. Factions battle over control and interpretation of research findings
2. Groups become engaged in the process of policy evaluation	2. End users of policies are indifferent to research; research is deemed obscure and/or useless
3. Close coordination between practitioners and researchers	3. Researchers and educators work in very different spheres
4. Users accept the results and apply them in their work	4. Policy evaluation is rarely consulted or used
5. Constituentive groups advocate for more funds and efforts to evaluate research on education policies	5. Interest groups are distant and indifferent
6. High trust between constituents and researchers	6. Little trust among constituent groups or researchers: • Advocacy over rationality • Hardened positions and long battles
7. Much learning from results; wide dissemination	7. Little learning; little acceptance and dissemination

Add-On versus Built-In Analysis.   Research on policy evaluation can be appended to a program years after it is implemented, or it can be conceptualized and begun almost immediately, building a baseline of information against which to compare progress.

Naturalistic versus Positivistic/Scientific Methods.   At the extremes, policy evaluation can be divided between meaning-generating or hypothesis testing models. McLaughlin (1987) made a strong case for contextual approaches, where participants struggle to define the meaning of their work and to place less emphasis on absolute measures of success. Thus, terms such as incrementalism, evolution, and subtle change are preferred to more absolute, dramatic, revolutionary, "slam bang" changes. Change may be marginal, "muddling through" (Lindblom, 1959), rather than absolute and dramatic. Meanings may be "bargained" and transformational, and not imposed or preestablished. Organizations, as they implement new policies, are in the act of "learning" and "reflecting," rather than being tested for preestablished outcomes. They are need-dependent, not independent of the context in which policies are evaluated.

Cross-Sectional versus Longitudinal Techniques.   Policy evaluations are often done cross-sectionally: taking a sample of students (or teachers) and then testing to see what change has occurred. Other researchers prefer a more long-term, cross-time approach, tracking change over a period of years, using the same co-horts of students. Several well-known studies, including the National Educational Longitudinal Study (1988), for example, trace learning and change over a long period of time, to see how programs worked for those students. Others prefer a larger, faster sample of students, taken at a single point in time (many state tests are cross-sectional).

Insider versus Outsider Evaluations.   Another common technical concern in policy research is whether the studies and evaluations should be done by knowledgeable people who work in the school district, state education depart-ment, or U.S. Department of Education, or by agencies from outside that are less "tied into" the system and have less to lose by releasing negative results. The problem with employing outsiders (e.g., consulting firms, university re-searchers, and independent research groups) is that no one may cooperate or take their results seriously. Perhaps a cooperative effort might work best, where groups of independent scholars and statisticians work closely with teams of ed-ucators and parents within the school who have a stake in the process and the results. Often, reports from outsiders, particularly if they are highly critical, are shelved and ignored.

Short-Term versus Long-Term Approaches.   Many argue that it may take three to five years to witness significant change and improvement in a school and stu-dent learning. Policy evaluations done during the first few years are advised, therefore, to examine formative qualities (e.g., implementation, acceptance, in-volvement) and leave the summative, results-oriented evaluations for the later years when the program has taken root. However, the problems with waiting three or four years are several: (1) valuable data available from the initiators of the program may be lost; (2) politicians may lose interest in an "old" program un-less it requires reauthorization, such as Title I, which has been around for over thirty-five years, and has been reauthorized eight times, meaning that some reevaluation is called for; and (3) results may come too late to revise unproduc-tive policies or to save effective ones.

Short-term, formative evaluations are likewise useful. They provide early warnings if problems arise, before it is too late. They are less costly and can main-tain the attention of researchers and policymakers perhaps better than a ten year study, for example. Hence, well-constructed formative studies can provide data on how well policies are initially understood, accepted, and being implemented, which allows school administrators to make periodic, mid-term corrections or modifications to policies and programs.

National/International Studies versus Local/Regional Approaches. The scope of the study remains an interesting question. Should the study be national or even international, providing baseline information across boundaries and time? Or, because education occurs locally and in schools, will national policy research reach down into the school and classroom, to see if changes are occurring in instruction and learning? Limitations in the United States include that states and localities give different tests over different time periods, leading to confusion when national and international comparisons are made. President George W. Bush's successful push for national legislation to test all children—3rd through 8th grades—using state-determined tests, may standardize who gets tested and how often, but not necessarily predetermine which tests are given, based on which curriculum. Because the curriculum is so different, the requirements vary, and the levels of equity and opportunity seem so diverse, one wonders just how useful national and international evaluations are for any one country.

But the "unit of analysis" problem is critical in policy research: what level is under study, whether the state, district, school, classroom, teacher, student, or combinations thereof? To what or whom are the results to be compared and benchmarked? How generalizable are results because localities vary in terms of school facilities, quality of teachers, levels of curriculum, and parental and community involvement and expectations?

Primary Analysis versus Meta-Analysis. Approaches may also vary as to whether research involves primary data collection or analyses of existing results across sites, times, and communities. Meta-analysis rests on the richness of preexisting findings: for example, researchers interested in how well after-school tutoring programs work for low-income students might consult numerous studies and databases on the results of these programs; these studies are then standardized and combined, to see what the common, comparable results are across numerous prior studies.

Case Methods versus Output Analysis. Research on policy evaluation also differs as to whether researchers focus on a single or multiple case studies (looking at the district, school, teachers, and students in an interconnected way), or study key variables (i.e., test results) across sites and states. Most state testing programs focus on outcomes and pay less attention to the settings, implementation, classroom activities, and student variations. Thus, when test scores improve, the state is hard-pressed to determine what changes at the school and classroom levels may have affected these outcomes, be it changing student demographics, test-retest effects, changing leadership, new curriculum and instructional methods, or a combination of these factors.

Researchers suffer from other practical problems when trying to evaluate a policy or program, a few of which are discussed in detail below:

Limited Access.   Researchers are not always welcome. They may find it difficult to gain access to students and schools, as school boards and superintendents are wary of researchers studying their children. With the laws governing research on human subjects, it becomes increasingly problematic to find schools, parents, students (parental consent is required), and teachers willing to be observed and surveyed. Because teachers and families may not see the advantages of policy research, and the results may not be useful, they may refuse to provide required "informed consent" and thus data are not made available.

Limited Controls over Variables.   Researchers also have limited to no control over the variables in their studies. Authentic studies with control groups and alternate treatments are usually impossible because families would never agree to having their children assigned to a control group like a lab rat, and given a placebo instead of the real thing. And students cannot be randomly assigned to treatments, schools, or programs, because districts will not let researchers dictate a student's program, teachers, or school assignment.

Competing Treatments.   Related to limited controls is the presence in most natural school settings of competing treatments that may invalidate a scientific study. Thus, how would researchers—who are subjecting one (treatment) group to a new program while another group either has no program (control) or a less respected version to test the effects—prevent students on the school bus from sharing their new learning with a control-group student, thus contaminating the study?

How can school researchers eliminate or control the effects of home, summer, camps, private tutoring, religious instruction in Sunday schools, and other programs (Boy Scouts, Girl Scouts) on what students are learning? Again, contamination is a problem in naturalistic, uncontrolled, quasi-experimental studies, so common in education research and policy evaluation.

Weak Results.   In addition, much of policy evaluation research produces moderate to weak findings for many of the reasons already discussed. Because researchers cannot control their own studies, they cannot expect to find strong results that are striking and significant.

When is Enough, Enough?   Finally, policy evaluation raises the question, When is enough study enough? Because it is virtually impossible to "prove" a policy is working, to control enough variables to show what is affecting what (curriculum, teaching, and programs affect student test scores), and to produce strong and significant results, policy analysts are either ignored or are requested to go back for more data.

Overcoming Barriers to Good Policy Evaluation

Policy evaluation is stymied by a combination of forces—some of which can be controlled, and some of which are beyond the reach of researchers and field personnel. For an evaluation to be valid, reliable, and credible, it must conform to basic tenets of scientific research practices and be practical in suggesting improvements. Education, of all human activities, is most difficult to isolate because learning goes on everywhere (at home, on vacation, on the bus, in front of the computer, and through television) and is hardly the sole purview of schools and teachers. Further, learning is influenced by a set of previous conditions, natural interests, motivations, and abilities that schools cannot control.

Five conditions are critical if policy evaluation is to be valid and useful: (1) general agreement on the purposes of the policy; (2) knowledge that the program or policy was uniformly implemented; (3) access to matched samples of end-users, to determine the quality of the program and its outcomes; (4) adequate measures of improvement; and (5) some agreement among policymakers and users that the results are related to the policy, programs, and student outcomes.

Yet for all the shortcomings and practical problems with doing valid, reliable, and acceptable policy research, we see signs of improvement. First, a number of large-scale national and state studies of education are ongoing and productive. Besides NAEP, NELS, and High School and Beyond, all longitudinal data collections on students across the nation, a number of states are getting into large-scale, high-stakes testing, which holds promise for both evaluating the curriculum of the state's schools and for actually helping to shape the curriculum through curricular alignment.

Second, with new technologies, data banks, and instant access, the opportunity to increase the availability of useful information has increased exponentially. Most importantly, politicians and the public are demanding more data on schools, and how well their programs and policies are working. Demand for good information drives supply, as schools, districts, and government strive to make better data available.

Research Organizations

Policy and program evaluations have been performed over the years by some key organizations, that are worth considering:

OERI.   The largest national education research organization is the Office of Educational Research and Improvement (OERI), the federal governmental arm of the U.S. Department of Education, charged with managing the billions of tax dollars devoted to education research, coordinating the work of regional organizations (labs and centers), and funding research. It lists as its mission to provide leadership for educational research and statistics: conducting research and demonstration projects; collecting statistics on the status and progress of schools nationally; and distributing information and providing technical assistance to those working to improve education.

Testifying before the U.S. House of Representatives, Vinovskis (1999) explained the history, background, and changes necessary in OERI to recognize its contribution and improve its performance:

> The federal government has been collecting, analyzing, and disseminating education statistics for more than 130 years. Over time, the focus shifted from data gathering to emphasis on research and development to find more effective ways of educating children at the state and local levels. But the quality of work in educational research and development has varied greatly. As a result, education research and development usually has *not* been held in high esteem by most academics and policy makers in the 20th century. (p. 2)

National Academy of Education (NAE).   Founded in 1965, the NAE seeks to promote scholarly inquiry and discussion concerning the ends and means of education, in all its forms, in the United States and abroad. Like the National Academy of Sciences, the NAE accepts outstanding researchers, now numbering about 125 members, and sponsors research and proceedings of meetings.

General Accounting Office (GAO).   This branch of the U.S. government has conducted some of the largest studies in education. As the goal statement of GAO explains:

> The General Accounting Office is the investigative arm of Congress. GAO exists to support the Congress in meeting its Constitutional responsibilities and to help improve the performance and accountability of the federal government for the American people. GAO examines the use of public funds, evaluates federal programs and activities, and provides analyses, options, recommendations, and other assistance to help the Congress make effective oversight, policy, and funding decisions. In this context, GAO works to continuously improve the economy, efficiency, and effectiveness of the federal government through financial audits, program reviews and evaluations, analyses, legal opinions, investigations, and other services. (U.S. Government Accounting Office [1986], p. 1).

National Research Council (NRC).   Organized by the National Academy of Sciences, the NRC dates back to 1916 and produces research and articles on concerns to educators. A recent example is Beatty, Neisser, Trent, and Heubert's (2001) *Understanding Dropouts: Statistics, Strategies, and High-Stakes Testing,* for the Committee on Educational Excellence and Testing Equity.

Improving Education Policy Evaluation

A number of lessons have been learned as we analyze the process of policy evaluation in education:

• *Build in evaluation early:* History shows the importance of policy evaluations and requires that assessment be done early, as part of the formulation and implementation processes.

• *Work nationally, regionally, locally:* The structural dimension dictates an understanding of the interrelationships and interactions of various levels in the policy process.

• *Ascertain the sufficiency of school resources:* Policy evaluation points to the importance of adequate resources because change cannot easily be accomplished without the reallocation of funds, staff, space, time, and effort.

• *Insiders and outsiders:* Effective policy evaluation is best accomplished when assessments are made by those closest to the reform, working in conjunction with external evaluation teams.

• *Long-term policy perspectives:* Change in education occurs over long periods of time: time for goals to be adjusted, schools to be restructured, staff hired or retrained, and programs to be implemented, tested, and refined.

• *Scientific and contextual perspectives:* No single model of policy evaluation works in all settings. Policy evaluators should be skilled in a range of research modes and models. Data, both qualitative and quantitative, are necessary if a program is to be adequately assessed.

• *Moving from evaluation to reform:* Crucial to the process is the ability to take evaluation information and transform it into new policies and more successful programs. It is the translation of "learnings" from the research into action in schools that fosters school improvement and justifies the effort to do careful, long-term research.

• *Knowledge of how policy was implemented:* Policy evaluation may be improved with greater analysis of just how a particular policy was translated from laws and regulations, into jobs and programs. The goal, then, of some policy evaluation is to ascertain whether in fact the program was established, schools were opened, classes taught, and new approaches used. Researchers Charters and Jones entitled a policy evaluation: "On the chance that a new policy was ever implemented in the first place" (1973, p. 6). Their concern was that evaluators would test the students to see what they learned, without determining whether the program itself was ever implemented and used.

Are non-English-speaking students, for example, being taught English by English-fluent teachers in bilingual programs? If not, what good does it do to test the English proficiency of students who were never given a real chance to learn English in school in the first place?

• *Shared understanding of policy goals:* Another goal of policy evaluation is to see to what degree participants understand and share the goals of the program. Just because teachers are asked to use a new reading program does not mean that they understand it or share its purposes. Policy evaluation should consider, then, the degree to which participants are buying in to the goals of the program and understand them.

• *Reallocation of resources*: For a new program to be implemented and to succeed, resources should be used in different ways, for different ends, and with different educators assuming new and different roles. A goal, then, of policy research should be an assessment of how time, space, materials, and funds are used.

• *Training and professional development:* Another way to improve policy evaluation would be to study and assess the quality and effectiveness of professional training and socialization. Few policies can be implemented without some new techniques and concepts, and teachers and administrators are called upon to be retrained. A goal, then, is to figure out what opportunities for learning occurred and how well participants came to understand the new program.

• *Creating better, stronger, more comprehensive policies:* A goal of policy evaluation is often to determine how to improve the policies and their effects. Because policymaking is an iterative process, one that is ongoing, changing, and contextual, it is important to understand how implementation under varying circumstances affects the way policy is made and improved.

Cizek and Ramaswamy (1999) found that "policy development in education is prompted by the presence of a crisis" (p. 497). However, these authors and others recommend that we become more attuned to the strengths of U.S. schools and direct policies, and their evaluations, toward what is useful to the practitioners who teach our children. As Kennedy (1999) explains, "One could argue that, given the relatively recent entry of research into the education landscape, it has had a remarkable impact. Many of the ideas that motivate contemporary policies, and . . . contemporary teaching, have come from research [and evaluation]" (p. 75).

Effects of Improved Policy Evaluation in Education

Normative Dimension

When policymakers have access to accurate, up-to-date information, perhaps over the web, they may come to agree on the usefulness of the information. Common values, beliefs, and approaches are more likely to occur when the data are public and widely debated. For example, the success of the "school report card" movement in the United States has been remarkable, as communities are demanding and 180 receiving better and more information on students (attendance, graduation rates, test results, incidents of school violence) and on schools (use, quality, needs, resources). The report card becomes a major tool of communication and evaluation, and can be expanded to provide ever more and better information and evaluations.

Structural Dimension

The structural qualities of policy evaluation cannot be ignored. Because policies are created and promulgated at one level and accepted and implemented at another, evaluation must reflect this reality. Improved coordination across jurisdictions is critical; close collaboration is only possible if all levels support the program and want to see it evaluated and improved.

Constituentive Dimension

Important to the future of policy evaluation is the "buy in" among diverse groups in the community and the school. These constituencies help to shape the direction of evaluations and to determine how well received they are. Engaging teachers in their own evaluations and the assessments of their administrators promotes support and a likely acceptance of the results. Creating statewide and national commissions including the key interest groups is widely used and should continue. The participants, however, need more than to protect their associations' interest. They should be responsible for disseminating results and improving school practices. We are thus aware of just how contextually contingent are program effects and our ability to observe these effects. Such concerns have led to the development of "evaluability assessment" as an important evaluation approach and considers further developments in types, methods, and applications of program theory and causation.

Technical Dimension

The technical dimension is where the details are—and thus holds the key to success. Without careful attention to the details, the techniques, and the methods of policy evaluation, little can be done to assess outcomes and improve programs and methods. However, much can be done to focus resources, ideas, and skills on the technical dimension of research, given that the political, normative, and constituentive/structural issues are dealt with and overcome. Improved policy-making in education depends, as this chapter has shown, on good information, analysis, and feedback.

Chapter Assignments and Activities _____

Field Investigation

Investigate pupil promotion policies in two school districts: one that is very strict, and the other, moderate or weak. What are their purposes, rules, and regulations, and how well have they worked to reach the goals of the policy? How did the districts evaluate their promotion policy before changing it? Write a 10-page analysis of the two districts, comparing their goals and purposes, organization and regulations, and effects and changes.

Case Study #1: Promotion and Retention Policy

The Board of Education of West River School District is considering major changes in its pupil promotion and retention policy. The Board has held hearings and learned that the teachers were divided about increasing the levels of retention ("It makes them look bad and doesn't help kids," they argued.) The proposal is that if students fail their subject tests, they will be required to enroll in eight weeks of summer school, and if they fail the retest, they will be held back.

Critics of this policy argue that, (1) repeating a grade does not mean that the student will learn more; (2) teachers are unprepared to handle large numbers of older repeaters; (3) students who are retained have little in common with their peers socially; and (4) schools are already overcrowded and "keeping kids back" means it will take more than twelve years to finish school, further burdening the system that cannot afford to teach these students for twelve years (much less thirteen to fifteen years).

The measure passed the Board in 1999 and has been implemented in most of the schools. Answer the following questions:

1. What is the *normative dimension* of this policy: what values are being pursued, and whose values are being subjugated or ignored?

2. Which groups (e.g., parents, teachers, unions, administrators, school board members) or *constituents* might have supported or resisted the promotion policy spelled out above?

3. How might the *structural dimension* of this policy tie into state standards, local standards, and other agencies such as the State Department of Education and the Association for Children with Special Needs, which resist retaining or failing students?

4. What are some of the potential practical or *technical dimensions* of this policy that might prevent it from working?

5. How would you set about *evaluating* this promotion and retention policy, and how would you know if the policy were working?

Case Study #2: Student Truancy

Turnpike High School has a serious truancy problem. Data show that on any given day, 44 percent of the students either play hooky from school, staying home for unexcused reasons, or cut class, missing a class or two during the day, hanging out in the hallways or the schoolyard. Efforts to patrol the halls have not worked, and stiffer punishments seem to make students dread school and become ever more truant.

Research by Cooper and Guare (in press) shows that students are highly selective in which classes they cut, treating school as a "take it, or leave it" proposition, much like other consumers.

1. What would you suggest Turnpike High School should do?

2. How would you investigate and evaluate the process of policymaking, implementation, and attendance outcomes? How would you determine if the policy is effective?

3. What are the strengths and limitations of the methods you selected?

Seminal Works

Most public policy textbooks contain chapters on evaluation. Two highly recommended overviews of the process are found in Thomas Dye's (2001) *Understanding Public Policy* and Guy Peters's (1986) *American Public Policy: Promise and Performance*. Students seeking a comprehensive treatment of evaluation (from start to finish) should consult Carol Weiss' (1998) classic, *Evaluation* (2nd ed.). Two user-friendly evaluation texts for schoolteachers and administrators are Boulmetis and Dutwin's (2000) *The ABCs of Evaluation* and Naftaly Glasman's (1994) *Making Better Decisions About School Problems*. Both sources offer easy to use, step-by-step procedures for conducting program and policy evaluation.

References

Aaron, H. J. (1978). *Politics and the professor.* Washington, DC: Brookings Institution.

Bailey, S. K., & Mosher, E. K. (1968). *ESEA: The Office of Education administers a law.* Syracuse, NY: Syracuse University Press.

Beatty, A., Nessar, U., Trent, W. T., & Heubert, J. P. (Eds.). (2001). *Understanding dropouts: Statistics, strategies, and high-stakes testing.* Washington, DC: National Academics Press.

Berliner, D. C. (2000). A personal response to those who bash teacher education. *Journal of Teacher Education, 51*(5), 358–371.

Berliner, D. C., & Biddle, B. J. (1995). *The manufactured crisis.* Reading, PA: Addison-Wesley.

Biddle, B. J., & Anderson, D. S. (1991). Social research and educational change. In D. S. Anderson & B. J. Biddle (Eds.), *Knowledge for policy: Improving education through research* (pp. 1–20). New York: Falmer Press.

Bolster, A. S. (1983). Toward a more effective model of research on teaching. *Harvard Educational Review, 53*(3), 294–308.

Bourgue, M. L. (1999). The role of the National Assessment of Educational Progress (NAEP) in setting, reflecting and linking national education policy to states' needs. In G. J. Cizek (Ed.), *Handbook of educational policy* (pp. 213–249). San Diego, CA: Academic Press.

Cahill, A., & Overman, S. (1990). The evolution of rationality in policy analysis. In S. S. Nagel (Ed.), *Policy theory and policy evaluation: Concepts, knowledge, causes, and norms* (pp. 11–40). Westport, CT: Greenwood Press.

Charters, W. W., Jr., & Jones, J. E. (1973). On the risk of appraising non-events in program evaluation. *Educational Researcher, 2*(11), 5–7.

Cizek, G. J., & Ramaswamy, V. (1999). American educational policy: Constructing crises and crafting solutions. In G. J. Cizek (Ed.), *Handbook of educational policy* (pp. 497–531). San Diego, CA: Academic Press.

Cook, T. D. (1985). Postpositivist criticisms, reform associations, and uncertainties about social research. In R. L. Shotland & M. M. Mark (Eds.), *Social science and social policy* (pp. 21–62). Beverly Hills, CA: Sage.

Cooper, B. S., & Doyle, D. P. (1989). *Federal aid to education: What future Chapter I?* New York: Falmer Press.

Cooper, B. S. & Guare, R. (in press). *Truancy as rational choice? A new perspective on an old problem.* Lanham, MD: Scarecrow Press.

Cronbach, L. J., & Snow, R. E. (1976). *Aptitude and instructional methods.* New York: Irvington.

Davis, B. (1996, October 11). Dueling professors have Milwaukee dazed over school vouchers. *Wall Street Journal,* p. A1.

Doyle, D. P., & Pimentel, S. (1999). *Raising the standard: Better education through higher standards.* New York: McGraw-Hill.

Dror, Y. (1968). *Public policymaking re-examined.* San Francisco: Chandler.

Dye, T. R. (2001). *Understanding public policy* (10th ed.). Upper Saddle River, NJ: Prentice Hall.

Easton, D. (2001). *A systems analysis of political life.* New York: Wiley.

Finn, C. E., Jr. (2000, September 20). Fixing education research and statistics (again). *Education Week.* Commentary, *20*(3), 33, 48.

Forester, J. (1984). Bounded rationality and the politics of muddling through. *Public Administration Review, 44*(1), 23–31.

Fry, B. R., & Tompkins, E. T. (Spring, 1978). Some notes on the domain of public policy studies. *Policy Studies Journal, 6*(3), 305–312.

Garson, G. D. (1986). From political science to policy analysis: A quarter century of progress. In W. Dunn (Ed.), *Policy analysis: Perspectives, concepts, and methods* (pp. 3–23). Greenwich, CT: JAI Press.

Glass, G. V. (1979). Policy for the unpredictable (uncertainty research and policy). *Educational Researcher, 8*(9), 12–14.

Greene, J. P., Peterson, P. E., & Du, J. (1997). *The effectiveness of school choice in Milwaukee: A secondary analysis of data from the program's evaluation.* Paper presented at the Annual Meeting of the American Political Science Association. San Francisco, August 30, 1997.

Hirschman, A. O. (1970). *Exit, voice and loyalty.* Cambridge, MA: Harvard University Press.

Hoff, D. J. (2000, February 16). Test-weary schools balk at NAEP: Seven states can't find enough interest. *Education Week, 19*(23), 1, 11.

Howell, W. G., & Peterson, P. E. (2002). *The education gap: Vouchers and urban schools.* Washington, DC: The Brookings Institution Press.

Howlett, M., & Ramesh, M. (1995). *Studying public policy: Policy cycles and policy subsystems.* Oxford, UK: Oxford University Press.

Kennedy, M. (1999). Infusing educational decision making with research. In G. J. Cizek (Ed.), *Handbook of educational policy* (pp. 53–81). San Diego, CA: Academic Press.

Kerr, D. H. (1976). *Educational policy: Analysis, structure, and justification.* New York: David McKay.

Kogan, M. (1985). Education policy and values. In I. McNay & J. Ozga (Eds.), *Policymaking in education: The breakdown of consensus* (pp. 11–24). London: Pergamon Press.

Kirst, M., & Jung, R. (1991). The utility of a longitudinal approach in assessing implementation: A thirteen-year view of Title I, ESEA. In A. R. Odden (Ed.), *Education policy implementation* (pp. 39–64). Albany: State University of New York Press.

Lasswell, H. D. (1963). *The future of political science.* New York: Atherton.

Lindblom, C. A. (1959). The science of "muddling through." *Public Administration Review, 19*(2), 79–88.

Lindblom, C. A. (1980). *The policy making process.* New York: Prentice Hall.

Loveless, T. (1998). The use and misuse of research in educational reform. In D. Ravitch (Ed.), *Brookings papers on education policy, 1998* (pp. 279–303). Washington, DC: Brookings Institution Press.

Lowi, T. J. (1969). *The end of liberalism: Ideology, policy and the crisis of public authority.* New York: Norton.

March, J., & Olsen, J. P. (1985). The new institutionalism: Organizational factors in political life. *American Political Science Review, 77,* 281–296.

Martin, R., & McClure, P. (1969). *Title I of ESEA: Is it helping poor children?* Washington, DC: Washington Research Project of the Southern Center for Studies in Public Policy and the NAACP Legal Defense Education Fund, Inc.

Mazmanian, D., & Sabatier, P. (1989). *Implementation and public policy.* Lanham, MD: University Press of America.

McLaughlin, M. W. (1987). Learning from experience: Lessons from policy implementation. *Educational Evaluation and Policy Analysis, 9*(2), 171–178.

Murphy, J. T. (1991). Title I of ESEA: The politics of implementing federal education reform. In A. R. Odden (Ed.), *Education policy implementation* (pp. 13–37). Albany: State University of New York Press.

Nakamura, R., & Smallwood, F. (1980). *The politics of policy implementation.* New York: St. Martin's Press.

Peters, B. G. (1986). *American public policy: Promise and performance* (2nd ed.). New York: Macmillan.

Peterson, P. E., Greene, J. P., & Howell, W. G. (1998). *Initial findings from an evaluation of school choice programs in Washington, DC.* Paper presented at the annual meeting of the American Political Science Association, Boston, September 1998.

Pile, W. H., as cited in Hudson, G. (1986). *Educational Research: A Sociological Study of its Development, Organization and Ideology.* Unpublished Ph.D. thesis. Department of Sociological Studies. Sheffield: University of Sheffield.

Popper, K. (1959). *The logic of scientific discovery.* New York: Harper & Row.

Pressman, J. I., & Wildavsky, A. (1973). *Implementation.* Berkeley: University of California Press.

Sanders, W. L. (1998). Value-added assessment: A method for measuring the effects of the system, school, and teacher on rate of student academic progress. *The School Administrator.* December, 1998, pp. 4–11.

Sanders, W. L., Saxton, A. M., & Horn, S. P. (1997). The Tennessee value-added assessment system (TVAAS): A quantitative, outcomes-based approach to educational assessment. In J. Millman (Ed.), *Grading teachers, grading schools* (pp. 137–162). Thousand Oaks, CA: Corwin Press.

Shapiro, J. P. (1988). Participatory evaluation: Towards a transformation of assessment for women's studies programs and projects. *Educational Evaluation and Policy Analysis, 10*(3), 191–199.

Shavelson, R. J., & Berliner, D. C. (1988). Erosion of the education research infrastructure: A reply to Finn. *Educational Researcher, 17*(1), 9–12.

Simon, H. (1958). *Administrative behavior: A study of decision-making processes in administrative organization.* New York: Macmillan.

Smith, M. J. (1994). Policy networks and state autonomy. In S. Brooks & A. G. Gagnon (Eds.), *The political influence of ideas: Policy communities and the social sciences.* New York: Praeger.

Visnovskis, M. A. (1999). *History and educational policymaking.* New Haven, CT: Yale University Press.

Visnovskis, M. A. (1999, October 26). What might be done to improve educational research in the U.S. Department of Education. Testimony presented before the U.S. House of Representatives, Science Subcommittee on Basic Research. Washington, DC: U.S. Congress.

Viteritti, J. P. (1999). *Choosing equality: School choice, the constitution and civil society.* Washington, DC: Brookings Institution Press.

Witte, J. E. (1998). The Milwaukee voucher experiment. *Educational Evaluation and Policy Analysis, 20*(4), 229–251.

Wholey, J. S., et al. (1970). *Federal evaluation policy.* Washington, DC: Urban Institute.

6

Better Governance, Better Schools

School Governance and Policy in Education

POLICY VIGNETTE • *Community Control in New York City*

African American parents were not happy; animosity toward the public school bureaucracy in New York City was running high, as their children were receiving substandard education in substandard facilities in racially segregated schools. Little had
changed despite the best efforts of these parents and other supporters to prod a lum-
bering educational bureaucracy to respond and change what parents had perceived
as racially motivated decisions.

   The demand was simple. African American parents wanted more control over
what happened in the predominately minority schools attended by their children. In
response to demonstrations and boycotts for a transfer of control from the central office to parents, in the summer of 1967, the New York City Board of Education authorized the creation of three experimental community districts in minority enclaves—the
Lower East Side of Manhattan, East Harlem, and Ocean Hill-Brownsville in Brooklyn.
Each district had its own board of education. In less than two years, this modest move
to decentralization and more local control had ended in a conflict that affected the entire city of New York. The beginning of the end occurred when the local board of education in Ocean Hill-Brownside fired thirteen teachers and most of the administrative
staff in May 1968. The teachers' union, the United Federation of Teachers, retaliated
by shutting down the entire New York City school system for several months in the
fall of 1968. Local control of schools, a threat to change radically the governance system of New York City schools, fell victim to the powerful teachers' union. This move
to decentralize power and control over education threatened the political position of
the teacher's union and the corresponding position to reallocate resources (Katznelson, 1981; Ravitch, 1983; Spring, 1994).

The General Concept of Governance

Governance is government in action. At its most basic level, governance is about power—the power to decide who wins and who loses (Lasswell, 1950). It is also about the degree to which this power will be centralized or concentrated in the hands of a few or decentralized and widely distributed to others. Governance involves organizational structures and procedures, which shape and direct power to make decisions that can affect the quality of life of millions of people. The governance process transforms individual and personal preferences into institutional and public policies. This power to create universal norms of social conduct can impose external constraints on individual liberty and environmental barriers to the exercise of individual freedom. These decisions often have a differential impact on individuals and other organizations, which can vary both in terms of magnitude and scope.

In the field of education, the key governance question is who controls education and the formal institutions called schools that are organized to carry out the critical process of social reproduction and creation of individuals. The answer to this question has profound implications for the future of society and the various social organizations and individuals that comprise a society. Education is the process by which a society with its own particular culture reproduces itself. Through education, norms for proper conduct are established, social life and political institutions are legitimated, and worldviews are created and justified. "Education, both in its content and pedagogy, is the cultural furnace where a particular image of mankind and the world is forged and a way of living is passed on" (Randall, 1997, p. 71). Simply an enormous amount is at stake when deciding who is to be educated, what will be taught, and who will control the process of educating the children.

In specific terms, governance issues in education center on the content of education and access to the content. Who, for example, gets to decide which topics or knowledge areas are taught and from which perspective, whether it is history or biology? The teachers, parents, or principals? Who determines, for example, how widely this curricular content will be distributed and the manner in which it will be presented to students coming from various backgrounds and with different needs, abilities, and motivation to learn? Local boards of education, the state office of education, or the federal government? To what extent is the power to make decisions delegated both horizontally or vertically within the various organizational levels in education? To what degree is governance decentralized within an organization, such as a state office of education, and to what extent is decision-making granted to external organizations, such as local school boards? In addition, the degree of decentralization, or lack thereof, is determined not just by the quantity of decisions others are allowed to make but the quality or the potential a decision has for making a meaningful difference.

A school could organize a parent committee to help make many decisions about the school. But if the substance of these decisions deals with matters peripheral to the educational process, such as what flavors of soft drinks should be in the vending machines, then shared decisionmaking has a hollow ring to it. As O'Hair, McLaughlin, and Reitzug (2000) state, governance is about "people, agencies, institutions, and factors involved in making decisions and developing policies that direct, guide, and sometimes control the work of schools. Essentially, governance refers to who makes and develops decisions and policies, which decisions and policies they make and develop and what processes they use" (p. 286). A number of potential actors and sources of influence in the governance process are found in multiple levels of government at the local, state, and federal level. Included are the various branches of government (executive, legislative, and judicial), and a wide variety of participants such as professional organizations, PTA, business groups, taxpayer groups, school advisory groups, textbook publishers, research associations, schools of education at universities, think tanks and policy organizations, teacher unions, parents, students, and the growing influence of a global economy (O'Hair, McLaughlin, & Reitzug, 2000).

The substantive issues in educational governance—with all of its political character and the myriad sources of influence in educational decisions—pose significant challenges to understanding and exercising governance in education (Sergiovanni, Burlingame, Coombs, & Thurston, 1999). But this is not a new phenomenon in U.S. education. If education is government, it is also, by its very nature, about politics and the exercise of political power to achieve social ends. The history of U.S. education and the social struggle for control of education are no exception to this axiom.

Historical Foundations of Governance

Governance in U.S. education has undergone a number of dramatic changes over the years, for governance structures and processes have historical roots and contexts, and have been shaped by a variety of social forces and events. We must avoid the myopic pitfalls of presentism where we see the "past [as] simply the present writ small" (Bailyn, 1960, p. 9). A small but excellent example of this need for history, which also has great bearing on our understanding of governance in U.S. education, is the meaning of two very common and seemingly simple words: public and private. The current conventional meaning of the term "public" describes something that is sponsored, supported, and controlled by the government, while "private" often refers to nongovernment entities and absence of government control, sponsorship, or support. However, these definitions are quite narrow in scope and did not exist prior to the middle of the nineteenth century. Bailyn reminds us that the concept of public before this time was anything that benefited the community as a whole, and in reference to educational institutions, only to designate the lack of legal barriers to entrance. Indeed, it is anachronistic even to say that private and public functions overlapped and merged before the nineteenth century: the distinction by which to make such a statement was absent (p. 133; see also Jorgenson, 1987, pp. 1–7; Katz, 1975, p. 23).

This section presents an overview of the basic changes in educational governance in the United States from the colonial era to the present, divided into three parts: Colonial to Common School (1620–1830); Common School to Modern School (1830–1910); and Modern School to Present (1910–2000). The thesis of this section in terms of governance in education has two points. First, massive power was transferred from individuals and nongovernment institutions to government institutions, from the private to the public sector. Second, the organizational character of education was transformed from a highly decentralized, idiosyncratic, private, and diverse source of educational services to a more centralized, structured, standardized, and almost monopolistic source of education.

Colonial to Common School (1620–1830)

Systems of governance do not arise of their own volition, but are spawned by historical events and social movements. The modern public school systems of today are of relatively recent origin and can be traced back to the Progressive Era of the early twentieth century. Many traditional accounts of U.S. education are celebratory in nature about our public schools and point with pride to their distinguished ancestors, the "public" schools of New England. Although it is true that many schools of a bewildering variety of types were established during the colonial and early national era, they had little resemblance to the public schools of today. This transformation is especially true of educational governance.

Immigrants came to America for many different reasons, but almost universally, they sought to replicate the culture and society they had left behind. In New England, for example, the Puritans came with the determination to establish a Protestant Christian commonwealth or theocracy. Through education, the inherently evil nature of children would at least be kept in check. Socialization and the possession of vocational skills were secondary to the Puritan goal of a "radically transformed personality . . . whose being had been transformed by the infusion of God's mercy and grace" (Hiner, 1973, pp. 5–6). Villages, ministers, women, and schoolmasters established schools. Each community addressed its own educational needs and governance in a multitude of different ways.

In the South, Anglicans sought to replicate the society of landed gentry in England and prepared offspring for public service as religious or government leaders. The formation of huge plantations worked against any system of education for hundreds of years. Tutors of the children of aristocratic families were the usual order for the day. The middle colonies, with their bewildering array of cultural and religious diversity, engaged in an uneasy truce of mutual coexistence and tolerance. Each community determined for itself the nature and content of education to preserve its particular cultural or religious worldview.

The role of the state in education during the colonial period was almost nonexistent and was primarily limited to the granting of charters, acts of incorporation, and the approval of teachers. The most common and primary requirement for approval was that the teacher be of the right religious persuasion. If one word captures the character of education during the colonial period, it would be openness, wide openness. Cremin (1970) observed that

> inevitably, the openness of the environment and the competition for clients made institutions themselves responsive, in that they displayed a characteristic readiness to introduce what the populace seemed to demand. . . . In the last analysis, it seemed less important to maintain traditional definitions of education than it did to accommodate those who desired it. Virtually anyone could teach and virtually anyone could learn, at least among whites, and the market rather than the church or the legislature governed through multifarious contractual relationships. (p. 559; see also Butts & Cremin, 1953; Jernegan, 1919)

Education during the colonial era was, indeed, highly decentralized, unstructured, and very diverse. There was no system and governance was personal, local, and diffuse.

Common School to Modern School (1830–1910)

Education in the United States did not really change much from the colonial model during the first fifty years of the new republic. However, the social unrest of the 1820s through the 1840s caused social reformers and nativists to look for a social structure to remedy social ills. In their eyes, the only way to bring cultural harmony, economic prosperity, and social justice to U.S. society was through the establishment of a state-sponsored, state-controlled system of schools attended by all. Systemic social problems required, in their minds, a systemic solution. The state was the only social agency that could create and sustain the type of universal community they envisioned in an efficient manner. Universality, equality, and efficiency were the rhetorical watch words (Randall, 1994; see also Cremin, 1951).

This task of radically changing the structure and governance of American education was no easy matter for these nineteenth century social reformers such as Horace Mann and Henry Bernard. Already in place were several competing governance approaches in education. In *Class, Bureaucracy, and Schools*, Katz (1975) argues that schools are "designed to reflect and confirm the social structure that erected them" (p. xvi). Governance systems in education are configured in such a way to ensure that the prevailing powers in society remain the dominant force in society. The structure of schooling—and thus the governance of education—reflects a particular set of social values and the use of education to reinforce and perpetuate these values. "Forms of organizational structure," Katz maintains, "are not and cannot be neutral. The relationship between bureaucracy, class bias, and racism are fixed" (p. xxii). The current bureaucratic structure of schooling was not inevitable or a natural development of the common school movement of the 1830s. Rather, it is the "best" organizational form to ensure certain values to undergird a socially stratified society.

Katz identifies four models of governance that competed with each other as government schools were established and a government system of education was created. He refers to these four models as "paternalistic voluntarism, democratic localism, corporate voluntarism, and incipient bureaucracy" (p. 5). It is useful to briefly examine each model and the values upon which it was grounded.

Paternalistic Voluntarism.   The first model discussed by Katz is paternalistic voluntarism and was best exemplified by the New York Public School Society. The society was established as a private entity in 1805 with the mission of providing free basic education for children from poor families. The governing board of the society was comprised of members from the upper class who served without compensation and desired to "offer themselves to the public as agents to carry out certain benevolent purposes" (1975, p. 8). The virtue of the society was in its not being an overt political organization, with no obvious personal gain for those who volunteered their time and services. It was, in the eyes of its founders, a "variety of *noblesse oblige;* it rested on faith in the individual talented amateur and, at an over-all administrative level, scorned the need for elaborate organization, state control, or professional staff" (p. 9). Although volunteerism was the case, the fundamental objectives of the society were class-based. The schools operated for the society only taught poor children and taught them in the least expensive way possible, such as through the Lancasterian system with the use of student "monitors," who supervised large squads of students. The directors of the society "attempted to ensure social order through the socialization of the poor in cheap, mass schooling factories" (Katz, 1975, p. 11).

Critics of this paternalistic model of school organization and governance voiced three major concerns. First, a private entity had taken upon itself a public responsibility essential to the democratic republic without affording the general public any voice in its operations. It was, in a word, undemocratic. Second, the system of schools set up by the society in New York was really not a voluntary system. The society assumed governmental powers it did not have in requiring children and parents to attend the society's schools. And third, the standardization of the educational system did not reflect adequate sensitivity to a wide variety of needs and desires of the clientele. The driving values of paternalistic voluntarism, as depicted in the case of the New York Public School Society, were efficiency and social control of segments of the impoverished population deemed to be a potential threat to the established social order.

Democratic Localism.   A second model, functioning as an optional governance model to paternalistic voluntarism, was democratic localism. The basic premise with this system of educational governance was faith in grassroots democracy and the ability of local citizens to govern themselves, including decisions about the education of their children. It did not matter whether the location was urban or rural. Small communities—existing naturally or created artificially, such as dividing a city into wards with each ward functioning as a totally independent school district—operated semi-independently, much like the village structure of Puritan New England in the seventeenth century.

The point was that those closest to the education of children, who would most directly feel the impact of decisions about education, should have the authority to make all educational decisions. The character of education in each democratic community would reflect the desires and values of that community. Orestes Brownson, a staunch advocate of democratic localism and vocal opponent of the common schools movement, maintained that a highly centralized, bureaucratic governance system of education violated a fundamental principle of U.S. political theory. U.S. citizens had the ability to govern themselves and did not need some sort of super school board to tell them what to do. It was through the efforts of Brownson and others of a similar mind that the State Board of Education in Massachusetts was done away with, albeit temporarily. Brownson wrote that schools should be "under the control of a community composed merely of the number of families having children in it" (as quoted in Katz, 1975, p. 17). The community would determine the adequacy of teachers and who was hired, regulate the affairs of the school, and the curriculum would reflect community values.

For those convinced of the rightness of democratic localism, the efficiency argument advanced by advocates of a state board of education held little weight. These democratic localists "subordinated both efficiency and organizational rationality to an emphasis on responsiveness, close public control, and local involvement" (Katz, 1975, p. 17). Proponents of democratic localism feared that centralizing control of education through the creation of state-level departments or boards of education would also result in the restricting of perspectives and worldviews and a commensurate decrease in local control. The natural tendency of a bureaucracy is self-preservation at all costs and the imposition of the one best system. "To the democrats," observed Katz, "the threat of a state educational apparatus was the essential fault in the centralizing viewpoint: the willingness to impose social change and to force attitudes upon the people" (p. 18).

Corporate Voluntarism. A third alternative approach to governance in education, which existed along with paternalistic voluntarism and democratic localism, was corporate voluntarism. Unlike paternalistic voluntarism and democratic localism, the use of corporate voluntarism in governing education was found not in elementary or grammar schools but was primarily used in secondary schools and in institutions of higher education. These secondary schools and institutions of higher education, such as colleges and academies, were established as a single individual organization, entity, or corporate body. In effect, each educational institution was an education business or corporation governed by a board of trustees. These private educational "businesses" supported their efforts through tuition and grant-creating endowments. Katz (1975) also notes how states such as Massachusetts and Pennsylvania actively promoted the formation of these corporate schools with land grants and financial support.

This approach to the provision and governance of secondary and higher education had several advantages for the state. With a modest investment, a source of secondary and higher education was provided to citizens without the attendant headaches and tasks of managing such enterprises. Such an approach was also used in other areas of public interest such as "finance, travel, and manufacturing" (Katz, 1975, pp. 24–25). This type of governance and provision of secondary education still continues today in some states such as Vermont and New Hampshire, where the local school board contracts out to a private high school to provide secondary education. Students can often choose among high schools if their town or village does not operate a public secondary school. Students can even cross the state line separating New Hampshire and Vermont to attend a school of choice under an Interstate Compact passed by Congress in 1968.

Arguments for corporate voluntarism centered around three points. In addition to claims of honest and "enlightened management" that avoided the pitfalls of politics, proponents of corporate voluntarism argued that it provided the means to adapt the content and provision of educational services to local conditions. This governance model also preserved the right of parents to direct the education of their children through the selection of an appropriate school and allowed each school to "conform to all the irregular demands of society, without destroying their individuality" (Edward Hitchcock as quoted in Katz, 1975, p. 27).

In summary, Katz (1975) observes that "corporate voluntarism did seem to combine the virtues of the other two models. Without the stigma of lower class affiliation [paternalistic voluntarism], it offered disinterested, enlightened, and continuous management that kept the operation of education out of the rough and unpredictable field of politics [democratic localism]. At the same time, by placing each institution under a different administrative authority, it retained the limited scope essential to institutional variety, flexibility, and adaptation to local circumstance" (p. 27).

Incipient Bureaucracy.   Despite the advantages offered by these three competing and contemporaneous governance models of education in the nineteenth century, none of them became the dominant governance model for education. The eventual winner was an emerging approach Katz labels as "incipient bureaucracy." The success of incipient bureaucracy as the dominant model of educational governance can be traced to three major factors. First, advocates of the statist, bureaucratic model such as Horace Mann were able to change the definition of "public" from its initial meaning of "anything that benefitted the community as a whole" or the "performance of broad social functions" to state ownership and control (Bailyn, 1960, p. 133; Katz, 1975, p. 23).

The modified meaning was a narrower and more self-serving definition of anything that was "established by the public—supported chiefly or entirely by the public, controlled by the public, and accessible to the public upon terms of equality, without special charge for tuition" (George Boutwell as quoted in Katz, 1975, pp. 27–28). In other words, public became equated with the state not only in funding education, but owning, controlling, and managing it as a virtual monopoly. Public education was transformed into education specifically sponsored by the state, controlled by the state, and funded by the state. Everything else, regardless of its contributions to the general welfare of society, was deemed "private" education. With this change in the meaning of public, the governance models of paternalistic and corporate voluntarism would only work in the private education sector and thus were summarily eliminated by definition as viable governance approaches for education in the public sector.

Second, the remaining competitor, democratic localism, was attacked for two major deficiencies. In a bit of Orwellian doublespeak, advocates of the incipient bureaucracy model, such as Horace Mann and Henry Bernard, argued that schools governed at the local level through democratic means were not really democratic. The reason was the tyranny of the majority. Only 51 percent of the voters could determine the structure and curricular content of the local school, to the potential detriment and dismay of the other 49 percent. Schools would become political battlegrounds where parents fought over differing points of view regarding religion, politics, and worldviews.

The other major critique of democratic localism was the issue of efficiency and the ability of common schools to perform their most important task of socializing the poor and the culturally and religiously unwashed into respectable citizens. The structure of democratic localism with numerous small communities, each making its own decisions about the nature of education, worked against any systematic attempt by the educational activists to reform U.S. society. Also, democratic localism did not respond efficiently to urban needs, where enlarging the span of control would avoid duplication of resources and services. "What other business of society," asked Henry Bernard, "could escape utter wreck, if conducted with such want of system—with such constant disregard of the fundamental principal of the division of labor?" (quoted in Katz, 1975, p. 33).

Mann and Bernard saw education as the savior of society, particularly an education system with "fully developed plans for systems of schools and elaborate architecture, curricula, and pedagogy. . . . Their goal was to uplift the quality of public education by standardizing and systematizing its structure and content" (Katz, 1975, p. 33). This developing educational system had one principal feature: the centralization of control by the state. Local communities, philanthropic organizations, and business could not be trusted with the key task of socializing the young into their proper roles. Only the power of the state could do this, assisted by an emerging class of education professionals whose expertise was needed to supervise and implement this new system.

Bureaucracies, by their very nature, require a division of labor and specialization. Mann and Bernard saw bureaucracy as a neutral arbiter of competing visions of the good life and the only mechanism that could efficiently raise education and schools above the fray of petty politics and properly socialize the young. Katz (1975) points out the great irony of it all.

> Schoolmen who thought they were promoting a neutral and classless—indeed, a *common*—school education remained unwilling to perceive the extent of cultural bias inherent and not incidental to the standardization and administrative rationalization of public education. . . . Cultural homogenization played counterpoint to administrative rationality. Bureaucracy was intended to standardize far more than the conduct of public life. (p. 39; see also Glenn, 1988)

Modern School to the Present (1910–present)

The incipient bureaucracy model of governance in education continued to grow throughout the remainder of the nineteenth century. The social reforms of the Progressive Era of the first three decades of the twentieth century only accelerated and entrenched this model of educational governance as public education blossomed into a large, expansive, and centrally controlled government organization. The foundation of the modern public school system of today was laid during the Progressive Era. The process of centralization continued from the Progressive Era as schools and school districts underwent massive consolidation, thus reducing local control even more. Compulsory education was instituted, certification was required of principals and teachers, and curriculum became mandated. Indeed, the modern school system was a far cry from even the reforms of the common school movement. U.S. public education had indeed become the "one best system" (Tyack, 1974).

As a backlash to the high degree of centralization and the mounting problems of schools unable to provide a quality education to children, movements to decentralize public education have been advocated. Among the most popular alternatives are organizational changes such as site-based management, charter schools, and the school choice movement. Policy changes included block grants directly to districts or individual schools.

Theoretical Foundations of Governance

Amy Gutmann and Michael Katz provide two useful frameworks for approaching and understanding the issues of governance in education, introducing the dilemmas and potential solutions. Gutmann's *Democratic Education* (1999) is theoretical and more philosophical in orientation, while Katz's *Class, Bureaucracy, and Schools* (1975) treats educational governance from a more structural standpoint.

In *Democratic Education,* Gutmann selects the normative theories of political philosophers—Plato, John Locke, and John Stuart Mill—to construct and critique three perspectives about the governance of education and who should have the ultimate authority in deciding what constitutes good education. She labels these three theoretical perspectives as the family state, the state of families, and the state of individuals.

Family State

In the family state, the state has total and absolute control over education, including educational content, its distribution, and means of distribution, with neither local control nor parental input. Shared decisionmaking outside the state apparatus is anathema and dangerous to social harmony and order. "The defining feature of the family state," asserts Gutmann (1999), "is that it claims exclusive educational authority as a means of establishing a harmony . . . between the individual and social good based on knowledge" (p. 23).

The assumption behind the family state perspective of educational governance is that only the state has the correct conception of what constitutes the good and moral life. Therefore, only the state has the knowledge and competence to socialize the young in this conception of the good and just society. The state takes on the role of the wise parent, albeit an artificial parent but, nonetheless, the entity possessing the wisdom and insight to direct children in their proper development as citizens and to learn the appropriate social roles, which are essential for their personal development and fulfillment. For Gutmann, the Platonic family state rejects both the sophistical relativism of the state of individuals and the collective opinions of educational authorities.

However, Gutmann's criticism of the family state perspective rests on two major points. First, is it even possible for anyone to discover the objective vision of the good life and the good and just society and construct an educational system commensurate with such a universal vision? It is precisely because of this nearly insurmountable difficulty that confusion and sharply divided opinions characterize much of the debate about what should be the nature of education. As Socrates noted some 2,500 years ago:

> At present opinion is divided about the subjects of education. All do not take the same view about what should be learned by the young, either with a view to plain goodness or with a view to the best life possible . . . Goodness itself, to begin with, has not the same meaning for all the different people who honour it . . . it is hardly suprising there should also be difference about the right methods of practising goodness. (Barker, 1981, pp. 333–334)

The second major criticism of the family state as represented in Plato's work, *The Republic,* is what is to be done with the older citizens who have been raised with entirely different notions of the good life and what should constitute a good education? Being too old to change or want to change, what will be done with the adults in society? Does the new philosopher king have the right simply to impose this newly found objective vision on everyone? Doesn't the right of adults and their claims to a competing and alternative worldview count for anything? Gutmann (1999) claims that while the philosopher kings and queens "may claim to have discovered what is good for our children . . . she [or state authorities] may not claim the right to impose that good on them without taking our good, both as parents and as citizens, into account" (p. 27). Therefore, concludes Gutmann, "as long as we differ not just in our opinions but in our moral convictions about the good life, the state's educational role cannot be defined as the realizing of *the* good life, objectively defined, for each of its citizens." Parents and citizens have a right "to share in social reproduction" of children and society at large (p. 28).

State of Families

Gutmann then turns her attention to the state of families, as represented by the writings of John Locke. In the state of the families, the locus of control in education is vested in the parents. Parents are in the best position to know the needs of their children and how these needs can best be met. In addition, parents have a vested interest in the success of their children and can be counted on more than anyone else or any other social agency to provide for the essential needs of children. With parents in total control of the education of their children, the family's values and way of life can be inculcated in the children. Gutmann challenges these assertions of the state of families and contends that children are not simply extensions of parents and members of families, but they are also members of society. Therefore, society also has a vested interest in the education of children. As no individual or organization is infallible, parents cannot always be counted on to provide their children with an adequate education, especially one, argues Gutmann, that will "equip their children with the intellectual skills necessary for deliberation" (p. 29).

Parents may shield their children from competing viewpoints, worldviews, and values that contradict parents' value systems and perspectives, or even teach their children falsehoods or perspectives that would cause harm to other individuals or to society. These perspectives could include bigotry, prejudice, and intolerance. Even aside from the ideological issues is the specter of child abuse. Furthermore, children have the right to self-determination, to decide for themselves what values and worldviews they want to embrace. Without exposure to viewpoints other than those held by their parents, children are denied the right to choose for themselves; society is put at risk with the potential of dealing with adults who were taught as children to embrace notions that work against social harmony, mutual respect, tolerance for differences and diversity, and the rights of others.

Society has a right to have some say about the education of children. Children are not "mere creatures" of parents nor are they "mere creatures" of the state (*Moore v. East Cleveland*, 431 U.S. 494, 499 [1977]; Randall, 1994; *Pierce v. Society of Sisters*, 268 U.S. 510 [1925]). As Gutmann puts it, "children are no more the property of their parents than they are the property of the state" (p. 33). Both parents and the state have rights to be involved in the decisionmaking process about the education of children.

State of Individuals

The third common and competing position for the control and governance of schools as presented by Gutmann is the state of individuals. The major weakness of the family state and the state of families is that some agency or group external to the individual is making decisions about the education of the individual and with this involvement comes the potential for bias and ignorance. In addition, these two approaches to governance ignore the agency of the individual and the right that each person has to self-determination and fulfillment. Thus, the state of individuals proposes to solve this fatal weakness by "championing the dual goals of *opportunity* for choice and *neutrality* among conceptions of the good life" (Gutmann, 1999, p. 34). Every child must have the opportunity to choose, without external constraints, his or her own notion of the good life. The role of the state and families in the state of individuals is to facilitate the ability of students for rational thinking and discourse and of taking a neutral stance with regard to worldviews and value systems.

In sum, the duty of educational authorities, whether parents or educational bureaucracies, is to maximize the liberty and freedom of individuals to create themselves. Gutmann points out the failings of the state of individuals—or the liberal state—by first attacking the notion of neutrality. Neutrality is an impossible position to assume, both in practical terms and theoretically. A neutral position is itself a position of choice, a choice loaded with its own set of values and predispositions. The final aims of education in the state of individuals—that of maximizing individual freedom, liberty, and rationality—are not neutral and are values in and of themselves.

In addition, allowing children to choose their own notion of the good life from a social smorgasbord of worldviews connotes a specific worldview grounded in relativism and that any worldview is just as good and valuable as another as long as it is freely chosen by the child. It is not difficult to see that such an approach could result in particularistic notions of the good life that pose a real threat to the lives of other individuals and the survival of society. Although some liberals would respond that such potential dangers can be avoided by the paternalistic oversight of adults, families, and social institutions, this caveat does not solve the problem for the obvious need of some minimum civic virtue or values to also be taught to children.

None of these three absolutist positions—the family state, the state of families, and the state of individuals—for centering educational authority has solved the basic problem of how we justify any particular type of education, which by its very nature is value laden. Education is and can never be value free and neutral. Its intrinsically nonneutral nature begs the question of whose values and standards will be used to determine the specific content and access to education (Randall, 1994). "We are left with the problem," states Gutmann (1999), "of finding another standard that can justify a necessarily nonneutral education in the face of social disagreement concerning what constitutes the proper aim of education. . . . None of these standards is sufficiently inclusive to solve the problem of justification in the face of dissent by citizens whose conception of the good life and the good society threatens to be undermined by the conception of a good (but necessarily nonneutral) education instituted by some (necessarily exclusive) educational authority" (p. 38).

Although Gutmann acknowledges that each of the three arguments or positions for allocating educational governance has some merit, none is, on its own, sufficiently adequate to solve the thorny problem of who should control education. The state—which includes professional educators, parents, and children—has a right to have some say in the nature and disposition of education, but no one group can ethically justify having exclusive and total control over education. If this is the case, that all three are necessary but insufficient alone in governing education, what principles and governance configurations can be constructed that take the positive contributions of each position and also make up for the deficiency of each perspective?

Democratic State of Education

Gutmann's proposed solution, a fourth alternative, is grounded in her version of a democratic theory of education, which she refers to as the "democratic state of education." The solution is built on two fundamental premises: "all citizens must be educated so as to have a chance to share in self-consciously shaping the structure of their society" and decisions about education are arrived through a shared governance approach involving government officials, parents, and students (1999, p. 46). Not only does this proposed arrangement acknowledge and respect the right of the three major stakeholder groups to have a voice in educational matters, but the very process itself reflects democratic ideals and strengthens our democratic society. This pluralist or shared decisionmaking model allocates authority across society and also requires that education enable individuals to participate effectively in the ensuing democratic dialogue and governance of schools.

Gutmann asserts that "the broad distribution of educational authority among citizens, parents, and professional educators, supports the core value of democracy: conscious social reproductions in its most inclusive form. . . . A democratic state is therefore committed to allocating educational authority in such a way as to provide its members with an education adequate to participating in democratic politics, to choosing among (a limited range of) good lives, and to sharing in the several subcommunities, such as families, that impart identity to the lives of its citizens" (1999, p. 42).

The democratic state requires a contraction of the absolute autonomy of the family state, the state of families, and the state of individuals, a sharing of political power, and a mandate to prepare all citizens in the democratic state to participate in the shared governance scheme. This sharing of educational authority and power works to preserve the democratic society by installing "firewalls" against the abuse of power, which could harm others, both individuals and society as a whole. The conscious cultivation of rational thinking and "critical deliberation" in children gives them the ability to avoid indoctrination, prejudice, bigotry, and "noncritical consciousness," and the ability to add their voice to educational deliberations and debates (p. 44).

Dimensional Foundations of Governance

There are five dimensions of governance in education: structural, functional, sectoral, contextual, and procedural. The structural nature of educational governance is found in the three levels of political government—the federal, state, and local levels. Within each of these structural levels of governance is a functional dimension, represented by the executive, legislative, and judicial branches of government. Cutting across all three structural levels and functional domains is a sectoral dimension, such as public versus private, profit versus non-profit entities, and schools versus parents and children. The fundamental governance issue in the sectoral dimension is determining the proper role of government in private organizations and the lives of individuals. In addition, the entire governance system is influenced by contextual environments of values, beliefs, and needs. The contextual environments are comprised of a very complex amalgamation of individual worldviews and belief systems about the nature of the good society, the substance of the good life, and what role the state should play, if any, in the realization of these individual and societal goals.

Finally, a procedural dimension permeates all other dimensions of governance. It is the ubiquitous issue of a centralized versus decentralized decision-making process, deciding to what degree authority should be centralized or dispersed, determining the amount of centralized versus shared governance of education. Since the beginning of the twentieth century, U.S. education has usually been characterized by a fairly rigid bureaucratic organizational structure with a rule-driven decisionmaking process. The constitutional right of private schools and home schools to exist alongside government schools works to attenuate the governance scheme of U.S. education by forcing the state to relinquish substantial authority over these private educational endeavors, as does the privatization of educational services (Randall, 1994). In addition, the creation of charter schools, a sort of hybrid between a government school and a private school, and various forms of site-based management of individual schools serve to disperse educational authority and move toward a more diffused scheme of educational governance.

Federalism

The American political system and governance structure can be best summarized by the concept of federalism with specific powers enumerated between the federal and state levels of government, and a system of checks and balances among the three branches of government at both levels. The federal constitution spells out the powers granted to the federal government. Outside of these constitutional parameters, the federal government cannot act and any and all remaining powers not specifically granted to the federal government nor prohibited by the federal government are reserved to the individual states through the Tenth Amendment of the U.S. Constitution.

Federal Level.   Education is not mentioned in the federal constitution in terms as a responsibility of the federal government. Thus, education is reserved through the Reserved Powers Clause of the Tenth Amendment for each individual state to oversee. However, all three branches of the federal government are involved in education and in some instances have dramatically affected the nature of education. For example, the federal judiciary, through the U.S. District Courts, the U.S. Circuit Court of Appeals, or the U.S. Supreme Court, reviews disputes regarding the infringement of fundamental rights protected by the federal constitution and subsequent amendments. The First Amendment with the Establishment and Free Exercise Clauses prescribes the proper role of religion in public schools and the rights for freedom of speech, press, and assembly. The Fourth Amendment protects students and staff from unreasonable searches and seizures. The Fourteenth Amendment requires that students and staff be afforded due process in actions taken against them, ensuring that the process, for example, of suspension from school or dismissal from employment is fair. The Equal Protection Clause prohibits students and staff from being classified in unreasonable ways such as by gender or race. It was the application of the Fourteenth Amendment that declared the segregation of African-American students from white students in separate but equal school facilities as unconstitutional (*Brown v. Board of Education,* 1954). The specific effect of the judicial branch of the federal government is found in decisions of the federal courts that require schools and school systems to protect the fundamental constitutional rights of students and staff.

As the legislative branch of the federal government, Congress passes federal statutes that shape U.S. education. Congress often justifies such legislation from the General Welfare Clause found in the preamble of the U.S. Constitution. These federal laws usually create compensatory programs that allow federal money to flow to state school systems to help disadvantaged students or to promote national policy. Examples of federal statues include the National Defense Education Act (NDEA) of 1958, the Elementary and Secondary Education Act (ESEA) of 1965, and the Individuals with Disabilities Act (IDEA) of 1992. To ensure proper implementation of these federal laws and programs, the executive branch of the federal government, through the U.S. Department of Education, sets forth administrative regulations and guidelines and monitors compliance. In addition, the Department of Education collects statistics on education and funds research.

State Level. A system of education, often referred to as a public school system, is authorized in the constitution of each state. The public school system is part of a state's governmental structure. It receives its funding and decisionmaking authority from the state government. The state constitution, statutes, and administrative regulations and rules specify the domain of responsibilities and purview of this state school system. All of the states except Hawaii have elected to subdivide the state school system into small organizational units called school districts.

Educational governance at the state level mirrors the basic structure at the federal level. The state legislature passes laws that define the structure and configuration of the state school system, authorizes various state government entities, such as a state and local boards of education, to perform certain educational tasks and functions, determines the annual allocation of state funds to districts, and often establishes special programs in education to address state policy goals or provide additional assistance to districts in problem areas in education such as at risk students.

The executive branch, through the formation of a state office of education and a state board of education, implements the educational program defined by the state legislature. State superintendents of instruction and members of the state school board are usually selected by election or through appointment by the governor's office. The judicial branch at the state level, through local municipal courts, state district courts, or state supreme courts, adjudicates questions and disputes over the application of state law to education within a particular state.

Local Level. At the local level, the governance structure somewhat resembles the same overall structure found at the federal and state level, but the system of checks and balances is diminished. The local school board, whose members are usually elected by citizens in the district, assumes both legislative and executive powers. Board members establish policy, set direction, make judgments, and hire administrators to carry out the board's directives. Superintendents and school principals are employees of the school board and do not form an executive branch with separate powers. However, boards of education must follow municipal and county laws as well as state and federal laws and regulations pertaining to education. Table 6.1 illustrates the levels and functions of educational governance in American education.

TABLE 6.1 *Governance in American Education*

Level	Legislative	Executive	Judicial
Federal	Congress	U.S. Department of Education	District, circuit, and U.S. Supreme Court
State	Legislature	State board of education	District and state supreme court
Local	School board	School board with district office and school site staff	Local, county, and municipal courts

Viewing Educational Governance through Different Policy Lenses

Normative Dimension

At the heart of educational governance are beliefs and ideologies about the power to make decisions regarding the nature of education and, by association, the kind of human beings and society that are desired (Begley, 1999; Randall, 1997). Implicit in these beliefs and ideologies about political philosophy and governance are notions about the nature of human beings and their capacity for self-governance and rationality. If human nature is seen as fundamentally flawed, degraded, and inherently evil, then good arguments can be made for constriction of personal choice and the need for social structures and organizations to impose external controls for proper behavior.

If the perspective of human nature is that of rational human beings with moral agency, who are equal and capable of self-governance, then the arguments for highly controlled and centralized decisionmaking become more difficult. Governance thus touches on fundamental questions of individual freedom and liberty and the extent to which external controls and restrictions should be placed on individuals and organizations (Bull, 2000). To what degree should individuals and organizations have a voice in decisions that profoundly affect their lives? Do principals, teachers, students, and parents have a right to share in the governance of schools and school systems? If so, is this right of equal magnitude for all these significant stakeholders?

These difficult questions need careful thought and analysis. In the end, the answers will not come through research or data alone. The personal beliefs and values of those making the analysis and the final decision will drive the answers. The reason education is such a cultural flashpoint is that these fundamental but challenging questions come quickly to the fore. Education is an inherently political and value-laden enterprise with much at stake. Governance is not only about administrative efficiency; it is about who will get to decide the content of education and who gets access to this content. Governance is about life and deciding what kind of human beings society should create and what kinds of society and social institutions are desirable. All of these are normative issues and questions. Governance, the sharing or lack of sharing power to make these kinds of decisions, which are so central to who we are as persons and the nature of the good society in which we live, plays a profound role in these questions and their answers. Governance is more than nearly anything else a normative enterprise (English, 1994).

Structural Dimension

The governance system of U.S. education is multi-layered, multi-faceted, and just plain messy (Owens, 2001). Part of the explanation for this rather complex governance structure is due to the nature of the U.S. form of government with its three branches and multiple levels. In addition, democracies and representative forms of government are not noted for their efficiency, nor for their timeliness in making decisions. The original rationale behind the U.S. form of government was to disperse power and decisionmaking authority; thus the three levels with three major functions serve to counterbalance each other. With the creation of state or government school systems, the governance structure of the public school system reflects the contextual structure of the larger political and governmental organization.

This feature makes the governance of public education a difficult and challenging enterprise with many people in various positions at different levels having some portion of responsibility or control over education. In addition, the very structure of U.S. education allows a variety of competing special interest groups to exercise some influence over educational decisions. At the same time, however, the bureaucratic organizational structure works against the meddling of outside influences. Paradoxically, educational governance in the United States is both highly centralized and highly decentralized (Weick, 1976).

Some of the educational reforms of the past twenty years have called for a more decentralized approach in educational governance (Danzberger, Kirst, & Usdan, 1992). The fundamental idea is that those who are closest to the problems know what the best solutions are and, therefore, should be granted greater autonomy in solving these context-specific problems. Instead of a top-down approach, where problem identification and resolution is mandated from above, those most affected and directly involved are invited to participate in educational problem solving (Bryk, Sebring, Kerbow, Rollow, & Easton, 1998).

These more participatory approaches in educational governance involve a sharing of the power to make decisions, as represented by such innovations as site-based decisionmaking, teacher empowerment, and parent councils that have either advisory or decisionmaking authority (Heck, Brandon, & Wang, 2001;

Malen, 1999; Malen & Ogawa, 1988). For example, local parent councils in Chicago schools were given the power to hire and fire principals (Hess, 1999). Other partnerships between parents and local school officials work collaboratively on textbook decisions, school discipline policies, finding additional funding, and extracurricular activities.

A major step toward decentralized governance is the creation of charter schools (Nathan, 1995; U.S. Department of Education, 2000). Charter schools represent a new alternative educational choice within the public school sector (see Chapter 11 for a detailed policy analysis of charter schools). These new schools receive public funding and are public agencies. Although charter schools are public schools, they are public schools of a very different character. They may be sponsored by public or private entities but governed and operated by private individuals or organizations. In one sense, they represent a hybrid between a public and private school. In exchange for autonomy from many local and state regulations, charter schools are held accountable for results. The assumption is that greater autonomy in deciding the means and context of education will result in better student outcomes. Thus autonomy and accountability form the conceptual foundation for the charter school movement. Failure to provide satisfactory outcomes will violate the charter of the school and cause parents to withdraw their children from the school. The charter school will then have to close its doors.

The next step toward a decentralized governance system in education is found in private schools, which educate nearly 12 percent of all K–12 children in the United States. The ultimate decentralized governance approach is found in homeschooling, where a parent directs and provides for the education of their children at home.

Constituentive Dimension

Many players participate directly or indirectly in the governance of education (Beadie, 2000). Legislators pass laws. Justices adjudicate the constitutionality of such and their application to specific educational situations. Administrators implement legislative mandates through programs, rules, and regulations. Elected officials, such as those who serve on school boards, wrestle with local policy issues and work with superintendents, district office staff, school principals, teachers, and a host of support personnel to provide educational services. Professional associations and unions for teachers, classified staff, administrators, and schools all jockey for position in the debate over education. At stake for them are positions of power, compensation, employment, working conditions, and retirement and benefits.

The business community looks for schools to provide a trained workforce at the lowest possible cost. There is the private sector with its wide array and variety of private schools, homeschools, and providers of supplementary or remedial education. A host of other special interest groups, often with competing agendas, seek to influence what is taught or not taught in schools and to increase or decrease educational expenditures. Society as a whole expects education to solve all of its social ills and problems.

And last but not least are the students and their parents, the consumers of whatever educational services are finally determined should be delivered. Although students and parents are the targeted recipients of educational systems, they often have the least voice or input in the nature of education. Their power base is much smaller as compared to well-organized and well-financed special interest groups. Only when parents join forces and create advocacy coalitions are they able to exert a significant effect on policy.

Technical Dimension

One of the major debates in U.S. education centers around which type of governance structure or approach can provide the best educational experience for children. The discussion usually centers on notions of efficiency and choice. Centralized governance systems, which are often highly bureaucratic in nature, are criticized for being inflexible to local needs, a one-size-fits-all for solutions, wasted resources on administrative overhead, and nonresponsiveness to local concerns.

Within the public sector, the technical dimension of governance consists of three primary factors: size, choice, and shared governance. A substantial body of research literature deals with the issue of the size of the education organization or its sub-units (Fowler & Walberg, 1991; Howley, 1996; Lee, Smerdon, Alfeld-Liro, & Brown, 2000). If we consider the classroom teacher as playing some sort of governing role in the teaching and learning experience, then the size of the class could affect how the teacher interacts with students and what form or approach of classroom management is employed. In terms of school size, a significant body of literature suggests that school size not only affects student achievement but staff morale and incidents of misbehavior and violence. Some literature suggests an optimal range for the size of elementary, middle or junior high schools, and high schools. As schools exceed the upper range of size, there appears to be higher numbers of discipline problems, lower achievement (especially for minority groups), and a feeling of student alienation from the school.

Perhaps part of the problem occurs because as organizations become larger, the basis of governance shifts from that of personal relationships and contact to an impersonal bureaucracy that is rule-driven and ill-equipped to take extenuating circumstances into consideration as decisions are made. There is less opportunity for participation of all relevant stakeholders in the key decisions. The same criticisms have been leveled at large districts whose size and bureaucratic structure, it is claimed, have made them fairly insular to the needs of students and parents.

The second technical factor affecting governance is the choice of students in determining the curricular emphasis they want to pursue or the school or district they wish to attend (Morken & Formicola, 1999). In some areas and districts of the country, little discretion is afforded to students and parents to decide the nature of their educational experience. Although some latitude is given within a school to pursue various curricular strands, it is often difficult to choose to attend another public school within the same district or a school outside of one's own district. Even in the rare cases where interdistrict choice is available, usually a substantial tuition surcharge is imposed. If a parent and student want to enroll in private education, the choice is allowed but the entire costs of such a choice, plus the continued payment of taxes to support the public schools, must be borne by the parents. While it may appear that certain educational decisions are being delegated and left up to parents, the ability to actually do what one would like to do is determined by the economic status of the family. The rich are able to exercise many more educational options and have a far greater level of participation in the governance of education than poor families (Coons & Sugarman, 1999; Cooper & Randall, 2001).

The third technical dimension is shared governance. Each level of governance of education has the latitude to decide the degree to which power and decisionmaking will be centralized or decentralized and who will be left out or included in decisions about education. At the federal level, the U.S. Department of Education can choose to attach detailed and burdensome regulations to various federal educational programs or allow more latitude at the state, district, or school site level. One indirect way of doing this is to give block grants to state and local educational entities that offer wide discretion to the recipients in how the funds are to be used rather than using many categorical programs where funds must be spent only for very specific purposes and targeted audiences.

This also holds true at the state level as the state department of education interacts with local school districts and schools. The state office of education could elect to give large amounts of discretionary decisionmaking to districts and schools through block grants or minimal rules and regulations, or the office could fund state programs categorically and with detailed rules regarding the expenditure of the funds. At the local level, superintendents and district office staff can centralize decisionmaking or delegate a substantial amount to school principals and teachers.

In addition, some variation of site-based management or governance could be put in place where many of the decisions about the operation of the school are made by a school council composed of the principal, teachers, staff, and community members. The exact composition of such site-based councils and the types of decisions they would be allowed to address would determine the degree of collaborative decisionmaking. Such shared governance systems appear to promote better communication, buy-in from stakeholder groups, and contribute to successful schools (Wagstaff & Fusarelli, 1999). Thus technical matters of organizational size influence educational governance, structures, and processes for making decisions, and defining the scope of shared governance.

Conclusion

Systems of and approaches to educational governance will always remain topics of controversy and contention for two basic reasons. First, too much is at stake with educational decisions in terms of individual development, socialization, and societal norms. Second, the nature of education in both its content and access is inherently political and permeated with fundamental values.

The major decision in governance centers on the centralization versus the decentralization of power and decisionmaking in education. Who gets to make what kinds of decisions is at the core of educational governance. A collateral issue is who loses and who gains in the various approaches to educational governance, issues explored by scholars using interpretivist lenses of policymaking. Whose personal beliefs and values are raised to become public beliefs and values, which all are asked or forced to accept, is what makes debate of governance so contentious.

Gutmann (1987) contends that the nature of our democratic society requires more of a participatory approach to educational decisions. The voices of various stakeholders need to be heard and carefully considered. Unilateral and authoritarian decisionmaking is antithetical to U.S. culture and education. Katz reminds us that the current as well as past governance structures and approaches in education have historical and social roots. The U.S. educational system was not foreordained, nor was it required by its nature to assume the current governance structure and philosophy. History informs us that there are a number of different and effective ways in which U.S. education can be governed and that the status quo of governing and operating the United States's schools can and should be examined.

Assignments and Activities _____

Field Investigation #1

Compare and contrast the governance structures and decisionmaking processes of two school districts. In what ways are they different and in what ways are they similar? Are these differences important for student learning and achievement?

Field Investigation #2

Compare and contrast how decisions are made in a traditional school and a school with site-based management or some other form of shared governance. In what ways are they similar and different? Are these differences of any importance? Do they matter in any substantive way? How is student achievement affected by the governance structure, if at all?

Seminal Works _____

As this chapter suggests, Amy Gutmann's (1987) *Democratic Education* and Michael Katz's (1975) *Class, Bureaucracy, and Schools* are classic studies of educational governance, the former from the perspective of participatory democratic theory, the latter a Marxist interpretation of educational governance and change. Diane Ravitch's (1983) *The Troubled Crusade* is an interesting exploration of the major forces (both internal and external) that influenced education from 1945 to 1980. Perhaps the best history of U.S. education is David Tyack's (1974) classic, *The One Best System*, which traces the political battles to control U.S. education from the founding of the common schools movement through 1940, with particular emphasis on urban education governance and reform.

References _____

Bailyn, B. (1960). *Education in the forming of American society.* New York: Norton.

Barker, E. B. (1981). *The politics of Aristotle* (ed. and trans. by Barker). New York: Oxford University Press.

Beadie, N. (2000). The limits of standardization and the importance of constituencies: Historical tensions in the relationship between state authority and local control. In N. D. Theobald & B. Malen (Eds.), *Balancing local control and state responsibility for K–12 education* (pp. 47–91). Larchmont, NY: Eye on Education.

Begley, P. T. (1999). *Values and educational leadership.* Albany: State University of New York Press.

Brown v. *Board of Education of Topeka,* 1954, 347 U.S. 483, 74 S.Ct. 686.

Bryk, A. S., Sebring, P. B., Kerbow, D., Rollow, S., & Easton, J. Q. (1998). *Charting Chicago school reform: Democratic localism as a lever for change.* Boulder, CO: Westview Press.

Bull, B. (2000). Political philosophy and the balance between central and local control of schools. In N. D. Theobald & B. Malen (Eds.), *Balancing local control and state responsibility for K–12 education* (pp. 21–46). Larchmont, NY: Eye on Education.

Butts, R. F., & Cremin, L. A. (1953). *A history of education in American culture.* New York: Henry Holt.

Coons, J. E., & Sugarman, S. D. (1999). *Education by choice: The case for family control.* Troy, NY: Educator's International Press.

Cooper, B. S., & Randall, E. V. (2001). Vouchers: Still (largely) untested and why. In H. D. Meyer & W. L. Boyd (Eds.), *Education between states, markets, and civil society: Comparative perspectives* (pp. 137–159). Mahwah, NJ: Lawrence Erlbaum.

Cremin, L. (1951). *The American common school: An historic conception.* New York: Columbia University Press.

Cremin, L. A. (1970). *American education: The colonial experience 1607–1783.* New York: Harper & Row.

Danzberger, J. P., Kirst, M. W., & Usdan, M. D. (1992). *Governing public schools: New times new requirements.* Washington, DC: The Institute for Educational Leadership.

English, F. W. (1994). *Theory in educational administration.* New York: Harper-Collins.

Fowler, W. J., Jr., & Walberg, H. J. (1991). School size, characteristics and outcomes. *Educational Evaluation and Policy Analysis, 13,* 189–202.

Glenn, C. L., Jr. (1988). *The myth of the common school.* Amherst: The University of Massachusetts Press.

Gutmann, A. (1987). *Democratic education.* Princeton: Princeton University Press.

Heck, R. H., Brandon, P. R., & Wang, J. (2001). Implementing site-managed educational changes: Examining levels of implementation and effect. *Educational Policy, 15*(2), 302–322.

Hess, G. A., Jr. (1999). Understanding achievement (and other) changes under Chicago school reform. *Educational Evaluation and Policy Analysis, 21*(1), 67–83.

Hiner, N. R. (1973, Spring). The cry of Sodom enquired into: Educational analysis in seventeenth-century New England. *History of Education Quarterly, 13,* 3–22.

Howley, C. (1996). Compounding disadvantage: The effects of school and district size on student achievement in West Virginia. *Journal of Research in Rural Education, 12*(1), 25–32.

Jernegan, M. W. (1919, May). The educational development of the southern colonies. *The Southern Review, 27,* 360–376.

Jorgenson, L. P. (1987). *The state and the non-public school, 1825–1925.* Columbia: University of Missouri Press.

Katz, M. B. (1975). *Class, bureaucracy, and schools: The illusion of educational change in America.* New York: Praeger.

Katznelson, I. (1982). *City trenches.* Chicago: University of Chicago Press.

Lasswell, H. D. (1950). *Politics: Who gets what, when, how.* New York: P. Smith.

Lee, V. E., Smerdon, B. A., Alfeld-Liro, C., & Brown, S. L. (2000). Inside large and small high schools: Curriculum and social relations. *Educational Evaluation and Policy Analysis, 22*(2), 147–171.

Malen, B. (1999). The promises and perils of participation on site-based councils. *Theory into Practice, 38*(4), 209–216.

Malen, B., & Ogawa, R. T. (1988). Professional-patron influence on site-based governance councils: A confounding case study. *Educational Evaluation and Policy Analysis, 10,* 251–270.

Morken, H., & Formicola, J. R. (1999). *The politics of school choice.* Lanham, MD: Rowman & Littlefield.

Nathan, J. (1995). *Charter public schools: A brief history and preliminary lessons.* Minneapolis: University of Minnesota, Center for School Change, Humphrey Institute of Public Affairs.

O'Hair, M. J., McLaughlin, H. J., & Reitzug, U. C. (2000). *Foundations of democratic education.* Belmont, CA: Wadsworth/Thomson Learning.

Owens, R. C. (2001). *Organizational behavior in education* (7th ed.). Boston: Allyn & Bacon.

Randall, E. V. (1994). *Private schools and public power: A case for pluralism.* New York: Teachers College Press.

Randall, E. V. (1997). Culture, religion and education. In T. C. Hunt & J. C. Carper (Eds.), *Religion and schooling in contemporary America* (pp. 59–81). New York: Garland.

Ravitch, D. (1983). *The troubled crusade: American education, 1945–1980.* New York: Basic Books.

Sergiovanni, T. J., Burlingame, M., Coombs, F. S., & Thurston, P. W. (1999). *Educational governance and administration* (4th ed.). Boston: Allyn & Bacon.

Spring, J. (1994). *The American school 1642–1993* (3rd ed.). New York: McGraw-Hill.

Tyack, D. B. (1974). *The one best system—A history of American urban education.* Cambridge, MA: Harvard University Press.

U.S. Department of Education. (2000, January). *The state of charter schools: Fourth year report.* Executive summary [On-line]. Available: www.ed.gov/pubs/charter4thyear/es.html

Wagstaff, L. H., & Fusarelli, L. D. (1999). Establishing collaborative governance and leadership. In P. Reyes, J. D. Scribner, & A. P. Scribner (Eds.), *Lessons from high-performing Hispanic schools* (pp. 19–35). New York: Teachers College Press.

Weick, K. E. (1976). Educational organizations as loosely coupled systems. *Administrative Science Quarterly, 21,* 1–19.

7

Better Policies for Improved Curriculum, Standards, and Testing

Few matters are more important than who makes curriculum decisions for the nation's schools. Students of the curriculum-making process not only study who does but also inquire into the question of who should. . . . One need probe into the question of who makes such decisions only a little to realize that state governors and legislators have a deep interest in what is taught and should be taught in schools. Their desire to be key players has been heightened in recent years by the degree to which our schools are seen to be instrumental in worldwide economic competition. Indeed, many politicians perceive themselves to have a public mandate to intervene in the goals and content of the K–12 curriculum. (Goodlad, 1991, p. 9)

Everyone, as explained by Goodlad above, seems concerned to improve education by creating better staff and programs, tougher standards and curricula, and recently, improved students' test results and graduation rates. Although curriculum policy and improvement are among the most complex areas of study and governance, they are also among the most important if children are to learn and grow. At the very heart of curriculum policy is the delicate balance between local interests and national (even international) and state goals, standards, and national tests—a classic tension between decentralized and centralized control and authority (McNeil, 1988).

Yet curriculum policymakers suffer from inadequate information, less time and resources than are needed, and often fail to discuss policy changes with those being most affected. Wilhoit explains, in his "Foreword" to *Mandating Academic Excellence,* "that policymaking is the art of making wise decisions within a time frame that is shorter than desired, with less information than one needs, and with less resources than one should have. With the advent of school reform, state education policymakers have assumed awesome responsibilities" (Wilson & Rossman, 1993, p. xi).

State, district, and school policymakers continue to take action on the curriculum, often without the benefit of a dialogue about the effects of various policies, trying to change the essential elements of education: standards affecting teaching, learning, curriculum, and outcomes. As such, policymakers confront a complex set of values, constituencies, structures, and practical and technical details in trying to create a concrete set of *curricular standards, programs, and assessments*—the three pillars of the schools' academic program. As Anderson (1997) explains, each change in curriculum and program tends to produce a whole new set of concepts and language, which practitioners learn and use—to sound current and relevant—and with which policy analysts struggle to understand and improve.

And curriculum experts themselves hardly agree about what kind of instruction, texts, and materials to use—and how best to teach. Take simple things, like selecting a textbook. Stodolsky (1999) explains that "too little attention has been given the nature of books in relation to their use" (p. 145). Despite decades of teaching millions of students, we know comparatively little about which policies work best to bring together the students (compulsory education), staff (compulsory certification and periodic relicensing), the classes (required courses and skills), activities and materials, and pedagogy to help students learn.

"Remarkable, the literature on the relationship between method and content is underdeveloped," Thornton (2001, p. 200) opines,

> and, if anything, the focus of methods textbooks is more diffuse than it was in the 1930s. Without a sound basis in methods suitable for children and adolescents, it is hardly surprising that teachers rely on the content and methods they experienced in their college courses and see institutionalized in the schools where they work. Far more attention to the pedagogical demands of subject matter that extends beyond mere simplification of the content and methods taught in college courses is urgently needed. (pp. 200–201)

And Klein (1991) focuses mainly on who makes curriculum decisions, looking at "the array of participants who are officially designated or who function through default to make decisions is complex enough, but the question centers around not only *who* makes them, but also what type of curriculum decision is under discussion" (p. 1).

To a large extent, then, the process of curriculum policymaking involves decisions about just how centralized, top-down, or prescribed the system should be, versus the level of local, ad hoc, and grassroots decisionmaking affecting the curriculum (Schubert, 1991). As Goodlad (1991) discusses, "Many politicians perceive themselves to have a public mandate to intervene in the goals and content of the K–12 curriculum. Most are aware that, in aggressively pursuing national or state interests in the quality of schooling and particularly in what is taught, they [politicians] ultimately will bump up against both the rhetoric and the substance of local interests and control" (p. 9; see also Goodlad, 1990).

This chapter explores policies that affect the curriculum, standards, and assessments—the *core technology* of education—commonly called teaching and learning, using the four lenses employed throughout this book: the normative, structural, constituentive, and technical dimensions.

Normative Dimension

Setting the standards, aligning the curriculum, and assessing (testing) the results are three interdependent, highly value-laden policy efforts. In fact, they are so normative and complex that policymakers are often confounded as to where to begin. Should states and districts, not to mention federal agencies, create higher standards first, then back them up with consequences for failure and rewards for success, and let the curriculum and teaching techniques follow?

Or, as is now happening, should states "raise the bar" on the difficulty of criterion-referenced tests, mandate that children take these examinations yearly or periodically, and then let districts and teachers react by focusing their curriculum and making higher demands on their students? In describing attempts to build a humanistic curriculum, for example, Eisner (1999) is a realist when he asserts that ideal curricula come down to earth when assessments begin

> in the real world, however, it is often the evaluation method [the test, folio, or application exercises] that determines which ends students will pay attention to. Students can afford to neglect lofty goal statements, but they cannot afford to neglect the ways in which they will be evaluated. When evaluation procedures reward forms of study that contradict the humanities prize—the ability to make rational judgments, the ability to critique incisively, to see things in context, and the ability to recognize and appreciate nuance—such procedures diminish humanistic learning. (pp. 298–299)

Whatever the curriculum, evidence mounts that the assessments, particularly "high-stakes" testing, can drive the curriculum and set standards, regardless of the values and philosophy of what's being taught and for those doing the teaching.

Recently, too, some states and school districts have "privatized" the standards and curriculum process by outsourcing the heart of the program: the curriculum. Increasingly, districts—particularly those with many at risk students—are buying a pre-set curriculum and instructional package, such as Success for All, Accelerated Schools, Knowledge is Power, or Open Court, and are letting the curriculum writers set the standards, organize the curriculum, and even "script" the pedagogy (e.g., lesson plans, activities, scope and sequence of ideas).

Often, these prepackaged, preprogrammed whole school reforms are attractive because they make claims that prescriptive, highly structured, preprogrammed "packaged" curricula will improve students' chances of passing and excelling on standardized (often high-stakes) assessment tests. New Jersey, for example, requires that the thirty poorest districts (the so-called Abbott Districts, which were affected by the state's finance equity suit, *Abbott v. Burke,* 1991, 1994, 1996) convert all their schools to a "Whole School Reform" model, and that they outsource their curricula to these enterprises.

Whichever step is taken first, the processes of trying to align standards, curriculum, and tests are both critical and difficult because different agencies are involved. And the leap from a general *standard* to a specific *curriculum* (lessons, materials, activities) to a valid and reliable *test* is rarely accomplished without tremendous trial and error. But who should set standards, write curriculum, and design and assign the tests? Who has the legitimate right and role to create, disseminate, and enforce the new curricular policies?

Legitimization

The process of legitimating what should be taught, how, and to what level of competence applies to all subjects and skill areas, and at all levels (national, state, and local), creating one of the least understood and most important areas of education policy analysis. Schoenfeld (2001) explains that this policymaking and policy-legitimating process in curriculum, teaching, and testing is already political and becoming more so:

> In the political arena, "standards" may be evolving from progressive to a conservative force. . . . Many states have instituted stricter testing regimens, threatening to retain students in grade if they fail the tests. . . . These accountability tests tend to focus on the mastery of facts and procedures, because that is what can be tested cheaply and easily. Because the accountability measures are "high stakes", teachers feel compelled to focus on them, with a corresponding de-emphasis on other aspects of learning (reasoning, representation, problem-solving, communication, making connections) that are not tested. (pp. 273–274)

Thus, truly no area in education policymaking is more critical—or more complex—than those policies and programs affecting what students are taught, under what conditions, how they are tested, and to what standard of individual and normative achievement. The curriculum, standards, and testing troika are highly value-oriented, resting on the legitimization by government, courts, administrators, and, most importantly, teachers.

- Who, after all, should set standards (teachers in their classrooms, administrators in their schools or districts, or governments at the state or federal levels)?
- To what levels of learning (absolute scales, value-added, growth or gain score) should students be held?
- And importantly, with what consequences should schools and districts, not to mention teachers be held, for those students who perform at-or-above standard and those who do not (failure, retention, social promotion, mandatory summer school)?

In fact, London (1997) argues that "as far as state [and local] *legitimacy* is concerned, the public school curriculum is perhaps the most controversial area of educational investigation" (p. 64). Kirst and Walker (1971) go so far as to say that the curriculum is not merely the *result* of politics: in fact, "it *is* a political process in important ways" (p. 80).

As Diana Pullin (1999) claims, "The curriculum of the public schools, now and always, has been heavily influenced by the social, cultural, and political forces at work at the time the curriculum is adopted" (p. 18). Fine (1993) describes a struggle among educators, policymakers, and parents over the control of the curriculum, and to what degree the learning and testing of children are to be teacher- or government-controlled.

Because the values and beliefs that underlie school curriculum policies are sometimes vague and often heavily value-laden, policymakers struggle to find a legitimate basis for what they do. London (1997) explains that "the search for minimal consensus and legitimacy by the state constitutes a key factor in the government's attempt both to engage legitimization strategy and to achieve the important goal of curriculum improvement" (p. 64; see also Weiler, 1983, 1990). Legitimacy—the authority and "right" to make and enforce curriculum policy— rests with four very different strategies, which can and are used in various mixes and measures.

Legitimization by Procedure.   First, using a rational planning model, government policymakers can take a step-by-step process through a legislature, a state or local education agency, or the courts. It is the weight of government, wherein each branch of government follows a set procedure, that gives force and reality to the policies.

Legitimization by Expertise.   Policymakers can also use "scientific research" to bolster their perspective and give weight to proposed programs. Weiler (1985) explains that whatever the outcomes, new curricular policies are given greater legitimacy by the appearance of being scientific experiments, "as long as they confer the dignity and prestige of the scientific enterprise on a given innovation or reform" (p. 137).

Symbolic Legitimacy.   Curriculum policy carries enormous symbolic value, evoking strong reactions from teachers, parents, and the community. Bring in a new superintendent or principal, and often they will seek to define and legitimate their roles by establishing "new" and thus "more" and "better" standards, programs, and assessments. Edelman (1964) believes that such symbols help to build confidence and to give the regime its own unique identity and legitimacy with staff and community. These beliefs "are not necessarily false, but it is the social cue rather than the factual accuracy of demonstrability that brings them into being" (London, 1997, p. 65).

Legitimization by Participation.   Here the idea is that curricular reform, and its highly value-filled, symbolic meaning, can only be effective if key stakeholders become involved in the change process. A number of states and local school districts are experimenting with school-site management and shared decisionmaking as devices for legitimating the process of improving school standards, curriculum, and assessments.

As Hess (1999) explains, "Site-based management (SBM) is the attempt to shift the control of schools from the central administration to individual school sites. . . . It is highly visible, appears to be ambitious, can be superimposed on existing arrangements, is less likely to inconvenience the community, and is not considered costly" (p. 113). The very process of sharing authority enhances the policies under consideration and defuses criticism from those at the top to those at the base of the organization, increasing the "buy-in." It virtually spreads the responsibility (vulnerability) and thus the legitimacy across the system.

Developing curriculum policy may be thought of as a set of four distinct, yet interrelated processes, as: (1) a *technical* process based on "the knowledge and skills required to accomplish certain objectives" (Wilson & Rossman, 1993, p. 201); (2) a highly *political* effort that includes issues of influence, power, and authority; (3) a cultural effort that "captures the values, beliefs, and norms of the organizations—the rules, roles, and relationships that shape daily life and determine what is and ought to be for organizational members" (Wilson & Rossman, 1993, p. 202); and (4) a set of *moral* choices to bring justice and fairness to education through the standards, curriculum, and testing of children.

Compulsory Education Policies

The requirement that all children attend school is a relatively recent phenomenon, growing out of early twentieth century progressivism and the child labor movement, the national effort of reform groups to remove children from the mines, sweatshops, farms, and factories and place them safely into schools. By 1922, states such as Oregon had passed laws that extended compulsory education policy to require attendance at public schools, or to schools with state-certified and paid teachers—in effect, making private schooling (and nonschooling) illegal.

The normative intent of laws requiring children to go to school was transformed by foes of private and religious schools (particularly Roman Catholic schools) from policies requiring some school attendance to mandatory public school attendance. The so-called Blaine amendments (to constitutions in twenty-three states) specifically prohibited public funds from being spent on attendance at private, religious schools.

Compulsory education, an important first step in making sure that children are delivered to school and exposed to its curriculum, also raises the policy question of the right of the state to control education—and mandate that all children attend only public institutions. In 1922, the state legislature in Oregon passed the

Compulsory Education Act, which required every parent or guardian to send children "to a public school for the period of time a public school shall be held during the year; failure to do so is a misdemeanor" punishable by fine or imprisonment. And thus in 1925, Governor Walter Pierce of Oregon signed into law a bill that required children not only to attend school from ages 8 to 14, but also to be enrolled in public schools only.

The private and parochial schools in Oregon sued the state, arguing that this law would put all nonpublic schools out of business and allow the state, not the parents, to determine the education of children. In *Pierce v. the Society of Sisters of the Holy Names of Jesus and Mary* (268 U.S. 510, 1925), the U.S. Supreme Court ruled that the compulsory education law in Oregon was unconstitutional, and children did not have to attend state-run schools only.

Poignantly, the court recognized the limited rights of the state and the basic responsibility of the parent: "The fundamental theory of liberty upon which all governments in the Union repose excludes any general power of the state to standardize all its children by forcing them to accept instruction from public teachers only. *The child is not the mere creature of the state;* those who nurture him and direct his destiny have the right, coupled with the high duty, to recognize and prepare him for additional obligations" [*Pierce v. the Society of the Sisters of Holy Names of Jesus and Mary*, 268 U.S. 510, 535 (1925); emphasis added].

School attendance itself, where and under whose auspices, is a fundamental question of social values; the *Pierce* decision limited the hegemony of the government in controlling the types of schools a child could legally attend. It was not until fifty years later that another right—to homeschool the child—was challenged and defended.

Homeschooling: A More Recent Case

An interesting and similar legal struggle occurred in the United States between 1975 and 1993 concerning the rights of parents to homeschool their children. In 1975, it was illegal in most of the fifty states and the District of Columbia for parents or guardians to educate their children at home. Like the battle for private education, proponents of homeschooling were trapped by the policies and laws concerning compulsory education in formal schools. As Somerville (2001), an attorney for the Home School Legal Defense Association, explained,

> Hard to believe, but as late as 1975, home schooling in most states was illegal, driving families into criminal activity to hide their children at home from the public school authorities. . . . Proponents of home schooling fought a four-front war: in *court* to argue for the rights of families to select the home; in the *state legislature* to get home schooling made legal; in local *communities* where parents work to build support networks for their children; and in the *U.S. Congress* to protect home schoolers from laws that might force children to take tests or engage in certain programs. (p. 1)

Constitutional Challenges.   A number of states had constitutions that were interpreted to require children to attend formal schools, not be educated at home, and not to use a curriculum of the parents' choosing. The Texas Education Agency (TEA), for example, enforced state policies, prosecuting homeschooling parents. In 1994, the state high court in *Texas Educational Agency v. Leeper* (893 S.W. 2d 2432, 1994) enjoined the state from arresting parents (many of whom were Evangelical Christians), the first major victory of the Home School Legal Defense Association, an advocacy group for the nation's approximately 800,000 homeschoolers (National Center for Education Statistics, 2000). In Pennsylvania, the court in *Jeffery v. O'Donnell* (702 F.Supp. 516, M.D. Pa., 1988) actually struck down the state's compulsory education law, allowing parents to keep their children at home for education. The homeschooling movement illustrates the impact of advocacy coalitions on shaping education policy.

Legislative Actions.   As courts began to legalize homeschooling, states recognized the rights of parents to control their children's education and started to regulate these activities, usually requiring evidence of academic achievement (e.g., some homeschooled students were expected to take standardized state tests). As shown below, these states passed statutes or regulations, starting in 1982, that recognized the legitimacy of home education in the following years:

> 1982:   Arizona, Mississippi
>
> 1983:   Wisconsin, Montana
>
> 1984:   Georgia, Louisiana, Rhode Island, Virginia
>
> 1985:   Arkansas, Florida, New Mexico, Oregon, Tennessee, Washington, Wyoming
>
> 1986:   Missouri
>
> 1987:   Maryland, Minnesota, Vermont, West Virginia, Texas
>
> 1988:   Colorado, New York, South Carolina, North Carolina, Pennsylvania
>
> 1989:   North Dakota, Hawaii, Maine, Ohio
>
> 1990:   New Hampshire, Connecticut
>
> 1991:   Iowa, South Dakota
>
> 1993:   New York, New Jersey

Types of Curriculum

Besides normative decisions about who should educate children (whether at home or at school, whether at public or private expense), perhaps the most difficult normative problem in curriculum policy is the nature of knowledge, what should be taught (which skills, disciplines, or subjects), and in what manner. These concerns involve a popular view of epistemology (nature of knowledge), philosophy of education, and the nature of pedagogy (the art of instruction). The history of curricular policy development in education has been well detailed and is not reviewed here. Instead, we capture the development of several trends in the U.S. school curriculum, including developmental curriculum, experienced-based, externally-controlled curriculum, progressivism, and more recent attempts to return to "basics."

Building a School Curriculum.   Schubert (1991) reviews the historical development of the field of curriculum, starting in the nineteenth century with the struggle between the medieval classical, liberal arts curriculum of "grammar, rhetoric and logic" (the so-called *trivium*) and "mathematics, astronomy, geometry, and music" (*quadrivium*), and the belief that the mind is best developed through practical and useful learning, around the stages of human development, needs, and interests. Many of these changes from an elite, highly intellectual slant on curriculum policy, toward a more universal, applied, and useful form of schooling, "emerged as local publics decided they needed a more educated populace" (Schubert, 1991, p. 101).

A number of key events, commissions, and researchers led to developments in curriculum policy; here are a few highlights (see Charters, 1923; Goodlad & Klein, 1974; Goodlad, Von Stoephasius, & Klein, 1966):

1839:   Henry Barnard served as secretary of the Board of Commissioners of Common Schools in Connecticut. Pressed for universal education.

1890s: William T. Harris served as superintendent in St. Louis, Missouri, as U.S. commissioner of education, and as a member of several key national commissions.

1893:   Committee of Ten of the National Education Association (NEA): group including·Harris and Charles Eliot (then president of Harvard University) focused on the curriculum for the emerging public secondary schools.

1895:   Committee of Fifteen, led by Francis Parker and William T. Harris, incorporated the ideas of Herbart, who stressed the developmental needs of children and problem-based learning, not the liberal arts tradition, within a decentralized education system.

1902–1916:   John Dewey stressed education based on community and experience and started the Laboratory School at the University of Chicago, based on integration of ideas, science, and democracy.

1918:   Franklin Bobbitt writes *The Curriculum* based on "activity analysis," which begins the formal study of curriculum and classroom pedagogy, based on what adults "do" in society.

1918:   Cardinal Principles of Secondary Education, led by Clarence Kingsley, went far beyond the traditional curriculum for high schools, and included health, worthy home membership, use of leisure time, ethical character, vocation, and citizenship.

1918:   States submit programs to the U.S. government for compliance with the new Smith-Hughes Act for Vocational Education of 1917, designed to teach young adults the basics of agriculture, home economics, trade, and industry, leading to the beginning of the "life adjustment" movement in curricular policy.

1919–1931:   Rise of "progressive education," including *The Eight Year Study*, looking at four years of high school and four years of college; a study released in 1942 showed the effects of the curriculum from high school through work (see Aikin, 1942).

1942–1948:   The aftermath of World War II and the Great Depression led to school and teacher shortages, the Cold War, and the Korean War, all triggering a reaction against progressive education, led by Arthur Bestor (1953), Albert Lynd (1953), and Admiral Hyman Rickover (1959). These leaders provided the foundation for the "back-to-basics" movement.

1953–1980s: Allan Bloom (1987), E. D. Hirsch (1987), Diane Ravitch and Chester E. Finn, Jr. (1987), and others criticize the "soft" feel-good curriculum, insisting on more content-oriented, traditional subjects.

1983:   *A Nation at Risk* (National Commission on Excellence in Education, 1983) urged U.S. schools to regain an international competitive edge, seeking a more rigorous, standardized curriculum.

All of these debates and policies, their norms and beliefs, can be translated into concerns about whether standards, curriculum, and tests should be highly centralized or decentralized. Lying behind the norms and values of curriculum policies, according to Schubert (1991), is the very nature of humankind and who should control the teaching and learning of children. He explains, "Thus, at the essence of the issues of curriculum centralization and decentralization lies the question of faith in human nature and its potential, and the amount of external or internal control needed for decision and action to be good and just" (p. 115).

Structural Dimension

Policies affecting schools' standards, curriculum, and assessment are often formulated at one level (e.g., the state) and implemented at another (the county, district, and school). An understanding of the structure of curriculum policy is important to policymakers and analysts, for the norms and culture of policy formulation may be very different from the settings in which policies are implemented and evaluated. It is critical, therefore, to track the policy, over time and by level, within the structural dimension.

A number of interesting case studies show the complexity of the state–local–school relationship in reforming school curricula. Should the state mandate change, reinforcing it with accountability measures such as tests? Or should policymakers treat these structural relationships as joint efforts and stress collaboration?

Wilson and Rossman (1993) made a strong case for fewer mandated programs and more partnerships—advice that many states have ignored as state requirements, high-stakes testing, state takeovers of "failing" districts and schools, and other requirements have actually increased in the last decade. The authors wrote:

> We call for the state to move away from the mandated change of the first wave of reform and to embrace a strategy of *capacity building*, and *system changing* that makes the state, local districts, and schools partners in experimentation and innovation. In such a model, the state's role would be no less crucial than it is in a top-down, mandated model: in fact, its role becomes even more crucial. The state would provide resources, train and offer technical assistance, encourage and facilitate innovation at the local level, and lead the way to restructured schools. (p. 203)

Collaboration between governmental levels, particularly in making and changing curricular policies, requires patience, a willingness to listen and share ideas, and importantly, the building of close, working inter-jurisdictional relationships. So often, however, agencies have neither the skills, patience, nor the resources to follow a policy through its stages (formulation, implementation, evaluation, and reformation) and over a number of years, at several levels in the policy structure.

One good example (exception), however, is Valentina Bali's (2001) analysis of the effects of Proposition 227 in California, a study of the results of a statewide policy "to dismantle the bilingual programs in public schools and replace them with programs emphasizing early English acquisition" (p. 295).

The Case of California's Proposition 227

In the June 1998 primary election, 61 percent of voters in California, one of the nation's most ethnically and linguistically diverse states, passed Proposition 227, which removed Limited English Proficient (LEP) students from separate bilingual programs. Passing in every California county except San Francisco and Alameda, "Prop. 227" discontinued the state's bilingual education programs; only children whose parents successfully received a waiver from the local district could continue to have instruction in their spoken (native) language.

Statewide, this policy change reduced the percentage of students in bilingual programs from 29 percent in 1998 to 11 percent by 1999—and lower in coming years (Rossell, 2000). As we know, it is easier to cut or destroy a program through policy at the state level than it is to start a new program from scratch, and attempts to evaluate the effects of state-level policy change on students in the classroom are rare and often inconclusive. For, "bilingual education is a racially and ideologically charged issue for voters, and it is also controversial for scholars . . . " stemming "from ideological bias, problematic methodology, and intellectual disagreements" (Bali, 2001, p. 297).

Researchers have been sharply divided over the effects and effectiveness of bilingual education. Rossell and Baker (1996) found that bilingual education was not better than English as a Second Language (ESL) programs or Structured English Immersion (SEI) programs; Ramirez (1992) determined that over four years, short duration programs worked better than long-term ones, but only for younger students. Thus, concrete, reliable information is available neither on the effectiveness of bilingual programs (versus other approaches) nor on the immediate effects on students who are removed from bilingual ELP programs and placed into English-only instruction (Hakuta, 2000).

Bali (2001) compared Limited English Proficient (LEP) students in a separate bilingual program with those in other immersion programs, and found controversially that "dismantling bilingual programs seems to have provided a small step toward equalizing educational outcomes between Hispanic and white [non-Hispanic] students" (p. 312). Furthermore, when she compared the performance (reading scores) of bilingual LEP students from Pasadena before Proposition 227 with those who were not in a bilingual program, the ones isolated in a bilingual environment "had lower scores in reading than non-bilingual ELP students." Once taken out of the separate program, she found the scores "were indistinguishable from those of their non-bilingual LEP peers, students who in principle already had a better command of English" (p. 312). The findings show, minimally, that removing students with limited English skills from a separate bilingual program did not "set bilingual students back." Data also indicate that over a four-year period, bilingual instruction had not been superior to English-based programs.

This kind of research is important: it takes students who are affected by changes in a state policy (e.g., Proposition 227 ending bilingual LEP classes) and tests the effects down the "structure" to district, school, and classroom (bilingual versus regular programs) to students. And Bali (2001) makes an interesting prediction concerning the effects of such policies on the structure and curriculum policies of other states and districts:

> From a political perspective, the passage and positive impact of Proposition 227 will likely lead to similar measures in other states. For example, Arizona passed such a measure in the 2000 general election. Interestingly, the diffusion of this policy does not just mean the dismantling of bilingual programs, but also the setting of a uniform standard in a state that adopts it. (pp. 312–313; see also Mintrom & Vergari, 1998; Ravitch, 2000)

When considering the structural dimension of curriculum policy, one that takes the level of political organization into account, certain paradoxes appear. For example, although conservative interest groups in California (perceived by many as being anti-immigrant and anti-Latino) are responsible for putting Proposition 227 on the ballot, the reform "was not detrimental and may have even benefited those whom it targeted" (Bali, 2001, p. 313) and shows the potential positive effects of state initiatives (plebiscites) over traditional legislative approaches to comprehensive state-level school reforms.

Whichever constituent group makes the key curricular decisions—whether politicians at the federal, state or local levels, school administrators or curriculum writers in the districts, or teachers in the classroom—each "layer" or type has a special relationship with other layers in a complex system of control and support. These levels of control, which are critical to understanding the centralizing and mandating of curriculum, create an interesting stair-step structure (Figure 7.1), where on one level, teachers, a key constituent, are in control over students; in the next "step" the teacher is in turn, being controlled by the level above. As Schubert (1991) explains, the history of the centralization of curriculum policy-making and implementation includes a series of internal and external controls that vie with one another, affecting the viewpoints of the stakeholders involved.

As shown in Figure 7.1, at Level 1, we see that the federal government, its courts, legislature, and executive agencies all act as an external force in shaping the policy environment for the states, their agencies, and constituents. Whether it's a critical court case, a new law or program, or the threat of withdrawing federal funding, the federal government is definitely seen as the most centralized and external in education, as a succession of "Education Presidents" have learned.

At Level 2, the state, which perceives itself as bound by federal mandates and laws, now acts as the external agency, lording over the local school districts in establishing boundaries, programs, funding formulas, and of course in affecting the curriculum of the district (state standards, programs, tests, and consequences).

At Level 3, local districts (school boards, superintendents, "central offices") become the external controlling agency to the schools, setting the standards, determining administrative and teaching staff eligibility, budgets, and programs. Interpreting federal and state curricular policies and mandates usually falls to curriculum coordinators at the district level, who act with the authority of the laws and policies of those levels above the school.

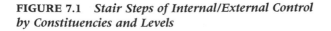

FIGURE 7.1   *Stair Steps of Internal/External Control by Constituencies and Levels*

Level 4, while internal to the school, may see principals and other building-level administrators who are hiring, supervising, tenuring, and removing teachers, as engaging in efforts to control the quality and scope of the curriculum (standards and testing) within each school. Hence, teachers, as Schubert explains, see their immediate supervisors as an external force in the conduct of the classroom. And finally, at Level 5, students may see their own teachers as representatives of the system, making the assignments, setting the standards and expectations, and assessing the students to see that they've reached a level of quality.

At best, control and authority should reside at the level where expertise is most obvious in determining "subject matter, social needs, and needs of learners as individuals" (Schubert, 1991, p. 99). For, as Schubert (1991) explains, "those who have expertise in each of these bases [levels] for curriculum development, depending on a particular problem [or goal] in a particular place, might be state officials, funding agents, school board members, central office administrators, parents, teachers, education researchers in disciplines, educational theorists and researchers, principals, teachers, students, or others" (pp. 99–100).

Constituentive Dimension

Another important frame for understanding policymaking in standard setting, curriculum making, and assessment is that of who should make these policies and where? Some would argue that it is primarily the classroom teacher who ultimately instructs students, interpreting their subject and skills in light of how they were taught to teach and were taught themselves. Others believe that as "one nation, under God, indivisible," the federal government and national leaders—starting with the President—should make education a top priority and use the "bully pulpit" and the White House to force education policy reforms.

But because federal legitimacy is difficult to create, and constituencies are unlikely to agree on the essentials of the curriculum, standards, and test outcomes, governments and other policymaking agencies have been slow to direct and manage the daily work of teachers. Among the nations of the world, the United States is, for example, one of the last to mandate *national* government (federal) standards, curriculum, and testing, unlike Great Britain, for example, which established a national curriculum with national tests in 1988 under the Margaret Thatcher régime (see Knight, 1992), building on the Ordinary or O-Levels, General Certificate of Student Excellence (GCSE), and Advance or A-Level national examinations.

Recently, however, the Bush administration began tackling national standards and testing policies, where the federal government uses its education funding, and the threat of withdrawing federal support, to force the states into setting their standards, administering standardized (norm referenced) tests initially in mathematics and reading, later in social studies and science, to every child minimally every year between the 3rd and 8th grades. As the *New York Times* reported (July 7, 2001), "The bills give schools 10 to 12 years to bring all students—black and white, middle class and poor, Anglo and Hispanic, and those with limited English—up to proficiency and to require states to report their performance of each such category of students and to set the criteria for proficiency" (p. A-10).

Responses to the Bush administration's education policy were rapid—and negative. Heads of the nation's two largest school districts, former Colorado governor Roy Romer, superintendent of the Los Angeles Unified School District (LAUSD), and former Citibank manager and lawyer, Harold Levy, Chancellor of the New York City Public Schools, both argued, interestingly, that the federal policies raising standards, test requirements, and the stakes might in fact have the opposite effect: a dilution of the meaning of "proficiency" and thus local standards, to increase the likelihood that urban children in Los Angeles and New York City would pass the tests and these two districts (and their respective states) would avoid the sanctions and continue to receive federal funding.

Even Republican governors were concerned about losing federal funding and fought with the president to eliminate this provision from the law. Governor John Engler (Republican-Michigan), a Bush ally, reported that "once you tie resources to state academic progress, you could create a perverse incentive to lower standards and states with high standards [like Michigan] could look bad" (Chaddock, 2001, p. 20). The White House backed off for fear of destroying the critical Republican–Democratic coalition necessary to get education policies passed in Washington. As Chaddock (2001) reported, "The White House and Senate negotiators say they made the changes after it became clear that the original language of the law would have resulted in unacceptably high numbers of failing schools [over a ten year period]. Senate projections showed that even in states that were acknowledged leaders in school reform—Texas, North Carolina, and Connecticut—large numbers of districts would fail a standard of proficiency for all students" (p. 1).

From a policy perspective, this reaction from leaders of the nation's largest public school systems, New York City and Los Angeles, a major constituent of school operations, as well as governors of key states, makes sense. After all, these states and districts (and other urban centers) educate a large portion of the poor, immigrants, and children of color in the United States and risk losing large sums of money from the federal government.

If the federal government allows each state to set its own standards and testing process, states and districts might dumb down the requirements to increase the chances that their children would pass and that federal funds would not be cut off. Levy noted that many of the "new policies" being pressed by the President and Congress were already in place, including magnet schools, public school choice, and holding schools accountable for student performance. He continued: "If the system's accountable, then I say the politicians and policy-makers also have to be accountable. With all the standards and reform, there's a need for adequate resources" (Schemo, 2001, p. A-10). Unless urban districts have sufficient funds to improve the recruitment and pay of teachers, then higher standards cannot easily be met.

Likewise, states are legislating curriculum at a rapid rate, putting state core curriculum standards and testing to work in attempts to raise the standards for all students in that jurisdiction. States have enacted laws throughout the twentieth century that required students to attend school (compulsory education), for so many days per year, taking certain subjects (the integrated, core curriculum), accumulating a certain number of Carnegie credits, and to certain levels of attainment (as determined by regular statewide testing), with certain sanctions for failure (e.g., no high school graduation).

National organizations, such as the National Association of Teachers of English (and math, and social studies), have set standards for their fields. Although these standards are not required or enforced locally, they do set a benchmark for the country and inspire states and local school boards to enact their own similar standards, citing the experts from these fields. And teachers are likely to take seriously the requirements and standards of their peers, even in the absence of laws and sanctions.

Another constituent group is private companies that write and distribute textbooks and materials, the "canned programs" that come from the big publishers. Stodolsky (1999) explains that "there is a widely held belief that classroom instruction in elementary schools is dominated by textbooks. Undoubtedly, textbooks are present in most classrooms most of the time. But the assumption that textbooks *drive* instruction because they are ubiquitous may not be tenable" (p. 143).

Whichever constituent group is involved in promoting and changing school standards and curriculum, teachers are the primary, and final, constituents that must live with these policies. As Schwartz (1991) explains, "Teachers typically emphasize the content of tests and test-taking at the expense of other educationally important activities, and formal curricula center on or are limited to those tested by the state" (p. 190).

Perhaps the most useful examination of the effects of curricular policy on local constituencies is the work of Brooks (1991). He generates a set of negative, even destructive "messages" that teachers, parents, administrators, and other local constituencies receive when the curriculum is taken over by outside agencies and interests:

Message #1:   "Curriculum development is not our responsibility."

Message #2:   "Testing drives instruction."

Message #3:   "It's more important to cover material than to learn it."

Message #4:   "Minimum competency is the desired outcome."

Message #5:   "We don't trust you."

Message #6:   "Past effectiveness does not matter."

Message #7:   "More, sooner, and quicker are better."

In effect, Brooks (1991) argues that the varying constituencies of school policy-making can create real problems for schools and teachers in reforming school curriculum and standards. Or, as he explains, "The imposition of centralized curricula by state education departments creates many needless problems for local schools, districts, educators, and students" (1991, p. 164). Who, then, should have responsibility for standards and curriculum?

Technical Dimension

The analysis of curriculum policy comes down to determining: Does the policy work? Are students better off under the new standards, curriculum, and testing than previously? Schwab (1970), for example, suggests a practical analysis that starts with the goals of the curriculum, includes the lessons, activities, and results, and works to settle real problems in the schools.

Elementary and secondary school curricula, and the policies that support each, are very different, and deserve some attention. In general, the elementary school curriculum is more skill- and concept-centered, not so much on particular disciplines, while the high school curricula (and the teacher training and licensing that goes with it) are more discipline-based, whether in science (physics, chemistry, biology), languages, English writing and literature, history (U.S., global, European), or vocation and health-related programs. Take, for example, the battery of tests that are required of high school students in New York.

As one New York high school reported, tests were required in English (11th grade), Global History (10th grade), U.S. History and Government (11th), Earth Science (9th), Biology (10th), Chemistry (11th), Physics (12th), Foreign Language (level 3, 10th), and Math I, II, and III (9th, 10th, and 11th). Thus, while elementary school students take tests in basic subjects such as Reading, Writing, Math, and Social Studies, high school pupils have more specific, subject-based tests at various levels (New Jersey requires these tests at 4th and 8th grades). Under federal legislation (No Child Left Behind Act), the nation's elementary and middle schools will soon be required to give tests in basic subjects in grades 3 through 8 or risk losing federal funds.

Technical analysis of curriculum policies rests on five related criteria to learn if the effort is really working: (1) Agreement: Do participants have a general consensus about what they are doing and why? (2) Clarity: Is there some sense of what is being accomplished and how? (3) Acceptance: Do participants buy into the program and use it? (4) Assessment and Results: Do policy participants have and use means for understanding the curriculum or programs? And (5) Effectiveness: To what extent does the curriculum work for various groups of students in improving their learning and even their grades and test scores?

Academic Standards

Increasingly, states are passing laws and policies that set standards for all students, often requiring that each local district "align" its standards to those promulgated by the state. States such as New Jersey have built a policy system that affects every subject (mathematics, science, reading and language arts, social studies) from grades one through twelve (Klaghotz, Schechter, & Reece, 1996). Called the State Core Curricular Content Standards (SCCCS), New Jersey's system of standards, curriculum, and testing is, at least on paper, highly *aligned*. In fact, each teacher's lesson plans must indicate which standard is being addressed and how that standard will be met.

The standards begin with the New Jersey state constitution, guaranteeing children a "Thorough and Efficient" (T&E) education; thus, the "core curriculum content standards are an attempt to define the meaning of 'Thorough' in the context of the 1875 New Jersey State constitutional guarantee that students would be educated with a Thorough and Efficient system of free education" (Klagholtz, Schechter, & Reece, 1996, p. 1). Although the state standards are meant to define the outcomes, they "are not meant to serve as a statewide curriculum guide" (p. i). That is, the core curriculum content standards attempt to define results— what students are to achieve—but they do *not* limit district and presumably school-site strategies to accomplish these ends.

However, besides a set of state standards, the New Jersey Department of Education also established curriculum frameworks, which became the structure around which the curriculum, teaching, and testing are aligned:

> To assist local educators, the standards will be further elaborated through curriculum frameworks. While also not a curriculum, these frameworks will bring to life the intent of the standards through classroom examples and a discussion of the underlying rationales. Local curriculum developers can use the frameworks as a resource to develop district curricula that best meet the needs of the students in each community. Curriculum frameworks also serve as a resource to classroom teachers and staff developers who want to modify instruction in light of the new standards. (New Jersey State Department of Education, May 1996, p. I)

The core curriculum content standards go a step further, beyond "framing" the curriculum; they also define what students "should know and be able to do" by subject and across disciplines. Hence, across the curriculum, *all students will show readiness to:*

1. Develop career planning and workplace readiness skills.
2. Use technology, information, and other tools.
3. Use critical thinking, decisionmaking, and problem solving skills.
4. Demonstrate self-management skills.
5. Apply safety principles.

Note that of these five workplace readiness standards, the first two are practical job preparation and the last two are care and self-discipline (i.e., deportment); only the middle standard—"critical thinking, decisionmaking and problem solving"—is directly related to cognitive or academic standards.

The New Jersey Department of Education recommended fifty-six standards that covered seven content areas:

1. Visual and Performing Arts
2. Health and Physical Education
3. Language Arts/Literacy
4. Mathematics
5. Science
6. Social Studies
7. World Languages

Thus, somehow, districts are expected to integrate the five "workplace readiness standards" into the seven "content" areas, meeting each standard in formal courses in school or "through experiences beyond the school walls, such as volunteer activities, job shadowing, and part-time jobs" (New Jersey State Department of Education, 1996, p. iii). With these standards in place, school districts are now required to build a curriculum and establish testing.

The Passaic Public Schools in New Jersey have established core curriculum content standards for each grade level, from kindergarten through 12th grade for each of the subject areas. *Number 4—Mathematics,* for example (see above), has sixteen separate standards that cut across the grades and require Cumulative Progress Indicators, Objectives, Suggested Activities for the class, Materials, and Evaluations (both "authentic performance assessment" and a "portfolio holistic approach"). Let's take Standard 4.1: for all students "to pose and solve problems in mathematics, other disciplines, and other experiences."

At the kindergarten level, this problem-solving unit in Math has the following Indicators, Objectives, Activities, Materials, and Evaluation:

Kindergarten Curriculum

Cumulative Progress Indicators	*Objectives*
By the end of Grade K, students will: Use discovery-oriented, inquiry-based, and problem-centered approaches.	1. Use discovery-oriented, inquiry-based, and problem-centered approaches to investigate and understand math content. 2. Explore a variety of puzzles, games, and problem-solving techniques. 3. Use manipulatives to solve math problems. 4. Use software to solve problems.

(continued)

Kindergarten Curriculum   Continued

Cumulative Progress Indicators	*Objectives*
Suggested Activities	*Materials*
1. Daily use of the problem of the day	1. Math in Action
2. Teddy Bears Trip	2. NCTM Addenda S Series
3. Shapetown vignette/Venn diagrams	3. Primary Bear counters
4. Various AIMS activities from "Primary Bears"	4. Teddy Bear counters
5. Technology: Note pad: Dot to Dot Jigsaw Puzzle: learning shapes and sizes	5. Jumpstart preschool knowledge adventure
Evaluation	*Evaluation*
Authentic Performance:	**Portfolios:** Holistic approaches
• Students engage in math task or investigation	• Journals
• Observe students as they question the processes used to solve the task	• Open-ended questions, scoring rubrics
• Examine final results	• Observations, interviews, conferences
	• Math chapter tests

This same kindergarten standard (4.1) has the same indicators, objectives, and evaluation methods at the 4th grade; only the Suggested Activities and Materials differ for 10- and 11-year olds. For each standard, in each subject, and at each grade level, the curriculum establishes the indicators, objectives, activities, materials, and evaluations, creating a giant grid that includes the readiness factors, standards, subjects, and benchmarks for each test—an enormous "superstructure" that many teachers and parents cannot easily understand and use.

4th Grade

Suggested Activities	*Materials*
1. Use of the Problem of the Day in Math in Action (MIA)	1. Math in Action and journals
2. "Sharing Cookies" from Math Frameworks: Shapetown vignettes, p. 95.	2. Pattern Blocks
3. Play Mancala	3. Beans, eggs, cartons, cups
4. Play Nimh with coins or toothpicks	4. Coins or toothpicks
5. Use activities and manipulatives	5. Pattern Blocks
	6. Tangrams
	7. Geoboards
	8. Sim City

Suggested Activities	Materials
6. Hands on the Pattern Blocks	**9.** Treasure Math Storm, Learning Co.
7. Moving on with Pattern Blocks	**10.** Other software
8. Hands on the Tangrams	
9. Moving on the Tangrams	
10. Hands on the Geoboards	
11. Moving on Geoboards	
12. Sim City	

Test Outcomes

Supporting these state standards and curricula are policies requiring regular state-designed assessments of student progress. The policies affecting testing—and the results of using these high-stakes measures—are finally receiving the attention they deserve. Firestone (2001), in his study of test outcomes in New Jersey, sets the tone for discussion of the technical effects of student assessment (e.g., state criterion-references tests), particularly on teachers and classrooms:

> As state testing becomes more pervasive, researchers and test developers are split as to how it affects teaching. In the early 1990s in particular, reformers argued that using more performance-based assessments and portfolios would encourage teachers to engage in intellectually challenging instruction of a sort that is atypical in most American schools (Resnick & Resnick, 1992). Both before and since then, considerable documentation of teaching-to-the-test has suggested a very different result. State tests are likely to encourage teachers to teach the content on the assessments, use items like those on the tests as instructional materials, and engage in even more rote instruction as a short-term strategy for raising scores. (p. 1)

Firestone explored the long-term effects of testing on math and science teachers over three years, using the New Jersey Elementary School Performance Assessment, surveying, interviewing, and observing teachers. The results were interesting but disturbing, as teachers tended to stress facts over concepts (even though the ESPA test requires concepts and approaches, not just "right answers"). The researchers report that "While ESPA may be raising consciousness about new, more challenging approaches to instruction, there is a long way to go before these approaches are broadly adopted" (2001, p. 3).

The RAND Corporation conducted a similar study of the effects of Washington state's education reform policies on teachers. Stecher (2001), working with the National Center for Research on Evaluation, Standards and Student Testing (CRESST) at RAND, surveyed principals and teachers to learn whether curriculum reforms, standards, and tests were being implemented at the local school level (see Stecher, Barron, Chun, & Ross, 2000). Two related questions emerge from looking at testing and curriculum: First, does aligning and reinforcing the curriculum in schools raise test scores of students, as intended? And, second, do tests in turn influence teaching?

This study discovered that changes in curricular policies affected the structure of classroom activities and emphases in what was being taught, although these changes were slow, deliberate, and uneven. As Stecher (2001) explains, "Teachers and principals feel considerable pressure for their students to perform well on the Washington Assessment of Student Learning (WASL). Schools have made institutional and organizational changes, such as instituting summer school. . . . Teachers have shifted instructional time and focus to subjects tested by WASL. Most teachers spend time preparing students for the test particularly as the test date approaches" (p. 8).

RAND found a disconnect between the goals of the new test, the curriculum, pedagogy, and results. In 1999, with greater curricular alignment came better test results—but not in 2000. Thus, on a technical level, policymakers and educators should be aware of three trends in the effects of curricular policy in schools:

• *Change is gradual:* It takes time, training, preparation, and persistence to see practical results, including improved academic outcomes. Teachers "buy in" slowly, and usually only when other teachers are using the program or preparing students for the tests. Firestone and Stecher both reported the slow pace of change in New Jersey and Washington state, respectively.

• *Change is erratic:* It appears that test results are rarely consistent. In the first year of a new test (like the Washington Assessment of Student Learning, WASL), academic results almost always go down. Then, over the next few years, outcomes improve as students and teachers become more comfortable with the type of testing and higher expectations. Yet, states that test yearly find that versions of the test may be more difficult or easier, and state test scores fluctuate, having little to do with classroom instruction or real student learning.

• *Change works both ways:* Importantly, policymakers, educators, teachers, and administrators have become aware that testing results are both *affected by* changes in curriculum policies, usually making gradual improvements in test results, and also *affect* the curriculum and classroom practices. Most research shows that teachers change their emphases, uses of time, activities, and content in response to new tests (particularly when these exams are high stakes and publicly released). Whatever the results, the technical dimension is a critical lens in understanding and evaluating policy analysis because it indicates what's working and how, exposing the day-to-day concerns of those who must live and work with changes in education policy.

The American Education Research Association (AERA), the largest professional association of academics in the nation, has taken a strong position on the nature of national and state test standards, stating that "the AERA seeks to promote educational policies and practices that credible scientific research has shown to be beneficial, and to discourage those found to have negative effects" (2000,

p. 2). AERA is particularly concerned about what is commonly called "high-stakes testing." In particular, AERA believes that testing requires the following:

1. *Full Disclosure of Likely Negative Consequences of High-Stakes Testing Programs:* Where credible scientific evidence suggests that a given type of testing program is likely to have negative side effects, test developers and users should make a serious effort to explain these possible effects to policy makers.

2. *Alignment Between the Test and the Curriculum:* Both the content of the test and the cognitive processes engaged in taking the test should adequately represent the curriculum. High-stakes tests should not be limited to that portion of the relevant curriculum that is easiest to measure. When testing is for school accountability or to influence the curriculum, the test should be aligned with the curriculum as set forth in standards documents representing intended goals of instruction.

3. *Validity of Passing Scores and Achievement Levels:* When testing programs use specific scores to determine "passing" or to define reporting categories like "proficient," the validity of these specific scores must be established in addition to demonstrating the representativeness of the test content. To begin with, the purpose and meaning of passing scores or achievement levels must be clearly stated. There is often confusion, for example, among minimum competency levels (traditionally required for grade-to-grade promotion), grade level (traditionally defined as a range of scores around the national average on standardized tests), and "world-class" standards (set at the top of the distribution, anywhere from the 70th to the 99th percentile).

4. *Opportunities for Meaningful Remediation for Examinees Who Fail High-Stakes Tests:* Examinees who fail a high-stakes test should be provided meaningful opportunities for remediation. Remediation should focus on the knowledge and skills the test is intended to address, not just the test performance itself. There should be sufficient time before retaking the test to assure that students have time to remedy any weaknesses discovered.

5. *Appropriate Attention to Language Differences Among Examinees:* If a student lacks mastery of the language in which a test is given, then that test becomes, in part, a test of language proficiency. Unless a primary purpose of a test is to evaluate language proficiency, it should not be used with students who cannot understand the instructions or the language of the test itself. If English language learners are tested in English, their performance should be interpreted in the light of their language proficiency.

6. *Appropriate Attention to Students with Disabilities:* In testing individuals with disabilities, steps should be taken to ensure that the test score inferences accurately reflect the intended construct rather than any disabilities and their associated characteristics extraneous to the intent of the measurement.

7. *Careful Adherence to Explicit Rules for Determining Which Students Are to be Tested:* When schools, districts, or other administrative units are compared to one another or when changes in scores are tracked over time, there must be explicit policies specifying which students are to be tested and under what circumstances students may be exempted from testing. Such policies must be uniformly enforced to assure the validity of score comparisons. In addition, reporting of test score results should accurately portray the percentage of students exempted.

8. *Sufficient Reliability for Each Intended Use:* Reliability refers to the accuracy or precision of test scores. It must be shown that scores reported for individuals or for schools are sufficiently accurate to support each intended interpretation. Accuracy should be examined for the scores actually used. For example, information about the reliability of raw scores may not adequately describe the accuracy of percentiles; information about the reliability of school means may be insufficient if scores for subgroups are also used in reaching decisions about schools.

9. *Ongoing Evaluation of Intended and Unintended Effects of High-Stakes Testing:* With any high-stakes testing program, ongoing evaluation of both intended and unintended consequences is essential. In most cases, the governmental body that mandates the test should also provide resources for a continuing program of research and for dissemination of research findings concerning both the positive and the negative effects of the testing program.

("AERA Position Statement Concerning High-Stakes Testing in Pre-K–12 Education," Adopted July 2000)

Making Better Curriculum Policies

In conclusion, making better policies affecting the teaching and learning of children remains a critical, unmet goal. Government, districts, and schools are experimenting with new curriculum packages, new levels of curriculum decisionmaking, including those at the school and teacher levels, and new means for assessing the quality of programs to meet new standards. Is the field still a mess? Yes. Are we beginning to assess the effects? Yes. Note the work of Bali on the results of Proposition 227 in California, one eliminating bilingual classes for limited English proficient students. Although the study was early and limited, it does provide a model for assessing students before and after a new policy is implemented, comparing cohorts of students—in this case, in the Pasadena, California schools.

The value issues remain divisive. The structural concerns remain complex as the United States struggles as a nation to create standards, quality, and testing at various levels in the system. The constituents are many and varied, from parents and community to professionals and politicians. And the practical problems are gripping, as districts and states, schools and classrooms struggle to build (as in New Jersey) a set of core curricular standards that underpin the curriculum and lessons for students, and that align the tests to the curriculum, and standards to results. The role of policy analysts, scholars, and practitioners remains critical in our growing understanding of how to make schools work better for students. As Anderson (1997) explains,

> Over the last decade, myriad policies and projects have been initiated with an aim toward improving the quality of education in public schools. There has been a tendency within the education research community to invent new models of educational change for different policy thrusts, rather than drawing upon and extending what has been learned from the past. There has been a tendency within the educational practitioner community to apply research-based models of educational

change uncritically. . . . There is still much to learn about the process of educational change among teachers [and administrators] in the organizational context of the school. (pp. 363–364)

Assignments and Activities

Assignment #1

Individually, or working in small groups, conduct interviews (in person or by phone) to learn the following, and write them up as reports or assignments:

1. What are the curricular requirements for students in your district and/or state? Set by whom? Benchmarked how, against what standards?

2. To what extent do teachers in your district (or a nearby one) understand the standards and curricular requirements—and how are these requirements and standards reflected in the curriculum, lessons, and activities in their classrooms?

3. Locate reports and other examples of how standards are assessed (e.g., local, state, and national tests including the Stanford 9, Iowa Tests, SAT, ACT, report cards by school and district, and other curricular audits) and assess to what extent:
   a. These tests are "driving" the curriculum in the eyes of teachers.
   b. These tests are believed to be "authentic" assessments or not.
   c. These tests are widely reported and consulted within and outside the school system (newspapers, political discussions, PTA groups, and realtors).
   d. The curriculum, standards, and tests are seen as "aligned" or at least mutually supportive.

4. Which groups and individuals in your district (or a nearby one) are the major constituents (stakeholders) in the setting of standards, creation of standards, and assessing of results, and how do they influence the process and policies or not?

Seminal Works

W. W. Charters' (1923) *Curriculum Construction* is a classic introduction to curriculum construction and development. M. Frances Klein's (1991) edited book, *The Politics of Curriculum Decision-Making* provides an excellent overview of the political issues inherent in curriculum revision, particularly efforts to centralize and standardize the curriculum. A more recent work analyzing the politics of curriculum policy is Margaret Early and Kenneth Rehage's (1999) edited work, *Issues in Curriculum,* containing selected chapters from yearbooks published by the National Society for the Study of Education (NSSE). Another excellent source on curriculum politics and policy is Lyn Corno's (2001) edited work, *Education Across a Century,* the One Hundredth Yearbook of the NSSE.

References

Aikin, W. (1942). *The story of the eight year study*. New York: Harper & Brothers.

Anderson, S. A. (1997). Understanding teacher change: Revisiting the concerns based adoption model. *Curriculum Inquiry, 27*(3), 331–367.

Bali, V. A. (2001). Sink or swim: What happened to California's bilingual students after Proposition 227? *State Politics & Policy Quarterly, 1*(3), 295–217.

Bestor, A. (1953). *Educational wastelands*. Urbana, IL: University of Illinois Press.

Bloom, A. (1987). *The closing of the American mind*. New York: Simon & Schuster.

Brooks, M. G. (1991). Centralized curriculum: Effects on the local school level. In M. F. Klein (Ed.), *The politics of curriculum decision-making: Issues in centralizing the curriculum* (pp. 151–166). Albany: State University of New York Press.

Chaddock, G. R. (2001, May 10). Bush education plan meets new foes: GOP governors. *Christian Science Monitor*, p. 1.

Charters, W. W. (1923). *Curriculum construction*. New York: Macmillan.

Corno, L. (2001). *Education across a century: The centennial volume: One hundredth yearbook for the National Society for the Study of Education*. Chicago: University of Chicago Press.

Edelman, M. (1964). *The symbolic uses of politics*. Urbana: University of Illinois Press.

Early, M., & Rehage, K. (1999). *Issues in curriculum*. Chicago: The University of Chicago Press.

Eisner, E. (1999). Can the humanities be taught in American public schools? In *Issues in curriculum: A selection of chapters from past NSSE yearbooks*. Ninety-eighth Yearbook of the National Society for the Study of Education, pp. 281–300. Chicago: University of Chicago Press.

Fine, M. (1993). [Ap]parent involvement: Reflections on parents, power, and urban public schools. *Teachers College Record, 94*(4), 34–55.

Firestone, W. A. (2001). The effects of testing policies on teaching in New Jersey. *PEA Bulletin, 22*(1), 1.

Goodlad, J. I. (1990). *Teachers for our nation's schools*. San Francisco: Jossey-Bass.

Goodlad, J. I. (1991). Curriculum making as a sociopolitical process. In M. F. Klein (Ed.), *The politics of curriculum decision-making: Issues in centralizing the curriculum* (pp. 9–23). Albany: State University of New York Press.

Goodlad, J. I., & Klein, M. F. (1974). *Looking behind the classroom door*. Worthington, OH: Charles A. Jones.

Goodlad, J. I., Von Stoephasius, H. P., & Klein, M. F. (1966). *The changing school curriculum*. New York: Fund for the Advancement of Education.

Hakuta, K. (2000). How long does it take an English learner to attain proficiency? [On-line]. Available: http://www.stanford.edu//-hakuta/SAT9

Hess, F. M. (1999). *Spinning wheels: The politics of urban school reform*. Washington, DC: The Brookings Institution.

Hirsch, E. D. (1987). *Cultural literacy*. Boston: Houghton Mifflin.

Kirst, M. W., & Walker, D. F. (1971). An analysis of curriculum policymaking. *Review of Educational Research, 41*(5), 479–509.

Klagholz, L., Schechter, E. M., & Reece, G. T. (1996). *Core curriculum content standards.* Trenton, NJ: New Jersey State Department of Education.

Klein, M. F. (1991). Introduction. In M. F. Klein (Ed.), *The politics of curriculum decision-making: Issues in centralizing the curriculum* (pp. 1–6). Albany: State University of New York Press.

Knight, J. (1992). *Institutions and social conflict.* New York: Cambridge University Press.

London, N. A. (1997). Socio-politics in effective curriculum change in a less developed country: Trinidad and Tobago. *Curriculum Inquiry, 27*(1), 63–80.

McNeil, L. M. (1988). *Contradictions of control: School structure and school knowledge.* New York: Routledge.

Mintrom, M., & Vergari, S. (1998). Policy networks and innovation diffusion: The case of state education reform. *The Journal of Politics, 60*(2), 127–148.

National Center for Education Statistics. (2000). *The condition of education.* Washington, DC: Author.

National Commission on Excellence in Education. (1983). *A nation at risk.* Washington, DC: U.S. Government Printing Office.

Pullin, D. (1999). Whose schools are these and what are they for? The role of the rule of law in defining educational opportunity in American public education. In G. J. Cizek (Ed.), *The handbook of educational policy* (pp. 3–29). San Diego, CA: Academic Press.

Ramirez, D. (1992). Executive summary. *Bilingual Research Journal, 16*(1&2), 1–61.

Ravitch, D. (2000). *Left back: A century of failed school reforms.* New York: Simon & Schuster.

Ravitch, D., & Finn, C. E., Jr. (1987). *What do our 17 year olds know?* New York: Harper & Row.

Rossell, C. (2000). *Bilingual education in California before and after Proposition 227.* Occasional Paper, Public Policy Institute of California, San Francisco.

Rossell, C. H., & Baker, K. (1996). The effectiveness of bilingual education. *Research in the Teaching of English, 30,* 7–74.

Schemo, D. J. (2001, July 13). School leaders contend laws may cause lower standards. *New York Times,* p. B1.

Schoenfeld, A. H. (2001). Mathematics education in the twentieth century. In L. Corno (Ed.), *Education across a century: The centennial volume: One-Hundredth Yearbook of the National Society for the Study of Education* (pp. 239–278). Chicago: University of Chicago Press and the National Society for the Study of Education.

Schubert, W. H. (1991). Historical perspective on centralizing curriculum. In M. F. Klein (Ed.), *The politics of curriculum decision-making: Issues in centralizing the curriculum* (pp. 98–120). Albany: State University of New York Press.

Schwab, J. J. (1970). *The practical: A language for curriculum.* Washington, DC: National Education Association.

Schwartz, A. J. (1991). Organizational metaphors, curriculum reforms, and local school and district change. In M. F. Klein (Ed.), *The politics of curriculum decision-making: Issues in centralizing the curriculum* (pp. 167–197). Albany: State University of New York Press.

Somerville, S. W. (2001). The legalization of home schooling in America: A quiet but persistent revolution. *Private School Monitor, 21*(4), 1–15.

Stecher, B. (2001). The effects of Washington education reform policies on schools and districts, 1999–2000. *PEA Bulletin, 22*(1), 4–14.

Stecher, B., Barron, S. E., Chun, T., & Ross, K. (2000). *The effects of Washington education reform on schools and classrooms.* CSE Technical Report 525. Los Angeles: University of California, Center for Research on Evaluation, Standards, and Student Testing (CRESST).

Stodolsky, S. S. (1999). Is teaching really by the book? In M. J. Early & Kenneth Rehage (Eds.), *Issues in curriculum. Selected Chapters from NSSE Yearbooks* (88th Yearbook reprint) (pp. 143–168). Chicago: University of Chicago Press and the National Society for Studies in Education.

Thornton, S. J. (2001). Legitimacy in the social studies curriculum. In L. Corno (Ed.), *Education across a century: The centennial volume: One hundredth yearbook of the National Society for the Study of Education* (pp. 185–204). Part I. Chicago: University of Chicago Press.

Weiler, H. N. (1983). Legalization, expertise, and participation: Strategies for compensatory legitimization in educational policy. *Comparative Education Review, 27*(2), 259–277.

Weiler, H. N. (1985). Politics of education reform. In R. L. Merritt & A. J. Merritt (Eds.), *Innovation in the public sector* (pp. 123–147). Beverly Hills, CA: Sage.

Weiler, H. N. (1990). Curriculum reform and the legitimation of education objectives: The case of the Federal Republic of Germany. *Oxford Review of Education, 1*(1), 15–27.

Wilson, B. L., & Rossman, G. B. (1993). *Mandating academic excellence: High school responses to state curriculum reform.* New York: Teachers College Press.

8

Accountability and School Improvement

Standards. Achievement scores. School report cards. International comparisons. And, of course, testing, testing, everywhere. Hardly a day goes by without educators, parents, students, and the general public being reminded about the performance of our nation's schools. (Fusarelli, 1999, p. 97)

In the world of education, increasing accountability tops the agendas of most key policymakers at the state, federal, and local levels. As Garn (2001) notes, "Few people argue against increasing accountability in public education" (p. 577). Everyone is talking about it, although it is by no means clear what they mean when they do. Nor is it clear for what purpose accountability systems are receiving so much attention. For example, is it performance-based accountability for the purpose of raising low student achievement? If so, then presumably school personnel—either teachers, administrators, or staff—are not doing their jobs well, or else student achievement would not be so poor. This type of accountability is punitive, requiring school personnel to be closely watched and monitored (a mindset based on decades-old assumptions about human nature, discussed by Douglas McGregor [1960] in Theory X). Related to this purpose is market-based performance accountability, where staff is rewarded for demonstrable gains in student achievement.

Other forms of accountability include standards-based accountability, a type of equity reform where all students are held to the same standards; resource accountability, a system to ensure that funds are properly allocated and spent; and choice-based accountability, where schools are held accountable through the decisions of parents as to which schools their children will attend. As an equity reform, standards-based accountability suggests that it is neither ethical nor just to expect different levels of achievement among *groups* of students—either along socioeconomic class, ethnicity, or gender lines. Recent research has found that "particular configurations of state accountability and standardized testing can

189

positively impact both teacher expectations and instructional practices intended to improve student achievement, particularly for children of color and children from low income homes" (Skrla, 2001, p. 1). Moreover, asserts Skrla, "the benefits may be cumulative, producing long-term effects that far transcend what is measured by a single-year assessment of academic progress" (p. 1).

Resource-based accountability addresses the question of the distribution of resources in schools. Are the level and distribution of resources adequate and fair? If not, "how many more resources would be needed in some districts or schools relative to others to achieve those goals?" (Ladd, 1996, p. 5). Choice-based accountability reforms, such as charter schools and vouchers, rely, in part, on indices of parental and student satisfaction as the accountability mechanism (a detailed description of choice vis-à-vis charter schools is contained in Chapter 11). This type of accountability places the onus of responsibility on the consumers of education (to make good, informed choices), rather than the providers (both in schools and within the state's regulatory system).

Unfortunately, much of the accountability rhetoric in education tends to coalesce around the punitive aspects of performance-based accountability. As Newmann, King, and Rigdon (1997) note, "Many politicians and policymakers today link school accountability and school performance" (p. 41). This reflects in part "a general preoccupation with managerial efficiency" for the purpose of increasing output with fewer inputs (Ladd, 1996, p. 1). Because this type of performance-based accountability has been the dominant theme of accountability reforms in education, this chapter examines the history and evolution of education accountability systems at the federal, state, and local levels, presents two case studies of accountability systems, explores recent developments and trends in performance-based accountability, and looks at accountability through different policy lenses. The chapter concludes with an assessment of the state of performance-based accountability in education today and offers suggestions for future directions of the movement.

Accountability in Education: A Brief History

Although improving education through increased accountability has been a dominant theme of recent education reform, accountability in education is hardly new. Education reform in the United States has a long tradition of achievement testing, use of behavioral objectives, and competency-based education. As a reform, accountability reflects the pressure in systemic reform simultaneously to loosen policies "mandating inputs while 'tightening' state oversight of outputs" (Cibulka & Derlin, 1995, p. 482). In the early half of the twentieth century, accountability was measured primarily as a function of inputs into the system. Traditional accountability measures have included class size, staff characteristics, expenditures, resources, and so on. Staff evaluations tended to reflect input-driven models as well: checklists were used to evaluate teacher lesson plans, how many times teachers asked questions, and wrote on chalkboards.

According to Jackson and Cibulka (1992), public demand for greater accountability in schools "began to surface in the 1950s, during the Sputnik scare" (p. 76). The movement continued to build throughout the 1960s and 1970s. During this period, educational policymakers' interest in theories of business and public administration, with their attendant emphasis on systems of planning, programming, budgeting, and management by objective, led state legislatures to enact accountability legislation—at least seventy-three such laws—between 1963 and 1974 (Rothmann, 1995). Most called for some type of assessment of educational performance (Rothmann, 1995). Accountability measures were also advocated as a result of increasing public anxiety over perceived declines in student achievement—clearly not just a recent phenomenon (Rothmann, 1995).

"The movement toward greater accountability in education has been one of the hallmarks of the 1970s" (Rich, 1978, p. 381). In the early 1970s, the goal of accountability systems was "increased efficiency through better management and improved fiscal procedures" (Pipho, 1989, p. 662). In essence, more bang for the buck. As Mazzoni (1995) observes, "'Accountability' for education—and educators—had been the subject of extensive legislative and regulatory action throughout the 1970s" (p. 55). In the 1970s and early 1980s, minimum competency tests were used as an accountability criterion. From 1973–1983, the number of states with some form of minimum competency testing rose "from 2 to 34" (Linn, 2000, p. 6).

Pressure for greater accountability increased with the release in 1983 of *A Nation at Risk* (Ginsberg & Berry, 1998). Accountability has been the cornerstone of nearly every major education reform of the last quarter century, including school-based management (decentralization), state takeovers (recentralization), and the drive for higher standards and high-stakes testing. Accountability rhetoric is usually couched in terms of the need to "drive up standards" (Ouston, Fidler, & Earley, 1998, p. 112). As Ginsberg and Berry (1998) note, "Much of the demand for stricter accountability emerged from agents or agencies external to school systems" (p. 43), a consistent facet of most educational reforms of the past century, driven in part by corporatist concerns for efficiency and excellence (Reyes, Wagstaff, & Fusarelli, 1999). Political and populist pressure for increased educational accountability comes largely from outside the educational establishment, while internal pressure for accountability comes principally from "school administrators, regulatory and accrediting agencies, professors and schools of education, and testing companies" (Cibulka & Derlin, 1995, p. 480).

The active involvement of big business in education reform throughout the 1980s and 1990s increased the pressure for system-wide, school-based accountability by linking reform to international economic competition (Jackson & Cibulka, 1992). As Cibulka (1991) observes, "international economic competition requires better information and improved performance" (p. 182). Increased emphasis on accountability has not been limited to the United States. Many industrial countries throughout the world are immersed in accountability reforms (Chapman, Sackney, & Aspin, 1999; Macpherson, 1998).

A dominant thrust of the reform movement was the use of "traditional state regulatory tools such as mandates and sanctions to assure local responsiveness to state reform goals" (Cibulka, 1989, p. 417). Some scholars predict that schools will place even greater emphasis on accountability in the coming years, due in large part to the efforts of neo-corporatist policy entrepreneurs pushing an "account-ability at all costs" philosophy (Reyes, Wagstaff, & Fusarelli, 1999, p. 197). There has been a shift in the focus and emphasis of accountability systems, with more emphasis on measuring student performance and assigning responsibility for re-sults (Pipho, 1989). One by-product of the renewed emphasis on accountability is a dramatic increase in testing (Hunter & Swann, 1999; Kuchapski, 1998). Most states rely heavily on commercially available standardized tests, although some states and districts have developed their own tests (Linn, 2000).

The Role of the Federal Government

Increased school accountability has worked its way into federal education policy initiatives as well. The Clinton administration advocated the creation and adop-tion of voluntary national standards, coupled with an examination system, in five core areas: English, mathematics, social studies, science, and foreign languages (Wong, 1995). Former president Clinton's Goals 2000 programs continued the trend toward increased accountability in education, reflecting growing concerns about low student performance, rising local tax rates, taxpayer rebellion to local school bond issues, and public dissatisfaction with public education, particularly in urban areas (Scribner, Reyes, & Fusarelli, 1995). The striking similarity be-tween America 2000 (former President George H. W. Bush's education platform) and Goals 2000 is evidence of the demands federal policymakers are placing on accountability at the local level. Continuing this theme, President George W. Bush signed into law the No Child Left Behind Act, which mandates state testing of children in grades 3 through 8, in addition to multiple other accountability pro-visions contained in the massive federal law.

More than a decade ago, Cibulka (1991) noted that performance reporting has reshaped educational politics and predicted a greater federal role in shaping the direction of accountability reporting. This prediction has come to fruition. During its reauthorization by Congress, amendments added to Chapter I, the major federal compensatory education program, included an emphasis on school performance accountability, requiring districts to identify low performing schools and develop comprehensive school improvement plans (Herrington & Orland, 1992). From the standpoint of educational policy, this suggests a new direction in federal involvement in accountability at the local level. The current emphasis on and pervasiveness of performance-based accountability distinguishes this era from pervious eras (Linn, 2000).

However, as Herrington and Orland (1992) point out in their study of the effects of the 1988 amendments to Chapter I on the policies and practices of large urban districts in Atlanta, Chicago, Florida's Dade County, and Dallas, these ac-countability provisions were already mandated by state or local mandate in three of the four districts. The result is that the federal accountability provision was seen as yet another administrative paperwork requirement to be complied with rather than as a tool to enhance program accountability and effectiveness. This example suggests that, although the federal government shares a concern about accountability with state and local policymakers, it is often behind the curve in efforts to implement stronger accountability policies in schools. Multiple state and local groups are leading the charge for increased school accountability nationwide.

State Accountability Systems

From the mid 1980s through the turn of the new century, state governments have become increasingly active in assessing student learning through accountability. Accountability measures include report cards, indices of program and school quality, expanded use of student test scores, and outcomes-based accreditation strategies and curriculum designs. Nearly every state mandates some form of statewide assessment system. Twenty-five states mandate school-level profiles (Mitchell, 1996). Student testing "has become the primary method by which states monitor curriculum and provide state accountability for education" (Blank & Schilder, 1991, p. 59). Cibulka (1991) identified three different rationales or purposes for accountability systems: (1) political responsiveness, (2) bureaucratic oversight and efficiency (rewards and sanctions), and (3) market efficiency (information to allow individual consumers to make better market choices).

Some policymakers argue that incentives should be provided to motivate schools to improve. Thus, schools with high test scores (the most common and easiest, if not most accurate, measure of performance) should be rewarded, either with more autonomy or cash bonuses (Sergiovanni, Burlingame, Coombs, & Thurston, 1999). Accountability programs offering incentives and rewards to individual schools and, most controversially, to individual school administrators and teachers have been implemented in several states (Cibulka, 1989). In some districts, the length of administrative contracts is tied to a performance evaluation.

South Carolina employs a School Incentive Program in which schools demonstrating exceptional gains in student achievement receive financial rewards. Principals and teachers (individually or as a group) may receive fiscal rewards for superior performance, based in part on accountability criteria (Cibulka, 1991). Schools and districts can be declared "educationally impaired" for failure to meet one or more accreditation standards (Cibulka, 1991, p. 188).

Accountability systems are expensive and have evolved through several stages. In Minnesota, local officials are required only to develop an accountability system tied to state graduation standards, while Kentucky has a highly centralized accountability system "of interlocking policies, tying the PR [performance reporting] system into rewards for teachers and schools and sanctions for poorly performing schools" (Cibulka & Derlin, 1995, p. 488).

In the mid 1990s, the Kentucky state legislature initiated a comprehensive statewide school reform (the Kentucky Education Reform Act—KERA), placing heavy emphasis on student and school accountability. Kentucky's statewide performance-based assessment system contains new curriculum (content) standards and curriculum frameworks and assessments, linked to a system of rewards and sanctions, which is tied to student achievement (Minorini & Sugarman, 1999).

In 1993, a new statewide accountability system was implemented in Texas, in which schools were placed in one of the following four categories: exemplary, recognized, acceptable, or low performing. Ratings are based on performance on a statewide test, the Texas Assessment of Academic Skills, and dropout and attendance rates. Exemplary schools receive cash awards. School report cards, which are becoming increasingly popular nationwide, are published in newspapers throughout the state.

Fuhrman (1999), in her analysis of "The New Accountability," argued that these new accountability systems share several common characteristics, including:

- A focus on student performance
- On schools as the unit of improvement
- On continuous improvement strategies
- Regular inspections
- More accountability categories
- Public reporting of results
- Real consequences attached to performance levels

POLICY VIGNETTE • *Accountability Policy in North Carolina*

In North Carolina, school performance is evaluated based on "expected growth," determined by a mathematical calculation completed by the state education department; expected growth is roughly equivalent to "one year's growth on standardized tests for one year of schooling" (Hunter & Swann, 1999, p. 241). Schools whose students achieve on average ten percent better than expected are designated exemplary, while schools whose students fail to meet expected growth levels are designated as "low performing" (p. 241). Teachers and assistant teachers in schools recognized as exemplary are eligible to receive bonuses of up to $1,000. Schools designated as low performing "receive state-level teams of instructional specialists" including "practicing and retired educators from public schools, universities, and community colleges for assistance in designing and implementing" school improvement programs (pp. 241–242). The state department of education assigns these teams to the schools; funding is provided through the state government.

Under North Carolina's "School-Based Management and Accountability Program" the State Board of Education has the authority to dismiss personnel in low performing schools, including "principals, assistant principals, directors, supervisors, and teachers" (p. 242). If more than half the schools in a district are low performing, the State Board of Education may suspend the superintendent and even, under certain circumstances, remove locally elected board members. In North Carolina, teachers in low performing schools are required to pass general knowledge tests.

POLICY VIGNETTE • *Milwaukee's Three-Tiered Accountability System*

The Milwaukee Public Schools have a three-tiered accountability system that includes statewide goals (focusing on student achievement and attendance), school-based goals (set collaboratively by the principal, faculty, and school site council), and an individual school narrative (Reeves, 1998). The system rewards improvement, allowing schools and districts that fail to meet statewide goals to achieve recognition for progress, while encouraging already high performing schools to find areas of improvement. The school narrative "allows principals to explain the meaning behind the numbers—the context, school climate, and professional environment" (p. 8). The school narrative enhances communication between school professionals, the media, and the public at large and "makes the essential case that accountability is more than test scores" (p. 8).

Despite the political popularity of using accountability reforms to improve education, criticisms of various accountability schemes include:

- Administrators are held accountable for variables not under their direct control, such as student achievement and attendance (Cibulka, 1989).
- Concerns have arisen about the validity of evaluation instruments and the evaluation process itself (Cibulka, 1989).
- Rejection of the values of efficiency and competition (Rich, 1978).
- Confusion about the purposes and role of testing in accountability assessment systems (Smith & O'Day, 1991).
- Unequal resources among districts and schools (Cibulka, 1991).
- Overreliance on tests fails to accurately or completely measure the varied missions of schools (Cibulka, 1991).
- Encourages teachers to "teach to the test," thereby narrowing the curriculum (Linn, 2000).
- Over-reliance on standardized tests stifles creativity and creates hostility between teachers and principals (Webber & Townsend, 1998).
- Ambiguity of the terms *success* and *accountability* (Webber & Townsend, 1998).
- Encourages test coaching and cheating (Linn, 2000).
- The argument that optimal performance results from threats and intimidation is dubious (Reeves, 1998).

Other criticisms include the following: (1) the system holds low and already high performing schools, which often have vastly different needs and student populations, to the same standards; (2) it assumes a cause-effect relationship exists between teacher and administrator performance and student performance; (3) the system unfairly rewards some teachers and administrators, while unfairly punishing others; and (4) these flaws raise serious scientific and moral questions (Sergiovanni, Burlingame, Coombs, & Thurston, 1999).

Recent Trends in Accountability

The Value-Added Approach

One of the most contentious issues in accountability is how to report test results. Some have suggested grouping together districts with similar socioeconomic and demographic characteristics. However, this approach has been criticized out of fear that it "lowers expectations or justifies existing performance differences" (Cibulka & Derlin, 1995, p. 484). Some states have adopted value-added schemes, while others de-emphasize comparisons by reporting information in alphabetical order. In recent years, the concept of value-added accountability has become increasingly popular. Under this system, schools compete with their own previous performance levels, rather than with each other. This approach balances concerns for equity and excellence by benchmarking performance on a school-by-school basis (Sergiovanni, Burlingame, Coombs, & Thurston, 1999).

State Takeovers

Another trend in accountability is state authority to take over chronically low-performing school districts. According to Swanson and King (1997), "Policies enacted in a number of states between 1983 and the mid 1990s authorized state education agencies to assume district operations" (p. 246). Twenty-three states currently have some mechanism for state takeover of individual schools or entire school districts (Hunter & Swann, 1999). In some cases such as Chicago, local municipal government is given the power to run the schools (Hunter & Swann, 1999).

In New Jersey, the state education department may dismiss and replace a democratically elected school board, superintendent, or district administrators. Of course, this assumes "that state-level officials can perform better than local officials" (Swanson & King, 1997, p. 246)—a policy assumption that is largely untested. State takeovers are based on the often erroneous premise that schools are low-performing because they are poorly managed. So far, the results of state takeovers have been mixed. As Hunter and Swann (1999) point out, state governments "often inherit difficult instructional problems but lack the expertise to solve them" (p. 246).

Public School Choice

A major debate in education is raging over accountability in charter schools. Thirty-eight states and the District of Columbia have passed charter school laws, permitting school administrators, teachers, parents, or members of the community to create their own publicly-financed schools. The basic premise of the charter school movement is that the bureaucratic nature of public education inhibits creativity and innovation, preventing school professionals from meeting the needs of schoolchildren. Thus, by freeing professionals from overly intrusive rules and regulations, we can create more effective, responsive public schools.

The focus of debate, however, centers on what criteria should be used to hold charter schools accountable to the public. Ostensibly, charter schools have a built-in accountability mechanism—either they fulfill the terms of their charter or they face sanctions and closure by the state. Manno, Finn, and Vanourek (2000) refer to this as "accountability via transparency" (p. 473). However, as Fusarelli and Crawford (2001) point out in their introduction to a special issue of *Education and Urban Society* devoted to "Charter Schools and the Accountability Puzzle," accountability in charter schools has multiple meanings and usages. According to the authors, accountability in charter schools involves much more than answering a straightforward technical question of whether student achievement improves or not. It is "inextricably tied to political, social, and ethic questions of social justice and equal educational opportunity" (p. 107).

At least five different types of accountability are found in charter schools nationwide (to differing degrees, dependent on location): (1) market-based or consumer-driven accountability (if consumers are not satisfied with the school's product, the school will close), (2) achievement-based (via meeting standards and improving test scores), (3) professional-based (placing substantial control and responsibility in the hands of teachers and administrators), (4) bureaucratic or regulatory-based (monitoring and control), and (5) political accountability (Fusarelli & Crawford, 2001). Political accountability is not used here in the traditional sense of being responsive to voters' preferences; rather, political accountability means that politics, political considerations, and pressure pervades all facets of the seemingly neutral, objective language of accountability, suggesting that decisions as to whether to sanction charter schools, close them, renew (or not) their charters, or increase (or not) the number of charter schools authorized by the state is based more on politics than on any objective measures of accountability per se (see also Fusarelli, 2001; Hess, 2001).

The type of accountability system utilized by a school district, state education department, or federal agency has a significant effect on educational policy and practice. For example, Arizona's charter school policy disregards professional accountability; there are "no procedures to ensure competence through teacher or charter school accreditation. The Arizona charter school legislation did not require charter school teachers to have state certification, a degree in education from an accredited school, or even a college degree" (Garn, 2001, p. 589). In his study of accountability in charter schools in Arizona, Garn (2001) found that "parental choice was the principal accountability mechanism" (p. 592).

Viewing Accountability through
Different Policy Lenses

Normative Dimension

Despite its technical, pseudo-scientific language, school accountability is immersed in highly value-laden, ideological, and contextual representations. Ouston, Fidler, and Earley (1998) observe that, "Often, accountability is presented as self-evidently 'a good thing' without any clear understanding of who is being accountable to whom, for what, by what process, and for what purpose" (p. 107). Despite the widespread adoption of various accountability systems throughout the United States and several other countries, the rationale for accountability reporting is unclear (Cibulka, 1991). As Kuchapski (1998) observes, "The pervasiveness of accountability as a method for reforming education may lead one to assume that a high degree of clarity surrounds the term, and a great deal of thought has gone into establishing the principles and elements that undergird the concept" (p. 185). According to Kuchapski (1998), "It is surprising to discover that no such clarity exists" (p. 185).

Accountability has traditionally been associated with the values of efficiency and effectiveness. However, renewed attention to performance gaps among ethnic groups has incorporated the value of equity into the development of accountability systems. When school report cards were first introduced in the states, many school officials complained that the system simply reinforced stereotypes about the high performance of affluent schools and the low performance of schools with poor, largely minority student populations (Cibulka, 1991). Although accountability theory rests in part on the idea that a system of rewards and sanctions will spur low-performing schools to improve, Ginsberg and Berry (1998) contend that "historically low-performing schools and districts tended to remain as the poorest achievers" despite reform efforts (p. 44). Thus, using accountability to improve schools raises several key questions in the normative dimension of policy—particularly when considering the values of efficiency, effectiveness, and equity.

Structural Dimension

As Smith and O'Day (1991) observe, "We do a terrible job of holding anyone accountable. In a typical situation, facing falling test scores, our local and state policymakers threaten, cajole, re-emphasize 'basic skills,' and adopt a new program as a panacea. Occasionally, a principal or superintendent is removed as a scapegoat, but rarely is the system altered in any significant fashion" (p. 252). A RAND study of principals' attitudes toward accountability found that many principals believe current accountability systems narrow the focus of public education (Mitchell, 1996). Principals expressed anxiety over incorporating rewards and sanctions into accountability systems, particularly given the limitations of traditional statewide tests and the lack of development of adequate measures of performance-based assessments (Mitchell, 1996). It is possible, looking at accountability policy from the structural dimension, that little structural change may occur—at least deep, structural changes. Change may occur at the margins—cosmetic changes that do little to alter the fundamental nature and character of education.

Sunderman (2001) examined how federal accountability mandates affected the design and implementation of Title I programs in Chicago, Cleveland, and Detroit. She found that the accountability systems in the three districts "were not as coherent or rational as reformers may have envisioned. Instead of a set of clearly articulated goals, they encompassed state-level legislation, regulations, and district-level reform initiatives . . . Rather than a stable system envisioned by reformers, these systems continue to be shaped by political and institutional factors unique to each state and district" (p. 512).

Judging from the accountability rhetoric coming from Washington, we would expect that school-based decisionmakers would be given the freedom and autonomy to adopt whatever strategies are most effective in increasing student achievement. However, as Mintrop, MacLellan, and Quintero (2001) found in their comparative study of accountability systems in Maryland, Kentucky, and San Francisco, most school improvement plans are very similar, suggesting institutional isomorphism. The Maryland and Kentucky state accountability systems "are driven by a few quantitative performance indicators, center on a largely performance-based test, have highly ambitious growth targets for all schools, focus on student achievement, and bestow rewards to and impose sanctions on schools based on quantitative performance records" (p. 205).

Constituentive Dimension

The United States, "with its tradition of popular sovereignty, the idea that 'the public has a right to know' is nearly unassailable. To resist it sounds undemocratic, elitist" (Cibulka, 1991, p. 182). Yet, as Cibulka (1991) observes, "It is far from clear for whose use performance information is intended" (p. 183). Although designed to improve education, few schools or districts are rated as low performing, educationally bankrupt, or educationally impaired under most state accountability systems. Whether it is a result of negative publicity, shame, or restructuring, nearly every state reports success stories of schools that went from low to high performing.

One of the original purposes of school report cards was to create an informed public who would, presumably, pressure local district officials to improve low-performing schools. However, as Cibulka (1991) noted in his analysis of accountability reforms in Illinois, "there is little evidence that this has occurred" (p. 191). Those most likely to use such performance reporting include those parents already active in schools, the media, and, not surprisingly, real estate agents eager to make their properties more attractive (Cibulka, 1991). Often, the media will purchase computer tapes and publish their own analyses. It is clear that along the constituentive dimension of policy, multiple actors stand to gain and lose from the implementation of accountability systems in school systems.

Technical Dimension

"The accountability impulse is built on the belief that once goals are clearly defined and stated in behavioral terms, they can be measured, and funding can be linked to these results" (Cibulka & Derlin, 1995, p. 481). Many states have created special divisions of accountability within state education departments. School performance reports are common in many states. School and district report cards are used to provide comparisons of student achievement, attendance, and dropout rates. In Illinois, annual school report cards contain information on student characteristics (demographics, plus attendance rates), student performance (statewide testing, graduation and retention rates), instructional setting (class size, average minutes of instruction, etc.), and financial information (Cibulka, 1991).

Under South Carolina's accountability system, school report cards containing information on student achievement, attendance, and dropout rates, as well as teacher attendance rates, are analyzed over three-year periods to assess school and district performance (Cibulka, 1991). Districts are evaluated by whether they meet minimum accreditation standards (e.g., teacher certification, instructional time, attendance) (Cibulka, 1991).

According to Berry (1996), "Most educational accountability systems draw upon relatively simplified indicators of student learning" (p. 233). However, note Ginsberg and Berry (1998), "even when multiple-indicator systems have been created, the evidence suggests that non-test score data get minimal attention" (p. 44). Effective internal accountability requires organizational capacity that many schools and districts lack (Ginsberg & Berry, 1998). Key barriers include lack of time and inadequate professional development (Ginsberg & Berry, 1998).

As Cibulka and Derlin (1998) note, new systems of accountability are in development throughout the United States. These new accountability systems have three distinguishing characteristics: (1) a shift from input (process) to output (performance) standards; (2) greater emphasis on what students should know and be able to do; and (3) a push to link often-fragmented state policies into a coherent framework (systemic accountability reform).

According to Richard Hunter, a comprehensive accountability system should:

- Consistently use and integrate measurable performance standards throughout the entire educational system (state, county, local, and school district levels).
- Implement school-based management and school improvement planning in all schools.
- Provide time for teacher planning and staff development.
- Involve parents, students, and the community as part of the accountability system.
- Offer significant financial rewards to teachers and staff of schools that exceed district and state performance goals (Hunter & Swann, 1999, pp. 247–248).

This method is consistent with that of Reeves (1998), who identified seven keys to effective accountability systems: "balance between achievement and improvement, specificity, focus on student performance, frequency, adaptation to individual strengths, rewards for the tough choices, and reflection" (p. 6).

The aforementioned examples suggest that attention to the technical dimension of accountability policy is crucial to the effective implementation and ultimate success of the reform strategy. Implicit in each model are assumptions of technical rationality, objectivity, and neutrality. However, as scholars examining policy through various interpretivist lenses have noted, assessment policy has "more to do with political spectacle and the struggle for power, position, resources, and the control over public schools than with empirical or rational analysis, moral imperative, or democratic debate" (Smith, Heinecke, & Noble, 1999, p. 157).

Accountability systems remain contested and controversial. When Illinois implemented performance reporting, much of the educational establishment opposed it, fighting the efforts of citizen advocacy groups who sought to broaden reporting criteria to include performance measures such as achievement data by ethnicity, gender, or educational classification (general or special education) (Cibulka, 1991). Administrator groups reportedly refused to use a state-developed video for parents explaining the school report cards (Cibulka, 1991).

Linn (2000) questions whether assessment-based accountability models actually improve education and concludes that the answer remains unclear. Reviewing previous literature on externally driven accountability systems, Ginsberg and Berry (1998) conclude that "much of the externally driven demand for accountability has not been terribly effective" (p. 45). The verdict is still out as to whether the renewed emphasis on accountability will actually improve schools (Cibulka & Derlin, 1998). The emphasis on accountability has forced school administrators, particularly superintendents and principals, to search for quick fixes to boost test scores. However, as Carter and Cunningham (1997) observe, "true excellence often requires time to stabilize and produce results" (p. 76). Given imperfect policy instruments, we believe continued emphasis on accountability in education, coupled with greater attention to performance differentials among socioeconomic and ethnic subgroups and the provision of appropriate resources and support, will produce better schools, thereby improving education for *all* schoolchildren in the United States.

Chapter Assignments and Activities

Field Investigation #1

Contrast and compare accountability policies in two school districts. What are their purposes, rules, and regulations? How are they similar? In what ways are they different? Do any differences affect the quality of education offered in the districts?

Field Investigation #2

Interview district officials, including the superintendent, about the district's account-ability policies. To what extent are they internally developed? To what extent are the policies and procedures externally mandated by the state education agency or the federal government? Ask how this affects the delivery of educational services to students. Is it beneficial or an impediment? In what ways? How are these accountability policies implemented in the district? Who is responsible and for what areas?

Current Events Project

Review newspaper articles related to accountability written within the last year. In addition to your local paper, *Education Week* (www.edweek.org) and the *New York Times* (www.nyt.org) are excellent sources of information on education-related policies. In your research, answer the following questions:

1. What normative questions are raised in these articles?

2. Which groups (e.g., parents, teachers, administrators, school board members, state and national policymakers) or constituents supported or resisted the drive toward greater accountability?

3. How is the policy tied into the structural dimension of policymaking in education? How does the governance structure of education affect the implementation of accountability?

4. What are some of the technical or practical problems that make implementation of accountability policies difficult?

Seminal Works

Educational research on accountability issues has a long history. Students seeking an examination of the multiple dimensions of accountability should review Helen Ladd's (1996) edited book, *Holding Schools Accountable.* Containing pieces by Richard Elmore, Susan Fuhrman, David Cohen, Eric Hanushek, John Witte, Helen Ladd, Caroline Hoxby, Jane Hannaway, William Clune, and Richard Murname, the book examines performance-based incentive programs, the effects of school choice and performance accountability, fiscal issues, and the costs of achieving high performance.

In addition, several excellent sources explore the politics of the account-ability movement. Scholars and students interested in an international, comparative perspective on accountability should check out R. J. S. Macpherson's (1998) edited work, *The Politics of Accountability,* the 1997 Yearbook of the Politics of Education Association. Containing selections from some of the leading scholars of school accountability, the book explores accountability reforms in the United States, Canada, England, Wales, and Australia.

References

Berry, B. (1996). Accountability, school reform, and equity: The troubling case of Sylvan school district. *The Urban Review, 28*(3), 233–256.

Blank, R. K., & Schilder, D. (1991). State policies and state role in curriculum. In S. H. Fuhrman and B. Malen (Eds.), *The politics of curriculum and testing* (pp. 37–62). London: Falmer Press.

Carter, G. R., & Cunningham, W. G. (1997). *The American school superintendent: Leading in an age of pressure.* San Francisco: Jossey-Bass.

Chapman, J. D., Sackney, L. E., & Aspin, D. N. (1999). Internationalization in educational administration: Policy and practice, theory and research. In J. Murphy & K. Seashore Louis (Eds.), *Handbook of research on educational administration* (2nd ed., pp. 73–97). San Francisco: Jossey-Bass.

Cibulka, J. G. (1989). State performance incentives for restructuring. Can they work? *Education and Urban Society, 21*(4), 417–435.

Cibulka, J. G. (1991). Educational accountability reforms: Performance information and political power. In S. H. Fuhrman & B. Malen (Eds.), *The politics of curriculum and testing* (pp. 181–201). London: Falmer Press.

Cibulka, J. G., & Derlin, R. L. (1995). State educational performance reporting policies in the U.S.: Accountability's many faces. *International Journal of Educational Research, 23*(6), 479–492.

Cibulka, J. G., & Derlin, R. L. (1998). Authentic education accountability policies: Implementation of state initiatives in Colorado and Maryland. In R. J. S. Macpherson (Ed.), *The politics of accountability: Educative and international perspectives* (pp. 79–92). Thousand Oaks, CA: Corwin Press.

Fuhrman, S. H. (1999). The new accountability. *CPRE Policy Briefs,* #RB-27, January 1999.

Fusarelli, L. D. (1999). Education is more than numbers: Communitarian leadership of schools for the new millennium. In L. T. Fenwick (Ed.), *School leadership: Expanding horizons of the mind and spirit* (pp. 97–107). Lancaster, PA: Technomic.

Fusarelli, L. D. (2001). The political construction of accountability: When rhetoric meets reality. *Education and Urban Society, 33*(2), 157–169.

Fusarelli, L. D., & Crawford, J. R. (2001). Introduction: Charter schools and the accountability puzzle. *Education and Urban Society, 33*(2), 107–112.

Garn, G. (2001). Moving from bureaucratic to market accountability: The problem of imperfect information. *Educational Administration Quarterly, 37*(4), 571–599.

Ginsberg, R., & Berry, B. (1998). The capability for enhancing accountability. In R. J. S. Macpherson (Ed.), *The politics of accountability: Educative and international perspectives* (pp. 43–61). Thousand Oaks, CA: Corwin Press.

Herrington, C. D., & Orland, M. E. (1992). Politics and federal aid to urban school systems: The case of Chapter One. In J. G. Cibulka, R. J. Reed, & K. K. Wong (Eds.), *The politics of urban education in the United States* (pp. 167–179). Washington, DC: Falmer Press.

Hess, F. M. (2001). Whaddya mean you want to close my school? *Education and Urban Society, 33*(2), 141–156.

Hunter, R. C., & Swann, J. (1999). School takeovers and enhanced answerability. *Education and Urban Society, 31*(2), 238–254.

Jackson, B. L., & Cibulka, J. G. (1992). Leadership turnover and business mobilization: The changing political ecology of urban school systems. In J. G. Cibulka, R. J. Reed, and K. K. Wong (Eds.), *The politics of urban education in the United States* (pp. 71–86). Washington, DC: Falmer Press.

Kuchapski, R. (1998). Conceptualizing accountability: A liberal framework. In R. J. S. Macpherson (Ed.), *The politics of accountability: Educative and international perspectives* (pp. 185–196). Thousand Oaks, CA: Corwin Press.

Ladd, H. F. (Ed.). (1996). *Holding schools accountable: Performance-based reform in education.* Washington, DC: The Brookings Institution.

Linn, R. L. (2000). Assessments and accountability. *Educational Researcher, 29*(2), 4–16.

Macpherson, R. J. S. (1998). (Ed.). *The politics of accountability: Educative and international perspectives.* Thousand Oaks, CA: Corwin Press.

Manno, B. V., Finn, C. E., Jr., & Vanourek, G. (2001). Charter school accountability: Problems and prospects. *Educational Policy, 14*(4), 473–493.

Mazzoni, T. L. (1995). State policy-making and school reform: Influences and influentials. In J. D. Scribner & D. H. Layton (Eds.), *The study of educational politics* (pp. 53–73). Washington, DC: Falmer Press.

McGregor, D. (1960). *The human side of enterprise.* New York: McGraw-Hill.

Minorini, P. A., & Sugarman, S. D. (1999). School finance litigation in the name of educational equity: Its evolution, impact, and future. In H. F. Ladd, R. Chalk, & J. S. Hansen (Eds.), *Equity and adequacy in education finance: Issues and perspectives* (pp. 34–71). Washington, DC: National Academy Press.

Mintrop, H., MacLellan, A. M., & Quintero, M. F. (2001). School improvement plans in schools on probation: A comparative content analysis across three accountability systems. *Educational Administration Quarterly, 37*(2), 197–218.

Mitchell, K. J. (1996). *Reforming and conforming: NASDC principals discuss school accountability systems.* Santa Monica, CA: RAND.

Newmann, F. M., King, M. B., & Rigdon, M. (1997). Accountability and school performance: Implications from restructuring schools. *Harvard Educational Review, 67*(1), 41–74.

Ouston, J., Fidler, B., & Earley, P. (1998). The educational accountability of schools in England and Wales. In R. J. S. Macpherson (Ed.), *The politics of accountability: Educative and international perspectives* (pp. 107–119). Thousand Oaks, CA: Corwin Press.

Pipho, C. (1989). Accountability comes around again. *Phi Delta Kappan, 70*(9), 662–663.

Reeves, D. B. (1998). Holding principals accountable. *The School Administrator, 55*(9), 6–12.

Reyes, P., Wagstaff, L. H., & Fusarelli, L. D. (1999). Delta forces: The changing fabric of American society and education. In J. Murphy & K. Seashore Louis (Eds.), *Handbook of research on educational administration* (2nd ed., pp. 183–201). San Francisco: Jossey-Bass.

Rich, J. M. (Ed.). (1978). *Innovations in education: Reformers and their critics* (2nd ed.). Boston: Allyn & Bacon.

Rothmann, R. (1995). *Measuring up: Standards, assessment, and school reform.* San Francisco: Jossey-Bass.

Scribner, J. D., Reyes, P., & Fusarelli, L. D. (1995). Educational politics and policy: And the game goes on. In J. D. Scribner & D. H. Layton (Eds.), *The study of educational politics* (pp. 201–212). Washington, DC: Falmer Press.

Sergiovanni, T. J., Burlingame, M., Coombs, F. S., & Thurston, P. W. (1999). *Educational governance and administration* (4th ed.). Boston: Allyn & Bacon.

Skrla, L. (2001). The influence of state accountability on teacher expectations and student performance. *UCEA Review, 42*(2), 1–4.

Smith, M. L., Heinecke, W., & Noble, A. J. (1999). Assessment policy and political spectacle. *Teachers College Record, 101*(2), 157–191.

Smith, M. S., & O'Day, J. (1991). Systemic school reform. In S. H. Fuhrman & B. Malen (Eds.), *The politics of curriculum and testing* (pp. 233–267). London: Falmer Press.

Sunderman, G. L. (2001). Accountability mandates and the implementation of Title I schoolwide programs: A comparison of three urban districts. *Educational Administration Quarterly, 37*(4), 503–532.

Swanson, A. D., & King, R. A. (1997). *School finance: Its economics and politics* (2nd ed.). New York: Longman.

Webber, C. F., & Townsend, D. (1998). The comparative politics of accountability of New South Wales and Alberta. In R. J. S. Macpherson (Ed.), *The politics of accountability: Educative and international perspectives* (pp. 172–184). Thousand Oaks, CA: Corwin Press.

Wong, K. K. (1995). The politics of education: From political science to interdisciplinary inquiry. In J. D. Scribner & D. H. Layton (Eds.), *The study of educational politics* (pp. 21–35). Washington, DC: Falmer Press.

9

Improving Teacher Personnel Policies

Better Teachers, Better Schools

Teachers are at the very center of education policies and school reform. Policies affecting these educators—their preparation, licensing (certification), hiring, remuneration (pay and benefits), working conditions, professional growth and development, recognition, and role in the education enterprise—are all crucial. From the very onset of free, public, compulsory, universal education, teacher-related policies have shaped who can teach which subjects, at what pay levels, and under what circumstances and conditions. Recent efforts to reform and improve the nation's schools have usually found their way back to schoolteachers and the policies that affect them. Even when bright and willing people enter teaching, we have no guarantee that they'll adjust, succeed, and remain in the profession.

As Firestone and Bader (1993) explain, "Underlying the florid rhetoric [of school reform] is a poorly formulated debate about whether to make teaching more bureaucratic or more professional" (p. 11). Policy analysis on school reform is not enough, as "the teacher must remain the key." Shulman (1989) goes on to explain: "Debates over education policy are moot if the primary agents of instruction are incapable of performing their function well. No microcomputer will replace them; no television system will clone and distribute them; no scripted lesson will direct and control them; and no voucher system will bypass them" (p. 5).

This chapter, then, analyzes teacher policies using the four dimensions: *normative*, as civil service employees striving for professional standing and practices; *structural*, as key targets of federal, state, and local policymaking; as *constituents*, in their efforts to shape policies in the key legislative, judicial, and executive arenas; and as *technical* concerns of how to prepare and promote teachers as critical actors in U.S. education.

Normative Dimension

As early as 1906, with the Carnegie Foundation for the Advancement of Teaching, teacher preparation came under scrutiny. When the movement for the "professionalization of everyone" (see Wilensky, pp. 1964–65) took hold, the Carnegie Foundation "became a major advocate of higher standards for teacher education and greater professional status for teachers" (Cremin, 1988, p. 499; see also Lagemann, 1983). "Yet, significantly," as Cremin (1988) pointed out, "even after teacher education had been dramatically upgraded in the 1960s, teachers, still articulating the rhetoric of professionalism, joined the union movement in large numbers and related to school administration through collective bargaining rather than professional colleagueship" (p. 500).

In the same vein, the Task Force on Teaching as a Profession (Carnegie Forum on Education and the Economy, 1986), in *A Nation Prepared: Teachers for the 21st Century,* warned that education improvement and success required higher standards, and that "the key to success lies in creating a profession equal to the task—a profession of well-educated teachers prepared to assume new powers and responsibilities to redesign schools for the future. Without a profession possessed of high skills, capabilities, and aspirations, any reforms will be short lived" (p. 2).

Ten years later, another blue-ribbon group, the National Commission on Teaching and America's Future (NCTAF), headed by North Carolina Governor Jim Hunt, reached much the same conclusion: that "without a sustained commitment to teachers' learning and school redesign, the goal of dramatically enhancing school performance for all of America's children will remain unfulfilled" (1997, p. 1).

The norms and values of policies affecting teacher personnel are complex and important. The so-called "slow revolution" (Grant & Murray, 1999) has occurred in attempts by teachers and their allies to grasp control over their professional practices. In part, this revolution involves teachers in controlling their own culture and determining with whom to work and how, even though many states and school districts are now trying to mandate (and control) collaboration.

This oxymoron of government-mandated teacher collegiality was questioned by Cooper (1989) when she asked, "*Whose culture is it, anyway?* If teachers are told what to be professional about, how, where, and with whom to collaborate, and what blueprint to follow, then the culture that evolves will be foreign to the setting. They will once again have a 'received' culture" (p. 47).

Yet Etzioni (1968) has argued that teaching is *not* a true profession at all. It is what he calls a "semi-profession," in contrast to "real" or "true" professions such as medicine, law, science, and engineering. As such, teachers' "training is shorter, their status is less legitimate, their right to privileged communications (e.g., attorney-client privileges) less established, there is less of a special body of knowledge, and they have less autonomy from supervision than 'the' professions" (p. v). Semi-professionals also tend to work in larger, more bureaucratic *organizations* (although with more pervasive health management organizations, this work-setting is changing even for physicians); are seen as civil servants and even as "employees;" and significantly the fields of teaching, nursing, and social work are predominately female, suggesting that fields dominated by women are accorded less professional status and recognition—a point made by feminist scholars. Thus, the struggle by teachers between an intense, internal desire to become professionals—with the concomitant pay, status, autonomy, and authority—and the external pressures from government policies that control their lives, is reflected in the ambivalence of teachers.

It is this tension that has sometimes divided the ranks of the teaching "profession" between those who accept their lower employee status and want to unionize and to take united political action, and those teachers who perceive themselves as members of a "helping profession" and who shy away from unionization, collective negotiations, and of course, illegal strikes. It is certainly important to keep this tension in mind when making and analyzing education policies affecting the lives, work, status, and beliefs of schoolteachers.

In summary, the efforts of teachers for control over their preparation and work has been complicated by:

- The sheer size and complexity of their occupation, numbering over 3.3 million teachers working in 15,000 school systems and over 96,000 schools.
- The ease and "flatness" of entry into the occupation (Lortie, 1975); unlike other professions, teaching lacks the increased status accruing to the promotion of senior law partners, doctors, accountants, and engineers.
- The limits of teachers' academic background, preparation, and knowledge base, which (unlike medicine and law) make the work itself hardly arcane or "life saving."
- Difficulties in proving that they are doing an effective job over the lifetime of their clients: children who are maturing into productive adults.

Policies affecting schoolteachers have come in three major forms. First, states and districts created policies and regulations about how teachers were to be recruited, prepared, assessed, licensed (certified), and hired in their first job. Since the 1900s, policymakers and analysts have tackled the problems of teacher preparation: Is it too long in duration? Too short? Too narrowly "professional" or too broadly "liberal arts?" Too theoretical or too practical? National commissions, state groups, legislatures, and state education departments have worked to raise the standard for new teachers while trying to ensure that the flow of qualified teachers is sufficient to meet demand.

Second, policies have determined the rights of teachers, as "employees," to form unions, to be recognized as exclusive agents for collective negotiations to co-determine with employers (school districts) their pay, benefits, and working conditions, and even to seek third party mediation or arbitration, should collective bargaining become bogged down and conflict-ridden. These policies, unlike those affecting preparation and certification, are relatively recent (since the 1970s) and treat the teacher as "worker" or "employee," not as trainee or professional.

Third, and most recently, policies affecting teachers have moved to engage teachers in their own school-site governance, shared decisionmaking, and professional collaboration. As part of this "new professionalism," to use a term coined by Kerchner and Mitchell (1988), teachers have come to participate on school-site councils or "teams" in setting school goals, formulating budgets, making recommendations on staffing, and working closely as colleagues. These three policy areas—teacher as trainee, teacher as employee, and teacher as professional decisionmaker (i.e., teacher preparation, teacher employee-relations, and teacher participation) have, since the turn of the twentieth century, all received considerable attention and continue to occupy policymakers across the country.

The structure of these policies, like the teacher-related policies themselves, has changed over the decades. Weiss, Altbach, Kelly, Petrie, and Slaughter (1989) noted the following:

> Historically, in the U.S. formal organizational control with the educational system has become increasingly nationalized and centralized while control of actual classroom practices [and teachers] has remained relatively diffuse and resistant to centralization. . . . Sustained, substantive changes in the content and daily practices of teaching and teacher education are less likely to be effectively mandated by upper echelons or external agencies. (p. 25)

Structural Dimension

This chapter also frames teacher personnel policies as a two-sided process, or as some might say, a two-way struggle. On one side, agencies of the government (e.g., school boards, state legislatures, governors, state departments of education) have written policies to control requirements for teacher preparation, access to the profession, pay levels (scales and schedules), rights to participate in union activity, and virtually every dimension of teachers' work lives, from recruitment to retirement, including participation in school-site decisionmaking. As the nation's largest civil service group, public school teachers number some 3.3 million, are located in every community, and are affected by a vast web of laws, rules, policies, and regulations as part of the larger public policymaking process. Teachers thus appear to be externally controlled by policies, agencies, and forces, rather than being managers of their own work lives and professional practices.

On the other side, however, teachers themselves, along with their colleagues and associations (e.g., unions), have struggled to gain greater, more direct control over their own work and self-concepts. Grant and Murray (1999), in their award-winning book, *Teaching in America*, explain this effort toward self-control as a "'slow revolution,' the gradual accretion of effort by schoolteachers to take charge of their practices" (p. 2). These authors recognize structurally, as do we in this chapter, that teachers are dually controlled and shaped: by these educators themselves and by policies and regulations over which they have only limited control. In this regard, Grant and Murray (1999) assert,

> Most education reforms have been mandated from the top and most haven't worked. We believe a second academic revolution is necessary because good teaching cannot be mandated or prescribed in a manual. Teachers need the proper authority and autonomy to nurture and assess good teaching. Students will not learn to be creative analysts and problem-solvers if they are taught by teachers who are not trusted to analyze and work out solutions to the problems of their own practice. (p. 3)

Without improved recruitment and preparation, better mentoring and support, and improved professional growth, however, teachers cannot hope to become acknowledged professionals. Policymakers are beginning to recognize this internal struggle against external controls and are trying to improve preparation and practice.

Teachers are also employees. They require decent pay and benefits, job security, and better working conditions. So, although teachers strive to improve their status as professionals, they have also formed local unions and become affiliated with one of the two powerful national and state associations: the American Federation of Teachers (AFT, of the AFL-CIO) or the National Education Association (NEA). In most states, laws permit teachers to form unions, to be recognized as exclusive, official bargaining units for teachers, and to participate in collective negotiations over pay levels and other contractual concerns.

Teacher education and certification remain primarily under the control of state policies, although a number of national agencies, commissions, and associations have attempted to span state boundaries and build a consensus and share practices.

1. The National Council for Accreditation of Teacher Education (NCATE): sets standards for schools of education and applies those standards in voluntary self-study processes.
2. Interstate Assessment and Support Consortium (INTASC): brings together thirty states to set standards for licensing new teachers and establishing common standards.
3. National Board of Professional Teaching Standards (NBPTS): gives national licenses to experienced, outstanding senior practitioners, working across the fifty states.

The process of setting policies to improve teacher recruitment and preparation, as well as continued professional growth, involves the following stages:

Attracting Good Teacher Candidates. Where can the nation find gifted college students who are willing to make teaching their careers? States use a number of incentive schemes to entice candidates into teaching, the most common being loan-forgiveness programs and scholarships. Data show, however, that these policies hardly work. A survey by the federal government found that about 50 percent of the undergraduates who prepared to teach in K–12 schools had not applied for a teaching job four years after leaving college. Of those who start teaching, 20 percent quit within three years. And undergraduates with the highest college admissions test scores are less likely to select teaching as a profession and more likely to resign from teaching if they do.

Recruiting Teacher Candidates.   What are the appropriate methods for locating and recruiting students to become teachers? When should they start their preparation: in undergraduate school, after graduation, in "fifth-year programs," or in alternative programs after college? What kinds of financial incentives can be and are used to attract the best and the brightest into teaching?

Pre-Professional Preparation.   What courses, undergraduate and graduate, should teacher trainees take in their teaching field and beyond? How much of a liberal arts (arts and science) education should they have before starting professional training?

Professional Education.   What courses in the history, structure, and development of U.S. education should students be required to take? How much pedagogy, curriculum design, testing theory, audiovisual, and technological techniques should trainees study? To what extent should students take courses in subjects such as Teaching of English, Teaching of Mathematics, Teaching of Biology, and Teaching of Reading, versus more general curriculum courses?

Practical Training.   When should teachers-in-training begin their exposure to real schools and classrooms, as tutors, interns, practice or student teachers, or teacher aides? How many hours, semesters, and even years of practical training should prospective teachers be required to take? Who should supervise and mentor these trainees? What's the relationship between the university faculty and the schoolteachers and program?

Initial Certification.   What should be the requirements for initial certification, including college courses, professional training, practical experience in the classroom, testing, and mentoring? How can policymakers balance the demand for more requirements, years of preparation, and costs, against the practicality of trying to recruit more and better students to become teachers?

Ongoing Professional Certification.   What are the best programs, practices, and experiences to ensure ongoing, lifelong professional growth and development? How might teachers' pay be related to their job experiences, competencies, and ongoing training?

National Certification. What is the role of national certification in improving local incentives, quality, and teacher leadership? How effective is national licensing in increasing the professional status, pay, and opportunity for teachers? Can states and localities learn anything about advanced assessment and certification from the national practice board?

Constituentive Dimension

Teachers do not control their training, although the national teacher unions are playing an ever-greater role in sitting on the boards of groups like the National Council for the Advancement of Teacher Education (NCATE). In fact, many agents (constituents) including the federal government, state education departments, universities and colleges, and these unions are having a hand in determining who becomes a teacher and how.

Thus, key teacher policies discussed in this chapter are those affecting the *recruitment, preparation,* and *licensing* of teachers, issues of great concern to the education profession, the universities and colleges that traditionally train teachers, and the public at large. The need for more qualified teachers has been stressed by every agency of government, as a national, state, and local concern. The National Commission on Teaching and America's Future (NCTAF) stated the issue as strongly as possible for teachers, schools, districts, communities, and the nation:

> America's future depends now, as never before, on our ability to teach. If every citizen is to be prepared for a democratic society whose major product is knowledge, every teacher must know how to teach students in ways that help them reach high levels of intellectual and social competence. Every school must be organized to support powerful teaching and learning. Every school district must be able to find and keep good teachers. (p. 3)

In its first publication of the new millennium, *Education Week* devoted a special issue to teaching, *Quality Counts 2000,* subtitled "Who Should Teach?" (2000, January 13), stating that "good teaching matters. And pressure to improve the quality of the teaching force has never been greater. Today, research is confirming what common sense has suggested all along: A skilled and knowledgeable teacher can make an enormous difference in how well students learn" (Olson, 2000, p. 12).

Policies on teacher preparation and certification have a strong constituentive dimension, because controlling access to a profession has been a concern since the rise of the guilds in the Middle Ages. Several key policy issues emerge from the process and results of teacher preparation, as defined by various key stakeholder groups. First, what courses and experiences should be required of candidates for a teaching license? Second, who should offer these courses—universities or other institutions? Third, what types of teacher quality assessments should be used and what is an acceptable level of attainment? Fourth, what research and information are used to shape teacher education and training?

POLICY VIGNETTE • *New York Teacher Preparation Reforms*

In 1998, the New York State Board of Regents issued its *Commitment: Teaching to Higher Standards*, which started with "stronger graduation requirements for students, more rigorous tests, and annual School Report Cards" (1998, p. 3). The Report continues:

> To ensure that students achieve those standards, we must also dedicate ourselves to building educational capacity where it counts the most—in the classroom, starting at the front of the classroom. The importance of good teaching cannot be overstated. Efforts to establish higher learning standards will only work if they are embraced by committed professionals who are ready and willing to help students meet the standards. (p. 3)

The **goals** of the New York State teacher improvement policies are as follows:

- All public school students have appropriately certified teachers who have met the high standards of rigorous teacher education programs.
- All teacher education programs produce high-quality teacher candidates.
- Teachers reflect the State's diversity.
- Programs are in place to ensure that hard-to-staff areas have access to highly qualified teachers.
- All teachers regularly participate in professional development linked to the learning needs of their students.
- Poorly performing teachers are given opportunities and assistance to improve their teaching, and where unsuccessful, are removed from the classroom in a timely fashion.
- All schools have educational leaders prepared to meet the challenges to school improvement.
- The state of teaching and teacher education is continually reviewed by all stakeholders: needed changes are made in a timely fashion. (pp. 3–4)

To meet these goals, a major constituent, the New York State Department of Education, recognized three "gaps" that required closing in teacher preparation and support.

Gap 1
New York does not attract and keep enough of the best teachers where they are needed most. Efforts must be made to find the best and the brightest, prepare them well, and support their teaching in the most difficult schools. More minority teachers are needed, as 45 percent of New York's students are minority while only 15 percent of the teachers are members of minority groups.

The new recruitment policies and programs should align supply with demand; monitor available positions by teaching field; create a *Teacher Incentive Plan* to attract and prepare well-qualified, certified teachers, including the following.

- *Undergraduate Scholarship Program:* $4,000 scholarships, annually, for four years; students will teach one year per scholarship year in an "eligible school."
- *Graduate Student Scholarship Program:* $10,000 scholarship for one year; students will teach for three years as repayment in an "eligible school."

- *Certified Applicant Scholarship:* $10,000 bonus with obligation to teach three years in a "high-need eligible school." Must have Permanent or Professional Certificates and strong recommendations. All awards will be indexed to changes in the Consumer Price Index.
- *College/University Incentive Program:* two-year competitive grants to colleges, working in collaboration with local schools, to improve teacher preparation and recruitment.
- *Business/Industry Challenge Program:* provide matching grants to help communities address issues that hinder teacher recruitment; create partnerships between local governments and the private sector to raise funds.
- *Master Teacher Program:* help outstanding teachers to obtain their Permanent or Professional Certificates and to gain their National Board for Professional Teaching Standards (NBPTS) certification.
- *Other Programs:* assist students in selecting teaching as a profession, initiate "jointly-registered" programs to shorten teacher preparation time; remove unnecessary barriers to becoming teachers; bring people with extraordinary qualifications and background into the profession. Curtail the issuing of "temporary licenses" using a schedule. No troubled or failing Schools Under Registration Review (SURR) will be allowed to hire temporary or provisionally licensed or temporary teachers.

The state recognized the extent of the teacher shortage when the rationale stated:

> The need to focus new financial resources on teacher availability and recruitment is well supported by the facts. A shortage of qualified teachers already exists in critical areas. . . . Adding to this problem, almost half of current teachers are expected to retire within the next decade. Other factors, such as increased enrollment, new universal pre-kindergarten programs and a reduction in the student-to-teacher ratio in the early grades, will require virtually all districts to increase the number of teachers. . . . New York City expects to hire approximately 8,000 new teachers in each of the next four years. (1998, p. 10)

Gap 2

Not enough teachers maintain the knowledge and skills needed to teach to high standards throughout their careers. The recommendations of the State Commissioner of Education include withholding an Initial Teaching Certificate until candidates receive their masters degree and pass all state certification examinations; new teachers will work with a mentor (senior teacher) during their first year of service. Certificates are awarded only after successfully completing another three years of teaching after their first year of mentoring.

Requirements for the Initial Certificate include:

- Completing an approved program of teacher education.
- Earning a bachelor's and master's degree with positive recommendations from an authorized institution awarding the master's degree, including the study of subject matter area and teaching methods at either undergraduate or postgraduate levels or both.

(continued)

POLICY VIGNETTE • Continued

- Achieving qualifying scores on the revalidated Liberal Arts and Sciences Test (LSAT), Assessment of Teaching Skills (ATS), and Content Specialty Test (CST).
- Completing all requirements for the master's degree in two years, including the mentored first year of teaching.

Effective in 2003, New York State is also extending the time and requirements for the Permanent or Professional Certificate.

Requirements for a Professional Certificate:

- Complete a year of "mentored" teaching.
- Complete three years of satisfactory teaching beyond the mentored experience, including annual professional reviews.
- Maintain their Professional Certificate in good standing based on satisfactory professional development by accumulating 175 hours of credit every 5 years.

The net effect of these new certification requirements is to extend entry and permanent licensing over at least five years (nine years if the bachelor's degree is included), that is, a one-year master's degree, one year of mentored teaching, and three years beyond the mentored year.

Furthermore, updated certification policies by the year 2003 include a greatly increased range of new, specialized teaching certificates: Early Childhood (Birth to Grade 2); Childhood Education (Grades 1 to 6); Middle Childhood Education (Grades 5–9); Adolescence Education (Grades 8–12 by subject); Special Education—Early Childhood, Childhood, Middle Childhood, and Adolescence; Teaching Hearing Impaired, Visually Impaired, and Language Disabled. The policy rationale for these new, distinctive, finely-tuned, licenses is stated as follows:

> During the past decade, distinguished national commissions have emphasized the importance of recognizing the needs of students at different developmental levels and then preparing staff and planning curriculum and instruction accordingly. For example, the Carnegie Council in *Turning Points: Preparing American Youth for the 21st Century,* recommended staffing middle schools with teachers who are expert at teaching young adolescents and who have been specially prepared for assignments to the middle grades. Nineteen states have already put in place certificates for early childhood education, a critical developmental level. New York's new certificate structure will respond comprehensively to the new research by establishing a framework for ensuring that certified teachers are prepared to teach to higher learning standards. (New York State Board of Regents, 1998, p. 21)

Because more formal preparation will be required under state policies, the State of New York is increasing regulations and "will raise the standards for teacher education to produce outstanding professionals with the knowledge and skills to meet the needs for their students" (New York State Board of Regents, 1998, p. 23). Steps in meeting the new standards include:

- *Accreditation:* A professional accrediting agency, such as the National Council for the Accreditation of Teacher Education (NCATE), will evaluate the quality of programs, using external and internal (self-study) review, after which the Board of Regents, on recommendation of the State Professional Standards and Practices Board (PSPB), will take action to accredit teacher education programs.

• *Minimum Standards:* At least 80 percent of graduates of teacher education programs must pass one or more examinations, or the program faces "de-registration;" periodic reviews might raise the passing rate to 90 percent. In the last year, only 12 teacher education programs in the State out of 113 colleges had a better than 90 percent pass rate.

• *Professional Standards and Practices Board:* The PSPB will advise the Regents and State Education Commissioner and will recommend the components of the first-year teacher mentoring program, annual teacher performance reviews, certification requirements, criteria for accepting alternative routes to certification, such as Teach for America, design a code of ethics, and find ways to attract and retain teachers in high-need schools.

Policymakers are also concerned with keeping standards high, not only during the initial period of certification but also throughout the career of teachers. As the New York State report stated:

> All teachers, to remain good teachers, must constantly extend their knowledge and skills. Yet recent surveys [by the National Center for Education Statistics, 1993–1994] show only a minority of teachers get enough on-going training to keep up with the demands of their profession. The State has not required teachers to continue their education throughout their careers, although the State certification signifies competence. To address the gap, the Commissioner will now require all new teachers to maintain their certification in good standing, based on completing professional development provided by school districts and other sources approved to address local student learning needs. (New York State Board of Regents, 1998, p. 29)

The steps in ensuring lifelong learning include district plans for professional development, related to School Report Cards for each school, which are collaboratively developed; other development plans, including such activities as mentoring new teachers or applying for advanced licensing through the National Board of Professional Teaching Standards; and completion of 175 hours of advanced training, starting with teachers licensed after the 2000 school year. Transcripts will be available on each teacher's professional development; those teachers found wanting will be afforded "due process" to explain their shortcomings, possibly leading to removal for incompetence under Education Law Section 3020-a.

This teacher improvement policy—involving other constituent groups—also places responsibility on districts to be accountable for their teachers' competence: included are standards for teacher performance reviews, supervisory training for administrators, the use of portfolios and videos of teaching, and the rating of teachers on rigorous performance criteria. School Report Cards will include the number of teachers given unsatisfactory ratings by administrators and supervisors. Cases will be reviewed by the State Professional Standards and Practices Board. Applicants for teacher certification will be fingerprinted to allow criminal background checks.

(continued)

POLICY VIGNETTE • Continued

The Professional Board will recommend a Code of Ethics for Teachers to be adopted by the Board of Regents.

Gap 3
Many school environments actively work against effective teaching and learning. Policymakers recognize that placing quality teachers into inadequate or poorly managed schools will not work. Solutions include the following changes in policy:

- Increase the aids for library materials, textbooks, software, and hardware.
- Improved school construction, maintenance, and repairs.
- Increased emphasis on operating aid over categorical aid to increase flexibility.
- Attention to closing unsafe, unhealthy schools.
- More Operating Standards Aid to high-need districts to meet new standards.

Other policies would lower class size and improve school leadership and climate. All of these policies will be examined and carefully evaluated, as explained in the new policy statement: "In 1999, the Professional Standards and Practices Board, in conjunction with Department staff, will initiate a process for formative evaluation of the adopted plan to improve teaching. They will report annually to the Commissioner, with recommendations, and begin a summative evaluation in 2005. . . . The purpose of the formative evaluation will be to recommend adjustments to parts of the plan, as needed" (New York State Board of Regents, 1998, p. 39).

The case of New York State is typical of efforts to improve the preparation and growth of teachers. Some questions might be raised about the difficulty of extending the length and cost of teacher education and delaying initial and permanent licensing during a teacher shortage. Will these additional barriers and higher demands actually reduce the number of candidates, forcing school boards to hire "anyone they can find" or the state to issue temporary or "emergency" credentials to fill classrooms?

Noteworthy in New York's policies, as in most other states, is the near absence of teachers in the process. One can imagine a similar process for licensing physicians or attorneys, where these professionals and their "societies" and associations (constituent groups) would be central to the deliberation, enactment, and enforcement of new standards. But as Etzioni and Lortie have noted, teachers are not yet true professionals, with the state bureaucracy—not the teachers' associations—making the policies and enforcing them. Teachers are concerned bystanders in determining who will teach, with what education and skills, and to what standard. The norms of the semi-professional appear alive and well in New York and other states' policymaking.

Technical Dimension: Teacher Education Policy Trends

Four routes appear in the policies for improving and enhancing teaching.

Centralized and Tough.   Perhaps the strongest, most centralizing, and demanding policies are those set forth by the National Commission on Teaching and America's Future (NCTAF). It invites states to join in an effort to raise licensure requirements, accreditation, and thus to standardize their teacher training procedures and lock out candidates who may become teachers in other ways: as Peace Corps volunteers, as teachers first in private and parochial schools, or programs such as TEACH for America, a private organization that places trainees into inner-city and impoverished systems to learn to teach on the job.

Yet even the states with the toughest teacher requirements and standards find that when they cannot recruit enough fully licensed teachers, they allow less prepared teachers to fill the classrooms, feeling that is better to have someone as a teacher than to over-pack the rooms of qualified teachers. Olson (2000) writes:

> As the ultimate arbiters of who is permitted to teach, states can help recruit and attract candidates. They can also keep good teachers in the classroom and weed out the bad ones by providing support and evaluating performance. But in each of these roles, states are falling down on the job. When it comes to teaching, many states play an academic shell game. They raise standards for who can enter the profession on the front end, while keeping the door cracked open on the back end to ensure that every classroom will be staffed come September. (p. 12)

Accrediting Training Institutions.   Another approach is voluntary, whereby colleges and university teacher training programs may be accredited, usually through a self-study process and then a review by groups such as the National Council for the Accreditation of Teacher Education (NCATE). While many states, under their policies, also oversee schools of education, NCATE approval is seen by some institutions as an additional quality check and a reassurance to increased numbers of potential students (a marketing force).

Decentralized, Deregulated Policies.   Another policy approach, advocated in *The Teachers We Need and How to Get More of Them* (Thomas B. Fordham Foundation, 1999), is to deregulate the process, based on the argument that "more regulation will not bring us better teachers, not, at least without inducing new and worrisome problems, such as deterring able and well-educated people from teaching" (p. iii). The decentralized approach to policymaking in teacher preparation devolves control over staffing to each school, and then holds the teachers and administrators accountable for the learning of students.

Types of Training.   Tom (1989) questions policies that require more general courses: "If we merely require more liberal arts courses of prospective teachers, the value of such work is dubious" (p. 58). Will students (our prospective teachers) simply select the easier, less-demanding courses, as research indicates they do? (See Galambos, Cornett, & Spitler, 1985.) In their survey of the fifty state teacher preparation programs and regulations, *The Quest for Better Teachers: Grading the States . . .* (1999), Finn, Kanstoroom, and Petrilli reviewed state policies on teacher training along four dimensions and found the states were lacking: (1) accountability for results; (2) school-site staffing autonomy; (3) subject mastery; and (4) multiple pathways, open doors to new teachers through a variety of routes. Of these four policy areas, only two deal directly with training—subject matter mastery and multiple pathways. The other two are broader than training and apply to everyone: accountability and autonomy.

Thus, the technology of teacher preparation and licensing speaks of increasing the quality and access of talented teachers; the policies are not so clear because some new policies are moving to increase the demand for courses, practice teaching, and testing, while others press for greater openness, more multiple pathways, and wider access. In the middle stand the states, which continue to license teachers and review teacher training programs, and national and regional groups such as NCATE that offer voluntarily to accredit programs.

Whatever the solution, policymakers will continue to struggle to find the right (technical) rules and regulations to ensure that the nation's schools have a rich flow of well-prepared, high-quality candidates for teaching. Perhaps the National Commission on Teaching and America's Future got it right when it wrote in 1997 that

> Teacher expertise—what teachers know and can do—affects all the core tasks of teaching. What teachers understand about content and students shapes how judiciously they select texts and other materials and how effectively they present material in class. Their skill in assessing their students' progress also depends on how deeply they understand learning, and how well they can interpret students' discussions and written work. No other intervention can make the difference that a knowledgeable, skillful teacher can make in the learning process. (Darling-Hammond, 1997, p. 8)

Goodlad (1990) captured the needs of the nation in producing an increase in qualified teachers: their recruitment, preparation, certification, and support:

> We do not know how much the exemplary education of schoolteachers would ameliorate the nation's problems, especially when education exerts only indirect leverage and schools are only part of a total educational delivery system. Nonetheless, we are probably on the right course in believing that elementary and sec-

ondary schools providing superb education do and will make a significant contribution over the long haul. The conduct of such schools presupposes a large corps of well educated and trained teachers and administrators. (p. 3)

Teacher Union Policies

Running counter (or at least obliquely) to the professional norms of teaching are the incentives to unionize, to gain collective rights, and to negotiate collectively for contracts protecting the rights of teachers (seniority, tenure, transfer limitations, review and supervisory restrictions). Kerchner and others have argued that teachers are finding something of an oxymoron, a "union of professionals" (Kerchner & Koppich, 1993), or as a book title expresses, "the united mind workers" (Kerchner, Koppich, & Weeres, 1997).

Teacher unions are relatively new organizations, among the last employee groups to seek and receive the right to collective bargaining. Under state public sector labor laws, teachers have fought long and hard to receive recognition as a work force, being granted the right to unionize, although the teachers' associations date back to 1857 for the National Education Association (NEA) and 1919 for the American Federation of Teachers.

These policies help to determine the pay scale for teachers, their right to grieve, to strike (or not), and to organize teachers and other employees of school districts (e.g., bus drivers, paraprofessional teaching personnel, and secretaries). The normative dimension rests on the belief that teachers—like other employees— have the right to negotiate salaries and benefits, to "protect" the rights of teachers to become active policymakers in their districts, states, and the nation as a whole. Or, as Firestone and Bader (1992) state,

> Employees give up control over their work in order to protect job security and access to work. This model for organizing is also based on the assumption that all workers should be treated equally. Industrial unionism has been criticized as inappropriate for education, and it has been suggested that models from craft unions, professional associations, and artists' organizations be substituted. All of these encourage teachers to take more control of and responsibility for the work they do, and several provide a basis for acceptance of both permanent job differentiation and collegial selection. (p. 214)

Today, over 2.3 million teachers are active members of the NEA and 950,000 of the AFT. This section explores the structure of the teachers' associations, their role in federal, state, and local politics, and the practical problems that arise when teachers play a key role in co-determining the policies and programs in their districts and states. While teachers are generally hardworking, dedicated professionals, they do "break the law," striking when their unions feel that management misunderstands their needs. This breakdown of "law and order" in education gives insight (see Liotta, 2002) into the conditions of work and the essential needs of teachers for respect and empowerment.

POLICY VIGNETTE • *Yonkers, New York, Teachers' Strike*

On October 1, 1999, strategically a Friday, the Yonkers Federation of Teachers (YFT), an affiliate of the American Federation of Teachers (AFL-CIO), the largest teachers' union in Westchester County, New York, and fourth largest in the state, went "ON STRIKE!" (Mickey, 1999) for five days. The issue was neither teachers' pay nor benefits—the usual cause of worker walkouts. Instead, teachers claimed that the Yonkers' superintendent, Dr. Andre Hornsby, recently arrived from the Houston public schools, had rammed block scheduling and a longer school day down the teachers' throats, without adequate involvement and discussion.

The YFT president, Steve Frey, explained, "the big thing is [scheduling] and the district's philosophy to impose things on us without consultation. There's a lack of respect for the opinion of teachers" (Halbfinger, 1999). Further, new teaching schedules were delivered in late August, not June, which was an "insult" to teaching professionals, Frey continued. As the contract expiration on October 1 approached, teachers threatened to strike, while the superintendent vowed to keep the schools open, replacing Yonkers' 2,100 teachers and going to court to seek an injunction banning the walkout. The proposed block schedule looked something like this at the ten middle schools and high schools in Yonkers:

7:20–7:41	Homeroom Period
7:52–9:18	Block One
9:21–10:47	Block Two
10:50–11:18	Lunch (alpha group)
11:20–12:48	Block Three
12:51–2:17	Block Four

Teachers would instruct on alternate days so as to cover the five or six required subjects in block form over a six-day period. As a pro-union statement in Letters to the Editor (Foley, 1999) explained:

> We are told by the superintendent, Dr. Andre Hornsby, that block scheduling is here to stay; but we are not told that no one, absolutely no one, has been guided as to how to handle 30, 40, 50 kids in a room for 84 minutes without the benefit of direction. Students and teachers go 4 and 5 hours without a break after having the lunch period at 8:45 in the morning. We are not told that under the current block schedules, students are actually spending less weekly instructional time with their teachers, and that time is hardly quality. We are not told that every single study done on block scheduling indicates that it cannot work unless there is ample preparation and planning. (pp. 7–8)

The effects would include:

1. Change from 42-minute periods, with each teacher instructing five periods per day, for 210 minutes of daily instruction, to three 84-minute "blocks" or 249 minutes per day.

2. Some teachers were concerned about having a 8:45 AM lunch period to accommodate the schedule.
3. Others worried about having three blocks consecutively with no time to rest, plan, or even go to the restroom.

The walkout lasted from October 1 through October 7, during which time both sides took action. The teachers' union held rallies, as "more than 1,000 teachers, parents, and students swarmed Board of Education headquarters, demanding that officials resign and the district return teachers to the classroom" (Liotta, 2002, p. 155). A host of related issues appeared during the course of the strike: (1) change from an appointed to elected school board; (2) personal verbal abuse of the superintendent: "Hornsby goes! Teachers stay!"; (3) candidates for elections joined in supporting the teachers' union, including presidential, mayoral, and city council candidates; (4) accusations that the union incited the students to fight and abuse the buildings, so that schools had to be closed; and (5) statements that the strike was racist.

By the second day of the strike, both sides agreed that without outside help, the situation might cause great harm to the students. Labor and management selected two outside mediators to help settle the contract and get the teachers back to work. While the two sides attempted to bargain a contract, the school board was seeking a contempt of court decision because the injunction prohibited the strike, which was already illegal under state labor policy.

By day three of the walkout, it was obvious that neither "side" could win. Union members faced dire prospects of losing money, going to jail, and mounting pressure from the community. The superintendent had learned that the YFT meant business and were willing to put their income and careers on the line. Mediators rushed back and forth, trying to forge an agreement that would bring the two sides together. Everyone got into the act. Yonkers Mayor John Spencer came forth to help settle the dispute, because under state policy, the mayor appoints the school board in Yonkers, rather than through elections as in most districts. As the newspapers reported, "Yesterday, Spencer stood alongside School Superintendent Andre Hornsby and Steve Frey, president of the Yonkers Federation of Teachers, as they walked out of the Board of Education offices to announce a tentative deal. Both sides credited the first-term mayor, who is up for re-election this fall, with playing shuttle diplomacy during the strike, helping them work out their differences" (Liotta, 2002, p. 155).

Who got and gave up what? The superintendent put aside block scheduling, the major bone of contention between management and the teachers, at least for the school year (1999–2000). In return, the union agreed to increase each teaching period by about five minutes and to shorten the lunch period: to work about forty more total minutes each day. And teachers will work one more day as part of the settlement and give up the benefits of seniority. Some argued that Dr. Hornsby softened his position, backing away from his "My way or the highway!" approach and coming to respect the teachers and to listen and involve them in making key decisions. One report said that in the interest of cooperation and for the benefit of the students, Superintendent Hornsby and YFT President Frey agreed "to make joint trips to Albany [the NY State capital] in search of more funding" (Halbfinger, 1999, p. 1A).

Law and Policy

Under New York's Public Employees' Fair Employment Act, Article 14, also called the Taylor Law after Prof. Robert Taylor who drafted the original legislation in 1967, teachers enjoy the right to unionize, to be represented, to bargain and sign agreements with school boards, but not to strike. Thus, teachers' strikes such as the Yonkers walkout are illegal.

The language of New York's Taylor Law is quite typical of labor laws in the public sector. First, it grants "public employees the right to form, join, and participate in, or refrain from forming, any employee organization [union] of their own choosing" (Section 202). Second, public employees have the right "to be represented by employee organizations, to negotiate collectively with their public employers in the determination of their terms and conditions of employment, and the administration of grievances arising thereunder" (Section 203). Third, public employers [e.g., school boards] are empowered to recognize employee organizations once certified or recognized as the "exclusive representative" of employees in that bargaining unit. Fourth, employers are "required to negotiate collectively with that employee group." Fifth, bargaining must occur "at reasonable times and confer in 'good faith' with respect to wages, hours, and other terms and conditions of employment" (Section 204.3).

While the Taylor Law guarantees public employees the right to unionize, engage in good faith bargaining, and have access to third party intervention (e.g., mediation and arbitration) in the case of impasse, the law also lays heavy penalties on public employees who stage a walk-out (Section 210). It states: "No public employee or employee organization shall engage in a strike" or "cause, instigate, encourage, or condone a strike."

Loss of Two Day's Pay for Every Day on Strike.   In the words of the Taylor Law, "the chief fiscal officer of the government [school district] shall deduct from the compensation of each such public employee [teacher] an amount equal to twice the daily rate of pay for each day or part thereof that he had violated this subdivision" (Section 310.f).

Temporary Loss of "Agency Shop."   The teachers' association will no longer have its membership dues automatically deducted from teachers' paychecks, a mechanism by which school districts collect union dues, relieving the union itself from having to bill and collect membership dues from each individual union member. In effect, the union loses rights granted under Section 208(b), rights "to membership dues deduction" by employers for a period of time specified by the local school board.

Court Injunctions, Fines, and Jailing Sentences for Striking Teachers and Their Union Leadership.   The state labor policy also provides a procedure for school districts to seek court injunctions against striking teachers, as stated in Section 211 of the state statute: "the chief legal officer of the government [school board] shall forthwith apply to the supreme court for an injunction against such viola- tions . . . to punish such violation." Actions can involve restraining orders, fines against strikers and their union, and even jail sentences for union leaders.

Loss of Prestige. Finally, strikes can be condemned in the public eye, as well as by the courts and school boards. In one of the first great strikes in the USA, the United Federation of Teachers (UFT) went on strike several times over the power of the community in Ocean Hill-Brownsville, in Brooklyn, New York, in 1968, to remove fourteen teachers. As Ravitch concludes in *The Great School Wars* (1974), "the union won the right to return its members to the classrooms of Ocean Hill- Brownsville, as well as strong procedural protection for the future. But its image as an idealistic and socially progressive union was tarnished among the liberal in- telligentsia and many black leaders. The union's victory established it as a politi- cal power in the city and state, but the price of victory was high" (p. 378).

As our case study shows, teachers unions, such as the Yonkers Federation of Teachers, are empowered by the New York State Taylor Law (Public Employ- ees' Fair Employment Law) to seek official school board recognition as the bar- gaining unit, and to be allowed to participate in "good faith" bargaining with the board. But, in exchange for the right to negotiate and the protections of collec- tive action, the Taylor Law makes public employee strikes illegal and imposes stringent penalties for unions that break the law.

Kerchner and Mitchell (1988) spell out the normative frame for under- standing teachers' union policies, and how they have affected the role and con- cept of teachers in the United States. They wrote:

> The new idea represented a shift in the social beliefs that legitimized teachers' pur- suit of self-interest, redefined their access and participation in decision-making and recast ideas about the propriety of teachers' engaging in political activity. The idea of a union also had an organizational dimension that shaped decision mak- ing and the norms by which the critical sub-groups within schools related to one another. Finally, the new idea concerned itself with the conception of teachers as employees and the definition of teachers' work. (p. 3)

Thus, the unionization of teachers was both a move toward greater unity and focus as an employee group, and less concerned organizationally about being perceived as professionals. However, as the "bread and butter" issues of pay, ben- efits, and working conditions were settled through collective bargaining, the teachers unions turned attention to education policies, attempting to increase their voice for better practices, stronger quality of education, and high academic results.

Kerchner and Mitchell (1988) conceived of teacher unions passing through three generations: First, "the meet-and-confer generation" was marked by infor- mal means by which administration "represented" and looked out for the needs of teachers. Data on these first generation districts show that despite an assumption of "bonds of trust, communication, and grants of mutual confidence by teachers and administrators, in fact the relationships were highly fragile, particularistic, and easily damaged" (p. 96). Because the relationships were "informal," they lacked, according to Kerchner and Mitchell, "institutional mechanisms" to manage labor-management conflict when it appeared (p. 97).

The second generation, coming with collective bargaining, was called the era of "good faith bargaining" and was based on a set of policies emanating from the state legislature and the state public employment relations act (PERA). Without legal backing, teachers had little power to force school boards to participate in good faith bargaining. And the third generation may involve teachers in professional activities, such as sharing in determining curriculum standards and programs. As Kerchner and Mitchell (1988) explain,

> If teachers are to behave as organized professionals, they must have some means of formulating and giving organizational authority to their collective professional judgments. They must be able to express their ideas about the proper goals, and the most appropriate strategies for handling education problems. Moreover, teacher organizations need to create more integrated work groups within the schools [shared decisionmaking], groups that share much more than common work rules and grievance mechanisms. They need to be organized around shared educational goals and integrated school programs. (p. 238)

The major themes of this chapter are captured in this statement: teachers' pervasive need to be treated and to act as professionals, their desire to participate as colleagues in determining the work and programs, and the ongoing interest in being "organized professionals," under a collective bargaining structure.

Teacher Participation Policies

The normative arguments for teacher collegiality and collaboration are important in understanding these new policies, "forming," as Hargreaves (1994) argued, "vital bridges between *school improvement* and teacher development" (p. 186). Proponents of improving schools through close teamwork by teachers, administrators, and even parents take as articles of faith that teachers (1) want to be part of the decisionmaking process; (2) have the skills to become working colleagues; (3) understand the collaborative process; and (4) are able to harness their shared interests to problemsolving in their schools. Policies for school reform, then, are building team management into their requirements, despite the lack of hard evidence that shared decisionmaking improves schools and enhances student achievement (see Malen, Ogawa, & Krantz, 1990).

Hargreaves (1994) sums up the normative expectations of teacher involvement as follows:

Collaboration and collegiality, then, form significant planks of policies to restructure schools from without and to improve them from within. . . . Consequently, while collaboration and collegiality are not themselves usually the subject of national, state, or provincial [Canadian] mandates, their successful development is viewed as essential to the effective delivery of reforms. (p. 187)

But, for all the desirability of enacting policies that bring teachers together as working colleagues, Hargreaves argues that real teamwork cannot be forced, mandated, or imposed, or these become what he calls "contrived collegiality." Teachers seem willing to share ideas outside their classrooms, around short-term projects, but reserve the right to close the classroom door and teach as they think best.

Thus, policies on teachers as professionals have made certain assumptions that have been questioned by academics, but less so by practitioners. Shared decision-making policies and laws in some states now require that each school have a site-based team or committee of teachers, working with parents and administrators, to help govern the school. The norms rest on a common belief that, like industry, schools would benefit from a closer collaboration among staff and community.

Teaching has long been an individual adult activity: in fact, Lortie (1969) argues that schools were designed to limit interdependence among the production units (classrooms) to allow for high teacher turnover and school growth. Individual teachers come and go without affecting classrooms across the hall. As a result, a culture of independence, if not isolation, emerged. Hargreaves (1994) writes that "the protection of their individuality, and their discretion of judgment, is also a protection of their right to disagree and reflect critically on the values and worth of what it is they are asked to collaborate about" (p. 191).

Critics of shared management policies fear co-optation most of all. They fear that policies actually will weld teachers to external, state-imposed rules and controls rather than to nurture a meaningful support system for teachers in their schools, departments, and districts. Hargreaves contrasts collaborative cultures with what he called "contrived collegiality." Table 9.1 shows the different qualities of true collaboration versus a more contrived relationship.

TABLE 9.1   *Collaboration versus "Contrived Collegiality"*

Collaborative Cultures	*Contrived Collegiality*
Spontaneous	Administratively regulated
Voluntary use of time as needed	Compulsory mandated prep time used
Developmental and personal	Implementation-oriented
Changing and dynamic	Fixed in time and space
Unpredictable	Predictable
Peer support and caring	Repressive supervision

Lieberman, Darling-Hammond, and Zuckerman (1991) see policies as important, restructuring schools "to create these learning opportunities within school organizations energized by collaborative inquiry, informed by authentic accountability and guided by shared decisionmaking" (p. 21).

The most recent policies passed by state legislatures and implemented by state departments of education and local boards of education affect the work lives of teachers—and their sense of professionalism and autonomy. These policies are efforts in states and districts to engage teachers in the decisionmaking process. Years ago, Shulman (1989) expressed this drive for involvement and collaboration as follows:

> Schools are asked to become like our best corporations, employing modern methods of management to decentralize authority, to make important decisions at the point where the street-level bureaucrats reside. Leadership is not monopolized by administration but is shared with teachers. (pp. 6–7)

Throughout the United States, state legislatures have passed laws requiring that schools become "self-governing." In New Jersey, for example, the policy requires that certain schools adopt a "whole school reform model" using School Management Teams (SMTs), comprised of teachers (as a minority voting bloc), parents, administrators (the principal), and for high schools, students. In New York, too, the policy stipulates site-based management and shared decisionmaking for all schools, with each key constituency electing its own representatives.

In 1991, the New York State Education Department in *A New Compact for Learning* stated in the words of the education commissioner, Thomas Sobel, that the Board of Regents acted "to bring about participation by teachers and parents in planning and decision-making for schools." Under the goal to promote local initiatives, the *Compact* explained that "the Regents will promote the participation of teachers and parents in making decisions about educational matters in all schools. The Regents will seek ways to increase the amount of time for participation in staff development, planning and decision making by relaxing the regulation on conference days and/or seeking funds for an extension of the work year" (1991, p. 5).

In all, "individual schools should be as autonomous as feasible within a context of shared purpose and support. As many operating decisions as feasible must be made by the principal, the teachers, the other staff members, and the parents whom the school unit comprises . . . Site-based decision making is not just a contemporary fad; it is a sound and enduring principle of institutional effectiveness" (*A New Compact,* 1991, p. 10).

These concepts of shared decisionmaking for teachers were then passed into law. Section 100 of the New York State education law (Title 8) specifies the policies on engaging teachers in the school management process, specifically: "The purpose of school-based planning and shared decision-making shall be to improve the educational performance of all students in the school, regardless of such factors as socioeconomic status, race, sex, language, or disability." The policy stipulates that a representative body, including the superintendent, members of the administrators and teachers "bargaining units," and parents, shall establish the shared management plan for approval. This plan shall specify the following:

1. The educational issues, which will be subject to cooperative planning and shared decisionmaking at the building level by teachers, parents, and administrators;
2. The manner and extent of the expected involvement of all parties;
3. The means and standards by which all parties shall evaluate improvement in student achievement;
4. The means by which all parties will be held accountable for decisions which they share in making;
5. The process whereby disputes presented by the participating parties about the educational issues being decided upon will be resolved at the local level; and
6. The manner in which all state and federal requirements for the involvement of parents and teachers in planning and decisionmaking will be coordinated with and met by the overall plan.

The effort to engage teachers in shared governance—in the presence of collective bargaining policies—introduces some interesting policy problems. How can teachers be part of a shared management team and continue negotiating collectively and autonomously with management about related issues of pay and working conditions? Section 100 recognizes this conflict, stating that "those portions of the district plan that provide for participation of teachers in school-based planning and shared decision making may be developed through *collective negotiations* between the board of education and local bargaining organizations representing teachers." In effect, the union rights of teachers override their participation as representatives of teachers in their particular school. Again, the effort to become professionals, democratic representatives, and unionists become entangled as different policies take effect.

Teacher Policies Reviewed

The three key policy concerns of this chapter have been the preparation, unionization, and collaborative leadership of teachers. As shown in Table 9.2, these areas have occupied education reformers and leaders, as well as teachers themselves, for years. Together, policymakers argue, better teachers, with better pay and support and a stronger voice in setting policies in their schools, should benefit students.

TABLE 9.2   *Key Policy Areas for Teacher Personnel Development*

I. Teacher Preparation and Licensing	II. Teachers' Job Rights & Remuneration	III. Teacher Collaboration & Shared Management
Recruitment policies	Pay levels	Representation on school councils/teams
Pre-prep. requirements	Benefits package	Shared decisionmaking
Professional requirements	Tenure and seniority	Site-based budgeting and management
Practical/classroom requirements	Recognition as a bargaining unit	Teamwork and true collegiality
Competency testing	Grievance procedures	Teacher leadership
Licensing procedures	Job protection	Collaboration
Post and relicensing	Third party dispute mediation	Mentorship and support
Professional growth	Improved working conditions	Role in vision-setting and implementation

Yet each of these three policy areas has different norms, different arenas and interest groups (constituents) involved, different levels of government (structures), and works on separate issues in teacher-related policymaking. Policies affecting teacher education and licensing take place quite apart from teachers themselves—usually imposed by the state and carried out by universities, colleges, and other education groups and institutions.

Unionization of teachers strives to balance the power of management and labor, as witnessed by the standoff in the five-day Yonkers' strike, where the YFT broke the law, staged a walkout, and tried to force the superintendent to change his policies.

Only recently, with site-based management, have policies attempted to bring teachers back into the education policy process in schools. Although shared decisionmaking is just starting, it does hold out some promise as a means to empower teachers and to bring them back to a concern for professionalism and autonomy, steps attributed by Kerchner and Mitchell (1988) to "Third Generation" labor relations.

Chapter Assignments and Activities

1. Examine the policies on teacher preparation, certification, and professional growth in your state and/or district. How are they working to balance (a) the need for more teachers to come into the field, (b) the drive for higher standards and more training time, (c) the rising costs of educating teachers,

(d) the testing of teachers, and (e) the means for assessing the quality of teachers?

2. What are the policies in your state that determine the collective rights of teachers either to unionize or not (the "right to work")? If the purposes of these laws are to give some equality of power to teachers and school boards, how well is this balance working?

3. What are the strong policy arguments for and against site-based shared decisionmaking? Do you agree with Hargreave's idea that much of this shared management is a form of "contrived collegiality," and not a real shared community of interest? What is it about teachers that makes them appear to be lone operatives, jealously protecting their independence and autonomy?

4. How might you explain the connections and the inconsistencies among policies that affect teacher preparation, collective bargaining rights, and shared, team decisionmaking? How might all three be improved, while supporting teachers' need to be treated like professionals? How might these three areas of policy work for and against one another, in part explaining the disconnect between teachers as professionals, as trainees, as unionists, and as political decisionmakers?

Seminal Works

Perhaps the most definitive study of the teaching profession is Dan Lortie's (1975) *Schoolteacher.* More recently, Firestone and Bader (1993) explored changes in the teaching profession in *Redesigning Teaching: Professionalism or Bureaucracy?* A related work drawing from the diverse scholarly literature is Andy Hargreaves' (1994) *Changing Teachers, Changing Times: Teachers' Work and Culture in the Post-Modernist Age,* which explores in detail the work lives and culture of teachers. More recently, Grant and Murray's (1999) *Teaching in America: The Slow Revolution* was awarded the Harvard University Press award as the outstanding work on education and society. Those interested in the role of teachers unions in shaping the teaching profession should read Charles Kerchner and Douglas Mitchell's (1988) *The Changing Idea of a Teachers' Union,* perhaps one of the best studies of teachers' unions ever written.

References

Carnegie Forum on Education and the Economy (May 1986). *A nation prepared: Teachers for the 21st century.* The Report of the Task Force on Teaching as a Profession. New York: Carnegie Corporation.

Cooper, M. (1989). Whose culture is it anyway? In A. Lieberman (Ed.), *Building a professional culture in schools* (pp. 36–52). New York: Teachers College Press.

Cremin, L. A. (1988). *American education: The metropolitan experience 1876–1980.* New York: Harper & Row.

Darling-Hammond, L. (November 1997). *Doing what matters most: Investing in quality teaching.* Washington, DC: National Commission on Teaching and America's Future.

Etzioni, A. (1968). *The semi-professions and their organization: Teachers, nurses, social workers.* New York: The Free Press.

Finn, C. E., Jr., Kanstoroom, M., & Petrilli, M. (1999). *Quest for better teachers: Grading the states, the teachers we need and how to get them.* Collingdale, PA: Diane Publishing.

Firestone, W. A., & Bader, B. D. (1992). *Redesigning teaching: Professionalism or bureaucracy?* Albany: State University of New York Press.

Foley, R. (1999, October 7). [Letter to the editor]. *Journal News,* pp. 7–8.

Galambos, L. M., Cornett, L. M., & Spitler, H. D. (1985). An analysis of transcripts of teachers and arts and science graduates. In W. D. Hawley (Ed.), *Breaking away: The risks and inadequacies of extended teacher preparation programs.* Nashville, TN: Vanderbilt University.

Goodlad, J. I. (1990). *Teachers for our nation's schools.* San Francisco: Jossey-Bass.

Grant, G., & Murray, C. E. (1999). *Teaching in America: The slow revolution.* Cambridge, MA: Harvard University Press.

Halbfinger, C. (1999, September 8). Yonkers teachers on strike. *The Journal News,* pp. 1B, 2B.

Hargreaves, A. (1994). *Changing teachers, changing times: Teachers' work and culture in the post-modernist age.* New York: Teachers College Press.

Hunt, J. (1997). *National commission on teaching and America's future.* Washington, DC: NCTAF.

Kerchner, C. T., & Koppich, J. E. (1993). *A union of professionals: Labor relations and educational reform.* New York: Teachers College Press.

Kerchner, C. T., Koppich, J. E., & Weeres, J. G. (1997). *United mind workers: Unions and teaching in the knowledge society.* San Francisco: Jossey-Bass.

Kerchner, C. T., & Mitchell, D. E. (1988). *The changing idea of a teachers' union.* New York: Falmer Press.

Lagemann, E. C. (1983). *Private power for the public good: A history of the Carnegie Foundation for the Advancement of Teaching.* Middletown, CT: Wesleyan University Press.

Lieberman, A., Darling-Hammond, L., & Zuckerman, D. (1991). *Early lessons in restructuring education, schools, and teaching.* Washington, DC: NCREST.

Liotta, M.-E. R. (2002). *The four great strikes of Yonkers teachers: An historical analysis of conflict and change in urban education.* Doctoral dissertation from Fordham University, New York.

Lortie, D. (1975). *Schoolteacher: A sociological study.* Chicago: University of Chicago Press.

Lortie, D. (1969). The balance of control and autonomy in classrooms. In A. Etzioni (Ed.), *The semi-professions and their organization: Teachers, nurses, social workers* (pp. 1–53). New York: The Free Press.

Malen, B., Ogawa, R. T., & Krantz, J. (1990). What do we know about school-based management? A case study of the literature. In W. H. Clune & J. F. Whitte (Eds.), *Choice and control in American education* (Vol. 2, pp. 284–343). Philadelphia: Falmer Press.

Mickey, K. (1999, October 2). On strike. *Journal News*, pp. 1A, 2A.

New York State Board of Regents (1998, July 16). *New York State's commitment: Teaching to higher standards.* Albany, NY: Author.

New York State Department of Education (1991). *A New Compact for Learning: Improving Public Elementary, Middle, and Secondary Education Results in the 1990s.* Albany: The University of the State of New York and New York State Education Department.

Olson, L. (2000, January 13). Finding and keeping competent teachers. *Quality Counts 2000: Who Should Teach? Education Week, 19*(18), 12–18.

Ravitch, D. (1974). *The great school wars: New York City, 1805–1973.* New York: Basic Books.

Shulman, L. (1989). *Alone, learning together: Needed agendas for the new reforms.* Conference on Restructuring Schools for Quality Education. Trinity University, San Antonio, TX.

Thomas B. Fordham Foundation. (1999). *The teachers we need and how to get more of them: A manifesto.* Washington, DC: Author.

Tom, A. R. (1989). A critique of extended teacher preparation. In L. Weiss, P. G. Altbach, G. P. Kelly, H. G. Petrie, & S. Slaughter (Eds.), *Crisis in teaching: Perspectives on current reform.* Albany: State University of New York Press.

Weiss, L., Altbach, P. G., Kelly, G. P., Petrie, H. G., & Slaughter, S. (Eds.). (1989). *Crisis in teaching: Perspectives on current reform.* Albany: State University of New York Press.

Wilensky, H. L. (1964–1965). The professionalization of everyone. *American Journal of Sociology. LXX,* 137–145.

10

School Finance and Equity

Better Policies, Better Use of Resources

The United States spent $699.7 billion in 2001–2002 on education at all levels, of which $423 billion went to the nation's elementary and secondary schools, public and private: that's 7.4 percent of the gross domestic product (the sum of the value of all goods and services produced in a year). Education at the kindergarten through 12th grade levels amounted to about $340 billion of that total, meaning that behind medical and health services, education is the second most costly public service enterprise in the country, employing 3.2 million teachers and administrators, engaging 52.2 million pupils daily, and consuming millions of hours of time. Virtually all educational policies involve money: funds to hire educators to carry out the program; money for equipment, buildings, and resources to prepare the next generation for a complex world ahead; and money for the testing and assessment of students.

Policies determine just how resources are generated, allocated, and used to produce education that society values—or why would voters agree to tax themselves on property, income, sales, and other activities (buying a home, a car) to support our schools? How much of the money actually reaches the students, their classrooms, teachers, guidance counselors, and librarians? What does this money buy, besides people and things? What about the use and usefulness of time in education: "time on task," contact hours, desk time, and detention time? What about the expenses of developing new ideas and technologies, the "investment costs" in education? And what are the costs of constructing, maintaining and upgrading schools (Cibulka & Cooper, 2002), their buildings, computers, equipment, and most importantly, their staffs? Without a clear sense of how money (tax allocations) can be converted to school-site and classroom resources (teachers, training, equipment, computers, textbooks, field trips), we may have problems determining the effect of these resources on student results (test scores, graduation rates, school attendance, civic pride, aesthetic appreciation, and good conduct).

Normative Dimension

Odden and Busch (1998, p. 3) prefaced their book, *Financing Schools for High Performance,* with the abrupt catchphrase of the 1997 movie *Jerry Maguire,* "Show me the money!" The norms of school finance echo these concerns: where's the money, how's it being spent, and to what ends? This chapter looks at four key norms that underlie policies in school finance:

> Norm 1: Education as a Public and Private Good
>
> Norm 2: Adequacy and Equity of School Spending
>
> Norm 3: Efficiency and Productivity of Education Spending
>
> Norm 4: Choice and Accountability in Education Spending

Norm 1: Education as a Public and Private Good

The education historian, Lawrence Cremin, researched the roots of education in the United States during the Colonial era (1607–1783) and discovered that education was available without public control and funds from our earliest history. Cremin (1970) explained:

> The accessibility of education in its many forms was doubtless enhanced by its diversification during the provincial era, for at the very least, as genuine options emerged, larger segments of the populace found themselves attracted to education in the particular terms of their own goals and aspirations. This was certainly true in the case of the churches, which reached out to the unaffiliated with novel styles and substance during the course of the awakenings. It was equally true of apprenticeships, as the range of possibilities increased with the proliferation of trades and crafts in the towns and cities. (pp. 551–552)

By the mid-1800s, however, increases in immigration and demand for schooling overpowered the financial capacity of private, familial, charitable, and church-supported institutions to educate the growing urban poor. Communities began to tax owners of local property to pay for the "free" or "common school," a movement that has captured the imagination of scholars and practitioners for over a hundred years. Tyack (1967) describes this crusade for universal, publicly-funded, compulsory schooling as follows:

> In the next few decades Americans would be much more specific about means as they translated their generalized esteem for education into the institution known as the common school. In the early nineteenth century, there were few sharp lines

between "public" and "private" education. States liberally subsidized "private" academies and colleges while towns and cities helped support "private" charity schools. (p. 120)

The big breakthrough in the history of financing U.S. public education oc-curred as communities and states harnessed their taxing power to the expansion and support of public schools. Where necessary, the states mandated communi-ties to tax themselves and later contributed state funds to the operation of local school districts. This formula (local effort, local real property taxes, state require-ments, and later state aid) contributed to the rise of public schools for all children. Butts (1978) asserted that "only direct taxation would supply the necessary funds and the most common form was, of course, the real property tax" (p. 84).

Private or Public?   Most children attend public schools; however, around 10 percent elect to use private and parochial schools. This nonpublic sector has re-mained strong and active, influencing finance policies in interesting ways.

Even though parents can elect to pay privately or take advantage of public schools, society sees education as both a private good (helping the individual to grow, be a productive citizen, earn a living) and a public concern for the benefit of all. Policymakers sometimes dichotomize this concept, trying to argue that ed-ucation is fundamentally a private good (up to the family and student), or a pub-lic (government) service. Education is quite obviously both: the meeting of individual, personal needs with and for the benefit of the total society. Friedman (1962) called this the "neighborhood effect," the benefits to the whole of the de-velopment of the individual.

Economists have been fascinated with how the education of individuals af-fects national productivity. The thesis is that as a society "invests" in its people ("human capital"), these adults become more knowledgeable, employable, pro-ductive, and hardworking, which should show up in the growth of national pro-ductivity. These economic modelers could care less about individual children and their schools; instead, education becomes a variable in their analysis, as another possible contributor to national economic growth, alongside more natural re-sources; enhanced capital development such as mines, oil wells, factories, electric power generation, harbors and bridges; better infrastructure such as railroads, highways, airports, telephone and other electronic hardware; new technological development; and extended political stability.

Perhaps the classic study of "human capital theory" was performed by Schultz (1963, 1981), who treated education as a kind of investment, both in the social sense, as when we invest in the happiness and well-being of our children, as well as in the economic sense of reaping financial benefits for the economy from putting money into education. In return for educational resources, the na-tion benefits in higher productivity, a stronger economy, more jobs, higher prof-its, and enhanced ability to adjust to changing demands and markets (Langelett, 2002).

POLICY BIOGRAPHY • *Theodore W. Schultz*

Human Capital Theory

In 1961, the Nobel Prize for Economic Sciences was awarded to University of Chicago economist Theodore W. Schultz for his study of national financial growth between 1929 and 1957. He tried to account for all the "inputs" into the economy in this period; but no matter what he analyzed, he was unable to determine why growth was 36 percent higher than anticipated once he took note of capital formation (trains, electric generating capacity, mines and smelting, industrial growth, shipping and trade).

His only workable explanation was that investment in people had "paid off" in economic growth: that one-fifth to one-fourth of all development was due to resources placed into educating the work force and the scientists, engineers, inventors, and technicians who made the society flourish. Confirming these findings of Schultz, Edward F. Denison found that between 1929 and 1948, education contributed 27.2 percent to the growth of "real national income," 18.1 percent between 1948 and 1969, and overall, between 1929 and 1969, he attributed 21.1 percent growth to schooling (see Schultz, 1960, 1963, 1981).

While the Schultz line of research is enlightening, it is so far removed from actual education (it's only a variable in Schultz's model) that educators cannot easily determine what to do. "Investing in education" is one thing; how to organize schools and teach children is quite another.

Lifetime Earning Streams.   Another line of research has shown that high school graduates make more money than secondary school drop-outs; college graduates do better economically than the non-attendees, and graduate work pays off economically—all over the lifetime of the educated student. This research is often called "lifetime earning streams" and shows significant differences by gross category (high school educated, college educated, post-graduate training).

Even though the government no longer collects data on lifetime earnings, the data seem clear. A 1972 study by the Bureau of the Census (1974) shows that individuals with a college degree, plus additional training, earned $823,759 on average, while those with only an elementary school background accumulated $279,997 over their lifetime. Missing from this analysis, however, are the costs of attaining this education (the "investment" side of the equation). Another way to examine this issue is compare the cost of education with its benefit—calculating the "rate of return." Here the data are less poignant: in fact, a number of studies around the world found that societies reap a rate of return on investments in elementary education of 27 percent (see Psacharopoulos, 1981, p. 133; Hansen, 1986, p. 63).

Like human capital theory, lifetime earning streams report data over long stretches of time (lifetimes), meaning that it is hard to pinpoint which part of these people's education has the strongest economic effect: reading and writing, math and sciences, music and art, School A over School B? Yet the pressure to attend college and gain a market advantage will continue to affect school spending, even if social scientists have difficulty pinpointing the exact advantages.

Thus, a central norm in finance policymaking is the tension between the private and public nature of schooling. Clearly, both the society and the individual benefit from the funding of education. But just how private or public education should be is open for debate. Efforts to ban private schools have failed; movements toward making public schools more "private" (vouchers, charter schools) have also been contested, as we discuss elsewhere in this book.

Norm 2: Equity and Adequacy in Education Finance

Public and universal funding of schools was given a special meaning: a democratic device for creating an egalitarian society. As Butts (1978) wrote, "Class distinctions [between rich and poor] could be obliterated only when a 'free school' no longer meant a charity school for the poor but one in which *all* children would be offered an education in common without fee or tuition. The only way that could be done was to support the schools by public taxes levied upon everyone in proportion to their ability to pay" (p. 84), the classic definition of "progressive" taxation ("regressive" taxes are those where the poor pay a disproportionately higher amount, such as a sales tax on food, where the poor pay a higher percent of their income than do the rich).

But some localities were slow to act or simply refused to tax themselves at all for education, particularly because churches, philanthropies, and special do-good associations seemed quite willing to apply private funding (charity) to schools—inadequate as these resources were for the burgeoning immigrant population. State legislatures were forced, then, to urge, cajole, reward effort, and lastly to require districts to tax their income and local property for schools. Butts (1978) explains: "And, finally, when legislatures could see no other way to carry out their constitutional mandates to provide 'thorough and efficient' systems of education for the whole state, they passed laws *requiring* local districts to tax themselves in order to support public schools" (p. 84).

Although equity is concerned to provide "fair" financial inputs, adequacy attempts to fund schools *sufficiently* to achieve certain academic and social outcomes. Guthrie and Rothstein (1999) explain that "'adequacy' suggests that something beyond equity is at issue. The 'something else' is the notion of *sufficiency,* a per-pupil *resource amount sufficient to achieve some performance objective*" (p. 214). So, although equity is usually calibrated against some norm or benchmark of local spending, adequacy relates money to certain results. Or, as Porter (1993) explains, adequacy is bundled with the drive for "opportunity standards."

Thus, we cannot understand the basic norms of school finance policies without taking into consideration arguments for both equity and adequacy. Minorini and Sugarman (1999) state the movement from equity to adequacy as follows:

> In the courts, the shift has been away from traditional "fiscal equity" cases (concerned with inequalities in school district per-pupil property tax base and the per pupil spending inequalities they yield), toward arguments focused on ensuring that all students have access to educational resources and opportunities adequate to achieve desired educational outcomes. In the education policy context, the shift has led to efforts to define what educational outcomes all students should attain and what resources are necessary to permit all students to achieve those outcomes. (Minorini & Sugarman, 1999, pp. 175–176; see also Clune, 1994; Heise, 1995; Underwood, 1995)

Whether a state or school district adopts an equity or adequacy perspective on school funding policies, the result is most often an overriding state program to allocate more funding to those local communities that lack the property or income tax base to provide either an *equitable* (fair and equal) or *adequate* (sufficient) funding to bring student learning up to some standard.

Norm 3: Efficiency and Productivity

The third norm is perhaps the most complex. To what degree do resources reach students (efficiency) and make a difference in their learning (productivity)? Although the United States has managed to increase spending on education almost every year over the last century, we cannot always say that policies ensure that funds are spent effectively. In economic terms, does more money lead to more learning for more children? "Productivity function analysis" has shown great promise of late, as statisticians try to show that x amounts of new money invested in education will produce y amounts of learning, in z time.

But again, this quest for a workable education "production function" takes us through a world of interesting research. Chubb and Moe (1990), for example, explored students' learning over their high school years (data were from High School & Beyond, a study done by the U.S. Government). These authors found that bureaucratic systems are less responsive than smaller public or private schools because the teachers in bureaucratic systems are not client-centered. Perhaps we can argue that more or less money is inconsequential unless those closest to and most concerned about students can control the funds. The answer, then, is not the amount of the money, its sources, or purposes; rather, it is putting greater resources and control into the hands of people who are more school- and student-centered, and less "system" directed (Chubb & Moe, 1990).

Public Spending.   As shown in Table 10.1, public education has grown in size (pupils) and funding levels for virtually every year since data were first collected.

TABLE 10.1   *Enrollment and Spending on Elementary and Secondary Education 1869–1999 (Does not include higher education)*

School Year	1. Total Pupils Age Cohort Percent	2. Total Spending	3. Per Pupil Spending Adjusted Dollars*
1869–1870	6.872 million students (64.7%)	$63 million (100%)	—
1899–1900	15.503 million (71.9%)	$215 million	—
1919–1920	21.578 million (78.3%)	$970.121 million (100%)	$533 per pupil
1939–1940	25.434 million (84.4%)	$2.260 billion (100%)	$1,202 per pupil
1959–1960	35.182 million (82.2%)	$14.747 billion (100%)	$2,547 per pupil
1979–1980	41.651 million (86.7%)	$96.881 billion (100%)	$5,098 per pupil
1994–1995	46.353 million (92.1%)	$273.138 billion (100%)	$7,104 per pupil
1996–1997	47.467 million (94.1%)	$349.979 billion (100%)	$7,371 per pupil
1998–1999	48.921 million (92.2%)	$446.126 billion (100%)	$9,212 per pupil

*Adjusted 1900 dollars.

Column 1 shows the numbers of public school children and the percent of 6- to 17-year-olds attending school. In 1869–1870, five years after the U.S. Civil War, enrollment was nearly 7 million or about 65 percent of the school-age population. Total spending that year was $63 million, with most in elementary schools (only about 80,000 out of 6.872 million total children were in secondary schools). By the turn of the century (1899–1900), the number in school reached about 72 percent of all children or 15.5 million pupils. Twenty years later (1919–1920), enrollment was almost 22 million (78 percent) and 1939–1940 saw a jump of about 5 million students attending public schools, up to 25.4 million from 21.6 million, reaching 84.4 percent of school-age students in schools that year.

This growth curve means that a rising percentage of 7- to 17-year-olds were in school for longer periods of time: from 65 to over 94 percent of the 6- to 18-year-old population eligible to attend U.S. public schools. Columns 2 and 3 in Table 10.1 show the phenomenal growth in total and per-student spending between

1869 and 1999. Again, taking count every twenty years, we see spending on public elementary and secondary schools rise from $62 million in 1869 to about $446 billion in 1999 nationwide. In dollars adjusted for the inflation rate (constant dollars), spending per pupil rose from $533 in 1919–1920 to over $7,104 in 1995 and to over $9,400 per student as a national average by 2002.

Changing Sources of Funds.   Another normative issue in school finance policy is the appropriate sources for the funds. On a national level, as shown in Table 10.2, changing amounts, ratios, and the percent of total were contributed by the federal, state, and local governments to education. The federal share in 1919 was minuscule, 0.3 percent, indicating that the government in Washington, D.C., had a minor role to play in education. In fact, education is never mentioned in the U.S. Constitution and only in a few other key documents of the founders of the nation (e.g., George Washington's "Farewell Address" in 1796).

In 1919–1920, the state portion of school funding was also small, at less than 17 percent, meaning that the local communities picked up the bulk of the costs of education, over 83 percent. By 1994–1995, the federal percentage rose from .03 percent to almost 7 percent or $128 billion, mainly for compensatory and special education programs. The states' share also grew from 16.5 percent in 1919 to virtually equal to the local share, each around 47 percent or about $127 billion out of total spending of $273 billion in 1995. Public education spending had become over 7 percent of the gross domestic product in just 75 years. The norms, here, are a growing awareness that education is a state and national issue; that local communities cannot be expected to foot the bill alone; and that our mobile

TABLE 10.2   *Public Funding by Source: Federal, State, Local Jurisdictions, USA, 1919–1995*

School Year	1. Federal Dollars and Percentage	2. State Dollars and Percentage	3. Local Dollars and Percentage
1919–1920	$2.475 million (0.3%)	$160.085 million (16.5%)	$807.561 million (83.2%)
1939–1940	$39.810 million (1.8%)	$684.354 million (30.3%)	$1.728 billion (68.0%)
1959–1960	$651.639 million (4.4%)	$5.768 billion (39.1%)	$8.327 billion (56.5%)
1979–1980	$9.504 billion (9.8%)	$45.349 billion (46.8%)	$42.029 billion (43.4%)
1994–1995	$18.582 billion (6.8%)	$127.720 billion (46.8%)	$126.836 billion (46.4%)

society requires greater equity among districts and schools—meaning a stronger role of the United States and state governments.

Totals Today.   By 1998, the United States was spending nearly $350 billion on education—and as the primary resource, money buys the goods, services, skills, and capital that children need to be able to learn in school. Education, as the largest public enterprise in the nation, involves 46.35 million public school children, another 5.86 million private school students (total in 1997 of 52.217 million students in kindergarten through 12th grade), about 3.2 million professional educators (teachers, administrators, librarians, nurses, coaches, guidance counselors, secretaries, bus drivers, and food service employees), not to mention the thousands of people who manufacture and sell the goods (e.g., desks, textbooks, and computers) used in schools. The nation's 3.1 million teachers alone—their salaries and benefits (pensions, unemployment, disability, and health insurance)—account for $160 billion of the $276 billion spent in 1996 on elementary and secondary schools. Jones (1985) drew a useful comparison because this much money is impossible to grasp on its own. He explained that $340 billion was "more money than was spent on public schools in all the years from the American colonial times (1774) until the Korean War (1952)" (p. 1), in unadjusted dollars (not accounting for inflation).

Norm 4: Choice and Accountability

The last set of norms that underlie school finance policies are the contending values placed on family choice, on the one hand, and the requirements for public accountability and social justice, on the other. In its simplest form, the debate is between the rights of the family to choose a school, and the responsibility of the society to ensure education for all.

But most communities are unwilling to trust parents completely and resist vouchers and other kinds of family controls and real choice. The result is the Great Compromise: shifting discrepancies in funding to local school districts (based on the wide differences in local property tax values and levels), without truly empowering parents to select a school and teachers to make major curricular decisions.

The result is a system that is neither rigorous, empowering, nor equitable. And the U.S. "system" is hardly a system at all, because it varies enormously by state (note differences between New Jersey at over $9,500 per student and Utah at below $4,000) and by district. The future trade-off, then, will be between a willingness to trust the family to make the "best" (most rational) choice for their children, while holding the system publicly accountable for all children. It's the old trade-off of social justice and individual rights. The No Child Left Behind legislation, the most complex federal education law in U.S. history, tries to do both: greatly increasing national accountability by requiring states to test children in grades 3 through 8, while also empowering parents to choose among public and private schools (through tax-free savings).

Structural Dimension

Throughout U.S. history, communities have wondered who should pay for the education of children: parents whose children benefit; federal, state, or local governments that seek political and economic gains; or a mix of public and private agencies and stakeholders. To what degree, then, is education a "public" concern and for what level of government? And because children and their immediate families are the main beneficiaries, and more education usually means better jobs, higher income, and greater political access and clout, why should the government become involved at all? Answers range from a safer, happier, and healthier community, to a better-informed electorate and stronger commitment to community improvement.

Thomas Jefferson wondered whether a democracy could survive without a well-informed electorate—as he wrote, "I think by far the most important bill in our whole code is that for the general diffusion of knowledge among the people. No other sure foundation can be devised, for the preservation of freedom and happiness" (Ford, 1904, p. 440). Today, in a large, diverse, multicultural and multilingual society, education may be even more important if the nation is to remain strong, unified, stable, and productive.

Government—and thus, taxpayers—should support education even though children and their families are the primary beneficiaries. Most modern societies, however, have good, logical reasons for spending public money on education of all children: education benefits all, in a concept called the "neighborhood effect" (Friedman, 1962). This theory contends that all citizens should pay for education, even without their own children benefiting—just as everyone is safer with a fire department on alert, even if a particular taxpayer never has a fire.

At the present, the United States is spasmodically trying to "decentralize" political control over funds and programs directly to schools. Rather mild administrative reforms include school-site management, budgeting, and shared decisionmaking. More radical means may drive education decisions to parents and schools through vouchers in Milwaukee and Cleveland, magnet schools in Kansas City and New York City, and charter schools in more than two thousand communities. At the same time, federal and state government policies continue to make demands on schools, with state standards, state curricula, and state tests becoming more common throughout the nation.

These mixed controls express the competing views of who should govern education, paralleling who should pay. Each level has a vital role; each puts in their two cents or more, and each extracts its influence and expectations. Over the last fifty years, the local school districts have watched their portion of spending erode, while state and federal funding has grown proportionally. But the trends are hardly clear, direct, or enlightening, as we look across 98,000 schools, 14,500 districts, and 50 states plus the District of Columbia. If money and control are inextricably linked (like the pun concerning the Golden Rule: those that have the gold make the rules), then school policies and finance should be examined together as a whole at four levels, with mixed and competing controls, regulations, and demands.

Controlled from Where?

The structural dilemma—what agencies should set the policies that control education—is typical of U.S. school finance, for we invest control at four levels at once: (1) local, meaning school-site, (2) school district, (3) state funding and oversight, and (4) federal initiative and leadership. This four-level approach creates confusion, conflict, and bewilderment as to where control resides. If we trace these four levels of control through funding, we see trends that underlie our ambivalence as to whose responsibility education really is.

The United States created its education system from the "bottom" up—that is, local communities began hiring teachers and building schoolhouses before the states were major players. Even the newer states would create districts (even before settlers had arrived), but the money was primarily raised by a local levy on real property (land, houses, and businesses). As late as 1970, the local share was 53 percent, state 39 percent, and federal 8 percent. Over time, the local contribution has dropped to 46 percent, the state share is now 47 percent, and the federal share is about 7 percent.

Education is everyone's concern: from the President of the United States to state governors and legislators, to local mayors, county commissioners, and, of course, local school boards. All three levels of government—federal, state, and local—help to pay for the education of children. However, the proportion has changed in several interesting ways.

Federal Aid.   The federal government is actually the newest provider of funds to education—and remains the smallest but hardly the weakest partner. For most of our history, the government in Washington, D.C., contributed less than 1 percent. Since the 1960s, the amount has risen to a high of 9.8 percent (1980) and went down to about 7 percent in the mid-1990s.

It was not until after World War II that the federal share of school funding went above 2 percent. Thus, federal support for education has grown from 0.3 percent in 1920 to 9.8 percent in 1980 to 5.8 percent in 1995. The increase was over 3,000 percent in just seventy years. Yet the federal share has never passed 10 percent—and has settled between 6 and 7 percent of total national spending on education. Meanwhile, the state and local portion has also shifted dramatically, from education being primarily a local service (83 percent paid for locally in 1920) and has moved to just about equal by 1996, when roughly 47 percent was local and 47 percent contributed by the state.

Looking at the rather meager contribution of the federal government (see Meranto, 1967), one might make the erroneous assumption that the roles of Congress, the president, U.S. Supreme Court, and U.S. Department of Education are limited in influencing policy in K–12 education. It is ironic that although the federal level contributes the least financially, it actually tackles the "big issues" and has a profound impact on our nation's schools. For example, it was the government in Washington, D.C. that led the way on school desegregation when the states were unable to break the racial education apartheid; it was the U.S. Department of Education that wrote many of the regulations on "inclusion" and "least restrictive environments" for handicapped and challenged children who had previously been locked out of mainstream public schooling. And don't forget bilingual, science, and vocational education, standards, and national and international research on school test results—all areas of major concern to Uncle Sam. So although the states and localities clearly have the important role of paying teachers, erecting and maintaining school buildings, and other operational costs, it's the federal government that breaks the barriers and sets new directions when local interests are perceived to be slower to act. Let's look back over the long history of the nation, and briefly trace the federal government's roles and policies in supporting education.

For example, federal aid was targeted for handicapped and challenged children in PL 94-142, which required the "least restrictive environment" be provided for children of all intellectual abilities, emotional needs, and physical and medical problems. Children in wheelchairs and those needing a gurney were guaranteed a "barrier free" environment under the Rehabilitation Act (Section 504). And children with "limited English proficiency" (LEP) were eligible for bilingual education services, classrooms where they could learn English and continue their education in math, science, and history in their own language. Native Americans received federal aid starting in 1924 with the Citizens Act, which shifted their education from church-related to federally-run public schools; in 1934, the Johnson-O'Malley Act gave states money to run vocational training programs for adults. After World War II, Congress passed the GI Bill to provide access to college for returning service personnel.

Thus, although the dollars may be small compared to support from the states and school districts, federal aid tackles the "big" problems in U.S. education, spreading a little money over thousands of jurisdictions and schools. Besides funding, of course, the federal level has used the courts and the "bully pulpit" to urge and require reforms. Hence, while funding is small, the visibility and range of federal programs are still impressive.

The States Step In

The fifty states bear the primary legal (fiduciary) and financial responsibility for education, creating and funding 14,500 local school districts. Since "education" is conspicuously missing from the U.S. Constitution, it devolved to the states under the Tenth Amendment and their constitutions to provide a free and effective education to all children. The local school districts, then, are "creatures of the state" and can be changed, consolidated, funded, and controlled by state legislatures and governors, as they see fit. As Burrup, Brimley, and Garfield (1996) explain, "Each state has been responsible for its own system of education, with power to delegate whatever degree of control it chose to local districts of the kind and number it desired. As a result, there have been 50 versions of how education should function in as many states. The federal government over the years has had very little real authority over education" (p. 168).

Thurston and Roe (1957) put the matter clearly when they wrote: "The solution [to the struggle for control of schools] seems natural—with the state maintaining legal supremacy and acting as the fulcrum to provide a proper balance for the local community on the one side, where the schools can be kept *close to the people*, and the national government on the other side, where the general welfare of the nation can be safeguarded" (p. 11). Note the reference to the Preamble to the U.S. Constitution, where the federal government shall "provide for the general welfare."

Historically, schooling itself began as a local function and passed through six phases (Burrup, Brimley, & Garfield, 1996, p. 211). These six phases are:

Phase 1: Local Responsibility

In colonial and the early republican periods in the United States, education was provided by local communities, relying on some public help but also on churches and charities to educate poor children in the basic subjects; wealthier families hired tutors or sent their children to private and proprietary schools. Although the Puritans in the New England Colonies passed laws such as the Old Deluder Satan Act of 1643 to require villages to open schools, by the 1800s the Puritans were a small minority and it took the likes of Horace Mann, Secretary of the Massachusetts state board of education (1832–1845), to promote local public support for the emerging "common schools." With the growth in the number of districts (to over 110,000 by 1900) and size of schools, the disparities in funding became so great that state leadership came to worry about how communities could possibly carry out state policy mandates to extend education to more children for longer periods of time (through high school). Funds were not always available at local levels to meet increased demand.

Phase 2: Grants and Allocations

By about 1900, states came to realize that local education would be weak and inadequate without a more active state role. A few states recognized the inequalities among districts, but little state aid was available. The leadership of Professor Ellwood P. Cubberley was critical here, although he stopped short of advocating full state participation in equalization.

POLICY BIOGRAPHY • *Ellwood P. Cubberley*

Ellwood P. Cubberley was one of the great scholar-pioneers in advocating for an enhanced role of the state in education. In 1906, Cubberley wrote his important book, *School Funds and Their Apportionment*, in which he prophetically wrote:

"Theoretically, all the children of the state are equally important and are entitled to have the same advantages; practically, this can never be quit true. The duty of the state is—

- to secure for all a high minimum of good instruction as is possible, but not to reduce all to this minimum;
- to equalize the advantages to all as nearly as can be done with the resources at hand;
- to place a premium on those local efforts which will enable communities to rise above the legal minimum as far as possible; and
- to encourage communities to extend their energies to new and desirable undertakings" (p. 17)

Cubberley realized that local districts would need help to carry out the mandates of the state—meaning funding and support. After all, children needed twelve years of schooling, 180 days per year, and a wider scope of subjects. The cities, with their accumulated wealth, were often able to meet these requirements; rural areas often could not. Inequalities among school districts were recognized as a major problem.

Cubberley was among the first researchers to gather data on local spending. To his chagrin, he found that state allocations not only failed to reduce inequalities in local spending, but also often increased the differences by aiding the wealthier communities more. He built six key principles that led the way for the twentieth century: (1) The state had a responsibility to fund schools; (2) the state should give additional help, not simply tax relief to districts; (3) state aid will actually make inequalities worse; (4) state mandates for more and better education should be supported with more state aid; (5) states should use "days in attendance" as the basis for state aid to encourage longer school years and days; and (6) states should base aid on the number of teachers per pupil to help poorer, less populated rural districts.

Even though most of Cubberley's concepts overlooked the dangers of state takeovers of local autonomy, the net result of Cubberley's work has been to alert states to their responsibility—not to run education but to supplement local ideas, efforts, and funds: that is, local effort, not state controls.

Phase 3: Foundation Aid

George Strayer and Robert Haig did extensive research on equality of school district funding in the state of New York in 1923. Their findings set the stage for the next seventy-five years of school finance policymaking. New York State, they learned, funded school districts on a per-teacher quota basis, favoring "the very rich and the very poor localities at the expense of those which are moderately well off." Strayer and Haig proposed a new concept of state aid: the "foundation" or minimum program. Based on what the richest districts spent, "each local school district would levy the amount of local tax that was required in the richest district to provide a *foundation*, or *minimum*, program. The rich district would receive no state aid; the other districts would receive state funds necessary to provide the foundation program" (Burrup et al., 1996, pp. 178–179).

Local districts could always tax themselves more and go beyond the foundation level; poor districts would have to extend local effort but would be rewarded by receiving more state aid. Foundation aid also encouraged the consolidation of smaller districts to increase efficiency. In practice, the foundation concept of Strayer and Haig was weakened by the tradition of "flat grants" to all districts, the drive in some communities to spend much more than the foundation or minimum amount per student, and the lack of sufficient state funds to equalize local spending.

Reformers such as Henry Morrison had more radical ideas. What if states formed one large school district, equalizing the tax burden and school expenditures, and shifting away from over-reliance on property taxes to state-level income taxes? Hawaii is the one living example of Morrison's ideas: a state with a single, statewide school system.

Phase 4: Power Equalization

In the last half of the twentieth century, mainly because of court cases discussed in the next section, "power equalization" became the overarching philosophy of school funding. Adequacy and uniformity extended both to students' rights to an equitable education and to taxpayers' rights to have their equal effort yield something like equal funding results. Thus, if a family with a $100,000 home in one district is taxed at 4 percent ($4,000 per year), which means local spending is $4,000 per student on education, then another homeowner, taxed at the same rate, should expect that his or her contribution creates somewhat equal spending. Equal effort should yield equal resources. But because housing values differ, the state may be called on to equalize the effect of the equal effort of taxpayers, creating a fiscally neutral (fair) system. We shall discuss equity in education finance next; at this point, we need only to realize that the state has taken responsibility for overcoming the inequalities built into a system of local education.

And, as Underwood and Verstegen (1990) explain,

> All but two states apportion revenue for public schools through a foundation school program (35 states), district power equalization approach (4 states), or a combination of these plans (9 states). Only one state uses full state funding to apportion state funding to apportion school aid, and one state uses a flat grant system—the plan used by a majority of the states prior to the 1920s [the Cubberley years]. Today, all states provide additional assistance to supplement basic costs for special education programs; 31 states give supplements for compensatory education; 24 states, for bilingual education; 31 states, for gifted and talented

education. Additional funding is provided for sparse or small schools/districts in 30 states; declining enrollment/growth adjustments in 24 states; and grade-level differentials in 24 states. (p. 180)

The role of the state has done much to overcome the inherent problems of a local system. But the tension between local control, state responsibility, and the federal role will never likely be resolved—and forms a backdrop for the future of U.S. education.

Phase 5: Decentralization and Privatization

The latest phase in the role of the state—at least in a few places—has been to support more radical departures from the traditional role of regulator and foundation aid provider. In a number of states in the 1990s, legislatures, governors, and state education departments created policies supporting the creation of charter schools, vouchers, and school-site management, budgeting, and decisionmaking. This fifth phase is just underway: 38 states and the District of Columbia have legislation creating charter schools: privately managed but publicly funded schools that allow greater choice for parents and regulatory flexibility for educators.

If the national average spending on education in 1997 was $5,540 per student for all 50 states, then how do states differ from that norm (mean or average)? One might assume that because education is about 47 percent state and 47 percent local, then poor states with impoverished local communities would spend less than rich states (high corporate and personal income and high property values). But the answer involves more than just the wealth of a state; spending on education is also a function of how much effort a community, region, or state is willing to put forth. How much are adults willing to tax themselves for the benefit of their children?

But this is a national average. Remember what finance professor Charles Benson used to say about averages: "With my right foot in a pot of ice water and my left in a pot of boiling water, why am I, ON AVERAGE, so uncomfortable?" This same adage is true about school finance; an average is just that: the total divided by the number of cases.

Data on state spending show that, indeed, the poorer states spend less on education than the rich states, although many of these low-spending states actually "try harder," that is, they set higher tax rates on their lesser wealth.

The State Contribution.   States also vary in how much they spend, versus local and federal. At the extremes are two very unique states. Hawaii, which has no local school districts or school boards, runs its system as one statewide unit. Thus, without local taxing power, 96 percent of the money for schools comes directly from the state for all 234 schools (the remaining 4 percent is federal). New Hampshire's schools are funded with less than 10 percent support from the state (meaning it's about 88 percent local, compared to the national average of 47 percent).

Why? Because New Hampshire has virtually no state taxes: no state income tax and no state sales tax, meaning that one could live in New Hampshire, earn a million dollars per year and buy a Rolls Royce, and owe the state no money for tax on either. Federal income tax is still collected, of course. Thus, New Hampshire leaves school taxation mainly to the local communities, which tax local property.

What state taxes does New Hampshire have? The five B's: (1) Booze—a tax on liquor purchased from state-run liquor stores; (2) Bets—a tax on dog racing and the state-run lottery; (3) Butts—a cigarette tax; (4) Bonds—a tax on profits from stocks and bonds sold in the state; and (5) Beds—a "room and meals" tax to capture money from the tourist trade. Although the five B's are a relatively painless form of taxation, and much of it may be considered "sin" taxes on evils like drinking, smoking, and gambling, these sources of revenue hardly generate enough income to support education, not to mention the other state functions (e.g., roads and highways, police, prisons, state government, motor vehicles, welfare). Of course, another way to rank states is by local support as a percentage of total spending. Here New Hampshire is first, with 96 percent, and Hawaii is fiftieth, with virtually zero local spending on schools.

Differences between District Spending.   Yet another way to view the averages and what they obscure is to analyze differences in district-to-district spending with any given state. Alaska, Vermont, Ohio, and Missouri have the greatest differences in spending among their districts, while Iowa, Nevada, and North Carolina have the least—in part because the state plays a greater role in funding schools, which means districts tend to spend similar amounts in the latter three.

Differences within Districts.   The most important differences in spending occur at the school level, for unless resources reach schools and classrooms, the steady increase over the last one hundred or so years will make little impact. The problem to date is that research on education spending stopped at the district (intra-state) and rarely went to the school level. In the early 1990s, we led a movement to develop a model that used the school as the unit of analysis, called the education micro-financial model, which became a software package called In$ite. We found greater differences in spending within districts than between them in single states (Cooper & Speakman, 1997).

Constituentive Dimension

What is the role of various constituent groups in the process and their effects on quality and equity? Equity in funding is the most constant and powerful theme in school finance in the United States—a serious concern for those dedicated to seeing that every child receives an equal educational opportunity. And like the New York City situation, the wealth of local parents, businesses, and properties are the main causes of inequality. If every family were middle class and owned an expensive home, then presumably the root cause of inequality would vanish and education of children would be much more equitable.

But it is not. States vary widely in their ability to raise money for education, as do communities and neighborhoods. Ironically, it seems, the very instrument designed for equalizing opportunity for all children, the public schools, is itself affected by the unequal distribution of wealth. Some critics argue that rather than reducing class differences among children, education reinforces these inherent advantages and disadvantages because the richest families provide the fanciest, classiest schools, and the poor, trapped in impoverished neighborhoods, suffer in the worst schools, with the least prepared teachers, in dilapidated buildings.

Thus, a third bone of contention in the U.S. funding of schools is the inequalities that plague the system: inequalities among states, districts, communities, schools, and now even classrooms. So while the nation argues for "equal education opportunity for all," the funding system reinforces the "savage inequalities" (Kozol, 1996) that exist between wealthy communities with large property tax bases and the poor districts with large numbers of poor, needy children and little tax base to support education. Eliminating inequalities may mean curbing or abandoning our dependence on local property taxes as the source of 45 percent of all money spent on schools in the United States—and moving toward some form of full-state funding, which may mean weakening local control, another value in U.S. education since colonial times.

Philosophically, then, we are committed to education equity, and "equal education opportunity for all" is the phrase often heard. Yet we maintain a highly diverse system of funding, with vast differences between states (Utah averages $3,600 per pupil while New Jersey's total was $9,321 per pupil in 1997), great ranges of spending by district within states, and still greater diversity between schools within districts. Even Hawaii, which has only one statewide district and thus absolute intra-state equity, found wide ranges of differences by school and classroom within the same state.

These inequalities are part and parcel of the U.S. education system because we are committed to funding schools from local taxes on residential, commercial, and utility property, which vary greatly from community to community, district to district, and state to state. Moves to abandon local property taxes for full-state funding schemes are resisted—even though inequalities emerge—because of the U.S. commitment to local control. So, we profess a belief in equal opportunity but unequal funding because we cling to keeping power and resources local and under the control of our neighbors and ourselves.

What is meant by equity (fairness)? Is it mainly synonymous with "equal"? If not, what's the difference? Why are funds so unequal among states, districts, and even among schools (see Cooper, Speakman, & Bloomfield, 1996)? And what have the legislatures, school districts, and recently the courts done to equalize school funding?

Defining Equity

On one level, if every child in the United States received a check yearly for education, raised from perhaps a combination of local, state, federal taxes on sales, income, property, luxuries, or whatever, would that be fair? No, unless all these children themselves were equal in need and ability. But because some children require more resources be spent on their schooling because of various challenges, for example, lack of English-speaking skills, physical handicaps, deficits in preparation, gifts and talents, or any number of other conditions, then the *equal treatment of unequals is not fair or equitable.*

Berne and Stiefel (1984) wrote a valuable book on equity in funding in which they differentiate between what they label as *horizontal equity* and *vertical equity.* Horizontal equity exists when all children, schools, or districts are roughly equal: the equal treatment of equals. Vertical equity begins with the assumption that children have differing needs and thus should cost varying amounts, depending on the weighting of each condition: the unequal treatment of unequals.

Horizontal Equity.   Imagine seeing a hundred students, all of whom are more or less similar in backgrounds, needs, problems, strengths, and weaknesses. This horizontal view rests on the principle, according to Berne and Stiefel (1984), that "students who are alike should receive equal shares. . . . When children are so treated, this principle requires equal expenditures or revenues per student, equal education resources for the basic education program, equal pupil-teacher ratios, equal mastery of basic competency levels, or equal contribution by schooling to long-term outcomes such as income or status in life" (p. 13).

State-to-State Equity.   Since the early 1970s, horizontal equity has occupied policymakers, analysts, and even judges. In most situations, horizontal equity was determined by comparing the spending of school districts within a particular state; however, the differences in spending on education between states are also dramatic. Table 10.3 shows the five highest and lowest spending states in 1994–1995 in adjusted dollars, compared to thirty-five years ago (1959–1960), based on the Consumer Price Index, although these data do not reflect the differences in inflation rates by each state.

Among the highest-spending states in the United States, New Jersey was tops in 1994–1995 at $9,774 per pupil, against the national average that year of $5,988. New York is next with $9,623 per student and was the highest in 1959–1960 at $2,875 per pupil in adjusted dollars, while New Jersey was not even in the top five thirty-five years ago.

The District of Columbia ($9,355), Alaska ($8,963), Connecticut ($8,817), and Rhode Island ($7,469) ranked next; although Alaska was second highest in spending in 1959–1960, it has fallen to third among the states and fourth if D.C. is included. All of these states except Alaska are located in the Northeast.

TABLE 10.3   *Highest and Lowest Spending States per Pupil, in 1959–1960 and 1994–1995 in Adjusted Dollars*

Ten States and D.C.	Adjusted 1994–1995 Dollars per Pupil	Adjusted 1959–1960 Dollars per Pupil
U.S. Average per Pupil	$5,988	$1,920
Top 5 Spending States		
1. New Jersey	$9,774	$1,984
2. New York	$9,623	$2,875
District of Columbia	$9,335	$2,207
3. Alaska	$8,963	$2,797
4. Connecticut	$8,817	$2,232
5. Rhode Island	$7,469	$2,116
Lowest 5 Spending States		
46. Arkansas	$4,459	$1,153
47. Alabama	$4,405	$1,234
48. Idaho	$4,210	$1,483
49. Mississippi	$4,080	$1,054
50. Utah	$3,656	$1,651

Among the lowest spending states, Utah was the bottom in the United States in 1994–1995 by far at $3,656 per student, even though it has the highest performance in the nation, with the strongest SAT scores, highest percentage of students taking Advanced Placement classes, and the lowest dropout rate. The Mormon influence (high investment in family and children), plus the homogeneity of the state, are often used to explain the low spending and high output, which we shall discuss under productivity analysis at the end of this chapter.

The next lowest spending, and the nation's poorest state, is Mississippi, which was fiftieth in spending in 1959–1960 at $1,054 and forty-ninth in 1995 with $4,080 per student. Idaho spent $4,210 per pupil at forty-eighth in the United States, Alabama at $4,405 at forty-seventh and Arkansas at $4,459 with $4,459 per student. Three of the poorest states are in the Southeast, and Idaho and Utah, both strong Mormon states, are in the Western Rocky Mountains.

Hence, the range in spending is $6,123 per student, from $3,656 to $9,779 per student between Utah and New Jersey, with New Jersey spending at 2.67 times that of Utah. When one compares the lowest spending district in Utah ($2,100 per student), to the highest spending in New Jersey ($17,000 per pupil), the horizontal inequalities are more than eight to one. Compare the lowest spending school in Utah with the highest in New Jersey, and even greater horizontal inequality emerges.

Local Property, the Root of Inequality.   Because about 46 percent of the money for public education comes from local property taxes, the basis of the inequalities results from some communities having vastly different residential, industrial, utility, and land values, creating what Kozol called "savage inequalities." Kozol (1991) contrasts public schools in a fancy suburb with those in the inner city, dramatically illustrating just how unfairly the United States funds its schools. Take New York City's schools: Kozol studied their spending and wrote regarding the results:

> Average expenditures in the city of New York in 1987 were some $5,500 [now up to $9,600 per pupil]. In the highest spending suburbs of New York (Great Neck or Manhasset), for example, funding levels rose above $11,000 [now $19,000], with the highest districts in the state at $15,000 [now $23,000]. "Why," asks the city's Board of Education, "should our students receive less" than do "similar students" who live elsewhere? "The inequality is clear." (p. 84)

The property-poor districts actually try harder, taxing themselves at a higher rate. But because their homes and businesses are less valuable, and often they have more children, the spending per pupil is considerably lower. State policymakers have long recognized these intra-state inequalities and have passed legislation to give state financial aid to the poorer districts—hoping to bring them up to some equal or at least "adequate" level.

The Courts Intervene

Horizontal Equity.   The courts have not stood idly by while districts spend vastly different amounts on local education. In fact, thirty-one of the fifty states have seen citizens in poor districts sue for greater financial equity and many have won. The first important court decision on equity of funding schools was the 1971 ruling in *Serrano v. Priest,* issued by the California Supreme Court. It declared the entire funding system of California in violation of the state and federal (Fourteenth Amendment) guarantee of "equal protection under the law."

In Texas, the state court followed the California decision in *Rodriquez v. San Antonio* (1973), ruling that children in that community were being denied their rights. However, unlike California, which accepted the decision, Texas appealed to the U.S. Supreme Court, which reversed the decision in *San Antonio v. Rodriguez.* While the high court recognized the seriousness of the problem—that children were losing out on an equal chance because of the low spending in some districts in Texas, while other, wealthier communities were spending much more—the judges were unable to locate a "suspect category" of children who were being denied their constitutional rights.

After all, the San Antonio Unified School District contained white, African American, and Latino children, rich and poor children, older people and younger children, Catholics, Protestants, and Jews. Without a recognized group (suspect category) being denied their rights, the Court bowed out, turning the problem over to state courts (where many constitutions did guarantee education equity, while the U.S. Constitution never mentions education at all). Following Texas, thirty-one other states have had *Serrano*-style court cases and twenty-two have ruled that their state funding was illegal and have moved to restructure the funding for greater horizontal equity. Few, however, have directly removed the property tax, which is at the base of the inequality, and no single principle of education equity funding has emerged nationwide.

From these court cases, five principles were established (see Burrup, et al., 1999, p. 228): (1) education is an important interest of the state; (2) the state, however, does not have to require equal spending; (3) although local property taxes discriminate against the poor, states are not required to eliminate property taxes as a source of funds for education; (4) schools may provide additional (unequal) funding for students who are worthy of special treatment; and (5) no specific plans mandate equitability in school finance formulas. Thus, attempts at equity may seek equal funding across systems but special extra funding is also critical to help children in need.

Vertical Equity.   Imagine a room full of children from different backgrounds, with diverse needs, problems, strengths, and shortcomings. To fund all these children's education equally is hardly fair, because a child with seeing or hearing impairments is challenged in ways that a sighted-hearing child is not. The need for specialized teachers, smaller class size, tutoring, counseling, and other help means that costs would be higher. Although experts agree that some children need more costly "treatment" than others do, little consensus exists about how much more each category of student needs to meet their special conditions.

Alexander and Salmon (1995) explain that "even among client programs universally accepted as requiring unequal or extra-ordinary costs, such as disabled children, there is little agreement regarding what constitutes either appropriate educational services or their respective costs. Each of the 50 states has established unique systems for providing and funding educational services to a varied array of client groups" (p. 234). Although we cannot reach consensus on how much more should be spent on a visually impaired child than an emotionally disturbed one, we do know in fact what some school systems spend, as a ratio to the "regular" child. Presumably, if all students had the same needs and were receiving similar funding, then the ratio would be one to one (1:1).

Berne and Stiefel (1984) state rather forthrightly that "the selection of the unequal groups of pupils is a value judgment that must be made regardless of the way vertical equity is to be measured. Furthermore, if vertical equity is measured with weighted dispersion measures, the appropriate treatment for the unequal treatments of unequals must be specified, usually in the form of pupil weightings" (p. 223). Table 10.4 shows a set of special students from the early

TABLE 10.4 *Vertical Financial Equity Weights for Students with Various "Challenges"**

Title of Condition	Vertical Weights (1.0 = Regular Education)
1. Educable Mentally Impaired	1.50
2. Trainable Mentally Impaired	2.00
3. Severely Mentally Impaired	2.00
4. Emotionally Impaired	2.70
5. Learning Disabled	1.50
6. Hearing Impaired	1.50
7. Visually Impaired	5.01
8. Physically and Health Impaired	3.00
9. Severely Multiply Impaired	1.29
10. Homebound and Hospitalized	1.60

*From Berne and Stiefel (1984), p. 224.

1980s, with their "title of conditions" (first column), although today these titles sound a bit outdated. Take, for example, "Trainable Mentally Impaired," the second category in Table 10.4. It received a 2.00, meaning that this vertical category would receive two times (double) the per pupil resources of "regular" students.

Recent research in several school districts (see Speakman, Bloomfield, Cooper, May, Sampieri, Holsomback, et al., 1997) illustrates the ratio of regular to special students spending. These data are the actual differences per student and are not necessarily the ideal or perfect level of vertical equity. To calculate the actual weights, we turn to the "Westerville Public Schools," in 1994–1995. First, we need to determine what the district spent on instruction for all children. Table 10.5 (Column 1) indicates that, overall, the district expended $3,040 per student for the General Education student (which we call the "General Education Marker," the baseline), and that these regular kids received no extra resources, leading to a 1.00 weighting, or the base level.

Column 2 shows the full-time Special Education children, who are not on the instructional base, but have their own program costs: $9,064 per student, which is 2.99 times the base of $3,040 per student. Column 3, the part-time Special Education students, do receive the "base" because they are in the regular classrooms, plus an additional $1,919 per student for extra pull-out services, for a total of $4,959, which is a 1.63 weighting. Bilingual was weighted 1.52 and Title I (Chapter I) students, 1.51. Whatever the weighting, we see just how complicated vertical equity can be. In effect, the United States tends to treat organizational units *horizontally* (states, school districts, and now schools) while attempting to provide services to individual and categories of students *vertically*.

TABLE 10.5   *Vertical Inequality by Program in "Westville School District"*

Cost Center	1. General Education Marker	2. Special Education FULL-TIME	3. Special Education PART-TIME	4. Bilingual ESL Program	5. Title I and II Program
Instructional base cost	$3,040	$0	$3,040	$3,040	$3,040
Program cost	$0	$9,064	$1,919	$1,579	$1,540
Total program cost	$3,040	$9,064	$4,959	$4,619	$4,580
Vertical equity weight (VEW)	1.00	2.98	1.63	1.52	1.51

Vertical and Horizontal Equity Together

A study of New York City school finances done in 1993–1994 provides useful data on both vertical and horizontal equity and reinforces the contention that both types of equity should be incorporated into finance policy. The average spending in the city's schools overall was $7,918 per student, including central office and school-site expenditures; but the Regular Education Marker—that is, funds reaching the typical or normal student—was $5,149 per pupil.

• Full-time special education ran $23,598 per student, or 298.0 percent of the system's total average of $7,918 per student and 458.2 percent of the General Education costs per student of $5,149. Because these full-time special education students are often treated in their own separate schools and programs, their costs are also separable. However, the remaining vertical equity groups (part-time special education, bilingual, Chapter I, etc.) are best compared to the average costs of the "regular education" student, totaling $5,149 per student. Because all the mainstream students receive the base resources, which are in turn "topped up" by special programs, the horizontal equity dimension becomes the basis for calculating the vertical differences.

• Part-time special education students in New York City public schools received $5,149 per pupil, as did all students, with an additional $5,059 per student added on, to total $10,208 per pupil or 128.9 percent of the system average of $7,918 per student and 198.25 percent of the General Aid spending per student ($5,149).

• Bilingual students got the $5,149 plus an additional $2,140 for a total of $7,289 per student, which translates into 92.1 percent of the total district expenditures and 141.56 percent of the Regular Education cost ($5,149) per student.

- Other categoricals, including Chapter I (Title 1), spent the base plus $2,252, for a total of $7,401 per student, which is 93.5 percent of the District total ($7,918) and 143.74 percent of the regular education costs.

Thus, we see from this example just how a real district weighted the general or regular education costs as 1.00, which could be considered the basis for considering horizontal equity (the equal treatment of equal students). The extra spending came in comparison to this base: full-time special education ran 458.3 times that amount, part-time or related services special education, nearly double (198.23), bilingual was 141.56, other categoricals were nearly the same at 143.74, and regular education at 1.00, as the baseline. It might then be possible to see if all part-time special education students received close to this 198.25, using horizontal equity within categories to test the differences between categories (vertical equity).

Whatever the method, U.S. schools are committed to fairness as a legal and policy doctrine, if not in practice, based in part on the constituency or group that an individual shares. The problem has been to define it, measure it, and then find legal means for enforcing equity. Thus, as this section has shown, perspectives on equity, adequacy, and efficiency are greatly colored by the needs of the individuals and which constituency they represent.

Technical Dimension: Does Money Matter?

A practical, technical battle is going on about whether "money matters." Do more funds for public education make a difference in school programs and student achievement? Or is new money "poured down old rat holes"? The argument about school productivity, first of all, depends to a large degree on whether those having the conversation can agree on the level of inputs, that is, the degree to which the United States is spending more, less, or the same, and if this money is reaching its target: the students. Opponents of public education tend to say, "Well, we've given more and more money to our education system; what have they produced?" Still others contend that we have spent more, but it never reached those who needed it most. And others admit that we simply do not know where the money is going, and could not control it even if we did.

Behind this controversy lie four ways of thinking about how public money is spent and whether it means improved education of children.

We're Spending Too Little— Needs Are Great and More Is Needed

One policy position is that education is underfunded, that millions of children are deprived of a decent education by a system that funnels resources to the middle class and leaves poor children, often children of color, in run-down, poorly administered, under-resourced, low-quality schools. For this group of critics, schools are not only underfunded, but also the lack of money affects the poor, to the advantage of the rich. And the courts, as we saw, have not stood idly by while districts spend vastly different amounts on local education. In fact, thirty-one of the states have seen citizens in poor districts sue the state for greater financial equity and many have won.

We're Spending More and More—Getting Less and Less

The opposing camp looks hard at the continuously rising costs and the falling or stagnant results and concludes that the United States is spending enough or too much money on schools for what our children are actually learning and benefiting. Hanushek, Benson, Freeman, Jamison, Levin, Levin, et al. (1994), some of the nation's leading economists of education, chaired a panel of experts, which concluded that

> Despite ever rising schools budgets, student performance has stagnated. Disappointing student performance, in turn, contributes to disappointing economic growth, stagnating living conditions, and widening gaps among the incomes of different social and ethnic groups. . . . The panel [of economists] concludes that school performance can be improved, without increasing expenditures, through a reform program guided by three broad principles: efficient use of resources, performance incentives, and continuous learning and adaptation. (p. xv)

We're Spending More, but Not on the Right Things

Several key scholars (Cooper, 1994; Rothstein, 1998) argue that although spending has risen in the last twenty years, little of this money is reaching the typical child in the typical classroom. Thus, it's hard to tell what the effects of money are on education because the new and extra resources have been lost or misdirected. Cooper's work on tracing resources to students is helpful in showing that raising district spending does not always guarantee that the new money is reaching its target: places where students learn and grow, such as the classroom, library, media and computer centers, and counseling and advising centers.

Rothstein (1998) analyzed spending trends over the last thirty years and concluded:

> While spending *has* risen substantially, the increase is both smaller and more complex than most assume: Real school spending increased by 61 percent from 1967 to 1991, only a little more than half the real growth conventionally assumed. And barely one-fourth of the increase was directed at "regular education," the traditional school activities whose outcomes can be measured in test scores, graduation rates, and so on. (p. 22)

Table 10.6 shows Rothstein's analysis of nine school districts' decreasing spending on general or regular education, while special education was absorbing much of the apparent increases between 1967 and 1991, an active twenty-four-

TABLE 10.6 *Nine District Analysis of Program Share Change and Share of "New Funds," 1967–1991*

Program	Share of Total, 1967	Per Pupil Spending, 1991	Change in Share, 1967–1991	Share of New Funds
Special Education	3.7%	17.0%	+13.3%	38.0%
Regular Education	79.6	58.8	−20.9	25.9
Food Services	2.0	4.1	+2.1	7.5
Attendance/Guidance	2.1%	4.1%	+2.0%	7.4
Vocational Education	1.4	3.0	+1.6%	5.2
Desegregation Funding	0.0	1.6%	+1.6%	4.1
Bilingual Education	0.3	1.8	+1.5%	3.9
Compensatory Education (Title I, Chap. 1)	5.4	4.3	−1.1%	2.9
Regular Education Transportation	3.9%	3.3%	−0.5%	2.8
After-School Athletics	0.4	0.7	+0.3%	1.1
Security	0.1	0.4	+0.3	0.9
Regular Education Health	1.3	0.9	−0.3	0.5
All Programs	100.0%	100.0%	—	100.0%
Overhead Allocation General Administration	9.4%	9.7%	+0.2%	9.8%
Operations & Maintenance	15.7%	14.2%	−1.4%	12.3%

year period of special education growth. For example, special education spending went from 3.7 percent of these districts' costs in 1967 to 17 percent by 1991, a jump of 13.3 percent of district expenditures—a 359 percent increase. To a large degree, this increase was "new funds," amounting to 38 percent, while regular education dipped from nearly 80 percent to about 59 percent, and captured only 26 percent of the new money during this period. Many of the programs for the regular student saw decreases (such as for regular education transportation, health, and even Chapter I). This information reinforces Rothstein's contention that it is patently unfair to attack U.S. education as wasteful and non-productive based on where all the increased money went—if most of these new dollars never reached the students being tested (the regular education pupil).

Tracking Money. Thus, a key component of the policy debate on school productivity is just how accurately we can trace resources to their target: the children being taught and tested. Because state and local governments have typically focused on the school district, not the school and classroom, as the setting for learning, we need a new system for analyzing costs where they actually occur. If General Motors cannot determine what it really costs to produce a Buick, how will it ever set a price for the work, hold each factory (even each assembly line) responsible for the quality of production, and tell how much it will cost to improve the design and construction? Price is essential to all forms of productivity, and yet education has been slow to create an acceptable "production function"—the means for relating cost inputs (funds, equipment, staff, buildings, and buses) to programs and student outputs (learning, test scores, attendance, promotion, and graduation rates). This slowness is typical of governments and doubly typical of large bureaucracies that are also near monopolies. Believe it or not, before the break-up of "Ma Bell," the telephone monopoly, the company did not even know what it really cost to make a phone call on the system.

But productivity begins with knowledge. Note the use of systems theory and language that relates the financial inputs of education to the systems outputs, such as high school graduation rates, academic achievement, and gains. Again, however, the "through-puts" (activities in the black box) are critical—how to convert funds into education activities and services that can be measured and analyzed—but are rarely addressed in the input-output models applied to school finance research.

POLICY VIGNETTE • *Western School District*

Using a typical, medium-sized urban school district in the western United States, we see how costs are structured in this real system—tracking resources to students. First, expenditure analysis separated "Central Office" and "School Sites," because resources need to reach the school before being used in the classroom for students. In the Western school district, Central Office cost 8.73 percent, and 79.72 percent or $5,707 per pupil out of a total district per-student cost of $7,159 was reaching the schools as a whole, as shown in Table 10.7.

TABLE 10.7 *Central, Other Commitments, and School Site Costs, by Dollars, Percent, and per Pupil in Western School District 1998–1999 (75,306 Students)*

	I. TOTAL Dollars	II. Percent of TOTAL	III. PER PUPIL
1. Central Office	$47,078,146	8.74%	$626
2. Other Commitments	$62,203,458	11.54%	$826
3. School Sites	$429,759,384	79.72%	$5,706
TOTAL	$539,040,988	100.00%	$7,158

TABLE 10.8 *School Site Spending by Functions in Western Public Schools, 1998–1999 (Pupils = 75,306, Total School-Site Spending = $5,707 per Pupil, District Total = $7,159 per Pupil)*

Functions	Total Cost	Per Pupil	% of School Spending	% of District Spending
Total instruction	$286,046,122	$3,798	66.5%	53.1%
Face-to-face teaching	$278,850,950	$3,702	64.9%	51.7%
Classroom materials	$7,195,172	$96	1.6%	1.4%
Total instructional support	$31,726,474	$421	7.5%	5.9%
Pupil support	$24,327,312	$322	5.6%	4.5%
Teacher support	$7,399,162	$98	1.8%	1.4%
School operations	$85,179,766	$1,131	19.8%	15.8%
School leadership	$26,807,024	$356	6.2%	5.0%
School-site total	$429,759,386	$5,707	100.0%	79.7%
Total district spending	$539,040,988	$7,159	NA	100.0%

School Site Spending

The next step is to analyze just how the money spent in school is used. Table 10.8, fourth column, shows that some 80 percent reached the schools as a whole, with about 53 percent used in the classroom for all purposes (face-to-face teaching was 51.7 percent; materials and equipment, 1.4 percent), counting all types and levels. Other functional costs in the schools included instructional support at 5.9 percent, school operations (heat, light, maintenance, transportation, and custodians) at 15.8 percent, and school-site leadership (principals and assistant principals) was 5.0 percent. Again, these are district averages spent in the schools by function.

Thus, of the $7,159 per pupil spent in the Western School District in the 1998–1999 school year, $5,707 per student went to the schools and $3,798 per student reached the classroom overall. Within the schools themselves, as shown in Table 10.8, Column 3, about two-thirds (66.5 percent) of the resources reached the classroom: that's $3,798 per pupil for instruction, out of school-site total per pupil spending of $5,707.

Instructional Costs

At the school level, we might look at instructional spending in particular, including the cost of teachers, substitute teachers, paraprofessionals (classroom aides), materials, and computers, examining still more closely spending that reaches all students on average in the Western Public School District. Of the 66.5 percent spent for instruction, as expected, most of this went to pay salaries and benefits of teachers, amounting to $3,474 per student out of school spending total of $5,707 per student, or 60.9 percent. It amounts to 48.5 percent of the Western Public School District's total per student spending.

School Outliers.   Yet another issue in policy decisionmaking is how much difference exists among school-site costs within a district or state, when all schools in a district or system are judged against the same benchmarks? Hawaii is an excellent place to compare schools because one presumes greater equity, as Hawaii is the only state without local school districts (which have been the traditional units of comparison when pursuing funding equity cases in court). Thus, we treat Hawaii, the state, as though it was the School District of Hawaii, allowing us to compare all the schools in the state with one another in spending.

We use the micro-financial model that tracks funds to schools and classroom instruction, as shown in Table 10.9. The high- and low-spending schools in and around Honolulu varied considerably from one another, and from the statewide average of all elementary schools. The Hawaii statewide total average spending on education was $6,360 per student in 1995–1996, which is total dollars for schools in the state, $1.187 billion, divided by Hawaii's 186,581 public school students. Of that amount, some 85 percent or $5,413 per student was spent in schools, while the remaining amount was expended for central administration and other non-school expenses. On average, about 51 percent ($3,237 per student) reached the classroom level for direct instruction (exactly the national average for other districts using this micro-financial model). Performing school-by-school analysis, however, we see the statewide averages converted to a wide range of high- and low-spending schools on classroom instruction. The Linapuni Elementary School was at the top of the spending chart (see Table 10.9) on instructional expenditures, while the Wailupe Valley Elementary School was at the bottom of the cost distribution:

TABLE 10.9   *Outlier Analysis Range of Spending Schools and "Classrooms" per Pupil within the School District of Hawaii, 1995–1996*

Cost Center	Percent of Total per Pupil ($6,360)	Per Pupil Costs	Dollars
State average total to schools:	85.11	$5,413	$1,009,983,835
Total state dollars to instruction	50.89	$3,237	$603,875,872
High spending (272 students) Linapuni Elementary School:	109.72	$6,978	$1,583,923
Linapuni instruction	70.60	$4,490	$1,019,158
Low spending (173 students) Wailupe Valley Elementary School:	90.60	$5,762	$996,900
Wailupe Valley instruction	39.20	$2,493	$431,241

- *Highest spending.* The Linapuni Elementary School expended a total of $6,978 per student, which was 110 percent of the statewide average of $6,360 per student. In turn, about 71 percent ($4,490 per student) went for direct classroom instruction, 20 percentage points higher than the statewide average of 51 percent.

- *Lowest Spending.* The Wailupe Valley Elementary School was a different story in 1995–1996, as shown in Table 10.9. While 90 percent of the per pupil cost, or $5,762 per pupil, reached the school, only $2,493 per pupil or 39.2 percent of the statewide average of $6,360 per pupil went for classroom costs (teachers' salaries and benefits; substitute teachers; textbooks and materials; and equipment and desktop computers for instructional purposes).

Thus, even though Hawaii spent almost $6,400 per student overall in 1995–1996, the lowest-spending school, Wailupe Valley Elementary School, had considerably lower instructional costs per pupil of $2,493 or 39.2 percent of the system spending. The range of costs, then, for classroom instruction in Hawaii's one system went from 71 percent ($4,490 per pupil) at Linapuni Elementary School, to only 39 percent ($2,493 per pupil) at Wailupe Valley Elementary School—a difference of over 40 percent. The range is still greater when elementary and secondary school costs for instruction are compared.

We're Spending More, but It's Unrelated to Learning

The fourth camp admits we really know neither whether money spent in education makes any difference for students' learning, nor how much more money increases learning and test results. As agnostics in the battle over more spending, this camp cannot quite show that more money leads to more learning, never mind whether learning leads to greater economic activity and higher productivity. These people are more than skeptics. It's difficult to prove that, for example, $500 more expended in schools brings about some small, positive, but measurable improvement in students' attainment.

Practical Issues: Improving School Productivity

The great quest, then, in education policy research is to relate money to results: more resources, better teaching, enhanced learning. A raft of research has sought to prove this relationship. A significant body of research supports the concept of school productivity, although these studies are often dated, contested, and inadequate for the modern debate on whether money matters and how.

Spending and Results

Research tries to show that systems that spend money on schools—to help them to change their programs, hire new staff, and create new cultures—have better results.

The burgeoning body of research on school change, reform, and restructuring—often around greater choice for parents—has made claims but has had real problems substantiating them. Although more money is spent on magnet schools, alternative schools, charter schools, satellite schools, and even vouchers for more family choice, researchers have been hard-pressed to prove that more funding for radical new reforms will produce better results.

In an ideal world, public policies would make more funds readily available from public and private sources to enable all children to attend quality schools that are appropriate for their needs. Money would be wisely spent, reaching children and educating them to their fullest capacity, turning them into productive members of a productive community, with jobs that bring them satisfaction and a decent income.

But we live in a less than ideal world. The financial support of education is a system of compromises, of competing interests and values that have produced one of the world's largest, most expensive, and most complex education systems. And the way money is raised, allocated, and spent reflects these compromises and this complexity, and deserves special attention. Compromises in what sense? In almost every one. Take these brief examples.

Compromising on Sources of Money for Education.   Education is mainly supported by taxes, although parents of 5.86 million students pay for their education privately, out of their own pockets, on top of paying taxes for other children's schooling. Some forms of taxation are more efficient and profitable than others. Tax on property is as old as civil life itself, because ownership of valuable land, sheep, and goats was the original wealth in societies where currency and coin were hardly used. But property wealth is inequitably distributed, with some communities having lots of land, factories, shopping malls, and high-priced housing, while other locations are property-poor. If school taxes are property taxes, as they are in most communities, then rich towns will have rich schools; poor areas, poor schools.

Yet eliminating the property tax is not an easy solution: here comes the compromise. Without tax income from local property, local communities fear the loss of local control, a highly valued quality in U.S. school finance. Five distinct compromises are made to attempt to equalize spending for poor districts:

1. *Supplement unequal local tax capacity with state school equalization aid, with the property-poorest communities getting the most help and the richest communities, hardly any at all.* Most states accept this compromise, although it "papers over" the basic underlying problem of inequalities based on taxing an unevenly distributed resource, real property, not eliminating the unfair structure itself.

2. *Regionalize property taxes on utilities and business/commerce, while allowing communities to keep their residential tax income.* This compromise hopes to allow us to have our cake and eat it too, by keeping the tax income on residential property within the community but creating larger taxing units (say, whole counties, as in Maryland) to help equalize spending between contiguous richer and poorer school districts. But towns with shops and industry hate to lose their income to poor communities; they argue that they put up with the pollution, overcrowding, traffic, and inconvenience of having commerce and industry in their districts and should reap the benefits of taxes on these resources.

3. *Create larger school districts that combine mixed income communities.* Larger districts may equalize the income but may increase the costs of operations—compromising to reach one solution (income equity) may just create another problem: school system size and inefficiency. Larger districts may create larger bureaucracies, longer distances to travel to school, and less community.

4. *"Cap" richer districts to keep them from constantly raising their spending on schools, while increasing state aid to poorer districts.* But some families argue that if they're willing to pay more for their children's education, what business is it of the state? Caps, one compromise, can bring on other problems: parents can withdraw from public schools and pay tuition for a local private or parochial school. Or parents can set up private foundations or trusts (off the "books") in public schools and spend more on their children's education, thus end-running the cap.

5. *Or even play Robin Hood and require that richer districts supplement poorer ones as a requirement for raising their own spending.* Say, for every dollar a rich district increases its per-student spending on schools, the districts must give 25 cents to a poor, neighboring district. These redistributive polices have been attempted in several states such as Texas but are resisted, because one district is subsidizing another.

These compromises are just that: an attempt to blunt the effects of unequal distribution of resources for education without actually changing the basic structure of school funding and governance: local money and local control.

Compromising Control over Resources.   We know that schools need to control their budgets and put money where it will most help their local students. But we also realize that because money comes from federal, state, and local sources, that control is usually shared among levels. Thus, multiple funding sources often mean multiple polices and mixed or shared control. The compromise is a highly complex model of control by higher levels over lower levels: federal over state and local; state over local; and districts over schools.

Each level of government (federal, state, local) has its own laws, policies, and requirements. To receive federal money for programs to help low-achieving children, for example, districts must spend the money in certain ways and report how. These regulations, then, hinder the discretion and autonomy of teachers and administrators—and mean that money cannot always be spent in the best way for students.

Compromising Equity for Enhanced Choice.   U.S. schools are, by design, inequitable: too many legal jurisdictions; too many different funding arrangements; and too much dependence on local property taxes that are in turn based on highly varying local property values. Even if every district in the nation were funded the same, we know from Hawaii and elsewhere that individual schools receive vastly different amounts of resources, have varying class size, and feed different levels of resources to students.

Compromising on Standards and Productivity.   Finally, the United States has never been committed to real quality for all students. Any suggestion of national policymaking—much less federal (governmental) standards—is rejected. And funding is so diverse and varying that lawmakers can never be sure whether local communities can actually afford the mandates (e.g., special education) they enact. Thus, the United States prefers a localist system: letting everyone off the hook. The federal government can relax because schooling is a state function. The state, despite years of court cases and effort, has delegated most responsibility to the districts, which may or may not turn control over to the individual schools.

Future of Education Resource Policies

The future of school finance policy rests with society's view of the role of education, its structure, controls, and outcomes. We appear to be moving in many opposite directions all at once: stricter standards in some places, more standardized curriculum and standards elsewhere, and more systematic testing of student results ("gates" programs to prevent students' being promoted to the next level until they can demonstrate knowledge and mastery) that depend on a stronger role for state and federal governments. We would also predict greater interest in full-state funding (like Hawaii currently has) and less emphasis on local differences.

Opposing this drive, however, is increased interest in school self-determination, charter schools, magnet schools, and greater choice for families. Funding, then, might move toward granting vouchers and other family-controlled devices, while at the same time the federal and state governments' share may decrease the control for parents. Full-state funding in states such as Hawaii has the effect of diminishing inequalities and increasing accountability, but giving less autonomy and choice to local schools and families.

Think, too, of having both at the same time: what if the state collected all the money, redistributing it equally and equitably among all the children in the state, using what Thomas Jones has called "child based funding" or CBF? As such, the raising and allocation of money are equalized—and the spending of the money on education is privatized or at least user-driven and user-friendly. Take several scenarios:

Scenario 1: State Vouchers

What if all property and income taxes were collected by the state, based on local property values and assessments? Then, using a weighted student education scholarship (WeSES), the state allocated the resources to the family in the form of a grant, scholarship, or voucher. The family could then cash in their scholarship, based on equalized value and special student needs (under-achieving, non-English speaking, or others), at a school of choice as long as the school was accredited. This plan has something for everyone: equity for the liberals and choice and enterprise for the conservatives.

Scenario 2: Open Enrollment— Money Following the Student

A slight modification of the WeSES concept would be to fund family choice, not the family itself. Already, resources are allocated by pupil enrollments, with larger schools receiving more money from federal, state, and local sources. By having a variety of local and regional schools, free transportation, and an inter-district transfer plan coupled with family choice, we would have both equity and choice: fair taxation and fiscal neutrality because children in every community, regardless of local wealth, could select a school and their tuition would follow them to that site, with the voucher going directly from the state and federal levels to the school based on enrollments and need.

Districts such as Edmonton, Alberta, Seattle, and Houston are experimenting with "weighted student formula" models, whereby each school is allocated funds based on the needs and conditions of each student, a kind of differentiated internal voucher that allows each school to plan its own program. We have some evidence that WSF schools have a greater sense of control, are able to tailor their programs to their students, and actually produce better results (see Ouchi, Cooper, Segal, & DeRoche, 2002).

Scenario 3: Full-State Charter Schools

Public money also follows children to charter schools, which are run by private boards but are often accountable either to the local district or the state education department. If these schools receive the average local per pupil costs as income, then they may be under-supported if they are a high school (because high schools spend above the local average per student) and over-supported if they are an elementary school (because these schools usually spend below the district average). Although parents may have greater choice with charters, they may have less funding for special programs unless the bilingual and Chapter I funds follow the student to these charter schools.

Changes in school funding may come all at once, as decisionmakers tire of trying the same old solutions: more money, more equity, more controls. We already see in places like Milwaukee and Cleveland where African-American communities want some of the same choices that the white middle class enjoys in education. Representative Polly Williams went to the Wisconsin legislature and came back with vouchers for a small experimental group of children, and other cities followed. Or, as has been the trend over the last century, changes in financing schools may come gradually, almost imperceptibly as costs rise, spending patterns are altered, and districts and schools gain more control over their funds. Jones (1985) notes that "the history of school finance reform has been marked by gradualism. Reforms begin with small amounts of money in just a few states, then spread and expand over time" (p. 262).

Three possible alternatives emerge, as Jones explains them: (1) using limited vouchers or tax credits for both public and private schools; (2) using vouchers only for supplementary educational services for the poor and handicapped first, then slowly expanding the concept to the less needy groups; (3) giving vouchers or credits in small amounts to a wide variety of individuals and allowing them to combine them into larger, more meaningful amounts.

To some degree since 1985, when Jones wrote these possibilities, all three have occurred somewhere. Minnesota gives tax credits to public and private school families. The poor in New York City, Cleveland, Milwaukee, and elsewhere have a few available vouchers (between 1,000 and 1,400 students per year), which are targeted for them. And charter schools allow a few families to take their children out of traditional public schools and to bring their money with them to the charter.

Whatever new policies in school finance may occur, the issues will be the same: How can we make funding more equitable? Equal for children who are somewhat equal in needs and abilities, unequal (greater) for kids who need more help? Should we fund private and public schools? And how can the nation see that the $345 billion dollars spent annually is reaching students, helping them to learn, and producing measurable results?

Until we are able to show just how much students benefit from additional resources—how more money means more learning—it will be increasingly difficult to pass policies for increasing school expenditures at the rate similar to the last thirty years. Called "production function" studies, such research has shown no consistent benefit from more spending, as Hanushek (1991) has argued: "There is no systematic relationship between school expenditures and student performance. This finding implies significant inefficiency in the operation of schools and has obvious and profound implications for discussion about altering school finance arrangements" (p. 425; see also Hanushek & Jorgenson, 1996).

This chapter has shown that most districts and states do not know how much money actually reaches children in services and materials. Instead, policymakers deal in national, state, and local averages and rarely are the school and classroom the primary units of analysis. This weakness is being addressed, as communities and taxpayers demand to know where their resources are going and who is benefiting, and the courts are demanding greater equity of spending on the education of all children. Knowledge and understanding of funding are the first steps toward effective finance policies in education.

Chapter Assignments and Activities

1. How does your state and district's spending per student compare with national and regional averages? How would you set a benchmark on these findings?

2. How might you determine the percent of spending in your district for:
   a. Salaries and benefits for teachers, administrators, and other groups?
   b. Special needs students, including handicapped, bilingual, or poor students?
   c. Staff development?
   d. Individual schools?

3. Over the last two or three years, what have been the dollar and percent changes (increases) in spending per pupil overall and for instruction, school totals?

4. Why is *equity* in funding of education a difficult if not impossible goal without major (total) restructuring of U.S. school organization, governance, and funding?

5. Compare vertical and horizontal equity and their key policies; how can school districts have horizontal (among equals) equity within categories of unequals (students with differing needs and problems)?

Seminal Works

Theodore Schultz's (1963) *The Economic Value of Education* offers an excellent overview of the economic benefits of an educated populace. Students interested in reading a good primer on school finance should check out Burrup, Brimley, and Garfield's (1996) *Financing Education in a Climate of Change* (6th edition). Julie Underwood and Deborah Verstegen's (1990) edited book, *The Impact of Litigation and Legislation on Public School Finance,* is a superb analysis of the legal and legislative aspects of school finance. Finally, Erick Hanushek and associates (1994) *Making Schools Work: Improving Performance and Controlling Costs* provides a definitive treatment of the complex relationship between costs and performance in U.S. education.

References

Alexander, K., & Salmon, R. G. (1995). *Public school finance.* Boston: Allyn & Bacon.

Berne, R., & Stiefel, L. (1984). *The measurement of equity in school finance.* Baltimore: Johns Hopkins University Press.

Burrup, P. E., Brimley, V., Jr., & Garfield, R. R. (1996). *Financing education in a climate of change* (6th ed.). Boston: Allyn & Bacon.

Butts, R. F. (1978). *Public education in the United States: From revolution to reform.* New York: Holt, Rinehart and Winston.

Chubb, J., & Moe, T. (1990). *Politics, markets and America's schools.* Washington, DC: The Brookings Institution.

Cibulka, J., & Cooper, B. S. (2002). Capital needs and spending in urban public school systems: Policies, problems and promises. In F. E. Crampton & D. C. Thompson (Eds.), *Saving America's school infrastructure.* New York: Information Age Publishing.

Clune, W. H. (1994). The shift from equity to adequacy in school finance. *Educational Policy, 8*(4), 376–394.

Cooper, B. S., & Doyle, D. P. (Eds.). (1989). *Federal aid to education: What future Chapter I?* New York: Falmer Press.

Cooper, B. S., & Speakman, S. T. (1997). The three R's of education finance reform: Re-thinking, re-tooling, and re-evaluating school-site information. *Journal of Education Finance, 22*(4), 337–367.

Cooper, B. S., Speakman, S. T., & Bloomfield, D. G. (1996). New model, new technology for improved school-site information. *School Business Affairs, 62*(2), 35–43.

Cremin, L. A. (1970). *American education: The colonial experience, 1607–1783.* New York: Harper & Row.

Cubberley, E. P. (1906). *School funds and their apportionment.* New York: Teachers College Press.

Denison, E. F. (1962). *The source of economic growth in the United States and the alternatives we have before us.* New York: Committee on Economic Development, Supplementary Paper No. 13.

Ford, P. L. (Ed.). *The works of Thomas Jefferson.* New York: G. P. Putnam.

Friedman, M. (1962). *Capitalism and freedom.* Chicago: University of Chicago Press.

Guthrie, J. W., & Rothstein, R. (1999). Enabling "adequacy" to achieve reality: Translating adequacy into state school finance distribution arrangements. In H. F. Ladd, R. Chalk, & J. S. Hansen (Eds.), *Equity and adequacy in education finance: Issues and perspectives* (pp. 209–259). Washington, DC: National Academy Press.

Hansen, D. A. (1986). Family-school articulations: The effects of interaction rule mismatch. *American Education Research Journal 2*(4), 643–659.

Hanushek, E. A. (1991). When school finance 'reform' may not be a good policy. *Harvard Journal of Legislation, 28*(2), 425–442.

Hanushek, E. A., Benson, C. S., Freeman, R. B., Jamison, D. T., Levin, H. M., Levin, R. A., et al. (1994). *Making schools work: Improving performance and controlling costs.* Washington, DC: The Brookings Institution.

Hanushek, E. A., & Jorgenson, D. W. (1996). *Improving America's schools: The role of incentives.* Washington, DC: National Academy Press.

Heise, M. (1995). State constitutions, school finance litigation, and the "third wave": From equity to adequacy. *Temple Law Review, 68,* 1151–1176.

Jones, T. H. (1985). *Introduction to school finance: Techniques and social policy.* New York: Macmillan.

Kozol, J. (1991). *Savage inequalities: Children in America's schools.* New York: Crown.

Langelett, G. (2002). Human capital: A summary of the 20th century research. *Journal of School Finance, 28*(1), 1–24.

Minorini, P. A., & Sugarman, S. D. (1999). Educational adequacy and the courts: The promise and problems of moving to a new paradigm. In H.F. Ladd (Ed.), *Equity and adequacy in education finance: Issues and perspectives* (pp. 175–208). Washington, DC: National Academy Press.

Meranto, P. (1967). *The politics of federal aid to education in 1965: A study in political innovation.* Syracuse, NY: Syracuse University Press.

Odden, A., & Busch, C. (1998). *Financing schools for high performance: Strategies for improving the use of educational resources.* San Francisco: Jossey-Bass.

Ouchi, W. G., Cooper, B. S., & Segal, L. G. (2003). The impact of organization on the performance of nine school systems: Lessons for California. *California Policy Options 2003* (in press).

Porter, A. C. (1993). Defining and measuring opportunity to learn. In S. I. Traiman (Ed.), *The debate on opportunity to learn standards: Supporting Works* (pp. 33–72). Washington, DC: National Governors Association.

Psacharopoulos, G. (1981). Returns to education: An updated international comparison. *Comparative Education Review, 17*(1), 321–341.

Rothstein, R., & Miles, K. H. (1995). *Where's the money gone? Changes in the level and composition of education spending.* Washington, DC: Economic Policy Institute.

Rothstein, R. (1998). *A race to the top? How states have hustled to spend more on schools: Some new ways of looking at data on school spending, 1970–1995.* Paper presented to the American Education Finance Association, Mobile, AL: March 1995.

Schultz, T. W. (1960). Capital formation by education. *Journal of Political Economy, 68*(2), 571–583.

Schultz, T. W. (1963). *The economic value of education.* New York: Columbia University Press.

Schultz, T. W. (1981). *Investing in people: The economics of population quality.* Berkeley: University of California Press.

Speakman, S. T., Bloomfield, D. C., Cooper, B. S., May, J. F., Sampieri, R. M., Holsomback, H. C., et al. (1996). Tracing school-site expenditures: Equity, policy and legal implications. In H. Walberg (Series Ed.), B. S. Cooper & S. T. Speakman (Eds.), *Optimizing Education Resources* (pp. 149–196). Greenwich, CT: JAI Press.

Thurston, L. M., & Roe, W. H. (1957). *State school administration.* New York: Harper & Row.

Tyack, D. B. (1967). *Turning points in American educational history.* Waltham, MA: Blaisdale.

Underwood, J. K. (1995). School finance adequacy as vertical equity. *University of Michigan Journal of Law Reform, 28*(3), 493–519.

Underwood, J. K., & Verstegen, D. (1990). School finance challenges in federal courts: Changing equal projection analysis. In J. K. Underwood & D. Verstegen (Eds.), *The impacts of litigation and legislation on public school finance* (pp. 177–192). San Francisco: Harper & Row.

Webster, N. (1790). *A collection of essays and fugitive writings. On moral, historical, political and literary subjects* (pp. 1–19). Boston: I. Thomas & E. E. Andrews.

11

Charter School Policy

Despite wave after wave of reform, the condition of education—particularly in urban areas populated by the most impoverished, disadvantaged children—remains in perilous condition. Reading and math scores in many large cities remain abysmally low (Ayres, 1994). From 1980 to 1990, nearly half of the students who entered high school in Chicago dropped out (Ayres, 1994), and there has been scant evidence of improvement since then. One-fifth of the public schools in Chicago and New York City are either on probation or in need of immediate intervention ("Saving Public Education," 1997). Performance data show wide, persistent gaps in student achievement. In Texas, in the 1997–1998 academic year, the performance gap between white and African American students on the Texas Assessment of Academic Skills was 36 points (Judson, n.d.).

Clearly, something needs to be done to improve the educational opportunities of at risk children. Dissatisfaction with repeated failures at educational reform has brought together "an unusual alliance of minority parents, conservative ideologues, and state legislators" searching for ways to reform public education "without totally destroying or abandoning it" (Fusarelli, 1999, p. 215). One reform that has become popular is the charter schools movement. Increasing numbers of educational reformers view charter schools as an opportunity to provide a more effective education to students who are ill-served by the public school system as it is currently structured—particularly in urban areas (Fusarelli, 1999). Support for charter schools comes from a wide array of groups, including conservatives who also support taxpayer-financed vouchers, business leaders who have lost confidence in non-responsive, bureaucratic public schools, African American and Hispanic civic groups, community leaders, and parents who view charter schools as an opportunity to escape failing inner-city schools (Hartocollis, 1998a). In New York City, partners include the Banana Kelly Community Improvement Association, El Puente, the Neighborhood Association for Intercultural Affairs, the Allen A.M.E. Neighborhood Preservation and Development Corporation, and the

East Harlem Council for Community Improvement. Currently, approximately 2,400 charter schools operate in thirty-nine states, and the District of Columbia, enrolling nearly 600,000 students. In Washington, D.C., nearly one-tenth of schoolchildren attend charter schools (Finn, Manno, and Vanourek, 2000), and the movement continues to grow as charters expand within each state.

Normative Dimension

The charter school reform movement has generated heated debate about whether this policy will improve student achievement, particularly in urban schools with large enrollments of at risk students. Advocates argue that freeing schools from the bureaucratic stranglehold of red tape will give school administrators and teachers the flexibility to devise effective education programs for students. Proponents assert that because charter schools can have their charters revoked if schools fail to meet stated performance goals, the schools are more accountable (and implicitly more efficient) to parents, students, and the public at large. By injecting an element of competition into the public education marketplace (because charter schools compete with traditional public schools for students), charter schools will spur reform within the public education system—a system notoriously resistant to change (Nathan, 1996).

Surveys of directors and founders of charter schools reveal several major reasons for establishing charter schools, including: (1) autonomy in educational programming, (2) a desire to serve a special student population, (3) realization of an educational vision, (4) a desire to provide a better teaching and learning environment, (5) instructional innovation, (6) a desire to involve parents, and (7) the autonomy to develop nontraditional relationships with the community (Kane, 1998; Medler, 1996). These responses offer the possibility that fundamental roles and responsibilities of key actors in the school organization will be altered or changed in charter schools, thus breaking the traditional factory model common in large urban school systems (Fusarelli, 1999).

Opponents of charter schools, and school choice in general, argue that competition will not improve public education because schools do not operate as markets do. Funds will be siphoned from already underfunded public schools. In an op-ed piece in the *New York Times,* Roger Bowen, president of the State University of New York at New Paltz, suggested that the passage of the New York charter school law starts the state "down the slippery slope toward increased privatization of education" (Bowen, 1999, p. A19). He stated, "Every dollar going to charter schools is a dollar not going to public schools" (p. A19). Many fear that competition will benefit only those students with the ability to move from one school to another, those students left behind will suffer in poorly-funded, dilapidated facilities. Good schools, they assert, will get the best teachers and students, leading to greater social stratification and segregation (Wells, Lopez, Scott, & Holme, 1999).

Structural Dimension: Examining the Policy Differences in State Charter School Laws

According to Vegari (2002), charter statutes differ dramatically from state to state with respect to the number of charter schools allowed, types of charter schools permitted, degree of exemption from state regulations (and thus degree of autonomy), and the conditions of accountability and charter renewal (U.S.D.O.E., 1998). Roughly half of the states place limits on the number of charter schools in a state or the number of students who may enroll in charter schools.

In most states, charter schools may be operated by public, private, or independent institutions of higher education, nonprofit organizations (such as museums and libraries), or governmental entities. Teachers, school administrators, parents, or community groups may operate their own charter schools, independent of local school district control. In some states such as Texas and New York, charters may not be granted directly to for-profit organizations, although such organizations may be contracted to manage or operate a charter school (Center for Education Reform, 1998a). Under most state charter laws, existing public schools may be converted to charter schools, and five states allow private school conversions. Usually, public school conversions require the approval of the local board of education. In eleven states, only the local school board can grant charters. Others require local school board and state board approval, while still others allow applicants to bypass the local school board entirely (U.S.D.O.E., 1998). However, home-based schools may not convert to charter status.

Charter schools are nonsectarian, considered part of the public school system, and must accept students regardless of where they live. Charter schools operate on an open-enrollment basis and may deny admission only to students who are adjudicated, convicted of delinquent conduct, or who have been removed from their previous school due to disciplinary reasons. In the event of over-enrollment, a process of random selection is used. Preference for enrollment may be given to returning students, siblings, and children residing in the local district. The length of the original charter and charter renewal varies greatly from state to state, ranging from three years in Utah to ten years in Missouri (Weber, 1998).

State laws differ with respect to where applications for charters are made and which agencies or organizations are authorized to grant charters. For example, in New York, applications may be made to any one of three charter entities: the boards of education of school districts (or, in New York City, the Chancellor of the Board of Education), the Board of Trustees of the State University of New York, or the Board of Regents. Under the law, the Board of Regents is the only entity authorized to issue a charter. Therefore, a charter approved by the board of education of a school district or by the Trustees of the State University of New York must also be approved by the Board of Regents. The State Board of Regents can approve an unlimited number of conversions of existing public schools. Public schools wishing to convert to charter status must gain the support of a majority of the school's parents/guardians as well as the approval of the local school board. The law prohibits private or nonpublic schools from converting to charter status. In Texas, the State Board of Education (SBOE) has the authority to approve charter applications after review by the Texas Education Agency (TEA).

In several states, preference is given to applicants who demonstrate the capability to provide comprehensive learning experiences to students identified as at risk for academic failure. The most recent survey of charter schools by the Center for Education Reform reported that forty-three percent serve minority populations of more than 60 percent (Center for Education Reform, 2002). Texas has a flexible cap that allows unlimited additional charters (beyond the state-approved cap of 120) if at least 75 percent of the students served by the charter school are at risk of dropping out.

Although open-enrollment charter schools are exempt from many state mandates, they are generally not exempt from regulations regarding class size, graduation and accountability requirements, laws related to bilingual and special education, finance, health, safety, and civil rights. In many states, tenure laws and state curriculum mandates are waived. Charter schools have the freedom to lengthen the school day, allow school uniforms, organize the school's curriculum around core academic subjects or a particular overall theme, and operate a single-sex school. Under New York' charter school law, if the charter school has fewer than 250 students, it will not be bound by union collective bargaining agreements. As the school grows, teachers are not required to unionize, although they may vote to do so. Schools with an initial enrollment of more than 250 students must comply with collective bargaining agreements. However, ten schools will be totally exempt from collective bargaining, regardless of size.

Such anti-union provisions in charter school legislation are not uncommon. According to Fusarelli (in press), "A number of states, including those with powerful teachers unions, have adopted what the Center for Education Reform calls 'strong' charter school laws—laws that allow great flexibility in creating and operating charter schools—including exemptions from collective bargaining agreements and relaxed rules on hiring certified teachers" (p. 221). Fusarelli concludes that "essentially, the 'strongest' charter school laws contain the most anti-union provisions" (p. 221), a finding that explains in large measure union opposition to charter schools in several states.

Equity in Policy Implementation

Despite the growing popularity of charter schools in the United States, student enrollment in charter schools represents less than 1 percent of the total student enrollment in public schools nationwide. Similarly, the 192 charters that have been granted since 1995 in Texas represent less than 3 percent of the total number of public schools (approximately 6,000) statewide.

The majority of charter schools are located in urban areas; many (at least half and as many as two-thirds) are specifically designed to serve at risk students. According to Brooks Flemister, former senior director of the division of charter schools for the Texas Education Agency, charter schools in Texas are "mostly an urban phenomenon. They do tend to congregate in areas where you have very large school districts as a choice to the large districts" (Waters, 1999, p. 19). Approximately forty charter schools operate in the Houston area, offering some students an alternative to the 235,000 students enrolled in the Houston Independent School District (Waters, 1999).

Charter schools are much smaller than traditional public schools, with an average enrollment of approximately 300 students. However, this number masks wide variation in enrollment in individual schools; some schools enroll anywhere from less than 10 students to over 1,000 (although the New York law requires at least 50 students per school). In New Jersey, which did not pass charter legislation until 1996, the average charter school enrollment is only 103 students (Kane, 1998). The U.S. Department of Education (1997) reports that

> about 60 percent [of charter schools] enroll fewer than 200 students, whereas only 16 percent of other public schools have such small student bodies. No matter what grade levels are served, a higher proportion of charter schools are smaller than other public schools. The difference is most striking at the secondary level. Almost four-fifths of charter secondary schools enroll fewer than 200 students, in contrast to one-quarter of other public secondary schools. (pp. 3–4)

Charter schools come in all shapes and sizes, which change nearly every year as schools add grade levels and student enrollment grows. A review of charter schools in Texas reveals astonishing diversity in terms of size and grade level served. Charter schools range in size from 23 students to 2,070 students, with an average enrollment of approximately 200 students (Texas Education Agency, 1999).[1] The average enrollment is misleading, however. Only six charter schools in Texas have enrollments greater than 400 students, and three-fourths of the schools have enrollments of less than 250 students. This is considerably smaller than the average enrollment (638) in a traditional public school in Texas (Charter School Resource Center, 1999). More than forty different grade level configurations can be found among charter schools in Texas, with slightly more than a quarter consisting of grades 9–12. This finding is consistent with a national survey of charter schools conducted by the U.S. Department of Education, which found that "many charter schools have non-traditional grade configurations" including "a higher proportion of K through 12, K through 8, and ungraded schools than other public schools" (U.S.D.O.E., 1998, p. 9). These configurations change year to year with continued charter school expansion.

---

[1]During their first three years of operation, average enrollment in charter schools in Texas has fluctuated from 147 (1996–1997), to 217 (1997–1998), to 198 (1998–1999) (Texas Education Agency, 1999).

As with school size, the student-teacher ratio is usually lower in charter schools than in traditional public schools. For example, charter schools in New Jersey have a student-teacher ratio of 9:1, with class sizes ranging from eight to twenty students (Kane, 1998). In Texas, however, class size in charter schools is slightly higher at 21.6 (compared to 15.5 in traditional public schools), although more than one-third of the schools had a student–teacher ratio of less than 15:1 (Texas Education Agency, 2000b).

The amazing diversity found among charter schools in terms of size, structure, and location, coupled with a corresponding shift in the demographic composition of students, faculty, administrators, and board members, reflects an attempt to "restructure, re-engineer, and reinvent" urban education in the United States (Fusarelli, 1999, p. 214). Many charter schools offer extended school days, biweekly Saturday classes, individualized instruction, problem-based learning, and an International Baccalaureate curriculum (which some traditional public schools offer as well). A few charter schools even offer opportunities for distance learning.

POLICY VIGNETTE • *Do Charter Schools Increase Segregation?*

The issue of diversity is a concern among public school leaders and critics who fear charter schools will further segregate students within the public school system. Do charter schools increase segregation, or is the policy a tool to reintegrate a deeply segregated public school system? Preliminary evidence suggests that in many cases charter schools serve a more diverse student population than traditional public schools. A study by the Hudson Institute found that half of the students enrolled in charter schools nationwide are members of minority groups (compared with a third in traditional public schools) (Manno, Finn, Bierlein, & Vanourek, 1998). A survey of 100 charter schools by the Education Commission of the States, along with Joe Nathan at the University of Minnesota's Center for School Change, found that enrollment in charter schools by major ethnic group is approximately 60 percent white, 19 percent Hispanic, and 10 percent African American (Medler, 1996), although the demographic makeup varies considerably from state to state and school to school. For example, in New Jersey, charter school enrollment is 46 percent African American, 22 percent Hispanic, and only 28 percent white (Kane, 1998). In a national survey of charter schools, a U.S. Department of Education study found that "only five percent of charter schools enroll a percentage of White students higher (by at least 20 percent) than the percentage of White students served by their surrounding district" (U.S.D.O.E., 1998, p. 11).

Compared with their overall enrollment in public schools in Texas, African American and Hispanic students are overrepresented in charter schools, while their white counterparts are underrepresented (see Table 11.1).

TABLE 11.1   *Student Demographics: Texas (2002)*

	Charter Schools	*Public Schools*
African American	40%	14%
Hispanic	38%	42%
White	21%	41%
Other	2%	3%
At Risk	66%	37%
Special Education	7%	12%
LEP	3%	13%
Male	56%	51%
Female	44%	49%
Enrolling from Private or Homeschool	7%	NA
Not Enrolled in School Previous Year (Pre-K, K, or Recovered Dropout)	8%	NA

Source: Texas Education Agency, 2000a.

Approximately 38 percent of students enrolled in charter schools in Texas are Hispanic and 40 percent African American, compared to 42 percent Hispanic and 14 percent African American in public schools (2002 data). The percentage of white students enrolled in charter schools is slightly more than half the percent enrollment in public schools statewide (21 percent to 41 percent, respectively). Nearly 66 percent of students enrolled in charter schools statewide are at risk of dropping out, compared to only 37 percent in traditional public schools (Charter School Resource Center, 1999). On the other hand, children classified as gifted and talented are underrepresented in charter schools: approximately 3.4 percent of students enrolled in charter schools are identified as gifted and talented, compared to 8 percent statewide (Waters, August 1, 1999).

In a study of charter schools in Texas, Taebel et al. (1997) noted "alternative education programs such as magnet schools are often charged with 'skimming' off the most able students, but in Texas the initial cohort of charter schools tends to serve students with the greatest educational difficulties" (p. 24). These findings are consistent with those of the U.S. Department of Education's survey of charter schools nationwide, which concludes that charter schools "serve the great racial and economic diversity of students that make up public education" with a racial composition roughly similar to statewide averages (U.S.D.O.E., 1997, p. 1).

POLICY VIGNETTE • *Do Charter Schools Serve Special Education and Limited English Proficient Students?*

Charter schools are touted as an alternative to the bureaucratic, cookie-cutter approach to education common in traditional public schools. One of the arguments of charter advocates is that charter school operators will use their newfound flexibility to more effectively meet the needs of at risk students, a number of whom are classified as special education or limited English proficient (LEP). Opponents believe special ed and LEP students will be ill-served in charter schools, asserting that charter founders are ill-equipped, unprepared, perhaps even unwilling to provide the necessary services. Using enrollment figures and student classifications from Texas, the issue is examined in the following case study.

Charter schools in Texas serve fewer numbers of special education and limited English proficient (LEP) students than public schools statewide. Only 7 percent of students enrolled in charter schools are classified as "Special Education," compared with a state average of 12 percent; only 3 percent of students in charter schools are LEP, compared to a state average of 13 percent (Texas Education Agency, 2000a). Because charter schools in Texas enroll nearly twice as many at risk students as traditional public schools, enrollment of special education and LEP students in charter schools should be *higher* than the statewide average. A U.S. Department of Education (1998) survey of charter schools found that students with disabilities are underrepresented in charter schools, although the percentage of LEP students enrolled is similar to those found in public schools in fifteen states with charter schools (plus the District of Columbia). Still, these data raise serious questions of equity and social justice, particularly insofar as children labeled as special ed or LEP are considered by many educators to be the children most difficult to educate (Fusarelli, 2002).

POLICY VIGNETTE • *Teacher Certification, Experience, and Staffing*

Another equity issue in charter schools concerns the areas of staffing and governance. With respect to staffing, one of the strengths of some state charter school laws, depending on one's perspective, is that teachers in charter schools need not be certified by the state. For example, students enrolled in charter schools in Texas are much more likely to be taught by a noncertified teacher: 54 percent of teachers in charter schools are noncertified, compared to only 4 percent in traditional public schools (Fusarelli, 2002). Teachers in charter schools in Texas also have fewer years of teaching experience (about six years) compared with an average of about twelve years for teachers in traditional public schools (Mabin, 2000).

Charter schools in Texas have higher percentages of minorities serving as faculty members, administrators, and board members than traditional public schools (Fusarelli, 2002). According to 1999 data provided by the state education agency, 33 percent of faculty in charter schools are African American and 21 percent are Hispanic, compared to only 8 percent African American and 16 percent Hispanic teaching in traditional public schools statewide. Similar results are found among administrators and board members in charter schools. Based on Spring 1999 data, 31 percent of administrators in charter schools are African American, 23 percent Hispanic; 28 percent of board members in charter schools are African American, 26 percent are Hispanic (Fusarelli, 2002).

Oversight and Accountability

Now that charter schools have been in existence for nearly a decade, recent debate has centered around different types of accountability for charter schools, principally, whether measures of student achievement should be the sole indicator of charter school success (Garn & Cobb, 2001). For example, some charter schools in urban areas operate as dropout recovery or "second chance" programs, for which traditional indices of accountability such as test scores may not be the most appropriate measure of effectiveness. There are those who would suggest that the market economy be the sole marker for accountability. If constituents (children and their families) are not satisfied with the educational product, they presumably will vote with their feet—although recent studies dispute this claim (Wells, Lopez, Scott, & Holme, 1999).

Others suggest that professional accountability should be a mechanism for measuring charter school success. Teachers and educators should be held accountable as professionals for student success. Finally, standards come into play. The American Federation of Teachers advocates the educational yardstick of the standardized test as the measure by which charter schools should be evaluated. The disagreement over who charter schools should be accountable to and who should be in control of determining the model of accountability generates a highly contentious debate, one with important implications for the success or failure of the charter school movement.

Charter schools, like other public schools, are rated by state's accountability system. In addition to participating in the assessment and accountability program, charter schools must design their evaluation programs to include more performance measures than traditional public schools, including achievement gains, nontraditional grading procedures, student products, and indices of parental and student satisfaction. The charter specifies how the data will be collected and submitted to the state education agency and the state board of education (Charter School Resource Center, 1998). Like traditional public schools, charter schools in New York must submit an annual report that includes indices of progress toward educational objectives, a financial statement, and indices of parental and student satisfaction. State standards and Regents requirements apply as they do for traditional public schools. Charter schools must meet or exceed the performance standards adopted by the Board of Regents. Generally, charters are renewable after three to five years.

Constituentive Dimension

A charter school can have its charter revoked if it is unsuccessful. Nationally, roughly 3 to 5 percent of charters granted have been revoked, although rarely, if ever, because of failure to meet student performance objectives (Hartocollis, 1999a; U.S.D.O.E., 1998). Seven charter schools in Texas have had their charters revoked, including one school that never opened. "Revocations have not been the result of low student performance or failure to meet student performance accountability requirements; rather, charters have been revoked for reasons such as inadequate fiscal accountability, including the accumulation of a large budget deficit," and violation of laws relating to open meetings, public information, inaccurate student attendance recordkeeping, and child nutrition federal program requirements (Fikac, 1999; Fusarelli, 2001; Fusarelli, 2002, p. 181; Hess, 2001).

Some states offer assistance or alternative interventions before making the decision to revoke a school's charter. For example, in Texas, before the SBOE decides to revoke a school's charter, "several options are available, including placing the school on probation for the duration of its charter, unilaterally modifying the existing charter, lowering the school's accountability rating (a shame type of punitive action)," or the commissioner may appoint a financial or program monitor or special master to oversee the operation of the charter school (Fusarelli, 2002, pp. 181–182).

In addition to state-mandated accountability procedures, charter schools are also subject to the ultimate accountability standard—parents whose children are enrolled in the charter school. According to Allan Parker, president of the Texas Justice Foundation, "In the public school system, bad schools continue to put out students year after year. These (charter) schools have the quickest accountability in the state. If parents don't like the school, they can take their kid out the next day" (Goins, n.d., p. A6). Manno, Finn, and Vanourek (2000) refer to this process as accountability-via-transparency. However, other scholars have questioned the highly stylized, rational, and seemingly value-neutral premises of charter school accountability. Applying a critical theoretical lens to charter school closures, Fusarelli (2001) argues that charter school accountability is driven less by performance results than by political considerations. Similarly, Opfer (2001) applied a Foucaultian, postmodern analysis to charter school accountability, finding that the overriding pressure on performance limits freedom and flexibility in charter schools, ultimately producing schools not unlike traditional public schools. As a result, the "panoptic effect of accountability" reduces to mere symbolism the freedom and flexibility promised by the charter school movement (Opfer, 2001, p. 209). The constraining effects of accountability provisions on charter schools, particularly its effects on teaching, have been noted by a number of scholars (see Crawford, 2001).

Technical Dimension: Evaluating Charter School Performance

Although little information is yet available on the impact of charter schools on student performance, preliminary results are mixed, as research by Vergari (2002) and others has found. According to the Michigan Association of Public School Academies (MAPSA), nearly half of all charter schools in Michigan doubled or tripled the number of students receiving satisfactory scores in one or more subjects on a statewide assessment exam, including a 24-point increase in fourth-grade math scores, compared to a 13-point overall increase in fourth-grade math scores for all public schools in the state (MAPSA, 1998). Manno, Finn, Bierlein, and Vanourek (1998) found that at six of eight charter schools in Massachusetts where students had been tested, "academic gains were greater than is typically found in regular public schools" (p. 540). The fact that most (nearly all) charter schools have had their charters renewed may itself be a measure of effectiveness, particularly given the close scrutiny they are under.

Other studies have found fewer beneficial effects from charter schools. A major study conducted at UCLA, *Beyond the Rhetoric of Charter School Reform*, of seventeen charter schools in California, concludes that charter schools are less of a "magic bullet" than proponents claim. Major findings of the study include: (1) wide variation in autonomy and public funding (even within the same district), (2) difficult working conditions for teachers, (3) no greater accountability in charter schools than in public schools in California, (4) no evidence that charter schools "do more with less" (the efficiency argument), and (5) no evidence that charter schools pressure reforms within the larger public system (Wells, 1999).

A study commissioned by the Texas State Board of Education found that nearly three-quarters of students attending charter schools specifically created for at risk students find the charter school they attend to offer smaller classes, be staffed by teachers who genuinely care about the students, give them more personal attention, and are of high overall quality (Texas Center for Educational Research, 1998). In 1998, the first year for which performance data on charter schools in Texas is available, of seventeen charter schools rated, only one received the second-highest state accountability ranking of "recognized;" nine were judged "acceptable;" and seven received low performance ratings based on test scores, dropout rates, and attendance (Fikac, 1999). In 1999, of twenty schools rated, three were classified as "recognized," twelve were ranked "acceptable," and only three labeled "low performing." No charter schools were rated as exemplary in 1998, whereas two schools were so rated in 1999 (Texas Education Agency, 2000).

Texas accountability ratings for 1997–1998 show that 59 percent (of seventeen) charter schools received an "acceptable" or higher rating, compared with 91 percent of Texas public schools in general (Texas Education Agency, 1998). Nine of the 17 charter schools enrolled a majority of at risk students. In 1999, the figure of "acceptable" or higher ratings among charter schools had jumped to 85 percent (of twenty rated). However, on all grade levels, in all subject areas, a significantly lower percentage of charter school students (56 percent), pass TAAS than students enrolled in traditional public schools (82 percent) (Texas Education Agency, 2002).

Under Texas's accountability system, charter schools rated as low performing are required to develop a detailed improvement plan and will receive increased attention (including site visits) from the TEA. "We will want to know how they are going to address the weaknesses that were found in their programs," said Debbie Graves Ratcliffe of the TEA (Stutz, 1998, p. 1). The poor performance of charter schools under the state's accountability system has fueled critics' claims that the state has rushed too quickly in expanding charter schools beyond the twenty schools originally authorized under SB 1 ("Charter Schools Worse on TAAS," 1999).

Although preliminary performance data on charter schools is mixed, the data itself may be misleading. Recall that student enrollment in charter schools represents less than 1 percent of total public school enrollment nationwide. What gets lost in student performance comparisons is the vast difference in the size of the test-taking populations. Each student taking a state exam in a charter school exerts a greater impact on the percent passing in each grade level because there are so few students taking the test, making valid comparisons difficult.

As a result, the mixed performance of students in charter schools may not be indicative of the low quality of the schools themselves. Because charter schools are so new, it may take years before solid, reliable school effects are reflected in student performance. As Vergari (1999) observed, preliminary student outcomes "may be more of a reflection of students' previous educational experiences than the performance of the charter school" itself (p. 400).

Not all indices of student performance in charter schools are poor; some individual charter schools reported significant gains on state tests. Brooks Flemister, former senior director of charter schools for the TEA, stated, "We have some [charter schools] doing a superb job and there are some that are not successful" (Waters, 1999, p. 19). Chase Untermeyer, chair of the Texas State Board of Education, concluded, "The world of charter schools in Texas . . . shows the full range from those doing brilliantly to those that are embarrassments and probably will be closed" (Fikac, 1999, p. E4).

Indices of parent and student satisfaction indicate that parents and students enrolled in charter schools tend to be pleased with the schools (Weiss, 1997). The most frequently cited reasons why parents choose to send their children to charter schools include educational quality, concern for children's safety, small size, innovative teaching methods, academic rigor, degree of individual attention, class size, and greater opportunities for parental involvement (Kane, 1998; Manno, Finn, Bierlein, & Vanourek, 1998; Taebel, Barrett, Brenner, Kemerer, Ausbrooks,

Clark, et al., 1997). A nationwide study of charter schools by the Hudson Institute found that parents and students are very satisfied with their charter schools (Manno, Finn, Bierlein, & Vanourek, 1998).

The Institute for Responsive Education reached similar conclusions in their evaluation of charter schools in Massachusetts (Weiss, 1997). Over two-thirds of parents report their charter school is better than their child's previous school "with respect to class size, school size, and individual attention from teachers. Over three-fifths say it is better with respect to teaching quality, parental involvement, curriculum, extra help for students, academic standards, accessibility and openness, and discipline" (Manno, Finn, Bierlein, & Vanourek, 1998, p. 546). In New Jersey, 90 percent of parents report satisfaction with the charter school their children attend (Kane, 1998). In Texas, approximately 85 percent of parents (both at risk and non-at risk) and nearly 80 percent of students express satisfaction with charter schools, giving them a grade of A or B (Taebel et al., 1997; Texas Education Agency, 1998). Nearly 75 percent of students attending at risk charter schools in Texas find their school to be better than the public school they would otherwise have attended (Taebel et al., 1997; Texas Education Agency, 1998). More than two-thirds of at risk students report that the at risk charter school they attend offers smaller classes, more personal attention, better quality teachers, and teachers who care more about their students than in the schools the students had previously attended (Texas Education Agency, 1998).

In a survey of charter schools in New Jersey, twelve of seventeen students interviewed believe the charter school they attend is better than the public school they previously attended (Kane, 1998). Students report receiving much more attention in charter schools than in public schools (Kane, 1998). Charter schools appear to be quite popular, with 65 percent nationwide reporting waiting lists of students (Center for Education Reform, 1998b). In Texas, more than three-quarters of charter school directors report having a waiting list of students (Taebel et al., 1997; Texas Education Agency, 1998).

Barriers to Expansion

The most significant barrier to creating a charter school is money—charters are severely undercapitalized enterprises. According to Loveless and Jasin (1998), "some states offer start-up monies, but most do not" (p. 11). Lack of start-up funds was the most frequently cited problem for newly created charter schools (U.S.D.O.E., 1997). Despite passage of charter legislation in New York, numerous obstacles remain. New York's charter law provides for a "stimulus fund" to help finance leases, renovations, and equipment, but as yet no money has been appropriated for the fund.

Lack of adequate start-up funding, inadequate facilities, and inadequate operating funds are the most oft-cited barriers to the creation and expansion of charter schools. These findings are consistent with research by Hill, Pierce, and Guthrie (1997), who found that barriers to creating charter schools include the cost and complexity of start-up, difficulty finding adequate space and facilities, problems establishing lines of credit and insurance, the need for legal counsel to create contracts, and lack of experience with budgeting and running what essentially is a non-profit organization. Manno, Finn, Bierlein, and Vanourek (1998) note that "finance, marketing, accounting, procurement, personnel management, complex logistical planning, and compliance with sundry local and state rules can cripple a school that has an outstanding curriculum and terrific teaching staff," and it is often difficult to find a staff that is adept at everything (p. 548).

Other factors tempering enthusiasm for charter schools are the incredible barriers that exist, making it difficult to sustain the movement. Despite the appearance of widespread bipartisan support, increasing opposition to charter schools is surfacing—although this opposition is tempered by the greater (and very real) threat of vouchers, which occupies much of the time and resources of opponents of school choice (Fusarelli, in press). According to Fusarelli (2002), "Local teacher unions, public school administrators, and school districts in many areas are openly hostile toward charter schools, erecting multiple obstacles in the path of the reform effort and attempting to block efforts at expanding and strengthening charter school laws" (p. 190). This resistance from the traditional education establishment may pose the greatest long-term threat to the reform movement.

Nationwide, some charter schools have been actively resisted by districts that have lost funding and, in a few cases, laid off staff as a result of the opening and expansion of local charter schools. As Loveless and Jasin (1998) observe, the system fights back. Many states, as part of the charter application, require a fiscal impact statement of the effect of the charter school on the neighboring district. In many rural and suburban areas, charter schools represent a direct threat to local public schools. Because charter school enrollment in urban areas constitutes a smaller proportion of the total student population, the fiscal impact of charter schools is significantly less in urban districts, although the cost to create the schools is much higher due to real estate costs (Loveless and Jasin, 1998).

In addition to the significant barriers to charter schools discussed above, officials in several charter schools in a growing number of states complain of limited autonomy, encroaching bureaucratic restraint, and government micromanagement, particularly in areas such as special education (Loveless and Jasin, 1998; Medler, 1996). Manno, Finn, Bierlein, and Vanourek (1998) report that one state department of education produced a hundred-plus page document of regulations applying to charter schools. Because charter schools are subject to many of the same legal and accountability requirements as traditional public schools, such state and federal government involvement may be inevitable.

Ultimately, the major issue with charter schools—and the determining factor as to whether the reform will last—is the issue of control. Charter schools hearken back to the days of community schools. In large, urban systems, this movement is pitted against the opposite trend of centralizing ever-greater control in the hands of a school superintendent, chancellor, or, in a growing number of instances, with the mayor. Chiara Coletti, a spokeswoman for former New York City School Chancellor Rudy Crew, said the cure to failing schools was not decentralized control but rather strong central control (in the hands of the Chancellor) (Hartocollis, 1998b). This "cure" is the very antithesis of everything the charter school movement represents.

Viewing Accountability through Different Policy Lenses

Normative Dimension

As a reform strategy designed to improve education, particularly in urban areas, charter schools are far less contentious than other forms of school choice such as vouchers or tuition tax credits. As evidenced by their widespread bipartisan support, charter schools occupy a politically safe "middle ground" between the increasingly untenable status quo and a full-blown voucher system that might fundamentally alter, for better or worse, public education in the United States.

This is not to say that charter school policy is a non-controversial, value-neutral reform. In fact, several aspects of charter schools raise significant normative questions. For example, is it fair that traditional public schools should have funds taken from their already limited budgets to finance experimental charter school reforms? What are the implications of relaxing rules and regulations, which presumably have some purpose? For example, do we really want our children educated by noncertified teachers? Or, for that matter, supervised by uncertified administrators? These questions constitute merely the tip of the iceberg when examining the normative dimension of charter school policy. Clearly, more research and study needs to be conducted to better evaluate the normative implications of charter schools.

Structural Dimension

Charter schools have the potential to alter significantly the public education system. How might the governance structure be altered through charter school policy? Preliminary evidence suggests that charter schools are significantly smaller than traditional public schools. What does this mean for students and staff? Will it lead to expanded role responsibilities for teachers and administrators? Will schools be structured and organized differently? Will it lead to increasing diversity in organization and approaches in public education? How will it affect teaching and learning processes in schools?

Conversely, there is the possibility that charter schools will go the way of other highly touted reforms such as the community schools movement of the 1960s, the school-based management reforms of the 1980s, and the whole school reform movement of the 1990s. It is possible that the structural dimension of education will not be significantly affected by charter school policy at all. If this is the case, then we need to examine the deep structure, the "hard truths" (Tye, 2000) of schooling. If this reform fails, then what?

Constituentive Dimension

Any reform policy that has the potential, fundamentally, to alter existing structural, governance, and pedagogical arrangements in schools (whether the impact is significant or not is immaterial—the mere threat is enough) has a significant constituentive dimension and must be analyzed accordingly. Although charter schools have bipartisan support—the reform is not strictly "liberal" or "conservative"—many groups, including teacher unions, are not entirely supportive of the movement. Teacher unions in several states are actively lobbying to amend "strong" charter school laws. In New York, for example, the American Federation of Teachers, together with its local New York City affiliate, the United Federation of Teachers, is pushing hard for the state legislature to substantially weaken what many consider to be one of the strongest charter laws in the country. Seldom an issue of the union newspaper goes by without an article or two decrying the evils of charter schools—how they will destroy everything the union has worked for and lead to educational disaster for everyone.

There is some truth to this argument. It is no coincidence that states with the strongest charter school laws contain the most anti-union provisions. When charter schools are touted as freeing schools from red tape, the red tape is usually the collective bargaining agreement. For example, as noted above, many state charter school laws do not provide blanket exemptions from federal civil rights, health, and safety regulations; several state regulations, including certain accountability provisions, are not waived either. What's left? The collective bargaining agreement. Thus, it is not surprising that unions across the country actively oppose and are seeking to amend the often significant anti-union provisions found in many state charter laws.

Technical Dimension

The technical dimension of charter school policy is closely related to its structural dimension. For example, how should charter schools be evaluated? How much weight should be given to student performance? Should performance be evaluated based on achievement tests or should alternative assessments be included in the evaluation? Should indices of parental and student satisfaction be considered? Is the logic of evaluation as clear as the rhetoric suggests? The evaluation of charter schools is far more complex than it first appears. Because charter school policy rests explicitly on the twin premises of accountability and responsiveness, the technical dimension of charter school policy becomes critical.

Conclusion

Charter school policy is a complex reform with multiple dimensions. As indicated in this chapter, the policy raises several questions about equity and social justice, as well as questions about the very structure of education reform efforts. Because the reform is still relatively new, it is too early to evaluate accurately the effects of the reform and its impact, if any, on the public educational system. To date, the movement has raised more policy questions than it has answered. To complicate matters further, many state charter school laws operate in highly contested terrain and are the subject of high profile amendment and reform efforts. In effect, the reform is under reform in several states. What this means for the future of the movement is as yet undetermined. What is clear, however, is that school choice as a reform strategy occupies center stage on the national education agenda and will likely do so for the next several years.

Chapter Assignments and Activities _____

Field Investigation

Visit a charter school in your area. Interview the director, the founders, and some teachers. Find out why they started and chose to work in a charter school. How much freedom and autonomy do they have? What rules and regulations are they exempt from? What are the challenges and difficulties of starting a new school? What lessons can be learned from their experiences?

Policy Analysis

Download a copy of your state's charter school statute. What are the strengths and weaknesses of the law? In what ways would a charter school be different than a traditional public school under the statute? If you were drafting a charter school law, in what ways would it be different than the current statute?

Seminal Works _____

Several interesting books provide a solid primer on charter schools. Joe Nathan's (1996) *Charter Schools: Creating Hope and Opportunity for American Education* and Bryan Hassel's (1999) *The Charter School Challenge* explore in detail the multiple dimensions of charter schools—what they are, how they operate, the challenges and promises of charter schools for urban education reform. Hassel's work also explores the politics of charter school programs. Finn, Manno, and Vanourek's (2000) *Charter Schools in Action* explores the question of whether charter schools are actually working, whether the schools are fulfilling their promise of providing a better education than under the traditional model of public schooling.

Seymour Sarason's (1998) *Charter Schools: Another Flawed Educational Reform?* and Sandra Vergari's *The Charter School Landscape* offer a more balanced view of the prospects of charter schools to improve substantially public education. Sarason discusses charter schools within the context of the creation of new settings, comparing charter schools to other new initiatives such as compulsory education, creation of a clinic, a hospital merger, and the Manhattan Project. Sarason ties these seemingly disparate projects together by exploring the difficulty of creating and building new organizations from the ground up. Vergari

(2002) offer the most comprehensive empirical analysis of charter school performance to date, with detailed reports on charter schools in eleven states and Alberta, Canada. Student performance in charter schools, compared to traditional public schools, is mixed at best.

References

Ayres, W. (1994). Navigating a restless sea: The continuing struggle to achieve a decent education for African-American youngsters in Chicago. *Journal of Negro Education, 63*(1), 5–18.

Bowen, R. W. (1999, January 13). "Charter schools, then what?" *New York Times,* p. A19.

Center for Education Reform. (1998a). Charter school legislation: Profile of Texas' charter school law. [On-line]. Available: www.edreform.com

Center for Education Reform. (1998b). Charter school survey 1996–1997. [On-line]. Available: www.edreform.com

Center for Education Reform. (2002). *Charter schools 2002: Results from CER's annual survey of America's charter schools.* [On-line]. Available: www.edreform.com

Charter School Resource Center. (1998). Accountability. [On-line]. Available: www.edreform.com

Charter School Resource Center. (1999). *Organizational plan.* San Antonio, TX: Author.

"Charter Schools Worse on TAAS." (1999, December 19). *Austin American-Statesman,* pp. 1–2.

Crawford, J. R. (2001). Teacher autonomy and accountability in charter schools. *Education and Urban Society, 33*(2), 186–200.

Fikac, P. (1999, July 4). "State's charter schools plagued by financial problems." *Houston Chronicle,* p. E4.

Finn, C. E., Jr., Manno, B. V., & Vanourek, G. (2000). *Charter schools in action.* Princeton, NJ: Princeton University Press.

Fusarelli, L. D. (1999). Reinventing urban education in Texas: Charter schools, smaller schools, and the new institutionalism. *Education and Urban Society, 31*(2), 214–224.

Fusarelli, L. D. (2001). The political construction of accountability. *Education and Urban Society, 33*(2), 157–169.

Fusarelli, L. D. (2002). Texas: Charter schools and the struggle for equity. In S. Vergari (Ed.), *The charter school landscape* (pp. 175–191). Pittsburgh, PA: University of Pittsburgh Press.

Fusarelli, L. D. (in press). *The political dynamics of school choice.* New York: Palgrave Press.

Garn, G., & Cobb, C. D. (2001). A framework for understanding charter school accountability. *Education and Urban Society, 33*(2), 113–128.

Goins, K. (n.d.). Pros, cons of charter schools in Texas still being debated. *North Central Sun,* p. A6.

Good, T. L., & Braden, J. S. (2000). *The great school debate.* Mahwah, NJ: Lawrence Erlbaum.

Hartocollis, A. (1999a, January 29). "Crew plans charter schools, his way." *New York Times*.

Hartocollis, A. (1998a, December 15). "Charter plan for schools makes gains." *New York Times*.

Hartocollis, A. (1998b, December 29). "Religious leaders plan schools with public funds in New York." *New York Times*.

Hassel, B. C. (1999). *The charter school challenge: Avoiding the pitfalls, fulfilling the promise*. Washington, DC: Brookings Institution Press.

Hess, F. M. (2001). Whaddya mean you want to close my school? *Education and Urban Society, 33*(2), 141–156.

Hill, P. T., Pierce, L. C., & Guthrie, J. W. (1997). *Reinventing public education*. Chicago: University of Chicago Press.

Judson, J. (n.d.). *The true state of Texas education*. San Antonio: Texas Public Policy Foundation.

Kane, P. R. (1998). *New Jersey charter schools: The first year 1997–1998*. New York: Teachers College.

Loveless, T., & Jasin, C. (1998). Starting from scratch: Political and organizational challenges facing charter schools. *Educational Administration Quarterly, 34*(1), 9–30.

Mabin, C. (2000, March 17). "Texas charter schools serve more minorities, study finds." *Austin American-Statesman*, p. 1.

Manno, B. V., Finn, C. E., Jr., Bierlein, L. A., & Vanourek, G. (1998). Charter schools: Accomplishments and dilemmas. *Teachers College Record, 99*(3), 537–558.

Manno, B. V., Finn, C. E., Jr., & Vanourek, G. (2000). Charter school accountability: Problems and prospects. *Educational Policy, 14*(4), 473–493.

Markley, M. (1997, May 16). "HISD board trustees approve 13 charters." *Houston Chronicle*, p. A29.

Medler, A. (1996). Promise and progress. *American School Board Journal, 183*(3), 26–28.

Michigan Association of Public School Academies. (1998). "Press release." [Online]. Available: http://www.charterschools.org/whatsnew/pr/meap98.html

Nathan, J. (1996). *Charter schools: Creating hope and opportunity for American education*. San Francisco: Jossey-Bass.

Nazareno, A. (1997, September 3). "Charter school ends shaky freshmen year." *San Antonio Express-News*.

Opfer, V. D. (2001). Charter schools and the panoptic effect of accountability. *Education and Urban Society, 33*(2), 201–215.

Peters, B. G. (1999). *Institutional theory in political science: The 'new institutionalism.'* London: Pinter.

Sarason, S. (1998). *Charter schools: Another flawed educational reform?* New York: Teachers College Press.

"Saving Public Education." (1997, February 17). *The Nation*, pp. 17, 18, 20–25.

Scott, W. R. (1995). *Institutions and organizations*. Thousand Oaks, CA: Sage.

Sibley, K. (1998, July 8). "NB charter school adds alternative." *San Antonio Express-News*, pp. H1, H9.

Stutz, T. (1998, September 4). "Low state ratings stir concerns about charter schools." *Dallas Morning News*, pp. 1–4.

Taebel, D., Barrett, E. J., Brenner, C. T., Kemerer, F., Ausbrooks, C., Clark, C., Thomas, K., Briggs, K. L., Parker, A., Weiher, G., Matland, R., Tedin, K., Cookson, C., & Nielsen, L. (1997). *Texas open-enrollment charter schools: Year one evaluation.* Austin, TX: State Board of Education.

Texas Center for Educational Research. (1998). *Open-enrollment charter school evaluation,* News Release.

Texas Education Agency. (1998). *Texas open-enrollment charter schools: Second year evaluation, 1997–98.* Austin: Author.

Texas Education Agency. (2000). Charter school accountability ratings for 1999. [On-line]. Available: www.tea.state.tx.us/perfreport/account/99/index.html

Texas Education Agency. (2000a). Snapshot 2000. [On-line]. Available: www.teas.stat.tx.us/perfreport/snapshot/2000

Texas Education Agency. (2000b). *Texas open-enrollment charter schools: Third year evaluation, 1998–99.* Austin: Author.

Texas Education Agency (2002). *Texas charter schools, summary information.* [On-line] Available: www.tea.state.tx/us/charter/states.html

Tye, B. B. (2000). *Hard truths: Uncovering the deep structure of schooling.* New York: Teachers College Press.

U.S. Department of Education. (1997). *A study of charter schools: First-year report, executive summary, 1997.* Washington, DC: U.S. Government Printing Office.

U.S. Department of Education. (1998). *A national study of charter schools: Executive summary.* Washington, DC: U.S. Government Printing Office.

Vergari, S. (1999). Charter schools: A primer on the issues. *Education and Urban Society, 31*(4), 389–405.

Vergari, S. (Ed.). (2002). *The charter school landscape.* Pittsburgh, PA: University of Pittsburgh Press.

Walt, K. (1998, September 5). "Charter schools called 'mixed bag' of success." *Houston Chronicle*, pp. A37, A38.

Waters, B. (1999, August 1). "Charter schools crop up across East Texas." *Tyler Morning Telegraph*, p. 19.

Weber, P. (1998). *Charter schools: A state legislative update.* Washington, DC: U.S. Department of Education.

Weiss, A. R. (1997). *Going it alone: A study of Massachusetts charter schools.* Boston: Institute for Responsive Education.

Wells, A. S. (1999). California's charter schools: Promises vs. performance. *American Educator, 23*(1), 18–21, 24, 52.

Wells, A. S., Lopez, A., Scott, J., & Holme, J. J. (1999). Charter schools as postmodern paradox: Rethinking social stratification in an age of deregulated school choice. *Harvard Educational Review, 69*(2), 172–204.

12

Future Policies, Better Schools

The future of school policymaking is as challenging as it is exciting. Education will continue to be important—even critical—as society changes, technology accelerates, and world economic competition intensifies. Yet, in some ways, the future is now: some parents are already questioning the hegemony of public control, moving toward charter schools and even vouchers. The federal government, long the sleeping giant in school policymaking, has passed the most complex and comprehensive (and some would say, intrusive) legislation in history, promisingly entitled, *No Child Left Behind.* Congress and state legislatures are enacting policies that not only raise standards but also place serious consequences on schools for failing to meet those expectations. Paradoxically, policymaking is moving toward greater nationalization and accountability, toward a system of fragmented centralization (Fusarelli, in press; Meyer, 1983), while at the same time empowering the family and breaking the mold of public school control.

The school standards race is on, as policymakers at all levels of government and the education system are responding to pressure for higher standards enforced by more comprehensive, high-stakes testing. Certainly the future of education policy must consider standards: what they are; how they are aligned with national and state standards; and how results will be assessed and used. Technology and all the educational, corporate, and management "systems" that go with it, are not only changing key policies concerning access, privacy, pedagogy, and financing of school renovations and modernization, but are also affecting the way policies are implemented and evaluated. After all, giving parents instant access over the Internet to their children's test results, homework, lessons, lunchroom menus, and soccer schedules, not to mention financial data on how much their children's schools are receiving and spending, is going to challenge existing power relationships within school districts, and between districts and their key stakeholders. Further, better technology should improve the quality of information and the effectiveness of services.

Running through these policy developments is classic tension between centralized control of education and the impulse to decentralize and empower those closest to schools and classrooms, including parents through more choice and teachers through increased decisionmaking, more sophisticated technology, better materials, and the latest pedagogical methods. Teachers and administrators are empowered to make key policy decisions about the curriculum, class time, funding and site-based budgeting; parents are using better information to change schools and to influence education policies at the school level.

Meanwhile, as governments build larger databases (national, state, and local test scores, attendance and graduation data), with more useful information, technology allows these standards and outcomes to be readily accessible to virtually anyone interested in education. As the public gains greater access, public school officials are held accountable in ways never before imaginable.

For example, in 1988, New York City schools spent only 33 percent of its budget in the classroom; when technology allowed the public to gain access, and good models were developed for tracking funds to students, the school district was pressured to increase resources, so today, 54 percent is now reaching the student (Cooper, Speakman, & May, 1998). Technology, then, will affect both the processes of making and evaluating policies and the way schools are run and students are taught. Few educators have taken management and pedagogical technology seriously; yet, the future is limitless, including the "virtual school" where courses and programs are delivered online; where students can study at scattered sites; and where resources are made available instantly across borders and time zones. Students and teachers have the ability to ask a question in one place and receive hundreds of answers instantly from elsewhere. The school is no longer the single most important purveyor of information, as the public hegemony of teaching and learning declines and learning is as close as the nearest computer or television.

Issues of equity and social justice are only exacerbated by new resources and new access to learning. The so-called "digital divide" may favor children from middle-class families and penalize students who have no computers (or even a telephone) at home; not knowing how to read, write, and compute are only made worse by being unable to use the computer, Internet, web, and other technologies. Although the federal government, and some states, have recognized the need to "wire" schools, make computers available, and help teachers to use computers in the classroom, the widening gap between rich and poor, able and disabled, may require radical changes in education policy, a common theme in recent education policy.

To some degree, of course, the recent reauthorization of ESEA builds on earlier concerns for social justice. Passed first in 1965 to narrow the gap between rich and poor, black and white students following from the Civil Rights movement (Meranto, 1967; Bailey & Mosher, 1968; Murphy, 1971), federal legislation has adapted to changing views of equity, from fairness in providing "inputs" (money, staff, programs, time-on-task) to a much greater concern about equality of "outputs" (test results, passing rates, graduation rates, and college admissions). Politically, too, ESEA spread the resources around, meaning that districts with even a small minority of poor children would receive federal funds to hire Title I teachers, provide better equipment, more training, and more staff. Thus, middle-class and poor districts benefited, and supported ESEA through its many reauthorizations—providing an excellent example of interest group behavior.

This coalition formed as much around the money as the needs of poor students, explaining in large part what happened when President Nixon tried repeatedly to repeal the law, and President Reagan pressed to "privatize" it four times through Chapter I vouchers for eligible children in private and parochial schools (Doyle & Cooper, 1988). Both presidents failed to kill or radically change the ESEA Title I (Chapter I) program, developments best understood using both the interest group theory to explain the broad coalition that supported ESEA and the critical, postmodernist perspective to show the ability of the middle classes to capitalize on programs designed for the poor.

Let's look now into the future, analyzing the far-reaching consequences and potential effects of the latest omnibus education law, the No Child Left Behind Act, signed into law by President George W. Bush, thus re-authorizing ESEA. As in the other chapters in this book, this final one will view this federal "law of the future" through the four analytical lenses: the normative, structural, constituentive, and technical dimensions. What are the values that underpin the articles of this far-reaching law? What are the structural and constituentive components of this law that affect not only the federal government's increasing role in education, but the way states and districts teach and test all children? What are some of the technical components of this law, as states and local districts work to comply with the requirements of the federalization of education?

POLICY VIGNETTE • *"No Child Left Behind Act" of 2002*

On January 8, 2002, the Elementary and Secondary School Act (ESEA) of 2001 was signed into law, the eighth re-authorization of ESEA, first enacted by President Lyndon B. Johnson in 1965 (Eisenberg & Morey, 1969; Murphy, 1971). The 2002 re-authorization for the next six years, the first major education law passed by the Bush administration, provides federal aid to state and local educational authorities, purportedly to help disadvantaged children achieve the same high standards as all other children. Subtitled the No Child Left Behind (NCLB) Act (Public Law 107-110), it provides a host of new policies and programs—a kind of omnibus bill—and authorizes the U.S. government to spend $28.4 billion (of which $22.3 billion was appropriated) for education.

What does the NCLB law mean for the future of education policy in the United States? How does this law fit into the framework for this book? And what can we

(continued)

POLICY VIGNETTE • Continued

learn from this law, both about the process of education policymaking and the development of education policy? Brown (2002) summarizes the potential effects of NCLB, exploring the purposes of the law as:

- To focus the states on setting higher standards and more technical assistance to districts, and to expand research strategies and compliance activities (Brown, 2002; Fege, 2002).
- To put teeth into federal legislation by threatening to withdraw federal funds to those states refusing to comply with federal regulations; for those states withdrawing from federal aid, they are vulnerable to "civil rights litigation" (Brown, 2002, p. 3).
- To improve data on student achievement and teacher qualifications, providing tools for school reform and providing a rationale for improving state accountability systems.
- To require Report Cards by 2002–2003 for each state's school performance, disaggregated by sub-groups (immigrants, poor, neglected and delinquent children, dropout prevention) and by school.
- To increase parental involvement so as to improve school support and shared decisionmaking.
- To improve family literacy through "Reading First" and "Even Start" literacy programs, supported by a $900 million appropriation for family literacy targeting early intervention to help smooth the transition from kindergarten to elementary school.
- To enhance teacher training and recruitment programs ($2.85 billion), based on the Eisenhower Professional Development effort. These include "Troop-to-Teachers" programs for armed services retirees, and other "Transition-to-Teacher programs."
- To expand the National Writing Projects ($14 million), Civil Education ($30 million), History Teaching, Math and Science Partnerships ($12.5 million), Technology ($700.5 million), and English Acquisition ($665 million).
- To offer sub-grants to Local Education Authorities (95 percent pass-through funds to LEA's for local activities), including professional development, tenure reforms, merit pay for teachers, and LEA improvement.
- To improve teaching through national activities, including the recruitment of teachers, school leadership, advanced credentialing, special education, and early childhood preparation.
- To assist districts in reducing school violence through the Safe and Drug-Free Schools and Communities Initiative ($746.8 million) by improving parent and community involvement, violence prevention, and character education.
- To increase community access to schools and libraries through the 21st Century Community Learning Centers ($1 billion) to enhance academic improvement.
- To promote Informed Parent Choice and Innovation ($385 million) to increase parental awareness and involvement.

- To address the unique needs of rural school districts through Rural Education Initiatives ($162.5 million) using competitive grants.
- To help improve schools serving American Indian students, Native Hawaiians, and Alaskan Native Education through the American Indian and Alaskan Education Programs ($102.4 million).
- To aid Public Charter Schools ($200 million) and Magnet Schools ($110 million), while expanding and guaranteeing services to private and parochial schools and prohibiting the federal government from exercising any control over homeschools.

Normative Dimension

Standards and the Future.   Title I of NCLB, Improving the Education of the Disadvantaged, with an appropriation of $12.384 billion, is the largest and most important of the ten titles in the act. It requires the states to test all students in reading and math immediately and administer science tests in five years, in an effort to raise standards of all students.

Raising standards is one thing; enforcing and reaching those standards, quite another. And these future trends converge in interesting ways. As the federal government requires states to set and meet their own standards—presumably to improve schooling nationally—the effect might be the opposite: states may actually lower standards initially, so as to make "adequate yearly progress" easier to show. Federal regimes (administrations) come and go. The twelve-year timeline of the No Child Left Behind (NCLB) legislation ensures that Bush will be long gone as president before his legislation completes its twelve-year cycle. This lag gives new administrations ample time to define and even to defuse the law, meaning that twelve years of progress is made unimportant if the law changes and the consequences of failure over this time period are removed.

Concerns for the Disadvantaged.   ESEA, and now NCLB, were designed to address the needs of poor students, students from isolated, rural areas, and children from special groups such as Alaskan Natives and American Indian groups. This dedication has remained constant, and the value of creating a more just, more socially equitable system continues and has been expanded. Reaction to the new law has been mixed. Former New York City schools Chancellor Harold O. Levy focused attention on the requirements of more and better assessment, with escalating sanctions for schools that fail to improve reading, writing, and math results. Levy explained in an interview that, "The good news is that schools will no longer be able to hide behind the performance of white, middle-class students." He notes that Connecticut purportedly had the highest test scores in the nation until results were separated by race: African American students in Connecticut had lower results than similar children in New York City.

Other critics fear more examples of "blaming the victim," demonizing poor and children of color, rather than working to improve their circumstances and their schools. Teachers, responding to pressure, will jettison the liberal curriculum and concentrate on test-prep subjects and skills, making school both less interesting and less engaging. Sports, music, art, foreign languages, and many of the sciences will be marginalized, while tedious rote and repeat answers will be valued as useful in raising standardized test scores. These issues are as old as public universal schooling; and the future will be no different.

More Federal Control.   NCLB involves the U.S. government in education as never before. Thus, a major value—local and state control—is being challenged. As Hanushek and associates (1994) explain, "Americans agree on the need for school reform, but that consensus is not matched by a consensus on the best approach to reform" (p. 1). Nowhere is disagreement stronger than in just how active and controlling the federal government should be in setting and enforcing standards in the states. Will the federal government have the will to withdraw federal funds from those states that (a) fail to assess their students adequately; (b) show weak or no progress over the twelve years in reducing the achievement gap; or (c) refuse to comply with the legislation? Already, a few states have withdrawn from the national testing effort, willingly forfeiting their federal assistance (e.g., Vermont).

Higher Standards, More Control.   Another set of values involves the force of federal control and whether raising standards nationally will work. While the NCLB law increases flexibility as states are able to transfer up to 50 percent of the funds for state-level programs among Teacher and Technology (Title II), Safe and Drug Free Schools (Title IV), and Innovative Programs Block Grant (Title V), it still means that strings are attached to the use of federal dollars—and states risk the loss of federal funds if they do not test children at grades 3 through 8, and if they do not use these funds to improve schools as the law requires.

Structural and Constituentive Dimensions

Implicit in the No Child Left Behind law is that the U.S. government is becoming a stronger player in funding and controlling education, changing the role of government and other constituents in the educational process. If the state and LEA's refuse to raise and test standards, increasing accountability in programs and teacher licensing and training, then districts face the possibility of the loss of federal aid. Standards must have at least three levels of attainment: failure, proficient, and advanced. The role of government and key stakeholders (e.g., teachers, unions, parents, and communities) is thus changing rapidly, as this book has shown.

This law, among others, raises the question of what is the appropriate role of the federal, state, and local governments in running and supporting education in the United States. As David (1990) explains:

> Imagine a circular jigsaw puzzle with students and teachers in the center, surrounded by rings of interlocking pieces representing the demands of local, state, and federal agencies. . . . Trying to change one piece of an interlocking set of pieces is not possible unless the other pieces are flexible enough to yield when the shape of neighboring pieces is changed. Continuing the jigsaw metaphor, previous reform efforts have added another piece to the puzzle or have tried to change one piece without recognizing the need to change neighboring pieces. Centrally defined and imposed reforms [such as this new federal law] typically have added new pieces with little effect on interactions between students and teachers. (p. 210)

Thus, we see a future filled with ambiguity, one where students, teachers, administrators, and communities must adjust to changes in laws, tests, programs, and roles about which we can only speculate. We clearly anticipate an era in which the federal and state governments will dictate standards, tests, and programs, where constituents will have to wrestle with external controls, while the government also encourages greater parental choice and where the nation also has increased charter schools, small-scale voucher programs, and other forms of privatization (e.g., outsourcing whole districts and schools, such as the case in Philadelphia). How will policymakers respond to an environment with such conflicting reforms?

Technical Dimension

We see a future, therefore, of crosscutting controls and demands, where educators are caught between demands for greater accountability *and* more choice and opportunities. As the U.S. Supreme Court ruled in the voucher case (*Zelman v. Simmons-Harris*) that public tax money can be spent by parents who select private religious schools, as is happening in Cleveland and Milwaukee (*Jackson v. Benson*, 1998) (see Howell & Peterson, 2002), we may witness a change in monopolistic public schools and a new era of choice for parents and greater competition for public education.

What will be the role of the government in funding and controlling private schools? How will these education reforms work as fifty states and the District of Columbia attempt to carry out these new policies? We foresee real conflicts between the federal government, which controls about ten percent of school funds, and states and districts, as they struggle to maintain "local control" while being accountable to new state and federal standards.

Under the new legislation, states are required to implement annual reading and math assessments for grades 3 through 8, on top of existing tests at lower and higher grade levels. Will states elect to calculate gain scores for each year, penalizing teachers, schools, and districts which fail to show a sufficient "value added" for each year of education? How will the details of this process work? What resources will be available to help failing schools? Florida has already granted parents a voucher to remove their children from low-achieving schools (two schools have already seen parents withdraw their children); other states may follow, particularly as the High Court ruled that vouchers for religious schools are legal under the *Zelman* decision.

Much research and analysis are required on the technical dimension of new education policies; the Howell and Peterson (2002) book, which examines the effects of vouchers on student achievement, is but the first of a series of new studies that examine the effects of privatization in education. In Philadelphia, the governor has forced the school district to restructure its schools, outsourcing a large number of failing schools to private and even for-profit corporations (e.g., the Edison Schools have been contracted to run twenty Philadelphia public schools).

Other policy areas are critical into the future. Keeping schools open longer (year-round education; after-school tutoring), making them safe and secure, drug-, alcohol-, and violence-free, providing sufficient, highly-trained teachers and staff, and improving the curriculum—among others—are all concerns for the future. But such improvements cannot be ensured unless issues of school governance, finance, and management are also worked out, in part ensured by better policy formulation, implementation, and evaluation. Better policies, better schools, goes hand-in-hand with better models for making and carrying out the decisions. It's a shared activity, across the nation, states, districts, and schools; among public schools, charter schools, and private schools. Better education is truly a national priority, for everyone.

Conclusion

The future of policymaking and analysis in education has already begun. The need for ongoing change, improvement, and policy analysis is more critical now than at any time in our history. Elmore (1990) foresaw much of this tension and excitement when he discussed the effects of school restructuring. He discussed three themes of our future in education: empowerment, accountability, and engagement in academic learning for teachers and educational leaders.

Empowerment refers to the reality that "technical and professional models stress specialized knowledge—both systematic and judgmental—as a source of legitimate power in schools" (p. 21). *Accountability* looks to sources of legitimacy for which reforms are working and how, focusing primarily at the school level, not at the federal, state, or district levels. He writes that school policy reforms "should consist in large part of inventing individual and school-level indicators of performance that reflect what teachers and administrators are trying to accomplish, rather than what external authorities [federal and states] think they should be accomplishing" (p. 23).

Finally, Elmore (1990) stresses *engagement in academic learning* as the end-all and be-all of education policymaking. Much like the recent federal legislation, he singles out academic achievement as a key indicator of school success. He explains that

> Sustaining a focus on academic learning in restructured schools depends heavily on the creation of setting and modes of discourse in which experts, professionals and clients debate and construct the meaning of academic learning. In the absence of such a dialogue, academic learning will become a political issue by which each interest group [constituent] attempts to assert control over the others: academic experts over teachers, teachers over parents, parents over teachers, and so on. (p. 24)

Ultimately, then, the future of education policy comes to rest in the schools, with children, teachers, and administrators. Without "dialogue" among the levels of government, between those who make policy and those who carry it out, we can predict that schools and children will not benefit from new legislation and regulations, wherever they may originate. This book has presented the big and little pictures, the local and federal governmental levels, as they struggle to define what a good, just, and meaningful education is for *all* children. Education is ultimately about providing a means for the next generation to take its place in a civil culture, ready to participate in the social, economic, and political life so important to the improvement of society.

Dionne (1991) concludes his provocative book, *Why Americans Hate Politics,* with a concern about the future of democracy. He writes,

> In our efforts to find our way toward a world role, we would do well to revive what made us a special nation long before we became the world's leading military and economic power—our republican tradition that nurtured free citizens who eagerly embraced the responsibilities and pleasures of self-government. With democracy on the march outside our borders, our first responsibility is to ensure that the United States becomes a model for what self-government should be and not an example of what happens to free nations when they lose interest in public life. *A nation that hates politics will not long survive as a democracy.* (p. 355; emphases added)

Critical to a robust, active political life—and a continuing commitment to democratic government and social justice—is a meaningful, effective education for all citizens—which reinforces the need for good education policy. As we look to our future and pursue our "republican tradition," to use Dionne's phrase, the importance of viewing policy from multiple perspectives continues. Public policy analysis is a relatively new academic field, even though policies affecting public life are as old as society itself. And the study of education policy is newer yet.

In his famous oration remembering the Athenian dead from the Peloponnesian War in 431 BCE, Pericles expounded: "Our ordinary citizens, although occupied with the pursuits of industry, are still judges of public matters. And instead of looking on discussion as a stumbling block in the way of action, we think it an indispensable preliminary to any wise action at all" (Hansen, 1991, p. 33; Dahl, 1998). This same argument for informed public involvement of parents and community leaders in the making of school policy is not a barrier to education improvement but is an "indispensable preliminary," to use Pericles' phrase, to building consensus and commitment in creating better schools through better policies.

Despite the importance of policies affecting education—as both a process for reaching decisions and a guide for implementing and shaping action—few books have applied models of policymaking systemically and critically to key policies in one of society's key public concerns: the education of its citizens. This book did just that; taking four key policy perspectives (we call them "dimensions"), the authors applied these differing views to six current policy issues: governance, curriculum, accountability, teachers and labor relations, finance, and charter schools. Analysis of education policy formulation, implementation, and evaluation are more complex than previously thought because changing lenses generates a wide range of questions, theories, and analyses. Each lens exposes a different set of issues and concerns, allowing us to understand the education policymaking process in a different light.

Looking to the future, we examined the important new legislation signed into law on January 8, 2002. How does this law fit into the evolution of U.S. education policy? What are the values, structures, constituents, and details of this enormously complex, diverse, and important piece of education legislation? And how does the No Child Left Behind (NCLB) Act capture the current condition of education in the United States and suggest directions for the future?

Klein (1991) argued years ago that education improvement is not possible without a balanced, coordinated role by level (federal, state, local), by key groups (teachers, administrators, parents, and policymakers), and by institutions. He explained:

> Schooling is clearly a concern of the state, local community, professional educators, and students, among others. The state must ensure that all students will receive an effective, relevant, balanced, current curriculum. The district must be held accountable to the local community that its students are receiving an equitable curriculum and one which includes all that is considered to be important in the educational process. The school faculty and each teacher with his/her students must have the freedom to develop some curricula or at least to modify curricula. All of these fundamental and interactive responsibilities must be coordinated and compatible, or difficulties occur. When one group usurps the right of the others, the resulting curriculum will be less effective than it could be. (pp. 223–224)

We are no doubt witnessing an exponential growth in our concern about schools and policies affecting them. More interest, greater activity, and more involvement will mean, as Lewis predicted, that policymaking in education "will not get any less complex in the future" (1998, p. 530). In fact, the meanings and processes of school policymaking are becoming a national concern, and this book has attempted to frame some of the arguments, to introduce key areas of policymaking, and to offer suggestions for better policies and schools in the twenty-first century.

References

Bailey, S. K., & Mosher, E. K. (1968). *ESEA: The Office of Education administers a law.* Syracuse, NY: Syracuse University Press.

Brown, C. G. (2002). *Opportunities and accountability to Leave No Child Behind in middle grades: An examination of the No Child Left Behind Act of 2001.* Washington, DC: Edna McConnell Clark Foundation.

Dahl, R. A. (1998). *On democracy.* New Haven, CT: Yale University Press.

David, J. L. (1990). Restructuring in progress: Lessons from pioneering districts. In R. F. Elmore and associates (Eds.), *Restructuring schools: The next generation of educational reform* (pp. 209–250). San Francisco: Jossey-Bass.

Dionne, E. J., Jr. (1991). *Why Americans hate politics.* New York: Simon & Schuster.

Doyle, D. P., & Cooper, B. S. (1988). *Federal aid to the disadvantaged: What future Chapter 1?* New York: Falmer Press.

Eisenberg, E., & Morey, R. D. (1969). *An act of Congress.* New York: Norton.

Elmore, R. F. (1990). Introduction. In R. F. Elmore and associates (Eds.), *Restructuring schools: The next generation of educational reform* (pp. 1–28). San Francisco: Jossey-Bass.

Fege, A. F. (2002). Overview of the Elementary and Secondary Education Act, entitled "No Child Left Behind Act of 2001" (NCLB), Public Law 107-110. Washington, DC: Public Advocacy for Kids.

Fusarelli, L. D. (in press). Tightly coupled policy for loosely coupled systems: Educational capacity and organizational change. *Journal of Educational Administration.*

Hansen, D. A. (1986). Family-school articulations: The effects of interaction rule mismatch. *American Education Research Journal, 2*(4), 643–659.

Hanushek, E. A., Benson, C. S., Freeman, R. B., Jamison, D. T., Levin, H. M., Levin, R. A., et al. (1994). *Making schools work: Improving performance and controlling costs.* Washington, DC: The Brookings Institute.

Howell, W. G., & Peterson, P. E. (2002). *The education gap: Vouchers and urban schools.* Washington, DC: The Brookings Institute.

Klein, M. F. (1991). Issues from curriculum theory in the centralization of the curriculum. In M. F. Klein (Ed.), *The politics of curriculum decision-making* (pp. 210–225). Albany: State University of New York Press.

Lewis, A. C. (1998). Policy making that made a difference. In G. J. Cizek (Ed.), *Handbook of educational policy* (pp. 523–532). San Diego, CA: Academic Press.

Meranto, P. (1967). *The politics of federal aid to education in 1965: A study in political innovation.* Syracuse, NY: Syracuse University Press.

Meyer, J. W. (1983). Centralization of funding and control in educational governance. In J. W. Meyer & W. R. Scott (Eds.), *Organizational environments: Ritual and rationality* (pp. 179–197). Beverly Hills, CA: Sage.

Murphy, J. T. (1971). Title I of ESEA: The politics of implementing federal education reform. *Harvard Educational Review, 41,* 35–63.

Index

California *(continued)*
    Proposition 227 in, 171–174, 184
    response to Bush education policy in, 175
    school finance in, 255
Cardinal Principles of Secondary Education, 169
Carnegie Foundation for the Advancement of Teaching, 208
Case methods, in policy evaluation, 121
Change
    in advocacy coalition theory, 30
    characteristics of, 182
    in neoinstitutional theory, 35
    and policy implementation, 92, 93
    resistance to, 93
    in systems theory, 30
Chapter I, of Elementary and Secondary Education Act, 5–6, 299
    and accountability, 192–193, 199
    evaluation of, 107, 117
    implementation of, 86
    and policy evaluation, 115–116
Charter schools, 275–291
    accountability in, 41, 196–197, 283–286, 289–290
    African Americans in, 280–281
    agenda setting and, 66–67
    applications for, 277–278
    for at risk students, 51, 275–291
    barriers to, 287–289
    control of, 288–289
    conversion to, 277–278
    dimensions of
        constituentive, 284–285, 290
        normative, 276, 289
        structural, 277–278, 289
        technical, 285–287, 290
    diversity of, 280
    enrollment in, 277, 279, 280–281, 281*t*
    equity of, 278–285
    evaluation of, 104, 283–287, 290
    financing of, 244, 250, 269–271, 287–288
    fiscal impact of, 288
    governance of, 154
    limited English proficient students in, 282
    in neoinstitutional theory, 33
    opposition to, 276, 288
    oversight of, 283–284
    parent and student satisfaction with, 286–287

    reasons for, 276
    revocation of charter of, 284
    and segregation, 280–281
    size of, 279
    special education in, 282
    staffing in, 282–283
    and student achievement, 285–287
    student demographics in, 280–281, 281*t*
    student-teacher ratio in, 280
    support for, 275–276
    teachers in, 282–283
    in urban settings, 279
Chicago, accountability in, 199
Children
    in state of families theory of governance, 147
    in state of individuals theory of governance, 147
Choice-based accountability, 189
Citizens Act, 246
Citizenship, 46
Class bias, and governance, 139–140
Class, Bureaucracy, and Schools (Katz), 139–140, 144–145
Cleveland
    accountability in, 199
    school choice in, 270
    voucher programs in, 117–118
Clinton, Bill, 192
Collaboration, among teachers, 210, 226–229, 227*t*, 230*t*
Collective bargaining, 226, 229, 278
Colonial period
    educational governance in, 138–139
    school finance in, 247
Colorado, and National Assessment of Educational Progress, 104
Commitment: Teaching to Higher Standards, 214–218
Committee of Fifteen, 169
Committee of Ten, 169
Committee structure, of neoinstitutional theory, 35–36
Common schools, 236
    1620-1830, 138–139
    1830-1910, 139–144
Compulsory education policies, 166–168, 236–237
Conceptual framework, of education policy, 43–45, 44*f*
    ethics and social justice in, 45–52

Conditions, distinguishing from problems, 65
Conflict, in neoinstitutional theory, 33
Connecticut, school finance in, 253, 254*t*
Constituentive dimension
    of accountability, 199
    of charter schools, 284–285, 290
    of curriculum policies, 174–177
    of education policymaking, 43–44, 44*f*, 76–77
    of governance, 154–155
    of No Child Left Behind Act, 300–301
    of policy evaluation, 106, 117–118, 119*t*, 127
    of policy implementation, 93–94
    of school finance, 251–259
    of standards policies, 174–177
    of teacher personnel policies, 207, 213–218
    of testing policies, 174–177
Constitution, and governance, 150
Constitutionality
    in agenda setting, 75
    in problem definition, 75
Consumer-driven accountability, 197
Content, governance of, 136–137
Context, effects on policy, 36–37
Contextual dimension, of governance, 149
Corporate voluntarism, 141–142, 143
Corporations, and accountability, 191
CRESST. *See* National Center for Research on Evaluation, Standards and Student Testing
Critical theory, 39
    definition of, 9–10
    emancipatory purpose of, 39
    in policy evaluation, 111*t*
    shortcomings of, 39
Cross-level alignment, for policy evaluation, 100–101
Cross-sectional techniques, of policy evaluation, 120
Cubberley, Ellwood P., 247, 248
Cultural values, language of, 72–73
Curriculum
    frameworks for, 178
    historical development of, 169–170
    privatization of, 163–164
    types of, 168–170

Focusing events, media and, 68
Formulation, in systems theory, 23
Foundation aid, for school financing, 248–249
Fourteenth Amendment, 150
Fourth Amendment, 150
Fourth grade, curriculum for, in New Jersey, 179, 180–181
Frey, Steve, 222, 223
Functional dimension, of governance, 149
Funding. *See* School finance

GAO. *See* General Accounting Office
Gender, ethics and, 50–51
General Accounting Office (GAO), 124
GI Bill, 246
Goals, of programs, 91–92
Goals 2000, 192
Goldwater, Barry, 42
Governance, 135–158
    actors in, 136–137
    of charter schools, 154
    and corporate voluntarism, 141–142
    decentralization of, 153–154, 156, 296
    and democratic localism, 140–141
    dimensions of, 149–150
        constituentive, 154–155
        contextual, 149
        functional, 149
        normative, 152–153
        procedural, 149
        sectoral, 149
        structural, 149, 153–154
        technical, 155–156
    at federal level, 137, 149, 150–151, 152t
    general concepts of, 136–137
    historical foundations of, 137–144
        1620–1830, 138–139
        1830–1910, 139–144
        1910–2000, 144
    and incipient bureaucracy, 142–144
    at local level, 151, 152t
    and paternalistic voluntarism, 140
    politics and, 136–137, 149, 150–151
    and school choice, 155–156
    shared, 155–156
    site-based, 156
    at state level, 151, 152t, 156

theoretical foundations of, 144–149
    democratic state of education theory, 148–149
    family state theory, 145–146, 147–148
    state of families theory, 146–148
    state of individuals theory, 147–148
Grants, for school financing, 247
Great Britain, testing in, 174
The Great School Wars (Ravitch), 225
Great Society, 84, 86

Handbook of Educational Policy (Bourgue), 104
Harris, William T., 169
Hawaii, school finance in, 250–251, 252, 264–265, 264t
Head Start, evaluation of, 106–107
Hispanics
    and achievement gap, 50
    in charter schools, 280–281
Historical institutionalism. *See* Neoinstitutional theory
History, effects on policy, 36–37
Homeschooling, 167–168
Horizontal equity, in school finance, 253, 255–256, 258–259
Hornsby, Andre, 222, 223
Human beings, nature of, 152
Human capital theory, 237–238
The Human Side of Change (Evans), 93
Hunt, Jim, 208

Idaho, school finance in, 254, 254t
Ideological theory, 41–42
    definition of, 10–11
    on Elementary and Secondary Education Act, 42
Illinois, accountability in, 200, 201
Images of Organization (Morgan), 11
Immersion programs, evaluation of, 117
Implementation. *See* Policy implementation
The Implementation Game (Bardach), 84
Improving the Education of the Disadvantaged, 299
Incentives, and accountability, 193
Incipient bureaucracy, 142–144

Industrial training, 25
Inequality. *See also* Equality; Equity
    in school finance, 252, 266–267
    societal, 4
Inequality (Jencks et al.), 4
Inputs, in systems theory, 20, 21f, 22, 99
Insiders, in policy evaluation, 120
Institutional perspective theories, interactions with other theories, 11–12
Institutions
    and agenda setting, 74–76
    as agents of change (*See* Neoinstitutional theory)
INTASC. *See* Interstate Assessment and Support Consortium
Interest groups. *See also* Constituentive dimension
    at federal level, 75
    and policy formulation, 76–77
    at state level, 75, 76–77
    in systems theory, 22
Interest group theory, 25–31
    definition of, 9
    in school reform, 29–30
    shortcomings of, 30–31
International studies, in policy evaluation, 121
Interpretivist theories, 38–43
Interstate Assessment and Support Consortium (INTASC), 211
Interstate highway program, spillover effects of, 94
IQ controversy, media's role in, 67

Jackson v. Benson, 301
Jeffery v. O'Donnell, 168
Johnson, Lyndon B., 19, 41, 42, 84, 86, 106
Johnson-O'Malley Act, 246
Judicial branch
    of federal government, 150, 152t
    of local government, 152t
    of state government, 151, 152t
Judicial policies
    implementation of, 85
    and school finance equity, 255–257
Justice, social, 45–52
    in policy studies, 49–52
    technology and, 296–297

Kentucky, accountability in, 193–194, 199
Kentucky Education Reform Act (KERA), 193–194
Kindergarten, curriculum for, in New Jersey, 179–180

Public schools
accountability in, 196–197
conversion to charter schools, 277–278
governance of, 137–138, 153
growth of, 240–242, 241t
incipient bureaucracy in, 142–143
school finance in, 237–238
at state level, 151
Public spending, on school finance, 240–242, 241t

Quest for better teachers: Grading the states, the teachers we need and how to get them. (Finn, Kanstoroom, and Petrilli), 220

RAND Corporation, 181–182
Rationalist model, of policy evaluation, 113
Reagan, Ronald, 6, 41, 297
Reality, in postmodernism, 40
Redistributive policies, 49
Reframing Organizations (Bolman and Deal), 11
Regional studies, in policy evaluation, 121
Regular Education Marker, 258
Regulatory-based accountability, 197
Religion, and educational governance, 138–139
The Republic (Plato), 145–146
Research, usefulness of, 109
Research organizations, for policy evaluation, 123–124
Reserved Powers Clause, of Tenth Amendment, 150
Resources
accountability for, 189, 190
equitable use of, 235–271
Rhode Island, school finance in, 253, 254t
Rickover, Hyman, 170
Right wing politics, 41–42
Rodriguez v. San Antonio, 255
Romer, Roy, 175
Roosevelt, Franklin D., 42

San Antonio v. Rodriguez, 255
San Francisco, accountability in, 199
SCCCS. *See* State Core Curricular Content Standards
School boards, and governance, 151

School choice. *See also* Charter schools; Voucher programs
and accountability, 196–197
agenda setting and, 66–67
dimensions of
contextual, 36
historical, 36
evaluation of, 104–105
governance and, 155–156
language of, 72
opposition to, 276
and school finance, 243, 268, 269–271
in urban settings, 66–67
School environment, in urban settings, 51
School finance, 235–271
accountability and, 243
adequacy of, 239–240
for charter schools, 269–271, 287–288
control of, 267
current figures on, 243
decentralization of, 244, 250–251
dimensions of
constituentive, 251–259
normative, 236–243
structural, 244–251
technical, 259–265
at district level, 251
and efficiency, 240–243
equity of, 235–271
definition of, 253–255
judicial issues in, 255–257
at federal level, 242–243, 242t, 245–246
future of, 268–271
human capital theory of, 237–238
inequalities in, 252, 266–267
misappropriation of funds in, 260–265, 261t
policy vignette of, 262–263
power equalization and, 249–250
privatization of, 250–251
and productivity, 240–243, 265–268, 268
and public spending, 240–242, 241t
public versus private, 237–238, 244
results of, 265–268
rising costs and, 260
and school choice, 243, 268, 269–271
and school outliers, 264–265, 264t
sources of funds for, 242–243, 242t, 266–267

and standards, 268
at state level, 242–243, 242t, 245–255, 254t
and student achievement, 265
systems theory of, 262
tracking of funds in, 261–262
and underfunding, 259–260
for voucher programs, 269
School Incentive Program, 193
School Management Teams (SMT), 228
School outliers, 264–265, 264t
School personnel, accountability of, 189
School reform
advocacy coalitions in, 29–30
equality in, 50
interest groups in, 29–30
language of, 71–72
at state level, 74
School report cards, 127, 194, 198, 199, 200, 201
School size, 155
School systems, organization of, 87
Schultz, Theodore W., 237, 238
Science, testing in, 181–184
Scientific approach, to policy evaluation, 109–112, 111t, 119
Secondary schools, curriculum in, 177
Section 100, of New York State education law, 228, 229
Sectoral dimension, of governance, 149
Segregation, 4, 64
charter schools and, 280–281
and desegregation, 26, 64
Semi-profession, teaching as, 208–209
September 11, 2001, terrorist attack of, as triggering event, 69
Serrano v. Priest, 255
Site-based management, 156, 166, 210
Slow revolution, 208
Smith-Hughes Act for Vocational Education, 170
Smith-Lanham Act (1914), 25
Smith-Lever Act (1914), 25
SMT. *See* School Management Teams
Sobel, Thomas, 228
Social construction of knowledge, 42–43
Social justice, 45–52
in policy studies, 49–52
technology and, 296–297